Out of Albania

OUT OF ALBANIA

From Crisis Migration to Social Inclusion in Italy

Russell King and Nicola Mai

Berghahn Books
NEW YORK • OXFORD

Published in 2008 by

Berghahn Books
www.berghahnbooks.com

© 2008 Russell King and Nicola Mai

All rights reserved. Except for the quotation of short passages for the purposes of criticism and review, no part of this book may be reproduced in any form or by any means, electronic or mechanical, including photocopying, recording, or any information storage and retrieval system now known or to be invented, without written permission of the publisher.

Library of Congress Cataloging-in-Publication Data

King, Russell, 1945-
   Out of Albania : from crisis migration to social inclusion in Italy / Russell King and Nicola Mai. -- 1st ed.
      p. cm.
   Includes bibliographical references and index.
   ISBN 978-1-84545-544-6 (hardback : alk. paper)
  1. Albanians--Italy. 2. Albania--Emigration and immigration. 3. Italy--Emigration and immigration. 4. Albania--Economic conditions--1992- 5. Albanians--Italy--Social conditions. 6. Albanians--Italy--Economic conditions. 7. Italy--Ethnic relations. I. Mai, Nicola. II. Title.
   DG457.A7K56 2008
   305.891'991045--dc22

British Library Cataloguing in Publication Data

A catalogue record for this book is available from the British Library

Printed in the United States on acid-free paper.

ISBN 978-1-84545-544-6

Contents

List of Tables	vii
List of Figures	ix
Preface and Acknowledgements	xi
1. Introduction	1
2. The Albanian Background	27
3. Albanian Migration	65
4. From Welcome to Stigmatisation	101
5. Albanian Migrant Lives	127
6. Social Exclusion and Integration	175
7. Return to Albania?	215
Bibliography	257
Index	275

LIST OF TABLES

1.1	Albanians in Rome, Modena and Lecce provinces: key data	8
1.2	Dimensions of integration of immigrants into a host society	17
2.1	Albanian population evolution 1923–2001	49
2.2	Albanian population: natural increase and vital statistics, 1950–2000	50
3.1	Albanian migration since 1990: annual estimates	70
3.2	Characteristics of temporary and permanent emigrants, by period of emigration, 1990–2002	75
3.3	Characteristics of temporary and permanent emigrants, by destination country, 1990–2002	76
3.4	Location of origin of temporary and permanent emigrants, by destination country, 1990–2002	76
3.5	Albania: selected migration statistics by district, 1989–2001	79
3.6	Albanians in Italy with 'permits to stay': end-of-year, 1990–2003	85
3.7	Albanians in Italy's regularisation schemes, 1986–2002	86
3.8	Foreign nationals in Italy: top ten origin countries for regularisation applicants (2002) and total permit-holders (2003)	87
3.9	Albanians in Italy: % females according to three sources, 1994–2001	88
3.10	Immigrants in Italy: indicators of family structure, Albanians and reference groups, 1992 and 2000	89
3.11	Albanian pupils in Italian schools 1991–92 to 2003–04	89
3.12	Regional distribution of Albanians in Italy according to the census and permit-to-stay records, 2001	91
3.13	Changing macro-regional distribution of Albanians and all immigrants in Italy, 1995–2003	94
7.1	Remittances to Albania, 1992–2004	227
7.2	Use and investment of remittances to Albania according to two recent surveys	230

List of Figures

1.1	Field sites in Italy	7
2.1	Albania: location map	34
3.1	Poverty map of Albania	73
3.2	Age–sex pyramids, 1989 and 2001	78
3.3	Internal and international migration outflows, by district, 1989–2001	80
3.4	Relationship between poverty and migration, by district, 1989–2001	83
3.5	Regional distribution of Albanians in Italy, 2001	93

Preface and Acknowledgements

Like many research monographs, this book derives from a funded research project. Our first debt of gratitude, therefore, is to the Leverhulme Trust, which financed the research project 'Albanians in Italy and Greece: A Study in Migration Dynamics and Social Exclusion' (grant no. F/00230/D) over the two years 2001–03. This research was based at the University of Sussex (Sussex Centre for Migration Research). Russell King was the grant holder, and he, together with Nicola Mai, worked on the Italian and Albanian parts of the project, on which this book is based. The Greek part of the study was carried out by Gabriella Lazaridis and Maria Koumandraki, then of the University of Dundee, now at the University of Leicester. It is important that we acknowledge here the input of Dr Lazaridis into the planning of the overall research project and the framing of some of the research questions.

Our fieldwork to collect the research material which forms the heart of this book took us to many parts of Albania and to three cities and regions in Italy: to Lecce in the southern region of Apulia, to Modena in the northern region of Emilia-Romagna, and to Rome. In each of these places we collected carefully monitored samples of in-depth interviews with migrants, together with interviews with various key informants. Three field visits were made to Albania: a reconnaissance trip at the beginning of the research, and two longer trips in which most of the interviews were taken. Most of the interviews were done by Mai, who worked full-time on the Leverhulme project; King participated in some of the fieldwork in Albania and Rome, as time allowed.

Although the Leverhulme research forms the core of this book, we also draw on parts of two other research projects in which we have both been involved. The first is Mai's Sussex DPhil thesis, which immediately predated the Leverhulme research, and was on the role of Italian television, received in Albania, in framing young Albanians' migratory projects and evolving identities. The second was research which we were commissioned to do by Oxfam into Albanian migration to the United Kingdom and its impact on alleviating poverty in Albania. This project, which ran alongside the latter part of the Leverhulme study (2002–03), enabled us not only to collect comparative data on Albanians living in the UK (many of whom had migrated onward from Italy) but also to spend more time investigating the Albanian context of outmigration and return.

Hence, although the book is mainly about Albanian migration to Italy, it also aspires to be a state-of-the-art sourcebook on Albanian migration generally. The fieldwork-based chapters on Italy (Chapters 4–6) constitute the heart of the book, Chapters 2 and 3 survey the overall history and geography of Albanian migration, whilst Chapter 7 deals with issues surrounding return migration, development and the future migration trends of Albania.

Many individuals showed a close and committed interest in our research, and helped in various ways. In Albania we owe particular thanks to three people: to Professor Kosta Barjaba, Director of the Department of Emigration in the Ministry of Labour and Social Affairs; to Dr Ilir Gedeshi, Director of the Centre for Economic and Social Studies in Tirana; and to Maurizio Busatti, Head of the Tirana office of the International Organization for Migration (IOM). In Italy we acknowledge the help and interest of Dr Franco Pittau of the Caritas team in Rome, Dr Ugo Melchionda of IOM's Rome office, and Professor Luigi Perrone of the University of Lecce, as well as many others too numerous to mention. At the Sussex Centre for Migration Research, four people contributed vital inputs into the research: Alessandro Drago, DPhil researcher, carried out several of the migrant interviews in Rome; Mirela Dalipaj, MPhil student and research assistant on the Oxfam project, did many of the household interviews in northern Albania and around Tirana; Natalia Ribas-Mateos, Marie Curie Post-Doctoral Fellow at Sussex, assisted with some Albanian interviews, especially with women; and Jenny Money made a magnificent contribution in editing, formatting and checking the final manuscript. We also acknowledge the time and commitment of the various individuals who transcribed more than two hundred interviews – the most important raw material for this book.

Our greatest debt, however, is to the people who agreed to participate in this research as migrant interviewees and key informants. Many showed keen interest in and a sophisticated understanding of our research. We thank them for allowing us to trespass on their lives, and hope that the publication of this book will help to diffuse a more balanced and realistic picture of their situation.

Russell King and Nicola Mai
Brighton and London
January 2008

Chapter 1

INTRODUCTION

Out of Albania

In the Silver Jubilee volume of the *International Migration Review*, Aristide Zolberg (1989: 405) opined that, if all the world consisted of Albania on the one hand and Japan on the other, there would be no need to study international migration, for it would not exist. Two years later, the world watched agog as pictures of thousands of fleeing Albanians crammed on to creaking ships dominated the newspapers and television screens for a few days in March 1991. Later that same year, in August, similar scenes were reenacted as another exodus of Albanian 'boat people' bore down on the coast of southern Italy. The pictures of the impossibly crowded ships containing the Albanian refugees desperate to escape a country collapsing into political and economic chaos became part of the iconography of global migration in the 1990s. The scene was cynically made into an advertising poster by the Italian clothing giant Benetton, it featured on the front cover of Myron Weiner's provocative book *The Global Migration Crisis* (1995), and it was reissued and replayed in countless magazine articles and television documentaries on migration.

In a sense this Albanian imagery was unfortunate. Whilst not wishing to deny the human drama and tragedy of Albanian migration, we suggest that most migration, even Albanian migration, does not take place in this way. As Castles and Miller make clear in their landmark study *The Age of Migration*, contemporary international migration is (and probably always has been) an infinitely complex and diversified phenomenon, deeply embedded within social and economic processes operating at a variety of scales. Since earliest times, migration has been a constant factor in human history, not an aberration or a crisis (Castles and Miller 2003: 278). People migrate as manual workers, trained specialists, students, entrepreneurs, or as family members of previous migrants. Some move as refugees, others have choice. For many poor people, however, choice is constrained: migration presents itself as the 'best option' for economic survival and improvement. All this rings true in the Albanian case, as we shall see in the pages that follow. In fact one of the key findings of this study is precisely the diversity and dynamism of the Albanian migratory experience.

The timing of Zolberg's remark was, of course, critical. His paper, ambitiously titled 'The next waves: migration theory for a changing world', was attempting to identify new theoretical frameworks that would help to explain the 'new waves' of migration beginning to emerge in the 1980s. What he could not anticipate was that 1989 would open up a new era of international migration in Europe – across the old migration barrier of the Iron Curtain. Yet here we find the first of a number of paradoxes concerning Albanian migration. It was widely thought at the time that the dismantling of the Iron Curtain would trigger a mass migration (Fassmann and Münz 1994; Layard et al. 1992). The logic of such a view was predicated partly on the recollection that the Iron Curtain had been initially created to contain westward migration from the Warsaw Pact countries, and partly on the fact that the immediate impetus for the breaching of the Hungarian barbed wire in May 1989 and of the Berlin Wall six months later was to allow Hungarians and East Germans to step into 'freedom'. Further strength for the view of impending mass migration derived from the obvious economic divide between East and West and from the presumed eagerness of much of the former's population to go and taste the hitherto forbidden fruits of capitalism.

By and large the threat of mass East–West migration failed to translate into reality. It is true, nevertheless, that a considerable amount of mobility has occurred. In Germany there have been the migrations of *Übersiedler* and *Aussiedler* – respectively migration from East to West Germany in the year between the knocking down of the Berlin Wall and unification, and migration into Germany of ethnic Germans from the former Soviet Union and elsewhere in Eastern Europe. There has been a fairly large-scale but geographically dispersed emigration from Poland, which had its origins in the somewhat more liberal attitude of the Polish communists towards travel abroad before 1989, and which has been boosted by Poland's accession to the EU in 2004. New systems of cross-frontier shuttle migration have sprung up, such as that between Poland and Germany, or Slovakia and Austria. More recently, there have been substantial migration flows from Romania, Moldova and the Ukraine; much of this is directed towards the newer countries of immigration along the southern flank of the European Union – Italy, Spain, Portugal and Greece. Yet most residents of the Warsaw Pact countries have been reluctant to tear up their roots.

The one undisputed case of massive East–West migration is that from Albania, the focus of this book. During the early 1990s around 10 per cent of the Albanian population emigrated, the vast majority of them to two neighbouring EU countries, Italy and Greece. By 2001, according to the Albanian Census, a net total of 600,000 Albanians had moved abroad in the previous decade, representing nearly 20 per cent of the Albanian population (INSTAT 2002). Some authorities, however, estimated the scale of the emigration loss as even higher, around 800,000 (Barjaba 2000a). Probably no other country in the world, certainly in Europe, was so deeply affected by emigration during the 1990s. The outflow has continued in the new decade, and by the end of 2004 the Albanian government estimated that one million Albanians were living abroad.

About the Book

This book explores the dynamics of Albanian migration since 1990, primarily to Italy but with some comparative reference to Greece and other countries. Based on the available statistics and on more than two hundred in-depth interviews in Italy and Albania, we explore the evolution of Albanian migration and settlement in Italy and impacts on the 'sending country', Albania. We look closely at migrants' employment, housing and social conditions in Italy, as well as actual and potential return to Albania. The study pays particular attention to the complex processes of social exclusion and inclusion and to the changing ways in which the host society has reacted to the immigration of significant numbers of Albanians (who are thought to number around 250,000 in Italy). Our analysis will show how the initial construction of Albanian migration as an 'heroic event' – of fellow Europeans escaping the terrible yoke of communism – was quickly replaced by a very different view based on a set of powerfully negative stereotypes. We will critically document, evaluate and deconstruct the discourses surrounding these stereotypes and, using a variety of field research methods, describe how Albanians have negotiated their way through and around various dimensions of stigmatisation, discrimination and exclusion. The final major theme we address in this study is the question of identity, particularly insofar as this is related on the one hand to the stigmatising narratives and behaviours imposed by Italian society, and on the other to the disruptive events in Albania where the exit from the nationalist-communist articulation of Albanianness destabilised existing notions of 'home' and 'belonging'.

Let us spell out our research questions and hypotheses in a more systematic fashion. The research had two major aims:

1. To build up a detailed profile of the Albanian migration to Italy encompassing migration processes, experiences of employment and housing, social networks and community structures.
2. To examine and to attempt to theorise the processes through which the stigmatisation and social and economic exclusion of Albanians have occurred and are constructed in Italian society.

More specific research questions nested within or extending from the two general aims include the following:

- What are the demographic characteristics of Albanian migration, and specifically that to Italy? Here we are interested in numbers, age,

gender and family structures, geographical origins within Albania, spatial patterning of settlement in Italy, and return migration. How have these characteristics changed over time?
- In what ways have Albanians been able to access employment in Italy; to what extent are they excluded from some types of job and confined to others; and to what extent are they engaged in illegal and semi-illegal activities? In relation to the existing literature on migrants and labour markets in Italy and southern Europe which shows the tendency of migrant workers to cluster in certain (often nationality- and gender-specific) niches in the parallel or informal economy (e.g., Baldwin-Edwards and Arango 1999; Iosifides and King 1996; Mingione and Quassoli 2000; Reyneri 1998), how do Albanians fare in comparison and in competition with other migrant groups? Have Albanian workers been able to improve their working situations the longer they stay in Italy?
- What are Albanians' housing and other social conditions in Italy, including their access to welfare, education and other 'citizenship rights'? Again, how have these housing and other social conditions changed over time?
- How have discourses of racism against Albanians evolved? What has been the role of the Italian media in stereotyping Albanians as 'undesirables', 'criminals' and 'others'? What are the other dimensions of everyday and institutional racism against Albanians? Extending this line of analysis further, how can the Albanian experience in Italy be theorised in relation to existing studies of the ethnic and racial aspects of migration? This is of particular interest because skin colour is clearly not a signifier of racism in the Albanian case, thereby confirming the position of Anthias and Yuval-Davis (1993) that any signifier, whether biological, cultural, linguistic or religious, can be used to construct 'racialised boundaries', and that 'hierarchies of whiteness' exist. Hence the importance of exploring how racism is experienced by Albanians in Italy, both as an intentional representation and as intersubjective prejudice.
- Building on the above questions, what are the dimensions of inclusion and exclusion experienced by Albanians in Italy, and how have they reacted to these conditions by drawing on their own social networks and cultural resources to combat racism, victimisation and stigmatisation? What has been the role of such networks in carving spaces of control and in building bridges between home and the host country? How have notions of Albanian community and solidarity been constructed? Here we must bear in mind that this construction has taken place across the abrupt post-communist transformation. With the demise of the communist state there was a general collapse of a collective moral, social and cultural universe, to some extent replaced by a foreign media-induced construction of a good life based on individualised and consumer-oriented values. Hence the most striking

aspect of contemporary Albanian culture, especially during the first post-communist years, has been its chaotic fragmentation and its failure to find a secure, shared ontological foundation to fill the vacuum left by the disappearance of the collective and the public as meaningful and all-pervasive bases for culture, economy and society. Similarly, in approaching the question of Albanian identificatory responses to victimisation and stigmatisation, it will be important to understand how Albanians' rejection of the communist celebration of nationalistic identity makes them potentially more likely to assimilate and interiorise a stereotypical and stigmatising description of themselves.

- Finally, what is the role of the 'Albanian background' in helping to understand migrant behaviour at various stages of the migration process, including return? We think this question is relevant at three levels. First, there are deep-seated traditions such as patriarchy, blood feud and the clan structure which, partially suppressed by communism, have resurfaced and taken on new forms since 1990. Secondly, there are more specific factors such as the breakdown of the Albanian collective system in the early 1990s, or the collapse of a series of pyramid investment schemes in 1997, which have acted as triggers for waves of Albanian emigration. Thirdly, there is the issue of the extent to which the current state of the Albanian economy, society and political system acts as an encouragement or, more likely, a barrier to return migration.

In working through the above research objectives and questions, a number of comparative dimensions will be introduced. Based on existing literature, some comparisons will be made firstly between Albanians in Italy and those in other countries, notably Greece; and secondly with other immigrant nationalities in Italy. A third comparative axis will be the regional contrasts of the Albanian experience within Italy: as will be seen in the next section of this chapter, the field methodology was set up explicitly to take this into account. Throughout our analysis, we will be sensitive to gender contrasts and to the danger of viewing Albanian migrants as an homogenous entity, or as simplistically dichotomised good/bad, criminal/non-criminal, legalised/undocumented, etc. As we will see, exclusion and inclusion are never absolute, but dynamic, contextual and differentiated.

Methods

Our approach is interdisciplinary, methodologically diverse and multi-sited. We are certainly not alone in believing that the best research on migration is 'intrinsically interdisciplinary' (Castles and Miller 2003: 21). This points us both in the direction of a combination and an integration of different disciplinary perspectives, and towards a variety of methods to gather data. Our research takes inspiration from Robin Cohen's eloquent words in the Prologue to his monumental *Cambridge Survey of World Migration*. Cohen (1995: 8) writes of his conviction that:

> the study of migration confirms, *par excellence*, the newer emphasis in the social sciences and the humanities on commensurability and mutual intelligibility across disciplines. This is witnessed in the increasing number of scholars who work comfortably across disciplinary divides ... The newer notion assumes that a consensus is emerging around social and cultural anthropology, law, sociology, politics, philosophy, economics (where humans still matter), history, human and population geography, social psychology and other cognate fields too numerous to mention ... [T]his new-found transparency should not be a licence for an 'anything goes' type of scholarship. Instead, systematic investigation, rigorous method, appropriate language skills, a combination of empathy and critical distance from the subject, attention to sources and to related research all acquire a new importance.

Our research approach in this study of Albanian migration to Italy is based around the cluster of disciplines made up of human geography, sociology, anthropology, and cultural and media studies, but we also bring in, where relevant, perspectives from history, politics, economics and psychology.

In addition to surveying a rapidly expanding literature on Albanian migration – evidence of a growing scholarly interest in the uniqueness, diversity and significance of the country's migratory experience[1] – we have kept a watchful eye on relevant official datasets. After a shaky start in the early 1990s, when much Albanian migration went unrecorded, the statistical hold over the dimensions and characteristics of the flows and settlement patterns, especially in Italy, has become more secure with the passage of time – as will become clear in Chapter 3.

Field Sites in Italy

Whilst the statistical picture is important in framing the broad outlines of Albanian migration and in providing the backdrop to our study, the main methodology we employ is based on extensive field research and in-depth interviewing. Field interviews were concentrated in three locations in Italy, in order to differentiate migrants' experiences in contrasting socioeconomic settings (Figure 1.1). These were:

- Lecce and the region of Apulia in southern Italy. Apulia (Puglia in Italian) occupies the south-east corner of Italy and contains the coastal cities of Bari and Brindisi where the 1991 arrivals of Albanian 'boat people' docked. Our field base was Lecce, a provincial city south of Brindisi. This southern part of Apulia has been the main landing point for the clandestine speedboat traffic of Albanian migrants and refugees

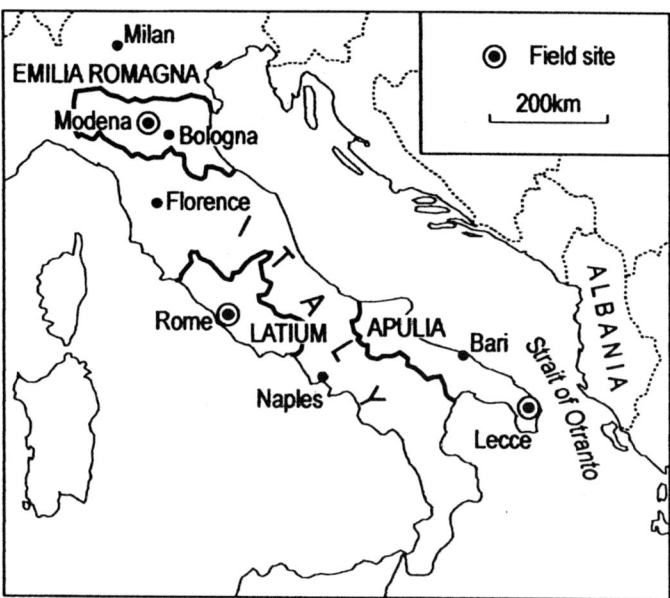

Figure 1.1 Field sites in Italy

across the Otranto Strait. Because of its closeness to Albania – indeed the region has been called Albania's umbilical cord to Italy (Caritas 2001: 416) – Apulia is a zone both of intense migrant through traffic, passing on to other parts of Italy, and of migrant settlement. The region has a mainly agricultural and service economy, which we will describe in more detail in Chapter 5. Most of the interviews were taken in Lecce city itself, with a few elsewhere in the region – in the countryside around the city and further north at Bari, Molfetta and Bisceglie.

- Modena and the region of Emilia-Romagna in northern Italy. This regional setting epitomises the wealthy north of the country. Modena and the adjacent city of Bologna (the regional capital) are amongst the richest cities in Italy (Dunford 2002). The economic structure of the region relies on a mix of industry, services and farming – all much more productive and efficient than their equivalents in the south. Moreover, the area has a long tradition of efficient local government, social responsibility and economic cooperation, the legacy both of its stable left-wing political heritage as part of the 'Red Belt' of central-northern Italy, and of a deeper historical tradition of city-republic governance traceable to the Middle Ages (Waley 1978). Interviews with Albanian migrants and key informants were centred on Modena, with a few taken in Bologna and in some villages in the hinterland.
- Rome. The capital city was added as a third field site. As indicated above, one of our main initial concerns was to bring out the north–south contrast in the Albanian migrant experience, given that

the north–south dualism has been such an indelible feature of Italian economic and cultural geography (King 1987: 173). Since a considerable amount of time had to be spent in Rome gathering statistical data and interviewing key figures at the national level, we took the opportunity to interview a quota of migrants in the city.[2] As Table 1.1 shows, the province of Rome (the city and some surrounding minor towns) had more than eight thousand Albanians at the end of 2000, but they do not represent such a large share of the total foreign population as they do in Modena and Lecce provinces – especially the latter, where Albanians account for over a quarter of all registered foreigners. The Roman situation is unique because the capital has both the largest number of foreign residents (more than 220,000 in 2000), and a greater variety of immigrant nationalities, than any other part of Italy.

In each of the three locations, we aimed to interview at least thirty Albanian migrants and at least twenty other 'key informants' – employers, social workers, activists, community leaders, etc. Table 1.1 sets out the eventual numbers of interviews achieved, plus some other data on Albanians in each of the three areas. It should be stressed that these official statistics are the figures for legally-resident Albanians, that is to say those who were in possession of a *permesso di soggiorno* – a 'permit to stay' – on 31 December 2000, just before we started the Italian field research, which took place during 2001 and 2002. These statistics do not necessarily match the situation on the ground, for various reasons which we discuss in Chapter 3.

The Interview Surveys

The main survey instrument employed in the field in Italy was the semi-structured interview with Albanian migrants. The semi-structured format gave some shape and purpose to the interviews, allowing the collection of systematic information linked to the research questions set out above. But the interview format was not rigidly composed, thereby allowing full rein for the interviewees to discuss topics which *they* thought were important. In this way a number of experiences and anecdotes emerged which were highly interesting and instructive.

Table 1.1 Albanians in Rome, Modena and Lecce provinces: key data

Province	Migrant interviews	Key informant interviews	Albanians legally present 31.12.00	Albanians as % of total immigrants in province
Rome	30	22	8,271	5.8
Modena	32	23	1,289	8.1
Lecce	35	22	2,391	25.8

The migrant interviews broadly employed a life-history approach. The following more-or-less chronological stages were covered in the schedule, although the sequencing varied from case to case according to how the dynamics of the interview unfolded:

- pre-migration background in Albania
- motives for migration
- mechanisms of migration – routes, mode of travel, cost, etc.
- arrival and settlement
- experiences of employment and work
- housing and welfare issues (education, health etc.)
- family, social and community life – contacts with other Albanians and with members of the host society
- experiences of racism, discrimination, stigmatisation, etc.
- issues of identity
- changing views of Italian and Albanian society
- hopes and plans for the future – to return or to stay?

It needs stressing that questions on these topics were phrased with appropriate neutrality and subtlety; they were not introduced brusquely or directly for fear of distorting the response. To give a concrete example, we did not ask the question 'Have you ever experienced racism?' since this would probably invite a simple 'yes' response and in any case is predicated on an assumption that the interviewee has the same definition and understanding of racism as the researcher. Rather, the question was posed along the lines 'Can you tell me of any incidents where you felt you were treated unfairly because of the fact that you are Albanian?' The interview schedule was carefully piloted, and changed very slightly as a result, in advance of the main surveys.

Initially we were concerned about the potentially high level of suspicion amongst Albanian migrants, given what we already knew about their precarious and stigmatised position in Italian society. In the event, this proved to be less of a problem than we anticipated; more of an issue was the logistical problem of setting up interviews with people who worked long hours in physically demanding jobs and who often had family responsibilities as well. The main technique for locating and selecting possible interviewees was to approach migrants through personal contacts and intermediaries, and then to use carefully controlled snowball chains.

We are not able to claim that we have interviewed a statistically representative sample of Albanians in Italy, or in the three locations surveyed. The migrant universe being studied is not fully known as regards its demographic and social parameters, and hence not amenable to a rigorous sampling frame. What we did was to endeavour to achieve intuitive representativeness by interviewing people across age groups and socio-occupational backgrounds, as well as including broadly equal numbers of men and women. Some of these respondent characteristics can be cross-checked with statistics on Albanians from the *permesso di soggiorno* and other records. This enabled us to have increased confidence that we were covering appropriate age ranges and gender distribution – therefore we interviewed a slight preponderance of males to reflect their numerical majority in the official data. However, we should not be too wedded to the official figures since they exclude undocumented Albanians, whose numerical size and characteristics are by definition unknown.

Most of the migrant interviews in Italy were conducted in Italian, a language most Albanians are fairly fluent in. This fluency comes not just from living in Italy but also from their experience in Albania of intensively watching Italian television, a practice dating back to communist times when foreign TV watching was, for many Albanians, a secret and obsessive pleasure (Mai 2001a, 2002a). However some interviews, or parts of them, were conducted in Albanian. The migrant interviews were tape-recorded, and subsequently transcribed and translated into English for further analysis.

Virtually all of the migrant interviews included in the quota samples enumerated in Table 1.1 were with individuals; just a few were with couples or pairs of friends. Beyond these quotas of recorded and transcribed interviews, several other conversations and discussions with Albanian migrants took place in various informal settings such as on train journeys, in bars, family groupings, etc.[3] These added to our overall insight into the Albanian experience in Italy.

Alongside the migrant interviews we talked to a variety of key informants in each field site (Table 1.1). These comprised Italian employers, landlords, administrative personnel, NGO workers, and many others. Also included were Albanian community leaders, journalists, activists and scholars living in Italy. These interview schedules, also semi-structured, were tailored to the particular respondent and his/her role or field of expertise regarding Albanian migration, employment, welfare, etc.

Fieldwork in Albania

A proper understanding of transnational migration involves researching both the context of arrival and the 'sending' context. Three visits to Albania took place. The first, at the beginning of the research in 2001, enabled us to interview a wide variety of key informants (academics, government officials, representatives of international organisations, local NGOs, etc.), mainly in Tirana, and to carry out a reconnaissance trip to make a general appraisal of the economic and social situation in different parts of the country. Several interviews with returned migrants were also gathered on this initial trip. Two longer field visits to Albania took place during 2003. During these three visits a total of seventy-three interviews were collected, most of them taped. The interviews were widely distributed across the country, reflecting the spatially widespread nature of emigration from Albania. Mirroring our strategy in Italy, we interviewed in selected areas of central, northern and southern Albania: Tirana, Durrës and their peri-urban squatter settlements in the centre; Kukës and Shkodër in the north; and Vlorë and Sarandë in the south.

These interviews took a variety of forms. Some were with individuals, especially returnees. But relatively few migrants have returned definitively at this stage of the evolution of the Albanian migratory phenomenon. So we interviewed many migrants who were on return visits, and many families or 'residual households' with one or more members abroad. The migrant interviews traced the same set of themes listed above, except that more emphasis was placed on return, resettlement, investment and plans for the future. For the family interviews we focused mainly on remittances, household survival, poverty alleviation, plans for the future and the possibility of return of the family members abroad.

In selecting the sample to be interviewed in Albania we tried again to achieve an approximate gender balance. However, given the conservative nature of Albanian society, especially in rural areas and in the north, often it was not possible to talk to women away from the rest of the family. Therefore many interviews conducted in these areas were family interviews, with the male head speaking on behalf of the family group. The atmosphere in the interviews was nearly always relaxed and friendly. The fact that the issues raised were not too controversial – unlike some of the topics covered in the Italian interviews – meant that all the family members could join in. These interviews often generated a lot of emotion: laughter and warm hospitality; but also anguish and tears as parents talked of their exiled sons and daughters and the likelihood that many of them would not return. Migrant and household interviews were conducted in Albanian, though English or Italian were used for some of the elite interviews in Tirana.

Some Key Concepts

This is not a highly theoretical book. Our analysis, in the main, is empirical and qualitative. Nevertheless, one of our main aims is to explain the processes by which Albanian immigrants in Italy have come to be so highly stigmatised, and to derive theoretical insights from this in terms of exploring and refining the nature of racism, social exclusion and integration, and migrant identity. Recognising the dynamism of Albanians' encounter with Italian society over the past fifteen or so years and, in particular, their success in improving at least some aspects of their economic and social lives in the host society, we need to be very cautious about how we define and operationalise these key concepts of social exclusion, integration, racism and identity. Above all, we want to move beyond an account which sees Albanians as ineluctably oppressed by their experiences of racism and exclusion and troubled by their own 'problematic' identity. As the evidence presented in this book will show, Albanians have been unfairly victimised by a whole set of condemnatory practices and discourses on the part of Italians; yet they have, in turn, reacted to this victimisation with patience and creativity, especially at an individual level, so that nowadays their story is on balance one of social inclusion rather than exclusion.

Each of the key terms we address has generated a wide-ranging literature and we do not have the space here to do justice to the full range of interpretations or to the details of the historical evolution of these concepts. What we try to do instead is to offer a brief critical discussion which sets out how we understand and employ these terms in order to shape our analysis of the situation of Albanian migrants in Italy.

Social Exclusion

We start with social exclusion. This term is of relatively recent origin. It gained currency in French discourse in the 1980s and was closely related to the public and policy debates on the 'new poverty' created by the post-Fordist crisis and economic restructuring, as a result of which increasing numbers of people – *les exclus* – found themselves unemployed, poor and without proper housing (Martin 1996). Following the term's adoption in official usage by the European Commission in 1988, social exclusion became part of the language of European social policy throughout the 1990s, inscribed in the Treaty of Maastricht and in the objectives of the EU Structural Funds. It also came to be used in initiatives promulgated by the Council of Europe and in the social policy discourses of several governments, including the UK Labour Government of Tony Blair. Its eclipse of other terms such as 'poverty' and 'deprivation' is interpreted by Berghman (1995: 16) in the following terms:

> The ... shift seems to have been political, as the member-states, who have a guaranteed minimum income deemed sufficient to cover basic needs, expressed reservations about the word poverty when applied to their respective countries. Social exclusion would ... be a more adequate and less accusing expression ... to designate ... existing problems.

Room (1995) analyses the dual origins of the term in the French and Anglo-Saxon traditions of social analysis. The Anglo-Saxon view focuses on unequal distribution of income arising through market competition and the economic division of labour, so that certain individuals end up lacking the means to achieve an acceptable minimum standard of living. In the French view, society is seen as a number of 'collectivities' bound together by sets of mutual rights and obligations that are rooted in a broader moral order, and social exclusion is the process of becoming detached from this moral universe. This latter interpretation derives from the Durkheimian view, whereby the individual is connected to society via the vertically mediating institutions of family, work, friends and welfare organisations; as a result social exclusion is 'the rupture of the social bond between the individual and society' (Silver 1994: 566).

The term social exclusion has been conceptualised at a variety of scales. Michael Samers (1998: 123) maintains that the 'grand discourses' which constitute the ideological foundation of nationhood continue to be significant in the social construction of exclusion; we shall see later how apposite this remark is to the Italian case. For Castles (1998) the contradiction between inclusion and exclusion is a global process differentiating between those who are 'full members of the new global order' and those, like poor and undocumented migrants, who are marginalised. Significantly, the single photograph in Castles' paper is of Albanian refugees in Italy, penned in behind barricades to signify their exclusion from the receiving society (Castles 1998: 182).

Miles and Thränhardt (1995) explore the dynamics of inclusion and exclusion of migrants as a specifically European process expressed via political and economic integration and linked issues of citizenship. These authors describe an EU-wide discourse of exclusion:

> Now that the struggle against communism is over, and given that there is no longer an economic case for the mass migration of unskilled labour ... the logic of exclusion predominates. Underlying and shaping the practice of exclusion are not only utilitarian economic considerations, but also racist conceptions of 'otherness'. (Thränhardt and Miles 1995: 3–4)

At this macro level, Europe and its various peripheries (and their populations) are structured into dialectics of inclusion and exclusion, with clear impacts on migration processes and migrant statuses. For those EU citizens inside this 'club of rich countries', the logic of inclusion is grounded in a set of common interests arising from joint participation at a similar level of economic development within the world economy: hence they are free to move anywhere within 'EU space'. Migrants from poorer non-EU countries – Turks, Moroccans, Albanians, etc., even if they have acquired some kind of qualified right of residence – are subject to the logic of exclusion as a result of their lacking the status of EU citizen (Thränhardt and Miles 1995: 7–8). This remains the case despite the recent shift in the economic and demographic arguments towards favouring further immigration into the EU.

In Italy the rhetoric of exclusion is made particularly clear by the distinction between *comunitari* and *extracomunitari* – terms (or their equivalents) not found in any other European country (Foot 1995). Initially applied to the image of black and dark-skinned immigrants from Africa and South Asia, the term *extracomunitari* has had to be adjusted to embrace 'non-black' immigrants from Albania and other East European countries, all of whom are regarded as 'excluded' and not 'one of us'. However, the social and ethnic construction of the term emphatically does not include 'desirable' non-EU citizens such as the Swiss or North Americans.

Many authors point out that there is no commonly accepted definition of social exclusion (Byrne 1999; Silver 1994; Yepez de Castíllo 1994); even that it is a 'chaotic concept' (Samers 1998). The following EU definition sees social exclusion as a 'structural phenomenon tending to establish within society a mechanism which excludes part of the population from economic and social life and from a share of the general prosperity ... The problem is ... not only one of disparity between the top and the bottom of the social scale (up/down), but also between those comfortably placed within society and those on the fringe (in/out)' (European Commission 1992: 7). This definition successfully integrates both the Anglo-Saxon and French/continental European approaches to the topic, but gives little idea of social exclusion's effect on the everyday lives of those who are excluded. Samers (1998) argues for a more hermeneutic approach to social exclusion, from the perspective of those supposedly socially excluded, and points to the emerging literary work on migrancy as a source for such an emic understanding. Certainly this is a view we would endorse, not least because we have made the point before, both in respect of general approaches to the study of migration (King et al. 1995) and in the context of Albanian migrants (King et al. 1998; Mai 2002a).

Samers (1998) also proposes a more dialectical and critical reading of social exclusion in which the distinction between exclusion and inclusion is far more ambiguous and nuanced than that presented by most academics and social policy analysts; once again we accord with this view. We follow Byrne (1999) and Samers (1998), amongst others, in appreciating the multidimensionality of social exclusion – a framework which manifests itself at three scales:

- the structural dynamics of national and supranational policies, economic processes and anti-immigrant discourses, including the hegemonic role of the media;
- the various dimensions of exclusion, including the labour market, housing, welfare entitlements, political rights, etc;
- the differential impact social exclusion has on individuals and the way it intersects with other social divisions such as race, class and gender.

Related to this, Stephen Castles' 'differential exclusion' model moves beyond the notion of a dual society in which some (the majority, above all national citizens) are included, and others (the unemployed, the poor, immigrants, etc.) are excluded. Differential exclusion is the situation in which immigrants become part of civil society in their roles as workers, consumers, parents, etc., but are excluded from full participation (Castles

1995: 294). In the case of Europe's former 'guestworker' countries such as Germany, Switzerland and Belgium, differential exclusion reflects the philosophy of migrants as temporary labourers whose possibilities for permanent settlement and full integration were (and to some extent continue to be) denied for a number of reasons – economic (to preserve low wages and flexibility of labour supply), social (to avoid demands on social services), cultural (threat to national identity) and political (fear of public disorder, neutralising the anti-immigrant vote, etc.). Castles suggests (1995: 295) that the differential exclusion model is also applicable to the newer immigration countries of Mediterranean Europe, where it is useful in understanding the contradictory character of state attitudes towards immigrants. On the one hand, migrants are tolerated because they are needed to fill gaps in the low-skilled labour market. On the other, countries such as Italy have been slow to see themselves as immigration countries and hence to introduce policies favouring migrants' integration and acquisition of citizenship rights (Anthias and Lazaridis 1999).

However, we do not see Albanian immigrants as passive victims of exclusion, but as increasingly dynamic actors who can challenge and negotiate the discourses and practices of exclusion, creating their own spaces of inclusion and avenues of integration into the host society. For this reason, in the analysis which follows, and which we pick up again more specifically at the start of Chapter 6, we prefer the term 'differential inclusion'.

Integration

To a large extent integration is the counterface of social exclusion, but it is also a term of broader resonance, linking to political debates (for instance on 'European integration') which operate at a larger scale than that treated here (cf. Geddes 2000; Hollifield 1997; Miles and Thränhardt 1995). Integration remains a nebulous and contested concept, subject to a multitude of definitions and overlapping to various degrees with competing alternative terms such as assimilation, incorporation, inclusion, etc. Moreover it implies, both in its essential meaning and in its prescriptive use as a 'desirable' policy outcome, a hegemonic relationship between immigrants as a minority population and the majority national society and culture into which integration is supposed to take place. In our use of the term in this book, we follow two pragmatic guidelines. First, we concur with Vermeulen and Penninx (2000) and Heckmann and Schnapper (2003) in their view of integration as an umbrella notion which covers a multitude of processes which occur over the long term. Second, we allow the migrant informants to define integration on their own terms. From this emic perspective integration, especially in the social, employment and cultural spheres, is seen as a highly desirable objective, not least because Albanians see themselves as 'close' to Italians – although this perception of affinity is not reciprocated by Italians themselves.

Questions relating to 'models' of integration are closely linked to the kinds of sociopolitical order maintained by the host society. Without going into too much comparative detail, the two main models are those of *assimilation* and *multiculturalism* or *pluralism*, exemplified by the United States and France in the first instance, and by Sweden, Canada and Australia in the latter. Integration is sometimes seen as a half-way house between these two; but also, as indicated above, as an overarching concept which embraces assimilation and pluralism as models of integration. The countries quoted above do not hold to uniform models of assimilation or multiculturalism, and there is a further differentiation between scholarship on this theme in the United States and in Europe (Schmitter-Heisler 2000). One well-known variant developed in the United States is *segmented assimilation* (Portes and Zhou 1993), or *segmented integration* in Schmitter-Heisler's term. Based mainly on research on the second generation in the US, this occurs when migrants are faced with three alternative pathways in the host society: towards the predominantly middle-class 'white' society; into an ethnically-mixed underclass characterised by poverty, low pay, unemployment and social marginalisation; or into an ethnic encave with its own internal homogeneity and structure.

Germany, Switzerland, and perhaps also Italy, are examples of another model, that of *partial or differential inclusion*, the flip side of the differential exclusion discussed in the previous subsection. In this model, immigrants are incorporated into some spheres of the host society, such as the labour market, but not others, such as full citizenship and political rights (Castles 1995). Italy's slow reaction to the reality of mass immigration, its lingering self-perception as a country of emigration and its frequent changes of government have prevented the emergence of a coherent policy on immigrant integration. So, to some extent, immigrants (and especially Albanians, as we shall see) have made their own integration, but highly differentiated across the various dimensions of entry into the receiving society's economy, society, culture and institutions.

Heckmann (2005) has put forward a cogent synthesis of immigrant integration processes within the European context, and we will use his framework to guide our empirical analysis later in the book. Four levels of integration are identified (Table 1.2):

- *Structural integration* involves the positioning of immigrant individuals and groups in terms of their membership and status within the receiving society's core institutions – the labour market and economy, education and qualification systems, housing, health and social welfare, and citizenship and political participation. In countries with good data systems, many of these immigrant integration characteristics

Table 1.2 Dimensions of integration of immigrants into a host society

Structural integration
- economy: labour market, ethnic economy
- education: academic qualifications, vocational/professional training
- housing
- health and social welfare system
- citizenship rights and political participation

Cultural integration
- language skills
- norms and values; attitudes and behaviour
- role models, e.g. gender roles
- religion
- mutual acculturation: change of culture of receiving society

Interactive integration
- friendships, social networks with host-society members
- partnerships, intermarriage
- membership of private organisations of receiving society

Identificational integration
- sense of belonging to, and shared identification with, the host society

Source: after Heckmann (2005: 28).

can be measured. This can only be done to a limited extent for Albanians in Italy, as we will see in Chapter 3. In any case such data are only good for recorded migrants. The axes of structural integration listed above and in Table 1.2 involve integration processes at a variety of scales – into the national, regional and local society, including neighbourhood effects. Alternatives to this multi-level entry into the host society are twofold: participation instead in the life and economy of the 'ethnic enclave' (which may stifle integration and socioeconomic mobility or could, conceivably, act as a nursery for economic activity leading to wider-scale integration at a later stage); or participation in a transnational system with internationally extended rights and greater support from the homeland. In both cases the potential for full structural integration into the receiving society is lessened.

- *Cultural integration*, also known as acculturation, concerns the transmission and acquisition of knowledge, cultural standards, language competence, and behaviour and attitudinal changes. Language is perhaps the most important variable here, in that it is key to so many other channels of integration. However, acculturation is an interactive process that, in theory, changes the receiving society as well, which has to learn new ways of relating and adapting to the needs of the migrants, and draws cultural richness from this interaction. So far, Italy has achieved little in this regard. On the other side, cultural integration does not mean that immigrant groups give up the cultural resources of

their home country; particularly for the second generation, bicultural identities and bilingual competence can be an asset.
- *Interactive integration* is the participation and acceptance of immigrants in the sphere of primary social relations and networks of the host society. Typical indicators (Table 1.2) are friendship patterns, partnerships and intermarriage, and memberships of clubs and organisations. Clearly the core competences of cultural integration, such as language and host-country cultural knowledge, are preconditions for interactive integration.
- *Identificational integration* only develops at a later stage in the integration process, building on the other three. Identification implies that the immigrant sees him/herself as not just an actor within a social system but also as having a sense of belonging with that collective body, a sense of 'we-ness' with the host society and culture.

Building on the above schema we may now advance a general definition of the integration of immigrants into a receiving society. Following again Heckman (2005: 15),

> Integration ... can be defined as a long-lasting process of inclusion and acceptance of migrants in the core institutions, relations and statuses of the receiving society. For the migrants integration refers to a process of learning a new culture, an acquisition of rights, access to positions and statuses, a building of personal relations to members of the receiving society and a formation of feelings of belonging and identification towards the immigration society. Integration is an interactive process between migrants and the receiving society, in which, however, the receiving society has much more power and prestige.

One dimension of integration omitted by Heckmann, but stressed by Fonseca and Malheiros (2005: 19–63), is geographical distribution or *spatial integration*, conventionally measured by indices of spatial segregation and location quotients. This aspect is quite well-covered by Italian statistics and, on this criterion, Albanians can be regarded as spatially well-integrated since, of all immigrant groups in Italy, their distribution most closely approximates that of the native population. Chapter 3 has full details on this.

Racism

As with social exclusion and integration, there is no common view amongst social scientists about the 'correct' definition of racism. If anything, the recent plethora of scholarship about race and racism has both exacerbated the lack of concensus, and led to a fundamental questioning about the very language and terminology we use when we discuss these topics (Bulmer and Solomos 1999: 5). The conventional definition of racism runs along the following lines: '[T]he process by which social groups categorise other groups as inferior or different on the basis of physical characteristics, cultural markers or national origin' (after Castles 2000: 174). Castles goes on to point out that:

> racism is not an aberration or a result of individual pathology. It is a set of practices and discourses which are deeply rooted in the history, traditions and culture of modernity. Racism exists in a variety of forms in all modern societies, and plays a crucial role in consolidating nation-states by providing an instrument for defining belonging or exclusion. (Castles 2000: 174)

There are several points here which resonate with the Italian case, especially as regards Albanian immigrants. The first concerns the assumption, common in the early years of immigration in the 1970s and 1980s, that Italians were 'immune to racism'. This was embodied in the complacent myth of *'italiani, brava gente'* – good, tolerant Italians, always welcoming foreign visitors (see Cole 1995: 9). From the late 1980s on, critical analysts such as Pugliese (1991) and Campani (1993) pointed out the uselessness and irrelevance of such high idealism when immigrants were (and still are) subject daily to exploitation, abuse and discrimination. Beginning with the murder of Jerry Maslo, a black African agricultural worker at Villa Literno near Naples in 1989, racist violence against *'extracomunitari'* has been shown to be endemic in Italy (Andall 1990).

Secondly, Italy illustrates very well the shifting meaning and practices of racism over recent years: from biological essentialism to cultural differentialism and social inegalitarianism. Paraphrasing Wieviorka (1994: 182–183), racism based on cultural factors considers the 'other' as 'different' and thus to be avoided; racism based on social differentiation considers the 'other' as an inferior being to be exploited. For many writers, this is the passage from the 'old' to the 'new racism', often now expressed in the postmodern plural – racisms.[4] With Lazaridis and Koumandraki (2001), who have written about the analogous context of Albanian migrants in Greece, we follow the arguments of Mac an Ghaill about the 'shifting meanings of racism at a time of wide and rapid social change', so that 'contemporary conditions are helping to produce multiple forms of racism and new ethnic identifications' (1999: 4, 7).

Racist attitudes in Italy were initially directed towards the easily-recognisable groups who made up the first major immigrant flows – above all those coming from Morocco, the Philippines and Senegal. Particularly emblematic was the black-skinned African street-hawker, the so-called *vu cumprà*, who became highly visible in tourist cities and on beaches in the 1980s.[5] The arrival of Albanians after 1990 challenged the notion of skin colour as the main signifier of immigrant status and racism. The racist stigmatisation of Albanians by Italian society as the 'new others' can be understood in relation to Italy's need to subscribe to new exclusionary discourses of European identity and 'civilisation': Albanians were targeted as the 'uncivilised other'. We return to this issue in Chapter 4.

The third point arising from Castles' statement concerns the variety and subtlety of forms of racism in contemporary Italy. Although institutional racism is certainly not absent, and nor are Italy's political leaders immune from making the most extraordinary racist gaffes (for example the Northern League politician Irene Pivetti, when Speaker of the Italian Parliament, suggested that Albanians landing in Italy should be 'thrown back into the sea'), what is more widespread, and therefore pernicious, is the 'everyday racism' of a multitude of familiar and hence unconscious practices, attitudes and conversations. Essed (1991: 52) defines everyday racism as a process in which socialised racist notions are integrated into meanings that make practices immediately definable and manageable; the repetitive nature of these everyday practices then reinforces underlying racial and ethnic relations. We shall see later how anti-Albanian racist practices are embodied in daily, routine behaviour and attitudes – in the street or neighbourhood, in the workplace, in school classrooms, etc.

Moreover these racisms are highly differentiated between immigrant groups, are regionally expressed and context-specific within Italy, and can be quite unstable over time. Strong ethnic (and gender) stereotypes are attached to different national groups of immigrants such as Moroccans, Senegalese, Filipinos and Chinese.[6] North–South differences in how racism is expressed and experienced within Italy have been suggested by Cole (1995: 100–129) and Daly (1999, 2001) amongst others. Our Albanian evidence will further explore these regional contrasts. We will also explore how racism towards Albanians is not only manifested in a wide range of material practices and anti-Albanian behaviour, but is also particularly powerful in the discursive realm. In Italy the term *albanese* ('Albanian') carries a heavy connotation of intolerance and derogatory attitudes which condemn all Albanians as unwelcome, uncivilised, poor, violent, criminally-inclined and untrustworthy.[7]

Summing up, then, racism is a key factor in understanding the social exclusion of migrants, including Albanians in Italy. Following Goldberg (1990: xiii), we observe the replacement of a single, monolithic racism by a multiplicity of racisms, each contingent on ethnic group, historical and geographical setting, and situational context. Like social exclusion and integration (and identity, which we examine next), racism is a multi-level phenomenon. It expresses itself at a variety of scales (structural, institutional, ethnic group, individual), in different domains (in the workplace, in the neighbourhood, in politics, in the press, in the legal domain, etc.), and in different forms (violence, discrimination, symbolically, verbally, etc.). Although most Italians remain highly conscious of skin colour as an index of their own racial attitudes, the arrival of the Albanians in the early 1990s saw a fundamental reworking of the nature of anti-immigrant racism in Italy (Vasta 1993). 'Cultural racism' came to be the key indicator by which to differentiate and inferiorise Albanians (cf. Wieviorka 1994). Albanians' ascribed cultural characteristics were deployed as justifications for their exclusion and for a widespread 'Albanophobia' within Italy (the same thing happened in Greece; Lazaridis 1996). In Italy, old colonial linkages, dormant for nearly half a century, were resuscitated as Italy examined not only its relationship with its Adriatic neighbour and former colony, but also with itself (Mai 2003). This forms part of the theorisation of Italians' ambivalence towards, and stigmatisation of, Albanians which we return to in Chapter 6.

Identity

Like racism, integration and social exclusion, identity is an elastic construct: complex and multi-dimensional, and the subject of huge debate in the humanities and social sciences. Indeed according to Stuart Hall (1996: 1) there has been a 'discursive explosion' over the concept of identity in recent years, and for sure the discussion is set to continue.

It is important to realise that identity is a contested concept, and is itself the focus of conflict and power. The very use of the term, especially when prefixed by qualifiers such as 'ethnic' or 'national', tempts one into essentialist readings of inherent values, fixed and static, without any acknowledgement of the role of agency, or of place, or of sociohistoric context. We refrain from using a prefix (ethnic, cultural, national, social, etc.) to the term identity because we want to detach any presuppositions from our empirical exploration of Albanian migrants' identity construction. In any case Albanians living in Italy tend to eschew any cohesive group identity or collective consciousness as Albanians.

The conceptualisation of identity that Stuart Hall proposes is not an essentialist, but a strategic and positional one:

> Identities are never unified and, in late modern times, are increasingly fragmented and fractured; never singular, but multiply constructed across different, often intersecting and antagonistic discourses, practices and positions. They are subject to a radical historicization and are constantly in the process of change and transformation. (S. Hall 1996: 4)

Hall goes on to point out that,

> Though they seem to invoke an origin in a historical past with which they continue to correspond, actually identities are about ...using the resources of history, language and culture in the process of becoming rather than being: not *'who we are'* or *'where we came from'*, so much as *'what we might become'*, *'how we have been represented'* and *'how that bears on how we might represent ourselves'*. (S. Hall 1996: 4, our italics)

Moreover, because identities are constructed within and not outside representation, through the narrativisation of the self and of the 'other', they are 'the product of the making of difference and exclusion', which means that they are 'constructed through, not outside difference' (S. Hall 1996: 4). This gives us a framework for our later analysis of the construction of Italian identity as contrapunctal to constructions of Albanian identity. Hall, again:

> Identities can function as points of identification and attachment only *because* of their capacity to exclude, to leave out, to render 'outside' the abjected ... The unity, the internal homogeneity, which the term treats as foundational, is not a natural, but a constructed form of closure. (S. Hall 1996: 5)

This approach to identity as a phenomenon which is both *exclusionary* and *inclusionary*, and both *processual* and *relational*, is very important for our analysis of Albanians in Italy, and of Italian society's reaction to them. It also provides an epistemological setting to locate the kind of research and fieldwork which we have carried out. Above all the approach provides an opportunity for us to:

- acknowledge the importance of both narrativity and performativity, and therefore of socially established practices of communication in the definition and strengthening (but also denigration and abandonment) of any identity;
- understand how the analysis of the construction of any collective or individual identity means mapping a set of scattered and fragmented micro-identities, corresponding to the various locales in which the self is conceived and performed in relation to various social forces and dynamics;
- operationalise the above via the various kinds of qualitative field research that we wanted to do, focusing on media and other discursive accounts of Albanians, matched with their own life-stories and narratives of events.

Identity, then, serves as an important nexus of our research: as a mediating concept between inclusion and exclusion, the external and the internal, the individual and society; and as a convenient tool through which to understand many aspects – personal, political, social, cultural – of Albanian migrant lives. We have quoted at length from Stuart Hall because we find his inspiring 1996 essay on the topic of identity corresponds extremely well with how we view the issue, and with how Albanian identities have evolved as fluid sites of contestation, myth-making, negotiation and manipulation (Schwandner-Sievers and Fischer 2002).

Of course, Hall is not alone in his rearticulation of the phenomenology of identity. Iain Chambers (1994), in his thought-provoking analysis of the relationships between 'migrancy', culture and identity, argues that all identities are continuously formed and re-formed throughout the journey of life and through processes that are never complete. Similarly, for Edensor (2002: 24, 29) identity is continuously evolving, reconstituted in a process of becoming by virtue of migrants' location in social, material, temporal and spatial contexts. For Albanians fleeing a material and ideological past which they tend to have rejected, the dynamic process of identity (re)construction, or identification, occurs both at a broader social and political level, and in their mundane, everyday lives, in private and communal spaces. Through the interactiveness of thought, discourse, action and experience, identification is both an individual and a collective act. Although we can agree with Eriksen (2002: 109) that in general terms the nation is the metaphorical space in which people locate their personal histories and thereby their identities, for Albanian migrants who have in many cases 'dis-identified' with their Albanian communist past, migrating to Italy (or to Greece, or elsewhere) is often about realising a new project of identity. But their initial glorification of Italy as an embodiment of the rich and pleasurable West is frustrated by their wholesale stigmatisation by Italian society. This forces them to adopt new identity outcomes, as 'Albanians in Italy'. Hence, more than most, Albanians are 'migrants of identity' (cf. Rapport and Dawson 1998), even 'identity-hoppers', and as Blumi (2003) shows, this is not a new process for them. Albanians' malleable self-identification, and the way in which an imputed Albanian identity has been used as a mirror to positively reflect Italian identity, will be themes echoing throughout the book.

A Summary of the Book

The structure of this book follows the migration cycle from Albania to Italy and back again. Six chapters follow this introductory one. The next two chapters are based mainly on secondary data and set out first the Albanian background to the migration flow to Italy, and second the evolution and patterning of that flow. Chapter 2 is an account of Albania's modern history which pays particular attention to the factors and events framing post-1990 migration. Although brief reference is made to the pre-communist era, our main focus is the later communist years and the chaotic period of transition to democracy and an open economy. We examine the evolution of Albania's population, the country's economic and social geography, its highly unusual political culture both before and after the break-up of the communist regime (in which elements of continuity were at least as important as elements of rupture), and the key political events that triggered, or helped to trigger, the various migratory phases. In the final part of Chapter 2 we focus more specifically on the role of Italian television as a force shaping Albanians' migratory aspirations and trajectories.

In Chapter 3 we trace the chronology and map the geography of Albanian migration post-1990, chiefly to Italy, but with some comparative reference to Greece, the other main destination for Albanian migration during these years. The account will be illustrated by several tables and maps which will enable us to discuss in some detail the spatial patterning of Albanian migration both within Albania and across the various regions of Italy. This will also help to set the scene for the empirical research which, as mentioned above, we concentrated in three contrasting Italian city-regions (Rome, Modena and Lecce) and in different parts of Albania.

Chapter 4 describes the Italian reaction to Albanian immigration, a reaction which passed swiftly from an initial welcome to a highly discriminatory securisation and repressive stigmatisation. Following Lazaridis (1996), we refer to 'Albanophobia' as a collective, strong, anti-Albanian feeling which embraces different sentiments – not only fear but also distrust, hatred, ignorance, condemnation and paternalism. The role of the media, and of certain political factions with links to the media (often 'owning' newspapers, television channels, etc.), is seen to be absolutely critical here. A review both of the media themselves and of the lively debate in Italy over their role in perpetuating negative stereotypes of immigrants enables us to identify a number of powerful discursive themes running through the media's treatment of Albanians, the most powerful of which is their criminalisation. The chapter concludes by attempting to theorise Albanian migration to Italy and Italians' stigmatisation of Albanians by reference to the colonial and neocolonial history of Italo-Albanian geopolitics and in relation to Italian nationalism and self-identity.

Chapters 5 and 6 are the longest of the book: it is here that we explore and synthesise the main corpus of migrant life-stories. We try to strike a balance between drawing out general themes from the interview narratives and giving due attention to unusual stories which, despite (or indeed because of) their uniqueness, are instructive in certain ways. We sample a diversity of types of migrant, both as regards demographic and socioprofessional background in Albania, and with reference to experiences in Italy. Especially in Chapter 5, on employment and housing, the bulk of the interviewees are ordinary working migrants – farm, factory, construction and service workers – doing low-status jobs for low rates of pay. But we also hear from many others – students, professionals, entrepreneurs, sex-workers – enabling us to explore the diversity of Albanians' experiences of life and work in Italy. The life-stories cover participants' pre-migration background in Albania, the migration and arrival phases in Italy, their experiences of work, housing, and family and community life, and their reactions to a range of Italian migration laws and regularisation schemes.

The migrant narratives continue in Chapter 6, which is on social exclusion and inclusion. Here we develop further, and in the Italian-Albanian context, Castles' notion of 'differential exclusion' – the situation in which migrants are incorporated into certain sections of society, for instance the labour market (albeit with limits set on progress up the employment ladder) but excluded from others, such as welfare provisions, citizenship and political participation (Castles 1995: 294). Acknowledging Albanians' dynamic progress within the host-society context, we choose to rephrase the concept as 'differential inclusion', a reorientation reflected in the book's title. The role of social networks and individual initiative is seen to be critical here, more so than Albanian associations and community organisations, which have developed rather slowly. We conclude the chapter with discussion on Albanians' renegotiation of their identity within their evolving diasporic space in Italy. We find that there is an 'Albanian paradox' in that Albanians remain the most stigmatised immigrant group in Italy, yet they see themselves, and aspire to be, very similar to Italians; and at an objective level do appear to be quite highly integrated at the individual, workplace and neighbourhood scales. The nature of this social integration does, however, vary between different parts of Italy. Hence, throughout Chapters 5 and 6 close attention is paid to the often marked variation in the migrant experience in the three field sites, and especially between the north and the south of Italy.

With Chapter 7 we return, with the migrants, to Albania. We find that, as yet, relatively few have returned, except on holiday and for family visits. This leads us into a discussion about the meaning of migration for the current survival, and the future, of Albania and its people. We examine the role of remittances, investment, and opportunities for small business development for returning migrants who have saved some capital. The poor infrastructure, still embryonic planning and the lack of trust, both towards the political elites and amongst ordinary people, remain significant obstacles to a productive deployment of migrant capital for the longer-term development of the Albanian economy. For the time being, migration begets further migration, but this process must soon exhaust itself. The critical challenge is for migration, remittances, return, investment, economic growth and political stability to achieve a synergy before the country slides into a downward spiral of depopulation and economic abandonment.

Notes

1   As an illustration of this expanding interest, a conference on Albanian migration organised at the University of Sussex in September 2002 by the two authors in collaboration with Stephanie Schwandner-Sievers of the Nash Albanian Studies Programme at University College London, attracted more than forty papers. For outputs of this conference based on revised and selected papers see King et al. (2005); Mai and Schwandner-Sievers (2003). A follow-up conference convened by King in Korçë, southern Albania, in September 2004 attracted a further twenty-five papers: see King (2005a).

2 This was facilitated by the presence in Rome of Sussex DPhil student Alessandro Drago, who carried out twenty interviews with our project interview schedule.
3 This was especially the case in Lecce where the more relaxed social environment of this southern city enabled Nicola Mai to meet several Albanian family groups for informal social intercourse, especially one family who 'adopted' him during his stay.
4 Given the vastness of this literature, this is not the place for an extensive review. For some examples see Anthias (1990), Balibar and Wallerstein (1991), Brah et al. (1999), Donald and Rattansi (1992), Goldberg (1993), Mac an Ghaill (1999), Miles (1989, 1993), Solomos and Back (1994).
5 The denigratory term *vu cumprà* derives from Italian stereotyping of the immigrant pedlars' pronunciation of *vuoi compare* – 'do you want to buy?'. Now this term has been condemned as offensive and has rightly been suppressed, except in anti-immigrant discourse. See Riccio (1999); Zinn (1994).
6 Conventional stereotypes in Italy associate Moroccans with drug-peddling, Albanians with criminal networks and prostitution, and the Chinese with being introverted and self-sufficient as a community. The Senegalese are seen as a group which is 'exotic' and 'different' but also relatively harmless. (Female) Filipinos are seen as hardworking and reliable but as a 'servant' class.
7 Such attitudes are remarkably widespread amongst the Italian population. King recalls a dinner-party conversation in a city in northern Italy with an eminent geography professor a few years ago: upon being told that we were to start some research on Albanian immigrants, he immediately interjected '*Stai attento! Sono pericolosi quelli*' (Be careful! They're dangerous, those Albanians). He was not joking or being ironic.

Chapter 2

THE ALBANIAN BACKGROUND

Introduction

Too often, when immigration is studied, the host-society perspective dominates, with insufficient attention paid to the migrants' country of origin. This chapter provides some background on the Albanian setting to the post-1990 trans-Adriatic migration flows. Of course, a full account of the history, geography, politics and culture of Albania is hardly possible in a single chapter.[1] Hence, we select those aspects of the Albanian context which are the most meaningful in understanding the driving factors behind the scale and nature of the Albanian migratory flows which are the subject of the next chapter.

We adopt a broadly chronological approach, from pre- to post-communism, supplemented by cross-cutting accounts which focus thematically on the economy, society, culture and demography – important structural factors framing the Albanian migration and the behaviour of the migrants. Our account weaves together history, politics, economic and social geography, cultural and media studies, and a little Freudian psychology.

In framing an explanation for the large-scale emigration of Albanians after 1990, the twin factors of poverty and economic instability are paramount. Despite its central position within Southern or Mediterranean Europe, with which it shares a common heritage of Greek, Roman and Ottoman cultural influences, Albania is different from all other European countries (Kressing 2002). The country's level of economic development and its physical and social infrastructures classify it as the poorest and most disadvantaged society in Europe, and more akin to the less-developed parts of Latin America and North Africa. The development gap which separates Albania from the European Union, which it aspires to join, is enormous, and made more dramatic by the country's neighbouring location to Greece and Italy.

According to the World Bank, economic indicators for Albania show the most widespread poverty of any country in Europe, the least diversified and most backward economic base, the pervasive threat of disappearing financial and human capital, inadequate fiscal resources, and the reluctance of foreigners to invest in the country. Nevertheless, the World Bank also notes positive features: good demographic indicators, such as high life expectancy and rapidly declining population increase; an industrious population, increasingly outward-looking and multilingual; a relatively rich resource base; fine coastal and mountain landscapes; and geographical proximity to wealthy countries. As a result, it is claimed that Albania has the potential to achieve fast, equitable and sustainable growth (De Soto et al. 2002: 1).

The post-1990 emigration was not without precedent in Albanian history; nor were the economic and social problems of the post-communist transition without their deeper historical origins. A brief glance at Albanian history is therefore necessary.

Pre-communist Albania

Early History: Illyria, the Ottomans and Skanderbeg

Most historians agree that present-day Albanians are descendants of the Illyrians, an ancient tribe that inhabited the western Balkans. Somewhat more conventionally, Albanian scholars claim that the Illyrians were the original inhabitants of the region and the oldest of the Balkan peoples. They argue that Albanians' historical identity and sense of territoriality are based on this Illyrian distribution which roughly coincided with the present-day Albanian-inhabited lands, long pre-dating the Slav migrations into the area (Buda 1985). One of the Illyrian tribes was the *Albani*, based around Durrës and from whom the country's modern name is derived.

Defeats in 229 BC and 167 BC brought the Illyrians largely under Roman rule; Christianity was introduced during the second century AD. When the Roman Empire split into its eastern and western parts in 395 AD, southern Illyria went to the eastern church and northern Illyria went to the western empire under the authority of the Pope (Hill 1992: 48). From the fourth to the sixth centuries AD the area inhabited by the Illyrians was subject to successive invasions by Huns and Goths, and from the sixth century Slavs began to settle on Illyrian territory, leading to a process of territorial 'involution' or 'compaction' (D. Hall 1994: 3). In Kosovo, lowland farmers withdrew into the mountains, laying the historical foundations for modern territorial disputes between Serbs and Albanians. From 750 AD on, the area was under Byzantine rule. Later came the Normans and the Neapolitans (the *Regnum Albaniae* of Charles of Anjou); the territory then became part of the large Serbian empire under Stefan Dušan. The Venetians took hold of the coast until the late fourteenth century, by which time the Ottoman Empire had begun its incorporation of the Albanian lands.

Assimilation into the growing Ottoman Empire was a gradual process; warfare continued as the larger and more powerful indigenous clans fought to retain their autonomy. The most important of these still-independent domains was that of the Kastrioti dynasty, based at Krujë, north of Tirana. Gjergj Kastrioti, son of the clan chief, was sent to the Sultan's court as a kind of hostage to guarantee the family's loyalty. Renamed Iskander-Bey (Skanderbeg), he nominally converted to Islam and fought several successful campaigns with the Ottoman army. However, in 1443 he returned to Albania, took over his father's citadel at Krujë and massacred those in the domain who refused to renounce Islam. For the next twenty-five years he united the Albanian nobles under his leadership against the Turks. His military successes against the Ottoman occupation evoked interest from the Papal States, Venice and Naples, who were only too willing to help him with arms and occasionally troops to fight the Muslim enemy (Vickers 1999: 8).

This period was the first time that what was to become Albania functioned more or less as a unified state. The Albanian people had found a patriotic hero who was well-known throughout Europe.[2] The Kastrioti emblem – the distinctive double-headed eagle on a red background – was to become the Albanian national flag.

With the death of Skanderbeg in 1468, Albania fell once more under Ottoman rule. Skanderbeg's own son was too young to take on his father's mantle, choosing instead to cross the Adriatic to live in the Kingdom of Naples. A large number of Albanian Catholics followed him, settling in numerous small towns and villages in Southern Italy and Sicily. Forerunners by more than five hundred years of the migrants of the 1990s, the Arbëresh (as they were called) retained their language and customs, and today number around 200,000 (D. Hall 1994: 50).

Back in Albania, Skanderbeg was succeeded by Lek Dukagjin, who became famous as the convenor of the legal system known as *Kanun*, which codified the customary laws and norms of the tribal society of northern Albania. The *Kanun* rigidly regulated issues relating to land, water, inheritance, marriage, theft and violence. Integral to its operation was the definition of behaviour related to 'honour' and the blood feud. The system survived for centuries until its partial eradication by the communist regime. However, it has been revitalised in new forms since 1990. We will assess its significance for modern Albanian society and emigration patterns later in this chapter.

Most writers interpret the Ottoman occupation of Albania in a thoroughly negative light. Logoreci (1977: 17, 22–36), for instance, refers repeatedly to the 'dark age' and the 'long night' of Ottoman rule. An alternative view stresses the tolerance of the Ottoman state towards its diverse populations and their various ethnicities, languages and religions

(Vickers 1999: 11, 16). However, during the seventeenth century a policy of Islamisation was put in train, as a result of which about two-thirds of the Albanian population converted to Islam, mainly to avoid the taxes levied against Christians. Nevertheless, 'crypto-Christianity' and religious syncretism were very common.[3] Today, as a legacy of these trends, around 70 per cent of the Albanian population is Muslim, 20 per cent (mostly in the south) belong to the Albanian and Greek Orthodox churches, and 10 per cent (mainly in the north) are Roman Catholic.

Albanian Nationalism and Independence

During the nineteenth century, the Ottoman Empire increasingly came under pressure from the mounting nationalisms of the conquered peoples in the Balkans. Launching the *Rilindja* or renaissance, Albanian nationalist leaders met in Prizren, in Kosovo, in 1878: a league was founded to promote a free, united Albania in all Albanian-populated lands. The league also sought to develop Albanian culture and education, and in 1908 the language was standardised, based on the Latin script (before, Muslim and Orthodox Albania had used the Arabic and Greek alphabets respectively).

Following the Ottomans' defeat during the First Balkan War, Albanian independence was proclaimed in 1912 and Ismael Qemali convened a temporary government. The post-war Ambassadors' Conference in London confirmed Albania's independent and neutral status, but because of strong pressures from Albania's neighbours, the Great Powers (Great Britain, France, Germany, Russia, Austria-Hungary and Italy) gave the Albanian-inhabited region of Kosovo to Serbia and much of the southern region of Çamëria to Greece. Albania's borders have remained unchanged, with roughly equal numbers of ethnic Albanians inside and outside the country. Soon, however, the First World War broke out; Austrian, French, Italian, Greek, Serb and Montenegrin armies occupied Albania, exploiting the country's lack of strong political leadership. At the Paris Peace Conference after the war, US President Woodrow Wilson vetoed a plan by Britain, France and Italy to partition Albania amongst its neighbours. Finally, in 1920, Albania was admitted to the newly-formed League of Nations, thereby gaining international recognition as an independent state.

During the 1920s Albania was deeply divided between two political groups: a conservative class of labourers and tribal chiefs, led by Ahmed Bey Zogu, who wished to maintain the status quo; and liberal/radical intellectuals, politicians and merchants, led by Fan Noli, a US-educated Orthodox bishop, who wanted to modernise. In 1924 a popular revolt against Zogu forced him to flee to Yugoslavia. Noli became head of the new government, and set out to build a Western-style democracy. Six months later, suffering from internal dissent and lacking international support, Noli was overthrown by Zogu, assisted by Yugoslavia. Zogu then reigned for fourteen years, first as president and, after 1928, as the self-proclaimed King Zog I. Zog's rule was marked by economic stagnation, although he helped create a modern school system and made the country somewhat more stable. He failed, however, to solve the issue of land reform, and the Albanian peasantry remained impoverished. Clan rivalries fractured rural society, especially in the north.

Italian Occupation and the Second World War

Albanians' mass migration to Italy in the 1990s was not without historical precedent, as we noted above. Nor were the migratory links between the two countries based purely on trans-Adriatic proximity. During Zog's reign, Italy exercised so much influence over its neighbour's affairs that Albania was virtually an Italian protectorate (Sjöberg 1991: 24). Mussolini saw Albania as part of his imperial vision – as a place to settle millions of Italians and as a strategic bridge in his plans to invade Greece. On the economic front, Italian companies were successful in reaching agreements with the hard-pressed Albanian government. Important agricultural schemes – drainage and irrigation of the coastal lowlands, reforestation of the uplands – were launched, several new roads were built and the layout of Tirana was remodelled. Even before the Italian invasion and annexation of Albania in 1939, Italians controlled every essential sector of the Albanian state: in 1938, 170,000 Italian men were working on agricultural and infrastructure projects in Albania (Vickers 1999: 137). Moreover Italy had virtual monopoly control over all of Albania's important mineral resources – chromite, copper, oil, etc. (D. Hall 1994: 104–105). Albania's dependence on Italy grew to such an extent that, by 1939, Italy accounted for 92 per cent of Albanian exports and was the source of 83 per cent of its imports.

The rhetoric of Italy's colonial venture in Albania is interesting because it foreshadows some of the discursive constructions of Albanian immigrants in Italy in the 1990s (Mai 2003). On the one hand Fascist propagandists stressed the shared Adriatic ethnic heritage of Italians and Albanians, deploying the slogan '*l'Adriatico è mare Italiano ed Albanese*' to frame Italy as the 'natural defendant' of Albania's territorial and cultural integrity. Hence, only under the 'imperial project' of Rome could Albania regain its true historical identity. This was used to justify the union of the two kingdoms (same fascist political regime, diplomats, armed forces, currency, customs union, etc.) as a cloak for Italian colonial supremacy and control.

On the other hand Albania was clearly regarded as a 'backward' and 'uncivilised' country whose people were to be 'progressively reformed' under Italian Fascist tutelage (Mai 2003: 83). In this way Albania was constructed as the 'colonial other' (but incorporated 'within' via unification with Italy), against which the 'civilised' status of Italy could be measured and confirmed.[4] We shall return to this ambiguous double construction of Albania and the Albanians in the context of recent immigration in Chapter 4.

The Second World War brought an end to Italy's chaotic colonial venture and to the quisling Albanian Fascist Party set up in 1939 in the shadow of the Italian Fascists. Mussolini's Albania-based invasion of Greece – ostensibly to 'liberate' Albanian irridentists in Epirus/Çamëria (northern Greece) – was easily repulsed and the Greek troops entered southern Albania, capturing Korçë and Gjirokastër, centres of the Greek-speaking minority in Albania. The German–Italian agreement of 1941 prescribed the formation of a 'Greater Albania', so that Italian occupation extended to all the Albanian-settled lands in Kosovo, Montenegro, Macedonia and northern Greece. However, after the Allied invasion of Italy in 1943, German forces occupied Albania and a bitter struggle by the Albanian partisans to oust the Italo-German fascist axis ensued. Albania was liberated in November 1944, shrinking back into its earlier borders.

Communism Albanian-style

Origins

According to Logoreci (1977: 71), the history of communism in Albania is 'as chequered and tortuous as the history of the Albanian nation-state itself'. Communist sentiments in Albania can be traced to the 1920s and 1930s; communist cells financed by the Soviet Union's Comintern were formed in opposition to Zog's monarchy and, later, to fascist currents. Typical members of such groups were students, intellectuals, artists and artisans, many of whom had been exposed to communist ideas abroad, notably in Moscow and Paris. In 1941, guided by the Yugoslav communists, the main cells from Korçë and Shkodër joined together to found the Albanian Communist Party (ACP). Party membership grew especially amongst those who had been neglected by the pre-war regime, such as peasants and young people: land reform, social change and economic improvement were promised as essential steps towards the creation of an egalitarian and democratic nation-state. The first issue of the ACP's newspaper, *Zeri i Popullit* ('Voice of the People'), appeared in August 1942, urging the people to wage a 'popular struggle' (Vickers 1999: 147). Communism, partisanship and liberation thus became united in a powerful mutually reinforcing movement: the supreme political force in Albania by the time the Germans were expelled in 1944.[5]

One further feature of communist origins in Albania deserves mention: its regional expression. This aspect is also important because, as we shall see later in the chapter, regional divisions are crucial to understanding the political cleavages in the country. The ACP was largely a creation of southern or Tosk Albanians. Enver Hoxha, leader of the Albanian communists, was born in Gjirokastër (see Figure 2.1) and it had been the children of the southern bourgeoisie who had received the best education, either at home or abroad, before the war. Tosk elements at the core of the ACP (renamed the Albanian Party of Labour in 1948) were able to successfully undermine the influence both of the southern landowning beys and of the northern clan hierarchies (Whitaker 1968: 282). As communism became the dominant political force in Albania, the balance of national political power transferred from the northern Ghegs to the Tosks who inhabited the central and southern regions south of the Shkumbin River (Figure 2.1).[6]

Enver Hoxha and 'The Regime'

Opinions differ sharply on the 'greatness' of Albania's communist patriarch Enver Hoxha who, installed as his country's leader in November 1944, ruled uninterruptedly until his death in 1985. Ramiz Alia's *Our Enver*, written by Hoxha's successor, was an exercise in deification. Weaving together the medieval nationalist myth of Skanderbeg with the utopian myth of Enver's communism, Alia wrote:

> Just as the battles and deeds of Skanderbeg inspired the Albanians' patriotism and spirit of resistance ... so the work of Enver Hoxha will remain through the centuries a banner of the struggles of our people for socialism and the prosperity of the Homeland ... With his majestic work ... [he] will always inspire the communists ... to ceaseless progress. He will always be present in the joys and worries of our society. The present and future generations will be guided by his teachings ... And Enver will help them. He will give them the answers through his work. (Alia 1988: 481–482, quoted in D. Hall 1994: 37, 39)

Western observers, even those with a special empathy for Albania, take a very different view. Derek Hall describes the Hoxha regime, his personality cult and the bible-like status accorded to his forty-seven-volume *Works* as 'programmed mass sycophancy' (1994: 37). Miranda Vickers' more prosaic epitaph provides what many would regard as a fair assessment of Hoxha's regime and signposts some themes which we expand on later in this chapter:

> For over 40 years he had ruled his tiny state isolated in its remote corner of the Balkans. His complex and contradictory personality had forged a unique and lonely path for Albania and left its imprint on every aspect of Albanian life. Although the country benefited from improved agriculture, industry, and in particular health and education, such initiatives were overshadowed by a horrific legacy of brutal repression, the full story of which has yet to be told. The Albanian people had been cowed into a fearful state of submission, which led them, like their country, to withdraw into themselves with their thoughts

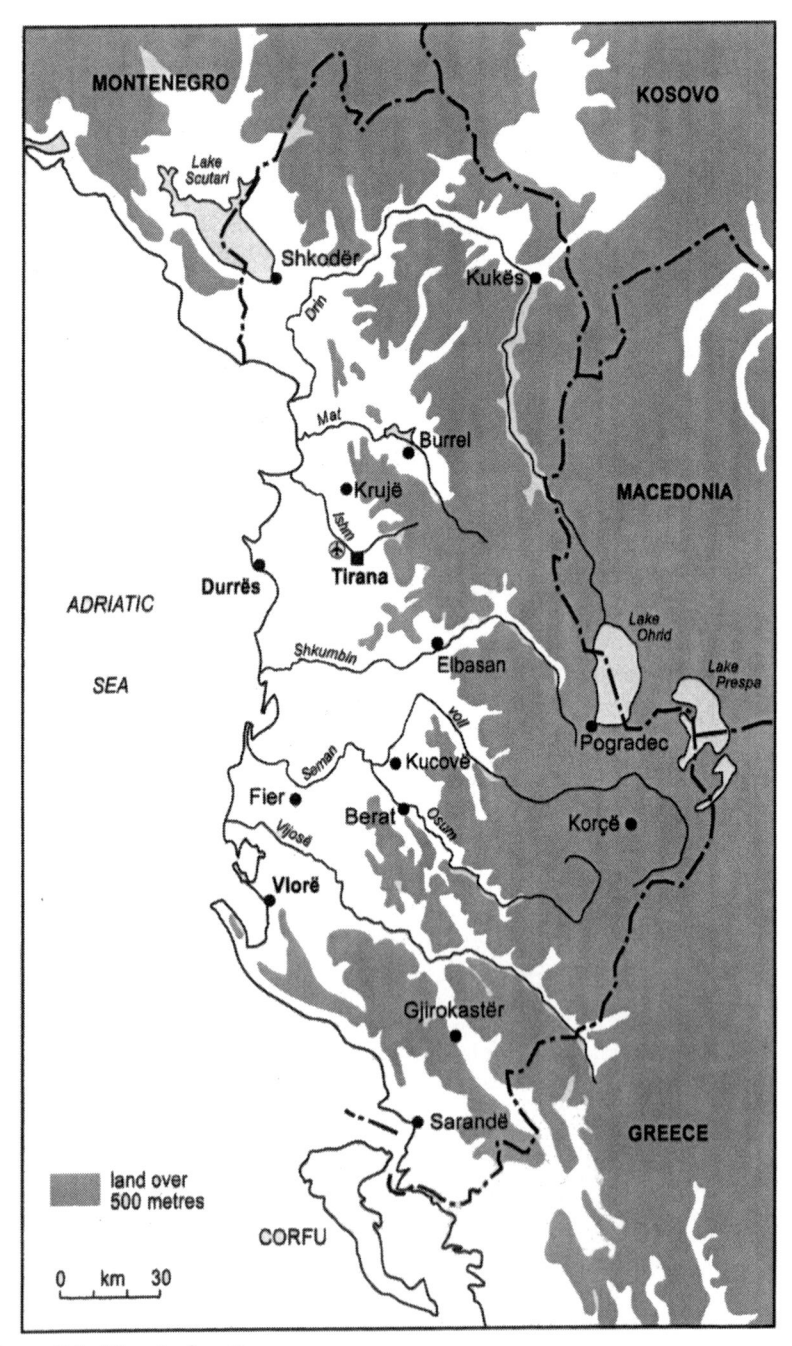

Figure 2.1 Albania: location map

kept secret, paranoid and suspicious of all around them ... Hoxha's policy of trying to practice 'socialism in one country' was totally impractical for Albania. The best he could manage was a policy aimed at mere survival. (Vickers 1999: 209)

The core of the Hoxha regime was an all-embracing Marxist-Leninist ideology which denied the autonomy of the individual in the service of the people. But this was a 'sleight of words', for the supreme moral authority of the state was not really invested in the people but in a single charismatic leader. The regime possessed a secret police force (the notorious Sigurimi), monopolised culture and mass communications, and centrally directed the economy. In enforcing obedience to the Party and ensuring internal security, a capillary network of cadres and informers reached all parts of the country. So-called 'enemies of the people' were badly treated, given the most menial jobs, banished to remote locations, and stinted in their allocations of food and fuel (Saltmarshe 2001: 59). Propaganda was intensively used to cow the population into a sense of defensiveness against the outside world. The border was sealed and militarised and 600,000 bunkers, one for each Albanian household, were scattered the length and breadth of the land. These 'concrete mushrooms' remain in the landscape today as an enduring testimony to Hoxha's defensive paranoia.

One indication of the regime's increasing control over Albanians' daily lives was the progressive purge on religion. Until 1967 the government tolerated the continuation of the three religions in Albania, although the numerically dominant younger generations, raised the 'new way' through school and by work in factories and agricultural cooperatives, set less and less store by religious belief, condemned as 'the opiate of the people' (Marmullaku 1975: 76). In 1967, as part of Albania's 'cultural revolution', Hoxha outlawed religion and created the world's first atheist state. All places of worship were closed down and turned into museums or youth centres; clergy were 'retrained', pensioned off, imprisoned or (in a few cases) executed. Hoxha argued that religion was a subversive force in the country, representing the 'trojan horse' interests of the historical predatory neighbours and enemies – Turkey (Islam), Greece and Serbia (Orthodoxy) and Italy (Roman Catholicism). Parents were discouraged from giving their children names with any religious significance; prescriptive lists of 'Illyrian' names were published (D. Hall 1994: 45). However, as before, crypto-religious behaviour, whereby Albanians outwardly went along with the regime's insistence on atheism but adhered to their original religion within the confines of their home and in secret gatherings, appears to have been quite widespread, especially in rural areas (D. Hall 1994: 45; Marmullaku 1975: 77).

An Era of Non-Migration

Another element of control was the heavy constriction on mobility. Only a very few people – the top Party elite – had passports. For the rest, travel abroad was not permissable. The borders were no-go areas, heavily controlled by electrified fences and watchtowers; potential escapees were arrested and imprisoned, or even shot on sight. Although there are some stories of 'heroic escapees',[7] flight was also discouraged by retribution meted out to family members left behind. Hoxha's propaganda machine banned emigration partly out of paranoia about contamination by the West; but official dogma was that emigration was a 'disease' of the capitalist system, which could not provide employment for all its workers. Albanians should not desire, in any case, to leave their communist paradise.

Internal mobility was also tightly controlled, although not as comprehensively as the complete ban on emigration. In fact, the few studies that exist on population movement at this time suggest that internal migration took place more widely than conventionally thought (Sjöberg 1989, 1992). One third of the population growth in urban areas during 1960–87 was due to rural–urban migration, especially in function of industrial growth. In addition, there was a kind of 'diverted urbanisation', occurring when people settled in peri-urban districts without authorisation, or when they obtained permission to transfer to a rural cooperative or state farm located near a city. Rural–rural migration also took place, notably from the north to the south and to the fertile plains along the coast.

Increasing Isolationism

Enver Hoxha's brand of communism modelled itself on 'ideologically pure' Stalinism. Rejection of all other forms brought about the progressive isolation of Albania, which broke off relations with Yugoslavia in 1948, the Soviet Union in 1961 and China in 1978. Hoxha himself never travelled outside Albania after he attended the world communist leaders' conference in Moscow in 1960.

Initially, Albania depended on neighbouring Yugoslavia for military and economic aid, but the relationship with Tito was always likely to be tense. The Albanian Communist Party had been founded under Yugoslav tutelage but there remained a fundamental geopolitical ambiguity: would Albania include Kosovo with its majority ethnic Albanian population, or was Albania itself destined to become part of the Yugoslav federation? In 1948, when Stalin expelled Yugoslavia from the Communist bloc for ideological reasons, Albania backed the Soviet leader. However, on the occasion of the Sino–Soviet rift in the early 1960s, and in light of the rapprochement between Kruschev's Russia and Yugoslavia, Albania supported China, which Hoxha viewed as more strictly adherent to his favoured Marxist-Leninist ideology. As Kruschev moved to discredit Stalin's legacy, diplomatic ties were broken between Albania and the USSR. Soviet aid, credits and technical assistance, which had allowed Albania to create a relatively modern industrial and agricultural base and enjoy a better standard of living, were cut off.

After 1961, the Albanian regime formed a close but geographically distant bond with China, which took the USSR's place as the country's main trading partner and supplier of economic aid. Various new industrial projects were completed, including the Mao Tse-Tung textile mill near Berat, a large ironworks at Elbasan and a plastics factory at Durrës (Figure 2.1). Chinese wheat bridged the shortfall in domestic production. Agricultural collectivism was finally completed, despite strong opposition from the clan-based population of the northern regions of Albania (Vickers 1999: 197). The Chinese presence in Albania brought a particular form of temporary immigration, commented on by Vickers (1999: 198, quoting various authors) in the following terms:

> By 1971, few industrial areas in Albania were without a population of Chinese … They have settled down well but the natives are not enthused about them … The Chinese community kept very much to itself. Work contracts were usually for six months to a year … and the workers were housed in flats in a self-contained quarter of Tirana with their own restaurants.

However, after the early 1970s Albania's relations with China became strained by China's détente with the United States and subsequent reforms after Mao's death in 1976. In 1978 China cancelled its trade and aid agreements with Albania, which thereby lost its only remaining ally. Albania then pursued closer economic contacts with Europe, but in terms of political, social and cultural ties, the country remained one of the most isolated in the world until the early 1990s.

Whilst the conventional (Western) view was that Hoxha's authoritarian and paranoid defence of the country's sovereignty forced the country to retreat into complete isolation, a study of the broader context leads to a more complex and nuanced interpretation. The Western powers, it seemed, could not begin to understand the ideological essence of the 'Albanian way', which they both demonised and exoticised. Marmullaku went further: according to him (1975: 70) the problem was not so much that the Western governments misunderstood Enver Hoxha, but that they simply did not wish to understand him. Other scholars were more willing to justify Hoxha's apparent paranoia by reference to Albania's history of cultural marginality, political and economic vulnerability, and geo-strategic attraction for foreign powers. Manipulation of these powers through the practice of shifting alliances was therefore the best (or the only) strategy in order to resist assimilation and to maintain independence right across the historical scenario from Skanderbeg to Zog, and from Enver Hoxha to Sali Berisha, Albania's first post-communist leader (Vickers 1999: 186).

Under the Hegemony of Homogenous Thought

The combination of Albania's history of marginality and the communist regime's ideological precepts produced a social, economic and cultural order characterised by extremely autocratic and paternalistic forms of power. Under the pressure of Hoxha's collective psychology of a communist utopia, individuals' desires and emotions were negated, or dissimulated into a secretive personal world. Hegemonic fantasies of unity and egalitarianism crushed the process of individual social differentiation and the development and expression of (to use a Freudian term) people's libidinal economy (see Mai 2002a: 120–140). During the regime, all forms of dissent and deviance from the Party line were repressed; sweeping purges ensured the regime's control. 'Generalised espionage, falsification of history, corruption of science, arbitrary imprisonment, psychiatric confinement, gulags, torture, murder and various forms of social exclusion' all took place (Saltmarshe 2001: 58).

This repressive libidinal landscape created an homogenous cognitive framework in which difference was regarded as an ontological problem, since it undermined the principle of common renunciation of pleasure and material wealth for the sake of the survival of the existing social formation. As many of those who have lived through communism have written (e.g., Solzhenitsyn 1972), this is the trade-off: on the one side unemployment, hunger, despair and class-based exploitation; on the other the promise of being provided for from cradle to grave; but the price to pay for such security and predictability was to live with institutional oppression, summary justice and shared austerity.

According to the Albanian philosopher Artan Fuga, there is an intrinsic relation between a cognitive order and a specific conception of political power, a reciprocal tie between a kind of social and political justice and a particular conception of truth (Fuga 1998). At the centre of this argument is the opposition between homogenous and heterogenous thought. Homogenous thinking is defined as a cognitive approach based on the appropriation of all the conceptual space by one of the poles involved in the process of intellectual confrontation. Heterogenous thought, on the other hand, is the cognitive approach that starts from an acknowledgement of the value of different views and works towards a synthesis of the arguments advanced by all the poles around which the debate is structured. Every philosophical logic operating with homogenous categories legitimates an authoritarian power, while democracy has been linked throughout the history of philosophy to heterogenous conceptual structures (Fuga 1998: 28).

This brief philosophical diversion has been worth making, we feel, because the upheavals and transformations that have characterised Albania's recent history are best understood against this binary. The two different social and moral worlds of homogeneity and heterogeneity have shaped Albanian politics, culture and mentality throughout the communist and post-communist eras. Moreover, they have had a major formative influence on migration decision processes, as we shall see later in this chapter.

Economic Geography

In 1944, at the start of the communist era, Albania's was overwhelmingly a rural economy. Almost nine-tenths of the population depended on agriculture, living under forms of customary law which regulated property, inheritance rights, and interfamily, generational and gender relations. In 1945 a land reform law was passed in order to destroy the power of the land-owning beys. Land redistribution was seen both as an egalitarian socialist measure and as a means of winning the support of the normally conservative peasantry for the fledgeling communist regime. As elsewhere in the communist world, however, the breaking up of large landholdings into small privately-owned lots was merely a prelude to the collectivisation of agriculture and rural life, which proceeded in stages, first under the Russian model and then under the Chinese. By 1967 the rural economy had been completely collectivised, with cooperatives and state farms replacing private property. Over time, under the influence of the Chinese communes, cooperatives were merged to form ever larger units; whilst state farms grew in both number and size, reaching a peak in 1988 when they accounted for a third of all agricultural production by value (D. Hall 1994: 119–121).

Despite some impressive achievements – extending the cultivated area by draining marshes and terracing hillsides, intensification, mechanisation and specialisation of production – agricultural planning was beset by several problems. Ambitious farm production targets were routinely undershot, and severe food shortages were endemic, especially of grain, meat, milk and eggs (Logoreci 1977: 141). The collectivised work regime led to lax practices and diminishing motivation and effort. Above all there was the difficulty of food output keeping up with a population that more than doubled between 1945 and 1975.

Alongside agricultural collectivism, industry and mining were the main prongs of the country's early five-year plans, built on the minerals which the Italians had already started to exploit during their brief spell as Albania's colonial power. An ambitious programme of electrification was also carried out in the 1950s, based on hydropower, for which the country's topography was well suited. In Vickers' view, the late 1950s were Albania's 'golden years' of industrial economic growth (1999: 183).

This period was accompanied by a transformation of many other human development indicators – literacy, health and education. A social security system was introduced, guaranteeing welfare payments and pensions. The early 1960s, however, were years of great hardship, as Soviet aid dried up and drought disrupted food supplies. Chinese aid eventually went some way to plugging the gap: it gave relatively more support to Albania's industrial development, helping to build up hydroelectric installations, oil refining capacity, copper and iron smelters, fertiliser production – in all some twenty-five industrial plants (see the map in D. Hall 1994: 112).

The break with China initiated a downward economic spiral which the increasingly autarchic policies of the regime only hastened. Obsessive self-sufficiency prolonged the inexorable economic decline until the end of the 1980s (Sandström and Sjöberg 1991; Sjöberg 1991: 118–122). Most authors are agreed that the failure of over-centralised planning to generate sustained economic growth was, ultimately, the single most important factor which undermined the regime's credibility and led to its collapse. Loss of competitiveness, failure to innovate, and missed opportunities to trade those products which had international market value were some of the key elements in Albania's growing economic crisis through the 1980s.

The year 1985 was highly significant for Albania, above all because of the death of Albania's 'great leader' after more than forty years in absolute power as one of the world's last major political personality cults. As Hoxha left the global communist stage, Mikhail Gorbachev rose to prominence in Moscow: *glasnost* and *perestroïka* were soon to follow. 'Albania, Eastern Europe, and the whole world order would never be quite the same again' (D. Hall 1994: 118).

The Post-Communist Transformation

Albanian migration to Italy (and to Greece) can perhaps best be understood as one of the main aspects of a complex process of political, social, cultural and economic change, namely the post-communist transformation, which both encompassed emigration, and was fostered by it. As with the previous parts of this chapter, we pursue a broadly chronological approach. We divide the period in question into three phases: the post-Hoxha years during which the communist regime struggled to survive under the leadership of Ramiz Alia (1985–91); the period dominated by Sali Berisha and the Democrat Party (1992–97); and the most recent period under the Socialist Party and Fatos Nano, ending with the re-election of Berisha in 2005. This historical-political narrative is interlaced with commentary on economic, social, cultural and migratory trends and events.

Transformation or Transition; Post-Communism and Post-Post-Communism

First, a note on terminology. We prefer the term post-communist 'transformation' to post-communist 'transition'. The latter implies a deterministic, teleological path which denies or obscures the full complexity of the interlocking dimensions of the collapse of communism. 'Transition' presupposes a linear progression between two opposed and well-known poles: a past and discredited communist system which is denied any social legitimacy; and a neoliberal interpretation of democracy built around the utopia of free-market capitalism. The use of the term 'transformation' acknowledges the open-endedness and contradictory nature of a process 'in which the introduction of new elements takes place … in combination with adaptations, rearrangements, permutations and reconfigurations of existing institutional forms' (Stark 1992: 22). This view encourages a more critical interpretation of how democratisation has been experienced thus far in Albania (and other post-communist countries). In fact the post-communist transformation should be seen as producing a new social reality of its own out of the interaction between the models transferred from Western democracy, the heritage of communist society, and the even more distant past of pre-communist Albania.

But the story does not end there. Nowadays Albania, following the other East European countries, has gone past both the phase of communism, when the West existed either as an ideal or an enemy, and that of post-communism when the West was associated with the 'shock of the new'. Albania now finds itself at the beginning of a different and subsequent phase which, following Steven Sampson, we call 'post-post-communism'. This is a phase in which the West, having already 'crept through' with its world of seductive 'visible manifestations', its material and cultural artefacts, 'enters in full force … it poses demands, it creates barriers, it offers opportunities, it facilitates or frustrates personal projects and strategies' (Sampson 1998: 156). In other words, whereas post-communism is a phase in which the West subsumes the East through globalisation, commodities, symbols and aid projects, post-post-communism is the stage where the West structures everyday life in all its aspects. The difference is evolutionary and qualitative, but important for our mapping and interpretation of the impact of migration on everyday life, both in this and in subsequent chapters.

Ramiz Alia and the End of Communism in Albania

Following the death of Hoxha, Alia inaugurated a period of cautious toleration and openness, an Albanian *glasnost* (Vickers and Pettifer 1997: 10–32). Foreign travel restrictions were eased slightly, trade relations were restored with many countries, and cultural and political debate allowed, albeit within limits dictated by the continuation of the one-party state.

Although a departure from Hoxha's hard-lineism, Alia's domestic reforms did not resolve the many problems of the Albanian economy, nor did they threaten the foundations of the Albanian system, except indirectly. The changes were meant to protect and strengthen the regime, rather than challenge it; but in reality the pace of reform was greatly outstripped by people's expectations and demands, so that every minor reform merely whetted the appetite of the populace for more fundamental structural change. Only a tiny minority of the population actually benefited from the relaxation of restrictions on intellectual and political debate; the vast majority were either agricultural labourers or factory workers, and still kept under heavy surveillance (Vickers and Pettifer (1997: 16, 24).

Three interlinked elements combined to break the stranglehold Alia's Party of Labour had over the Albanian people:

- the increasing freedom to access foreign, especially Italian, television, which gave Albanians a window onto a very different world of freedom, leisure, wealth and beauty;
- the key emerging role of young people, who in the past had been denied a voice or any role of responsibility within Albania's strange combination of patriarchalism and egalitarian communism;
- the issue of access to foreign countries, which emerged as a powerful symbol of the cultural and political challenge to communism.

The semi-secret watching of Italian television produced a xenocentric fascination for Western countries and their consumer lifestyles, denied to Albanians for so long. It shaped the desired destination for much Albanian migration, and on a wider scale came to have a politically subversive function by presenting to the Albanian people alternative models of life, above all of political, economic and social empowerment. However, it would be a mistake to regard Italian television simply as a magnet drawing Albanian migrants across the Adriatic Sea. Rather, television watching functioned as a *catalyst*, facilitating and accelerating a process of individual uprooting from a world of repression and collectivism. The diverse narrative scripts broadcast by Italian television shattered the existing homogenous cognitive world of Albanian communism. Meanwhile, from a libidinal point of view, watching Italian television tempted and led Albanian young people into an entitlement to individual desire which deeply challenged the collectivist ethos of the communist regime (Mai 2002a: 267). We pick up these issues for more detailed treatment in the final part of this chapter.

Second, young people emerged as a social and political force in Albania – although the real extent to which this has occurred remains debatable in a society still governed by a patriarchal mentality. In his essay 'For a critical spirit', Fatos Lubonja takes a pessimistic stance. In his view, the most salient feature of contemporary Albanian youth is its lack of rebellion against authority: '[Y]oung people's relations with authority are characterised by a mechanism of compliance and hatred. Although compliance seems to be the dominant element, this leads to a seething hatred deep in the unconscious' (1997: 27). This description can be seen to apply to all Albanian young people down through the generations, denied a voice both under the pre-communist tribalism and familism, and under communist authoritarianism. After 1990, Lubonja argues, Albanian youth's 'main preoccupations revolve around entertainment, money, and wangling a trip abroad', and they are 'ready to get up to any trick to achieve these aims' (Lubonja 1997: 25).

In general we concur with Lubonja's views on the passivity of Albanian young people as a consequence of their subjection to the paternalistic and familistic culture which has been hegemonic throughout Albanian history. We do contend, however, that Albanian young people have now become different from their parents in certain ways. Television watching and migration have been the strategic practices through which they have both resisted and complied with the double pressure exerted by the despotic and paternalistic state and by repressive and authoritarian family traditions. Viewing foreign television became a central practice within the identification of young people as a distinct social group, marked by different priorities, tastes and life objectives. This group emerged in relation both to the consumption of foreign products and lifestyles, and to the desire to migrate in order to attain those goods and experiences that Albanian culture had historically been unable to provide, or indeed had explicitly banned (Mai 2002a: 142–143).

The issue of migration – the third element in our trio – returns us to the specific events of the last years of the Alia regime. Alia's reforms did not resolve what was seen by Albanians, especially the young, as a fundamental oppression: their inability to travel or work abroad, or to own passports. Any attempt to cross the external frontiers of Albania remained highly dangerous, and a 'shoot-to-kill' policy was still operated by Albania's border security guards (Vickers and Pettifer 1997: 25). It is not by chance, then, that the first openly dissident act against the Albanian one-party state took place 'from within', in relation to access to the only 'foreign space' within Albanian territory: the embassies in Tirana. Under Hoxha the embassy district had been heavily guarded and was out of bounds to ordinary Albanians. Alia removed this security screen and in February 1990 a family from Korçë scaled the wall and entered the garden of the Italian embassy, taking refuge in a shed where they lived for several weeks. When the embassy refused to hand them over to the police, the Albanian authorities suddenly appeared vulnerable. By summer about 4,500 Albanians were encamped in various West European embassies in Tirana.

Soon, the economy imploded. As winter approached, food and power shortages became critical. Cooperatives and state farms were being dismantled and destroyed, all the main industrial complexes were paralysed by strikes, and street protests and student demonstrations were escalating. Alia formed an emergency committee of Party intellectuals to attempt to manage the mounting crisis: one of its key members was Dr Sali Berisha, a well-known cardiologist from Shkodër, later to become Albania's first non-communist president. It is very significant that the first opposition in post-communist Albania originated from an attempt at mediation between the one-party state and the student movement. When political pluralism was finally granted in December 1990, Berisha, who had been sent by the emergency committee to negotiate with the students, went over to their side, became their leader, and set up the 'Party of Youth and Intellectuals', later renamed the Democratic Party (DP). This process of opposition formation from *within* the communist system confirms the behavioural tradition of continuity in Albanian politics, where all decisions are taken by a restricted political elite: in Martelli's words, 'a carefully managed schism leading to the creation of two segments of this same elite, two forces competing for the same aim, that of avoiding mass revolutionary action' (1998: 161).

In the early months of 1991 events escalated in a number of directions. The economic crisis deepened and food shortages became more acute. In February ten thousand people converged on Durrës in order to commandeer ships to cross to Italy; only a pitched battle with the police prevented the migration from taking place. In Tirana seven hundred students and lecturers went on hunger strike, demanding an end to military conscription and to the compulsory study of Marxism-Leninism, and calling for Enver Hoxha's name to be removed from the University of Tirana. A crowd of 100,000 students and workers massed in Tirana's Skanderbeg Square and threw down Hoxha's giant statue. Then, on 7 March, the first big migratory exodus took place; over the next few days some 25,700 Albanians crossed the Otranto Strait to Italy, landing on the shores of Apulia in a flotilla of craft of every type. A larger-scale but more dispersed and unrecorded migration took place across the southern mountains to Greece.

The first multi-party elections in postwar Albania were held at the end of March 1991. The clear winners were the Albanian Party of Labour, later to be reconstituted as the Socialist Party. Whereas the Democrats won all of the urban constituencies, the rural population voted mainly APL. This reflects the significance of the rural–urban divide in Albanian politics and society. In addition there was (and remains) a regional split in political allegiance: northern Albania is mainly Democrat (Berisha is from Shkodër), the south, home of the Communist Parti elite, mainly votes Socialist.

Between April 1991 and the next elections held in March 1992, convincingly won by the Democratic Party, Albania witnessed harsh confrontations between the two political factions, which were not resolved by the formation of a succession of coalition governments of 'national unity'. Summer 1991 saw the country once again on the verge of economic collapse, marked by volatile political instability. A second migratory crisis ensued as twenty thousand people attempted to migrate to Italy; those who landed were eventually repatriated. Winter 1991–92 was a 'repetition of the nightmare of the previous year' with widespread hunger, anarchy and dissatisfaction with the way, and pace, that change was being introduced in the political and economic system of the country (Vickers and Pettifer 1997: 75). The Western powers voted $150 million in emergency aid, to be managed on the ground by five hundred Italian soldiers under 'Operation Pelican'.

Sali Berisha, Neoliberalism and the Pyramid Crisis

Berisha's election victory in 1992 ended almost five decades of communist rule. A period of relative stability and economic improvement ensued as Albania received high levels of Western aid and pursued a neoliberal market-led strategy which saw the closure of inefficient ex-state industries and the springing up of new, mainly service-type enterprises. According to UNDP (2000a), Albania benefited from the highest level of official development assistance of all the former communist states – $116 per capita per year in the early to mid 1990s. The United States and the West European powers were anxious to support Albania as a zone of stability in a volatile region, as events in Bosnia and Kosovo started to unravel. Whilst Berisha was able to project Albanian economic success as 'his' achievement, an alternative view (Korovilas 1998) sees this success and improvement in living standards as due above all to the mounting inflow of remittances from the large number of Albanian emigrants working abroad, thought to be around 400,000–500,000 in the mid 1990s.

By 1994 the Berisha government was regarded as increasingly corrupt, and the authoritarian behaviour of the leader had become a focus for opposition. The 1996 elections, in which Berisha claimed a sweeping victory, were widely regarded as flawed, with copious evidence of intimidation and vote rigging (Olsen 2000: 24). The Western powers protested, but took no action: indeed, until the formation of an interim government in March 1997, the West's endorsement of the Berisha regime was impervious to its obvious flaws in poor governance and human rights abuses (Abrahams 1996). Post-election demonstrations were brutally put down, the opposition Socialist Party, led by Fatos Nano, was denied its rights to organise and gather, journalists were being harassed by the police, and the government increased its control over the media. In other words, Berisha was assuming much of the behaviour and the trappings of a dictatorial ruler of a one-party state, albeit under a different economic model.

Two other worrying trends marked the Berisha years, one of which was to lead to the collapse of the regime. The first trend was the growth in criminal and illegal activities (Chossudovsky 2000). The abrupt change from half a century of dogmatic authoritarianism under Hoxha to a free-for-all situation of complete institutional, political and economic disarray in the early 1990s led to Albania becoming a focal point for smuggling and trafficking. Initially there was a boom in the smuggling of stolen vehicles from Western Europe – private car ownership had been banned under Hoxha. Sanctions imposed on Serbia-Montenegro led to profitable opportunities for smuggling oil, arms and other goods across the border. As illegal activity become more organised, trafficking in people, arms, drugs and other contraband by local gangs became increasingly integrated with international criminal networks (Saltmarshe 2001: 62).

The second negative development was the growth of private pyramid savings schemes, in which unsustainable rates of interest were promised to investors on the basis that the number of savers would continue to grow more or less exponentially. Banking deregulation, fostered by the IMF and World Bank, allowed the mushrooming of these savings scams without any regulatory management. Many believed that government officials had major stakes in the financial pyramids and that this explains why nothing was done to curb the exorbitant short-term profits being made, nor to avert the impending crisis.

The pyramids collapsed in spectacular fashion in early 1997; maybe half of Albanian households lost their life savings. Much of the capital invested derived from migrants' remittances: years of hard labour in Italy or Greece were thus wiped out virtually overnight. The World Bank estimated the loss in personal savings to be in excess of $1 billion, equivalent to half of Albania's 1996 GDP (Olsen 2000: 24).

Widespread disorder followed the pyramids' collapse. The government declared a state of emergency and imposed a curfew throughout the country, which only provoked further opposition and unrest. The situation slid into anarchy; large parts of southern Albania (Socialist Party territory) were effectively outside government control, in the hands of local gangs with looted firearms. For a time the country was on the verge of civil war. Many people's lives had been ruined by the pyramid losses and made impossible by the general climate of violence and insecurity in which three thousand died and countless more were wounded. This was the background to another mass migratory exodus in March 1997. As before, the migrants/refugees fled in two main directions: across the Adriatic to Italy and over the mountains to Greece.

In response to this renewed migratory episode, Italy led a UN-backed, six-thousand-strong military-humanitarian mission, Operation Alba, to deliver aid to the once again destitute and strife-torn Albanian people.[8]

New elections in 1997 saw the return to power of the Socialists under Fatos Nano. A measure of stability was restored, boosted by the passing of Albania's first post-communist constitution in 1998.

Recent years

Since 1998, Albania has enjoyed steady economic growth; the political situation, although rather fragile and polarised between the DP and the SP, has certainly been more settled than the upheavals of the early 1990s or the later Berisha years. However, during 1999, the influx of more than half a million Kosovan refugees exacerbated economic and social stress in Albania's poorest northern districts. The presence of NATO troops and large contingents of aid workers helped to ease the burden; now the refugees have either been resettled to Kosovo or have moved on to other countries.

After their dramatic decline as a result of the pyramid fiasco, remittances have once again risen to make a vital contribution to Albania's economic survival, exceeding $500 million per year in 2000 and $1 billion in 2004, according to Bank of Albania figures. During the five years 2000–04 remittances contributed, on average, 14 per cent of total GDP, were worth $250 per head of the Albanian population, were double the value of visible exports, and made up 55–60 per cent of the trade deficit (see de Zwager et al. 2005: 21, Table 2; Nikas and King 2005: 254, Table 4). We will have more to say on remittances and their role in household and national economic progress in Chapter 7.

The 2001 national election, with the SP victorious, passed off without major incident and was pronounced broadly fair by international observers. Similar judgements were made about the 2003 local elections, also won by the SP, but with a narrowed majority and a low turnout. In her report on this latter election Miranda Vickers (2003: 55) diagnoses important weaknesses of the continuing political scene. 'With each passing election', she writes, 'Albanians are becoming increasingly apathetic towards the political progress and towards their political leadership in particular'. Sali Berisha (DP) and Fatos Nano (SP) are still very much associated with the fear and uncertainties of the past decade: '[W]ith these two dinosaurs of the transition period still at the helm, the population has no belief that anything will change for the better'. Both main parties continue to nurture a political climate dominated by aggressive rhetoric, claim, counter-claim, and insults. In 2005 the electoral pendulum swung back in the Democrats' favour, when splits within the Socialist Party brought the DP back into power in the July election. Despite being compromised by his mishandling of the 1997 financial scandal, Berisha is once again Albania's prime minister, heading a government now populated by a remarkable number of young, foreign-educated technocrats.

According to Olsen (2000: 26), one of the biggest problems faced by Albanians is their inexperience with the democratic process and its accompanying debate, dialogue and necessity to compromise. They see the role of the state as merely to curb the excesses of individuals and society as a whole, thereby discouraging the development of individual and collective responsibility. Governments are not properly held to account for their actions or what they say. Such behaviour has made the development of civil society in Albania painfully slow, reinforcing instead the old mentalities based on confrontation and clan-party loyalties. As a result, economic reform also remains slow. No government has yet managed to reorganise infrastructures and utilities, which continue to serve the population badly. Water and electricity supplies are notoriously unreliable. Much of the population still lives in poverty, suffering a lack of jobs, extremely low rates of pay for those who are in employment, minimal pensions and almost nonexistent social welfare. In such circumstances, emigration is still seen as the most rational route to self-improvement.

Demography: Background to Migration

One of the 'root causes' of Albanian emigration that is not generally given the attention it deserves is the demographic factor: before the 1990s population increase continually outstripped the economic resources of the country. The policy of full employment at any price decreased productivity and real incomes since a structurally weak economy could not cope with a net annual addition of 40,000–50,000 people entering the labour force during the 1980s (Sandström and Sjöberg 1991: 935–36).

Table 2.1 sets out census totals and other key demographic data for the period 1923–2001. Averaging 2.5 per cent per year, Albania's rate of population increase between the Second World War and the collapse of the communist regime was the highest in Europe. Broadly, the population tripled during 1940–90 and doubled over the period 1960–90. Given that international migration between 1945 and 1990 was virtually nil, these changes were entirely due to the natural increase of the population. The most recent census, when the population dropped for the first time, reveals the impact of large-scale emigration during the 1990s. Because of the dramatic change in demographic dynamics brought about by mass emigration, the following account is divided into two parts, before and after 1990.

Population Development 1945–90

The geographers Michel Sivignon and Örjan Sjöberg are the authors of a substantial body of literature on Albania's demography during the

Table 2.1 Albanian population evolution 1923–2001

Census	Total population ('000)	Average annual change since previous census (%)	Males (%)	No. of households ('000)	Persons per household	Urban population (%)
1923	814.4		51.8	143.1	5.7	15.9
1930	833.6	+ 0.3	51.5	146.2	5.7	15.4
1945	1,122.0	+ 2.3	50.8	196.9	5.7	21.3
1950	1,218.9	+ 1.7	51.3	211.6	5.8	20.5
1955	1,391.5	+ 2.7	51.3	251.8	5.5	27.5
1960	1,626.3	+ 3.2	51.1	279.8	5.8	30.9
1969	2,068.2	+ 2.7	51.4	346.6	6.0	32.3
1979	2,590.6	+ 2.3	51.6	463.3	5.6	33.5
1989	3,182.4	+ 2.1	51.5	675.5	4.7	35.8
2001	3,069.3	− 0.3	49.9	726.9	4.2	42.1

Sources: INSTAT (2002: 19); Sjöberg (1991: 34, 42); note, however, that different sources give different figures for the 1923 and 1930 censuses, and misprints exist in the INSTAT source (corrected where possible).

communist era (Sivignon 1970, 1983, 1995; Sjöberg 1989, 1991: 41–79, 1992).[9] Part of the fascination of Western scholars for this topic derives from the fact that the population of Albania presented substantially different characteristics from those of any other European country (Sauvy 1980). Demographic parameters were in a unique combination. A strongly pronatalist policy was in place until the 1980s, with prohibitions on contraception and abortion.[10] Until 1990 this produced a population increase of 'Third World' dimensions (reaching more than 3 per cent per year in the late 1950s and early 1960s) combined with a 'European' social demography of low mortality, high life expectancy, high literacy and high gender and income equality.

Table 2.2 disaggregates the key elements of natural change at ten-year intervals since 1950, together with other vital statistics on life expectancy, infant and child mortality and age structure. High rates of natural increase up to 1990 were driven by mortality falling faster than fertility. The latter remained high, both in terms of birth rate (peaking at 43.3 per thousand in 1960) and absolute number of births (peaking at 82,125 in 1990). A key factor in mortality decline has been the progress made in decreasing infant and child mortality. In 1950 one quarter of all children died before the age of four; by 1990 this proportion was only 6 per cent, and by 2000 it had fallen to 3 per cent, if the official figures are to be believed.

Albania's demographic transition, which started around 1960, began much later than in all other European countries, and remains incomplete today. One reason for this is the continuation of a high birth rate until 1990

Table 2.2 Albanian population: natural increase and vital statistics, 1950–2000

Year	Fertility (births per thousand)	Mortality (deaths per thousand)	Natural increase (per thousand)	No. of births in year	% population aged 0–14	Infant mortality (per thousand)	Child mortality (per thousand)	Life expectancy at birth	Life expectancy at 15 yrs
1950	38.5	14.0	24.5	47,295	38.7	143.1	105.3	51.6	53.9
1960	43.3	10.4	32.9	69,686	41.1	96.6	58.6	62.0	58.6
1970	32.5	9.2	23.3	69,507	42.2	89.1	22.2	66.5	60.1
1980	26.5	6.4	20.1	70,680	35.9	74.1	17.4	68.0	60.1
1990	25.2	5.6	19.6	82,125	32.6	45.4	15.5	70.7	60.6
2000	14.7	4.8	9.9	50,077	29.3	22.8	9.1	74.6	62.4

Note: Infant mortality is deaths before age 1, child mortality is deaths at age 1–4 years.
Sources: Bërxholi (2003: Table 12); INSTAT (2001: 8–9; 2002: 22).

and, as a result, the survival in the population of a large share of young people who, in turn, ensure the continued natural growth of the population. In 1990 one third of the population was under the age of fifteen years. Nevertheless, data in Table 2.2 do show clear signs of demographic deceleration, even before 1990. Fertility fell from 43 to 25 per thousand between 1960 and 1990, natural increase fell from 3.3 per cent to less than 2 per cent over the same period, and the share of 0–14 year-olds decreased from more than 40 per cent to 33 per cent. The trend in absolute numbers of births reveals a somewhat different profile: constant at around 70,000 per year for 1960, 1970 and 1980, then increasing to 82,000 in 1990. This may appear counterintuitive given the other trends just noted, but is explained in the context of the overall growth of the Albanian population (doubling 1960–90) and the continued weight of young, reproductively active cohorts in the population structure. One more demographic statistic helps to complete the picture: the total fertility rate (TFR, the average number of children born to a woman over her reproductive life-cycle) was around six in the years 1950–60, but had fallen to three by 1990. A halving of the TFR over a period in which the population doubles is consistent with maintaining births at a high absolute level.

To sum up: in 1990 Albania still had the fastest growing population in Europe, with the highest crude and total fertilities, and the youngest age structure – factors which ensure a potential supply of emigrants for some years to come.

Returning to Table 2.1, the extreme right-hand column shows that, throughout the communist period, the urban population increased its share from one fifth to one third of the total population. Thus, Albania remained an overwhelmingly rural society. During 1960–80 the rate of rural population growth was twice the urban rate, with the result that the rural population in 1980 (1.75m) was greater than the country's total population in 1960 (1.61m). Particular restrictions were put on the growth of Tirana, so that the capital's share of both national and total urban population fell (Carter 1986). Derek Hall (1996) pointed out that Albania was unique in Europe in those decades as the only country where so little rural–urban migration was taking place, where the rural population was increasing rapidly in absolute terms (from 883,000 in 1945 to 2m in 1989), and where the capital was growing more slowly than other towns.

Two interpretative conclusions can be ventured from the above. First, the substantial 'diverted' rural–urban migration during later communist times set a model for rural to peri-urban movement in the post-communist years. We return to this issue in the final chapter. Second, and more speculatively, the blocked aspirations of rural Albanians to urbanise under communism led to pent-up pressure to modernise and settle in towns and cities in the years following the fall of the regime, with the result that some of this aspirational migration to urban modernity could only be satisfied by going abroad. So, in post-1990 Albania rural–urban migration was directed not only at Tirana and Durrës, but also at Athens and Thessaloniki, Bari and Milan.

Post-1990: A New Era for Albanian Demography

The collapse of communism and the opening up of Albania to the outside world, above all through emigration, brought about fundamental change in Albanian demographic trends. Scrutinising Tables 2.1 and 2.2, we highlight the following:

- a fall in population of 3.6 per cent between 1989 and 2001, reversing the long-term trend of rapid population growth;
- males become the minority sex, in contrast to the rest of the historic census record when they are a majority; the obvious explanation is their greater propensity to emigrate;
- sudden reduction in the average size of households, due partly to the onset of fertility decline but also to the removal of one or more household members due to migration;
- the urban share of total population increases sharply to 42 per cent, due to the lifting of restrictions on internal migration;
- fertility declines rather dramatically between 1990 and 2000 – crude fertility from 25.2 to 14.7 births per thousand, and the annual number of births from 82,000 to 50,000 – due in large part to the removal of many young adults abroad;
- infant and child mortality continue to improve (the former halving during 1990–2000), whilst life expectancy increases to 74.6 years at birth.

It needs stressing that not all the above changes were due to emigration alone. The last on the list represents continuing improvements in Albanian demographic health which had been ongoing for decades. What is most interesting here is the fact that the improvements were sustained across the post-communist transformation, given that in other Eastern bloc countries, notably Russia, life expectancy, mortality and other health indicators witnessed a deterioration (see Gjonça et al. 1997).

The 2001 Census offered a first estimate of the scale of emigration occurring over the previous decade: a net loss of 600,000: 350,000 males and 250,000 females, most aged under thirty-five (INSTAT 2002: 19, 29). It is important to note that this figure excludes temporary emigrants away for less than one year: such short-term absentees were recorded as de jure residents of Albania. We shall have further discussion on the question of numbers of emigrants in the next chapter.

The Seductive Role of Italian Television

Earlier in this chapter we briefly noted the strategic, catalytic role of foreign, especially Italian, television in the later years of communist rule; indeed this 'invasive influence' of the West was one of the key areas of the passage to post-communism. We argue that Italian television had four effects:

- it functioned as a periscope out of the isolation of the Hoxha regime, enabling Albanians to peer into a landscape of material wealth, freedom, eroticism and beauty;
- it had a politically subversive function, not so much directly in that it conveyed explicit political messages or propaganda, but because watching it was regarded by the regime as a 'seditious act' (and therefore illegal), and because the individualistic and heterogenous lifestyles portrayed challenged the homogenous and collectivist identity formation of the communist regime;
- it gave young people a new role as a distinct social group marked by different tastes, aspirations and life objectives, above all focused on Western products and lifestyles;
- it opened up a fierce desire to migrate out of Albania, both in search of material wealth but also, more importantly, because only by moving to Italy or another Western country could young Albanians 'find themselves' and express their 'true identities'.

In closing this chapter we investigate the role of Italian television in a little more detail, for it is clearly one of the framing mechanisms for migration to Italy. This also allows us to introduce our first ethnographic material, derived from an in-depth study of television watching in Albania by one of the authors (Mai 2002a).[11]

Italian Television in Albania in the 1970s and 1980s: Laying the Foundations for Future Migration

After the early 1970s, watching foreign television became an increasingly widespread activity amongst Albanians. Many households had a black-and-white set, which cost the equivalent of a year's wages for a skilled urban worker or two years' income for a rural farm worker. Italian TV signals could be received throughout western Albania, where most of the main towns and densely populated agricultural areas were located (Figure 2.1); in these comparatively richer parts of the country, around three-quarters of families possessed a TV set in the mid 1980s (Dorfles 1991: 7).

Until 1990 Albanian national television consisted of one channel broadcasting four hours a day, 6 to 10 p.m. The programming was dominated by documentaries and news features praising the achievements of the regime. Even the one weekly film 'was invariably political, patriotic and didactic and aimed at indoctrinating audiences rather than entertaining them' (Prifti 1978: 131). News about foreign countries, whether 'revisionist socialist' or 'Western imperialist', was limited, but inevitably portrayed them as beset by the contradictions produced by their own moral decay and ideological mistakes (Dorfles 1991: 10). Efforts were made to curtail the reception of Italian and other foreign television channels (Yugoslav and Greek) by jamming their signals and prosecuting people caught in possession of an aerial which received foreign broadcasts. Such aerials were hidden indoors and put out only at night. They were linked to a crude but effective tuning device called a *canoçe* (tin-can in Albanian), which contained a couple of transistors and a condensor fitted inside a tin.

In the early 1980s the authorities unjammed the Italian signal for half an hour every evening to allow Albanian audiences to watch the Italian news on RAI 1, the main Italian state channel.[12] Further relaxations on watching foreign broadcasts were made after Hoxha's death in 1985. However, right up to the end of 1990, tuning in to a foreign TV or radio programme, while no longer explicitly forbidden, could be considered a politically dangerous act, whilst talking about the contents of foreign programmes could be punished (by up to eight years in prison) as an attempt to spread 'subversive propaganda' (Dorfles 1991: 8–9).

Evidence on the scale and intensity of clandestine television viewing suddenly became apparent with the first migratory arrivals in Italy in March 1991. A survey carried out with these pioneer migrants found that 97 per cent had watched Italian television regularly in Albania, and 89 per cent had learnt Italian from watching Italian TV (Dorfles 1991: 14). The power of foreign media to break down the country's self-imposed isolationism and to open up alternative perspectives, especially for the young who increasingly distanced themselves both from the regime and from the values of the older generations, was apparent on all sides. Virtually all of the two hundred young people interviewed by Mai in Tirana and Durrës during 1998–2000 declared two things: that they wanted to go abroad to work or study, at least for a time; and that watching foreign television was an important factor in their desire to emigrate (Mai 2002a: 167).[13]

Watching Italian television during communism was remembered with a mixture of emotions: nostalgia, excitement, but also feelings of secrecy and danger. Given the risk involved in contravening the wishes of the regime and its local informers, hours of viewing were often rationed within the family setting. This first set of interview clips recalls the secrecy and the primitive technology used to access foreign channels:

> Before 1991, I remember we had a black and white TV equipped with a special aerial which we had made by adapting something like a tin ... I don't remember exactly because I was just a kid. (Female, aged 21, Tirana)

> I remember that we used to get together at my auntie's and raise the aerial secretly, hidden from neighbours or those who at the time were called the head of the neighbourhood councils. (F22, Durrës)

> Before 1991 we used to watch foreign television but with a lot of difficulties and under the control of my parents, who used to tell us, 'Be careful and don't watch that channel too much'. (M18, Tirana)

The next sequence of quotes (and others which follow later) gives information about the types of programme watched: cartoons, soaps, detective series, sports, and two types of broadcast that seemed to feature prominently in almost all recollections – advertisements and 'Sanremo'. The Sanremo song festival is held annually and has cult status as a lavish and spectacular 'show', whilst the TV adverts carried special appeal as they represented the consumer and lifestyle paradise that was the very antithesis of life in Albania.

> I used to watch the Italian and Yugoslav channels often and it was mostly because of Italian television that I learnt Italian. At the time I was a kid and I usually watched cartoons like Tom & Jerry ... I also watched a lot of soaps, usually from Brazil and Argentina ... and Beverly Hills, which I liked very much. (F24, Tirana)

> One day, I think it was in 1989, Dad came home with a *canoçe*, and we could watch RAI 1, RAI 2, and sometimes the Yugoslav channel... Dad used to arrange everything ... Above all I remember the TV adverts and 'Inspector Derrick' ... I remember them as if it were now. How much I liked the TV adverts! I mean, I was a kid, still in primary school. Whenever I saw the adverts for toys I began dancing and jumping around. (M18, Tirana)

> It was something very special for us. I remember 'Sanremo' very well. We did not get to watch much television in those days. There were (black and white) sets, but colour TV ... there must have been only two or three in Tirana and only their neighbours or relatives could enjoy them ... I once went with a cousin of mine, she had a neighbour, and it was something coloured that looked like a dream ... I remember that watching a colour TV gave us such joy that we talked about it all year long. We had watched 'Sanremo' on colour TV! (F18, Tirana)

Other interviewees, who were older, were more explicit about the political and ideological impact of watching Italian television, which became the embodiment of Albanians' aspirational Westernness:

> On Italian television there was freedom, diversity of opinions, lots of different programmes, whereas on Albanian TV we could only watch propaganda war films, biased documentaries ... a lot of lies. (F32, Durrës)

People remembered how foreign television programmes became the subject of conversation, although the possibility of watching Italian TV or talking about it varied from neighbourhood to neighbourhood, depending on the proximity or strictness of the local Party representative.

> As far as my generation is concerned, there was a bit of liberalisation only after the death of the dictator Enver Hoxha, there was liberalisation in access to foreign television and in the conversations about it. We organised parties amongst classmates and we started talking freely about the desires of the new generation. (F30, Tirana)

'Italy is Beautiful'

When asked what they liked most about Italian television in post-communist times (remembering our specific definition of this epoch as encompassing the later years of the regime), most interviewees replied that they were fascinated by the *beauty* of the people and the material environment presented on the screen. Quite simply, 'Italy was beautiful' (*bella, bellissima*), and this cultural landscape of beauty, pleasure and freedom contrasted with the cultural monotone offered by both Albanian television and Albanian society (Mai 2001a).

> I didn't like anything about Albanian TV, whereas Italian programmes were real programmes ... I liked them because they were beautiful, they showed beautiful things and talked about beautiful things in a beautiful way. (M26, Tirana)

> In communist times Albanians preferred foreign and in particular Italian television because it showed a beauty which we could not find in Albania ... We were looking for happiness, we wanted to see beautiful things ... better things. (M29, Durrës)

Beyond their display of colour, wealth and beauty, the appeal of Italian television programmes must be understood in terms of their potential to make tangible certain aspects of life that were decidedly lacking in Albanian society. Even more than their other Western counterparts, Italian networks, both public and especially the private channels which mushroomed at this time,[14] are characterised by the spectacularisation of beauty (especially of the female form), by a strong emphasis on fun and pleasure, and by the continuous celebration of the satisfactions and achievements which are allegedly there for the taking in Italy's consumer capitalism. For many interviewees, it was the adverts – the epitome of the spectacularisation of Western consumption – which were remembered most clearly and were, for some, their favourite 'programme':

> When I first saw adverts I thought they were a programme in themselves, that one had to watch normally. They were very entertaining and I used to watch them with enormous pleasure. (M18, Tirana)

> Adverts were extraordinary, they were the thing that attracted us the most ... I remember we used to wait impatiently to watch them, for the fact that they were so pleasurable to see. (F25, Tirana)

> Yes, I liked the adverts ... like a forbidden fruit ... it was a bit like see and not touch ... because there was no way that we could touch! In particular I liked the light, people's faces, the abundance on those tables, in those shops, the colours of the products, the way people reacted, the music ... (M22, Tirana)

Viewed through the prism of Albania's deprivations, Italian television appeared to offer seductive access to radically different ways of being, having and behaving (Mai 2002a: 178–183). This returns us to our Freudian perspective introduced earlier. Italian television watching challenged the 'ideo-aesthetic' and 'ideo-emotional' requirements of an authoritarian regime based on the repression of individual desires for the sake of the survival of the collective moral community.[15] By turning their desiring gazes away from the official moralised, naturalised mediascape, Albanian people started disembedding themselves from the regime's authoritarian libidinal economy which denied them existence as individual desiring subjects.

Italian Television and the Cultural Construction of the 'Migratory Project'

The watching of Italian and foreign television emerged as an act of libidinal political resistance which, initially, could happen in the only two spaces which were safe from the regime's repressive apparatuses: the privatised family household, and the individual subconscious. The images and messages conveyed by foreign TV, however, quickly opened up a yearning for a third space – abroad – where the desires fostered on the one hand by isolationist repression, and on the other hand by the televised cultural landscape of freedom, pleasure and prosperity, could be accessed.

Several of the interviews collected by Mai (2002a) reveal this desire to 'know' this yearned-for 'other world', which had been closed off to Albanians for so long. Two typical quotes:

> It was curiosity, first of all it was curiosity ... and the fact that seeing abroad there was something better ... that the living standards were higher ... it was this kind of curiosity, something new, this was an important factor. (F30, Tirana)

> Of course, one must remember that our senses at the time were very closed ... so this started the desire and the curiosity of the Albanians, who were used to schematic formats with standardised programmes – news, culture, etc. Then there was also something different, that great desire to know the unknown, to see what is happening over there ... (F26, Tirana)

Beyond this 'natural curiosity' lay more important and enduring rationalisations for moving abroad: a better standard and quality of life, especially in material terms (the economic rationale which is often portrayed as *the* paramount migration factor), and a channel and a space for self-realisation (a sociopsychological rationale which is less apparent in the migration literature). The following interview excerpts reveal how watching foreign, especially Italian, TV shaped both the desire to leave Albania and the process of cultural construction of Italy as a 'familiar' destination for Albanians' migratory projects in post-communist times.

> Well, a big, big world … I mean, such a beautiful thing … over there, there was a higher concentration of psychological and spiritual life … and such great luxury … an economic situation that was so much more developed than ours, particularly because in the early 1990s our poverty was at its peak … and (here) psychological and spiritual life was not taken into consideration. (F19, Tirana)

> Look, the enduring attraction to Italy is not only because there are more possibilities to go there across the sea, but also for the fact that Albanians are like Italians. They are two countries that get along well; we fit each other, so to say. Greece as well is very close, but most Albanians have a very bad opinion about Greeks … while Italians are friendlier, and warmer … and in a way it was them who imposed on Albanians such a great desire to go there (through Italian television). (F21, Tirana)

Whilst we do not discount the possibility that some of the 'nice' things said about Italy (and less nice things said about Greece) reflected the presence of an Italian interviewer, it is abundantly clear that Italy enjoyed the status of the country most likely to provide a 'solution' to local needs, to offer refuge from the growing disappointment and disillusionment of Albanians' own dim prospects at home. Because of the constant and 'subversive' presence of Italian television within everyday family life, Italy was the imagined space onto which frustrated Albanians mapped their hopes and desires. In the process of this idealised projection, Italy is configured not only as culturally closer to Albania than other Western nations, but also as a more advanced version of local culture. A common 'Mediterranean identity', structured around a shared history and the primacy and centrality of the family in both societies, is often invoked to explain this feeling of affinity – which, as we shall see in later chapters, is not reciprocated from the Italian side.

Towards a More Critical Stance: From Post-Communism to Post-Post-Communism

Alongside the celebratory and emancipatory aspects of Italian television, there is also a perception of its more sinister side. One interviewee offered the bluntest of judgements that 'Italian media raped Albanian young people' (F26, Tirana). Whilst this might be seen as an obvious reference to the erotic and pornographic displays that suddenly became available via foreign channels, what this interviewee was also referring to was the falsification of the real nature of Italian society by remorseless reference to the tropes of leisure, beauty and boundless wealth as the only meaningful categories in people's lives.

In fact, Italian television has offered Albanians a very illusory and ultimately disempowering narrative of Italian/Western society. By projecting utopian inclusionary discourses related solely to the spheres of consumption, pleasure and abundance, it implicitly underplayed the key roles of labour and production, let alone the dynamics of marginalisation and exclusion which are so characteristic of Italian society (and which, ironically, are directed above all at Albanian immigrants). Moreover, beyond this reductive image of the Western world as a place in which consumer goods, entertainment and pleasure can be attained with little work and sacrifice, one can easily read the projection onto Western capitalist democracy of the communist utopia of a world free of material hardship, discrimination and inequality – the historical promise Enver Hoxha failed to deliver.

This adoption of a more critical stance towards the realities that Italy offered also came about through Albanians' direct experience of migration there. Much of the rest of this book is about those experiences, so we will not go into further detail here, except to make two final points: first about the development of a more mature, discriminating evaluation of Italian television during the 1990s, and second about the passage from post-communism to post-post-communism.

As a consequence of the wider circulation of information about the lived experiences of migration – from relatives, friends or their own direct experiences – Albanians are now disillusioned, both about the actual possibilities offered by emigration to Italy (and to Greece), and about the reliability of the information provided by Italian television in relation to these opportunities. Two quotes sum up this reappraisal:

> At the time, we saw them (Italian TV channels) as a superlative world ... (but) they were exaggerating ... Now we know things are very different. But then we used to hyperbolise the lifestyle over there, because we had no other source of information. (M25, Tirana)

> Whereas in the early 1990s Italy was like a miracle in the eyes of Albanians, now this has changed because a person goes there and then tells his own experiences to others, he has understood that Italy is a place like any other place, that in order to live you have to work, to do something ... It's not that people enjoy themselves only, they have to work hard. The only difference is that the possibilities to find a job and the wages are much better than here. (M23, Tirana)

This also means that television-watching habits have changed; no longer is Italian TV the privileged 'window on the world' for Albanians. Nowadays satellite dishes are a pervasive element in Albanian urban and village landscapes, giving viewers an unparalleled choice of viewing, local and international, public and private. Indeed, it is as if the dishes' receptive concavity enacts the people's revenge against the aggressive convexity of the 600,000 concrete mushrooms which Hoxha erected to assuage his paranoid fears of foreign occupation! As a result:

> Now you can watch as many channels as you want. It is enough that you have a satellite dish and you can see the whole world ... The choice depends only on your taste and preferences ... [And so] the way I watch Italian TV channels has changed. Now I watch them like any other channel, like I watch (Albanian) private channels. Maybe also because for me the language is not a problem and I watch them normally like an Italian would watch them. I don't have any feelings towards it or more curiosity than an Italian would have. (M29, Tirana)

This change in behaviour as regards watching and interpreting Italian and other television networks over the past two decades or so corresponds also to the evolution from post-communism to post-post-communism – a transition which we defined earlier as being characterised not so much by the intensity but by the *nature* and *quality* of East–West relations. Particularly as regards television (but not migration, which was only possible after 1990), the post-communist period both precedes and follows the actual collapse of the communist state, since TV was the first 'direct encounter' between the two worlds. Thus, during post-communism (in Albania lasting approximately from the mid 1980s to the early 1990s), the West (primarily Italy) was experienced in its *absence* through TV as a fantasised and utopian 'place one escapes to', in contrast to the grim reality of everyday life under the regime and during the post-1990 economic and political chaos. During post-post-communism, the West (and its media and lifestyles) becomes an overwhelming *presence* within people's lives and 'the principle economic, political and cultural force (reproducing) conditions of life' (Sampson 1998: 156). If one looks at Albania today, the presence of Italy is so pervasive that one could say that 'Italian culture is an integral part of Albania' (F22, Tirana).

This may be true, but it does not acknowledge the way in which the evolution from post-communist to post-post-communist articulations of late modernity in Albania was accompanied by a switch from a utopian to a more pragmatic world view. This passage transformed the cultural formation of Italian television watching, the way this related to the migratory project, and the very nature of the migratory project itself. *The key moment in this passage was the encounter with the 'real' opportunities and contradictions enforced by Albania's post-communist aspirational and constitutive other, Western late modernity.*

This encounter took place both externally, through the lived or narrated experiences of migration, above all in Italy and Greece, and internally, in the predicaments caused by the introduction of neoliberalism in Albania and by the reactionary 'Albanian' interpretation of liberal democracy. The defining event of this passage was the 1997 pyramid-selling crisis. For Albanians, this represented a dramatic and painful release from a self-indulgent utopian understanding of capitalist modernity which had taken place under the 'pleasure principle', and a shift to a potentially more pragmatic articulation of their identities and ambitions under the 'reality principle' (Freud 1958).

However, this disengagement from collective pleasure-seeking did not happen for all Albanians at the same time; especially significant are the enduring urban–rural differences which we noted earlier. In isolated rural environments, as well as in socially marginal peri-urban areas which are often linked by internal migration to the deprived rural districts, repressive and patriarchal regimes of subjectification and a reactive utopian world view are still common. In these socioeconomic environments of poverty, marginalisation and poor educational standards, foreign television is less critically evaluated and is still associated with an 'imagined rural escape' leading to mass rural–urban migration and international migration (Fuga 2000: 153). According to Fuga, these areas exemplify 'peripheral' identities in relation to the 'centre' of both Albanian and Western social, economic and cultural space. Therefore this culturally and socially peripheral identity is still consistent with a utopian, uninformed and materialistic migratory project, which is more likely to be disappointing or unsuccessful.

On the other hand, Albanians from urban, non-peripheral contexts, having benefited from a relatively more plural and cosmopolitan social world, including better education, have had many more chances to break out of the previously homogenous sociocultural order. Their ability to access and to appreciate cultural heterogeneity in post-post-communist times enabled them to 'find their bearings' in new sociocultural contexts, including foreign television watching and their own migratory projects, planned or real. This dual central vs. peripheral background context is important to bear in mind when we encounter Albanian migrants in Italy in the next few chapters, and when we return, with the migrants, to Albania in the final chapter.

Notes

1   For in-depth surveys, a number of books can be cited. D. Hall (1994) is the seminal study; also authoritative are Vickers (1999) and Vickers and Pettifer (1997). Typical of an earlier generation of general texts are Logoreci (1977), Marmullaku (1975) and Prifti (1978). Recent critical studies of the post-

communist era include Biberaj (1998), Clunies-Ross and Sudar (1998), Kressing and Kaser (2002), Schwandner-Sievers and Fischer (2002), and Vaughan-Whitehead (1999).

2   Skanderbeg's true status as a 'hero of the Albanian nation' is hard to pin down, due to the lack of primary sources. He has been constructed as a national figure by both non-communist Christian Albanians and by the atheist communists alike. See Lubonja (2002: 92–93, 96–97) and Misha (2002: 43); also D. Hall (1994: 31–37); Winnifrith (1992).

3   Crypto-Christianity refers to the practise of professing Islam in the public sphere whilst continuing to practice Christianity in the private sphere of home. Religious switching has been a recurrent feature of Albanian social history. Cross-religious marriages have also been quite common. For further details, see Logoreci (1977: 31–33), Vickers (1999: 15–18).

4   There is a parallel and more historically permanent example here with North Italians' racist views of Italian Southerners, who were also seen as a colonised and backward people to be modernised and incorporated into modern, united Italy, yet who were likewise rejected as Italy's own 'internal other' (Pandolfi 1998; Verdicchio 1997).

5   This unity should not be exaggerated, however. See Logoreci (1977: 75–80) for a more detailed discussion of the complex political and military landscape of the late war years, including reference to the conflicts between the dominant communist partisans, northern clan chieftains and royalist guerilas.

6   Physical geography divided the Albanian population into two distinctive cultural groups. North of the Shkumbin River, including Kosovo, was the territory of the Ghegs, whose social organisation was tribal, based on a closely knit system of clan loyalties and a dispersed settlement pattern of isolated homesteads and hamlets, many of which were fortified. Ghegs, especially in the north-east highlands, were the most faithful followers of the *Kanun* principles of honour (*besa*), hospitality and the pursuit of the 'blood feud'. Albania south of the Shkumbin was inhabited by Tosks, who had abandoned the tribal system by the time of the Ottoman conquest in favour of a village-based social organisation of landlords, peasants and landless workers. Tosks have been consistently more open to foreign, especially Greek and Italian, influences and most of the pre-communist emigration was from this area. For more on Ghegs and Tosks see D. Hall (1994: 27–28) and Vickers (1999: 5–6).

7   Such as the case of a man who managed to swim underwater across one of Albania's interior border lakes to Yugoslavia breathing through a reed pipe; or the young man who drifted across the Corfu Strait with his head inside a large floating watermelon.

8   Operation Alba, following Operation Pelican in 1991, exemplified Italy's humanitarian neocolonialism in Albania, reviving memories of Mussolini's colonial ventures in the country. Italy's influence in Albania during the 1990s extended to most spheres of economic life – not to mention the cultural influence of Italian television. At the eve of the pyramid crisis, five hundred Italian entrepreneurs operated in Albania. Italian firms employed sixty thousand Albanian workers. Italian investments in Albania ($200 million between 1992 and 1996) accounted for more than two-thirds of all foreign private investment in the country; and in 1996 Italy accounted for the largest

share of Albanian exports (51 per cent) and imports (37 per cent). Data from Morozzo della Rocca (1997: 100); UNDP (1998: 27).
9   It would be unfair to Albanian population experts not to point out that the work of Sivignon and Sjöberg draws extensively on Albanian-language sources such as Misja and Vejsiu (1984) and Misja et al. (1987). Albanian scholars have also published some of their research in West European languages (see Meksi and Iaquinta 1991; Misja and Vejsiu 1982).
10 However Sauvy (1980) noted that the practice of contraception was spreading amongst the urban population, and a United Nations Fund for Population Activities mission to Albania in 1989 reported a high incidence of illegal abortion (UNFPA 1991).
11 This study, Mai's doctoral thesis, remains largely unpublished apart from a preliminary summary (Mai 2001a).
12 Even with the news, politically contentious issues, or anything related to the Pope or the Vatican, would be blocked out.
13 Of course, asking Albanian young people (respondents' ages ranged between 16 and 35 at the time of interview) about their television-watching habits and tastes before 1990 meant recalling both a different stage of their own lives (often when they were children) and a different historical period. But the memories were often crystal clear, not least because of the cultural significance of foreign television, and the fact that it came to completely dominate the leisure hours for many people.
14 Notably those controlled as part of the Mediaset empire of media mogul Silvio Berlusconi, later to become Italy's Prime Minister. That Berlusconi could simultaneously be in control of the country's media and of its government, and be the richest man in Italy, is a devastating indictment of Italian politics and society, we believe.
15 The expressions 'ideo-aesthetic' and 'ideo-emotional' derive from Enver Hoxha's writings, in which such terms were very common. Here is a typical quote: '(T)he moral image of our new man (sic) cannot be conceived without the *formation of sound ideo-aesthetic tastes about what is beautiful* in art, in nature, in work, and in life. The problem of tastes is not a purely personal matter for individuals ... *tastes always have a social character*, being formed under the direct influence of social and economic relations, ideology and culture and social psychology. *Hence it is clear that they have a class character.* Therefore, in essence, our tastes are the complete opposite of bourgeois-revisionist tastes. Our communist taste is imbued with the revolutionary ideal, with proletarian simplicity, with noble sentiments and pure moral virtues' (Hoxha 1973: 837; emphasis ours).

Chapter 3

ALBANIAN MIGRATION

Introduction

Chapter 1 opened with references to the iconic status of Albanians' seaborne flight to Italy in 1991. We pointed out that this was a partial view, and emphasised the diversity of the Albanian migratory flow to Italy that developed throughout the ensuing decade. We also noted the apocalyptic scale of the Albanian migration, estimated at between 600,000 (by the census authority INSTAT 2002) and 800,000 (by the Ministry of Labour and Social Affairs; see Barjaba 2000a) for the decade. Further elaborations by INSTAT (2004) revealed that the 2001 population, recorded by the census at 3.07 million, would have been 3.78 million had no emigration occurred – a difference of 710,000. Clearly, there is some consistency in the estimates for the scale of Albania's emigration during the 1990s. The lower estimate of the 2001 Census – 600,000 – is not incompatible with the Ministry's enumeration of 800,000 because the census excluded people who had been abroad for less than one year, and it is well-known that some Albanian migration, especially to Greece, has a short-term character. Whether these temporary emigrants should be included as part of the Albanian resident population is a moot point.

Albanian emigration has continued in the new decade, so that the figures quoted above are now somewhat out of date. A more recent estimate is given in the Albanian government's *National Strategy on Migration*, published at the end of 2004. This suggests that the scale of emigration has risen to one million (Government of Albania 2004: 40).

The purpose of this chapter is to trace the evolution of Albanian migration and to map its geography.[1] We concentrate mainly on the migration to Italy, but we make some reference to other key destinations, especially Greece. The chapter synthesises, tabulates and maps a wide range of Albanian, Italian and other data, and is structured in three parts. The first part documents the history of Albanian emigration, its nature, motives, demographic characteristics, and geographical origins and impact within Albania. This first section of the chapter should be read with half an eye on Chapter 2, which provided the Albanian background to emigration. In the second part of the chapter we follow the migration across the Adriatic Sea to Italy, tracing the development of this migratory flow since 1990. Particular attention will be paid to Albanians' geographical distribution within Italy, and to their changing social and demographic characteristics as revealed by the available data. The third section looks more briefly at Albanian emigration to other countries.

History of Albanian Migration

The epic nature of Albanian migration in the 1990s has tended to blank out reference to earlier histories of Albanian migration before the long-lasting ban on movements abroad during the communist era. Mention of these earlier migrations is important for two reasons, beyond completing the historical record. First, there are some historical parallels and connections between pre-communist and post-communist migrations, despite the length of the intervening period. Second, the discursive framing of these earlier migrations – the nomenclature and their role in Albanian culture – has been revived in the current migration epoch. A well-known Albanian saying maintains that 'a man becomes a man out in the world, a woman becomes a woman over the cradle'. Quite apart from what this proverb says about traditional Albanian gender roles, the clear implication is that travel and migration 'out in the world' constitute a rite of passage for Albanian men. The act of going away and being distant from home – known as *kurbet* – reflects the frequent travel and sojourn of Albanians within the borderless Ottoman Empire. These absences took place for many reasons, including military service and banishment. But by far the most common motive was economic – to seek work in order to support the family back home (Barjaba 2003; Tirta 1999). Over time, the practice of kurbet acquired a strong moral connotation: the *kurbetlli* (the emigrant) was viewed as energetic and fearless, in contrast to those who stayed behind. In Gilles de Rapper's ethnographic analysis of migration patterns in the Lünxheri district of southern Albania, the era of kurbet is remembered as a time of prosperity and development, due to the remittances and resources conveyed back home by the emigrants (de Rapper 2005). Today, particularly in rural Albania, the recollection of pre-communist migration is still clear, and this memory of kurbet, kept alive in folksongs and oral narratives, gives cultural meaning to the themes of migrancy, absence, loss and gain which have acquired a new intensity since 1990 (Papailias 2003).

Pre-communist Period

Chapter 2 provided the historical backdrop to the first major trans-Adriatic migration: that of the Arbëresh. Albanian Catholics fleeing the

Islamisation policies of Ottoman rule settled in a scatter of hill and mountain villages in southern Italy and Sicily. The main migration took place in the late fifteenth century, following the death of Skanderbeg in 1468, but movement to Italy continued in dribs and drabs for the next two hundred years. Other Albanian Christians migrated north and south, to Dalmatia and Greece respectively.

By the eighteenth century the Arbëresh in southern Italy were estimated to number 100,000 and, by the first Italian censuses of the late nineteenth century, the fifty or so Arbëresh villages and small towns returned a combined population of around 200,000, a figure that has remained fairly stable ever since, despite substantial emigration to the United States at the beginning of the twentieth century (D. Hall 1994: 50).

Jumping forward in time for a moment, some of the post-1990 Albanian migrants have settled in Arbëresh communities. The encounter between the 'old' and the 'new' diasporas has been one of mutual curiosity and suspicion rather than coethnic bonding. The Arbëresh language is an Albanian from the Middle Ages, substantially different from modern Albanian; and recent immigrants, who are mainly Muslim or secular, have little interest in the Christian religious rituals which are faithfully preserved in Arbëresh villages. Eda Derhemi's fascinating study of the linguistic and social encounter between the Arbëresh of Piana degli Albanesi, a town of some seven thousand inhabitants in Sicily, and around seventy new immigrants from Albania reveals some of the tensions between the majority, who see themselves as the 'aristocrats' of traditional Albanian culture, and the recent arrivals who live in low-standard rented accommodation and do menial jobs in and around the town. Derhemi (2003) found little solidarity between the two groups who are, in reality, too separated in time to have that much in common. Indeed the Arbëresh tend to replicate the standard Italian stereotypes of Albanians as low-class immigrants prone to criminality and prostitution – although objective evidence of Albanians' engagement in these activities in the town is lacking.

Meanwhile, back in Albania, during and at the end of the Ottoman Empire, poor and destitute peasants emigrated far and wide: to Turkey, Romania and Egypt; later to Greece, Bulgaria and Russia; and then to France and the United States. Significant Albanian communities formed in some cities, notably Istanbul. Towards the end of the nineteenth century, Albanians participated in the large-scale southern European migrations to the United States. The migrants were mostly young men from southern Albania seeking work, experience and money in the 'land of opportunity'. Boston was the initial centre of settlement (here the first Albanian Orthodox Church was founded) but soon Albanians settled in other major cities with good employment opportunities, such as New York, Detroit and Chicago (Nagi 1988; Trix 2001). By the 1920s this migration had changed character somewhat: some single migrants had returned, and migration subsequently consisted mainly of family units. At the same time the US government's imposition of immigration quotas and the perceived improvement of conditions in newly-independent Albania brought this phase of emigration to an end.

This brief review of Albanian emigration prior to 1944 demonstrates that the post-1990 exodus was not an isolated migration episode devoid of historical precedent. Indeed, the recent emigration contains elements of continuity with these earlier migration patterns and traditions. Thus, the period of 'non-migration', 1944–90, can be seen as an artificial interlude set within the longer-term historical framework of the migration of the Albanian people.

Post-1990

The first act in the drama of Albania's post-communist migration unfolded within the twelve months spanning the summer of 1990 to summer 1991. As Kosta Barjaba (2000a: 57) recounts, the six young men who crossed the Adriatic Sea in a flimsy raft in the summer of 1990 and who were welcomed with curiosity and amazement by the Italians who met them were the harbingers of a new season of Albanian migration. A few days later, several embassies in Tirana were entered by thousands of Albanians wanting to leave the country by any means. Two mass departures on crowded ships bound for southern Italy took place in spring and summer 1991. Meanwhile tens of thousands of migrants were hiking across the mountainous frontier with Greece.

Although emigration has been a more or less continuous process since 1990, most authorities agree that it has been structured around a number of political and economic crises (Barjaba 1997: 12; Del Re 2000: 12–24; King 2005b: 137–138; Pastore 1998: 2–5). Key moments and phases were as follows:

- proto-migration and the 'embassy invasion', 1990
  Early small-scale clandestine 'escapes' took place across the Adriatic Sea to the Apulian coast, across the narrow Corfu Strait, over the mountain passes to northern Greece, and across the northern and interior borders with Yugoslavia. During June and July several Western embassies in the capital were squatted by upwards of 4,500 would-be migrants,[2] many of whom were granted exile in Italy. Larger-scale attempts to commandeer ships were thwarted by the Albanian security forces in the seaport of Durrës.
- mass departures stimulated by political and economic crisis, 1991
  Chaos preceding Albania's first democratic elections led to the first 'boat-people' exodus in early March 1991. A flotilla of massively overcrowded craft converged on the Apulian ports: 25,700 Albanians were accepted by Italy under 'emergency' measures and were

dispersed and settled in various parts of the country, including rural areas. Continuing economic crisis, strikes and general insecurity provoked a second boat exodus in August, but most of the arrivals were sent back by the Italian authorities. The Italian government argued that, whilst the earlier wave of migrants could be accepted as refugees fleeing a repressive communist state, the second wave were leaving a country with (by then) a democratically elected government, and therefore could not be granted refugee status. Meanwhile a much larger-scale exodus was taking place to Greece, especially of ethnic-Greek Albanians from the southern border provinces. This transfrontier movement attracted less international media interest because it was hidden from view – often under cover of night. As noted at the beginning of Chapter 1, the ships arriving at Brindisi and Bari, jammed with desperate and raggedly dressed Albanians clinging to every part of the vessel, provided a spectacular media image.

- collapse of the pyramids, 1997
  Since 1992 Albanians had been investing in privately run pyramid savings schemes offering unrealistically high rates of interest. In early 1997 these pyramids collapsed, leading not only to widespread bankruptcy and economic distress, but also to the collapse of the Berisha government and to a period of virtual civil war. Desperation and lawlessness triggered another migratory episode: across the Otranto Strait to Italy (10,600 boat migrants received by Italy in March) and over the mountains to Greece (numbers unrecorded, but certainly much greater). According to Del Re (2000: 22), the Italian authorities assigned permits to stay to 8,662 Albanians during March. Subsequent sea-borne migrations to Italy were blocked, sometimes in tragic circumstances.
- Kosovo, 1999
  During the Kosovo crisis, Albania hosted 450,000 Kosovan-Albanian refugees who traversed the mountainous frontier into north-eastern Albania, putting enormous strains on the country's poorest region. After a period in hastily erected camps, most Kosovars were eventually able to return, but many moved on to seek asylum in other countries. Precise details are impossible to obtain, but it seems that many Albanians were also involved in these onward migrations, enhancing Albanians' ability to spread beyond their primary destinations of Greece and Italy to other European countries such as France, Belgium and, especially, the United Kingdom.[3]

Whilst some authors stress the close relationship between 'migration' and 'crisis' in Albania (Pastore 1998), others argue that emigration has been equally significant during the years of (relative) normality – 1993–96, 1998, post-2000 – when migrants have been able to plan their departures (and returns) in a calmer atmosphere (Barjaba 2003). This remains an

Table 3.1 Albanian migration since 1990: annual estimates

Year	Net annual migration	First-time temporary emigration	Permanent emigration New cases	Permanent emigration Cumulative
1990	90,618	4,355	12,032	12,032
1991	128,329	22,069	23,899	35,931
1992	80,024	45,451	18,512	54,443
1993	(3,022)	63,360	19,072	73,515
1994	25,311	68,661	16,088	89,603
1995	19,857	74,190	23,897	113,500
1996	9,441	82,067	28,671	142,171
1997	13,478	101,219	37,071	179,242
1998	22,785	116,941	56,135	235,377
1999	13,475	98,801	48,556	283,933
2000		98,834	49,645	333,578
2001		89,813	50,773	384,351
2002		94,467	71,931	456,282

Sources: net annual migration from Ricci (2004: 124) based on Caritas/Migrantes estimates; all other data from Stampini et al. (2004: 23) based on Albanian Living Standards Measurement Survey 2002.

unresolved question, as there are no official or reliable data on annual departures, only estimates based on partial information. Table 3.1 sets out these estimates. The first column, based on data assembled by the Italian Caritas/Migrantes organisation, confirms the oft-quoted figure of 300,000 departures in the three years 1990–92. It then estimates a small net return migration for 1993 followed by an annual net emigration averaging 17,400 for the rest of the 1990s, including a peak of 22,785 in 1998, after the pyramid crisis. The remaining three columns do not factor in return migration, but do draw out the distinction between short- and long-term emigration, based on grossed-up results from the Albanian Living Standards Measurement Survey (LSMS), which contains important information on migration.[4] In the LSMS schedule, temporary migrants are regarded as members of the household by the interviewee: they must have been abroad for at least one month and have lived in Albania for at least six of the prior twelve months. Permanent emigrants are those declared by the interviewee to have left the household definitively and be living abroad (Stampini et al. 2004: 6).[5] It is important to realise that the LSMS provides information only for households still residing in Albania. Thus – a vital point – households that have moved abroad entirely and no longer have parents living in Albania are not counted. This is one reason why figures for migration derived from the LSMS are lower than those from other sources. The cumulative total for permanent emigrants during 1990–2002 – 456,000 – is substantially below all other estimates noted earlier.

The two sets of estimates in Table 3.1 hardly offer a consistent picture. The Caritas/Migrantes data stress the mass departures of 1990–92 and surely under-estimate the scale of departures thereafter. The LSMS suggests a steadier rhythm of emigration, reaching higher levels of departure in the late 1990s; but the scale of the early-1990s exodus is under-recorded.

Overall, however, the mass scale of emigration during the decade 1990–2000 remains clear: Albania experienced *relative* rates of departure 4–5 times as high as other newly democratised East European countries such as Poland, Romania and Bulgaria. Likewise, Albania recorded much higher rates of outflow than those from less developed countries in other parts of the world (Barjaba 2000a: 61; Ricci 2004: 104).

Motives and Nature of Migration

For the post-communist period, Barjaba (2000a, 2000b, 2003) has posited an Albanian migration model which has the following characteristics:

- it is *recent* (post-1990) and *intense* (emigration of at least one in five of the population within a decade);
- it has a *high degree of irregularity*, with clandestine departures and a large proportion of migrants classed as 'illegal' or 'undocumented' in host countries such as Italy or Greece;
- it is largely *economically driven* and can be described as 'survival migration' or a 'route out of poverty' for the Albanian people;
- it is *dynamic* and *rapidly evolving* with an increasing variety of migration types and destinations.

Of these four key features, the first has already been described above. The second will be dealt with later in this chapter when we look at statistics on Albanian immigration in the main destination countries. For now, we explore the third and fourth features.

Poverty is the single most important 'push factor' for Albanian migration. In the World Bank's important study on *Poverty in Albania* (De Soto et al. 2002), this cause-and-effect relationship is largely analysed in *qualitative* terms, with descriptive data and migrant testimonies drawn from interviews and focus groups in various parts of the country. Beyond standard threshold measurements of the existence of poverty and extreme poverty (surviving on less than $2 and $1 per head per day respectively), poverty in Albania is multi-dimensional and includes: feelings of physical insecurity; lack of hope for the future; exclusion from social and commercial life; lack of education and health-care; and inability to continue cultural traditions such as baptisms, weddings and funerals (De Soto et al. 2002: xii–xiii). For the *very poor*, poverty primarily means not getting enough to eat, not being able to purchase clothes, lack of information, not being able to fulfil cultural practices, and feelings of hopelessness, fear and humiliation. Their principal problems are lack of food, clothing and shoes, and poor water quality; their sparse diet causes health problems which in many cases have worsened since 1990; child malnutrition in this group is estimated at 50 per cent. Lack of income and severe unemployment are the main causes of these problems. In contrast to the very poor, the *poor* are better fed and suffer less from health and psychological problems of stress. Their principal problems are infrastructure-related – lack of transport, electricity, water supply, etc. They receive more from migrants' remittances than the very poor, although not as much as the non-poor – a clear indication of the role of migration in differentiating classes of poverty and well-being in Albania.

According to standard *quantitative* measures of the incidence of poverty, the Albanian population is very badly afflicted. In absolute terms 46.6 per cent of Albanians fall below the poverty line of $2 per capita per day, and 17.4 per cent are below the extreme poverty line of $1 per day. Following the unmet basic needs (UBN) criteria of poverty, 41.6 per cent of the population are classed as poor, including 14.4 per cent as extreme poor.[6] These data are from surveys of 1998 and 2000–01 (Albanian Center for Economic Research 2002: 48, 93). However it is measured, poverty is much more widespread in Albania's rural areas and in the interior and mountainous regions; it has a lower presence in towns and in the coastal districts. UNICEF's map of poverty in Albania, based on data for communes and municipalities, shows the clear spatial expression of Albanian poverty – concentrated above all in the north and in the interior regions (see Figure 3.1).

Whilst the cause–effect link between poverty and migration appears clear in the Albanian case, this is not the end of the discussion. Two further questions remain. How does poverty, and related economic factors such as unemployment, rank alongside other stimuli of Albanian migration? And how does the incidence of poverty determine exactly who migrates and who does not? Existing literature helps us to answer these questions, albeit partially.

Surveys based on questionnaire and interview samples confirm the overriding importance of the economic dimension of Albanian migration motives. The World Bank research quoted earlier found that 39 per cent migrated due to unemployment, 26 per cent due to economic insecurity, 20 per cent due to insufficient income, and 16 per cent to obtain a better future for their children (De Soto et al. 2002: 45). Whilst one can argue about the extent to which these motives can really be regarded as discrete one from the other, it is clear that economic motives – the first three, combining to 85 per cent – constitute the overwhelming force for departure. Likewise, a questionnaire survey of 1,500 households (one person interviewed per household, but incorporating information also on 708 household members living abroad) showed that, of reasons to emigrate, 87 per cent were economic, the rest being mainly social or political (Kule et al. 2002: 233).

Albanian Migration | 73

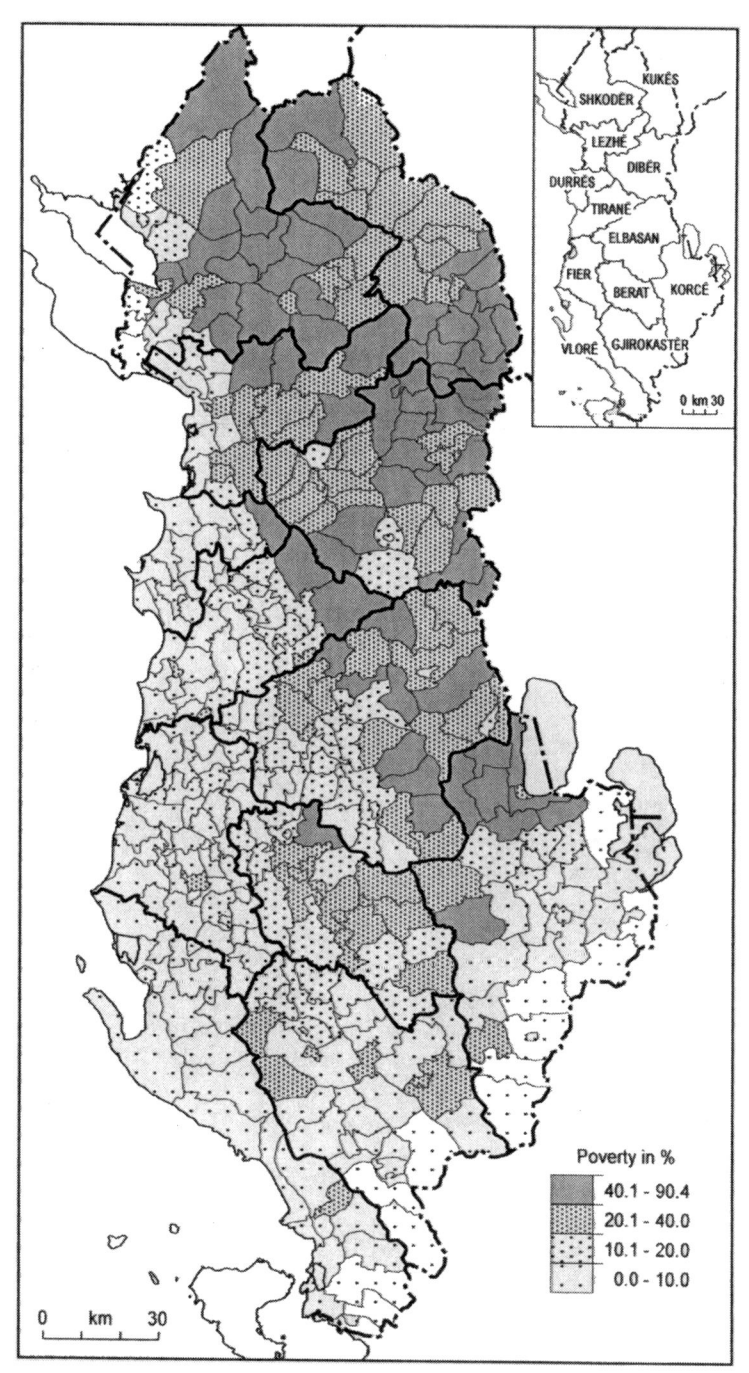

Figure 3.1 Poverty map of Albania: percentage of households classed as poor in each municipality, 2000 (inset: prefectures)
Source: UNICEF (2000).

Who is most likely to migrate? A recent analysis of the 2002 LSMS data by Castaldo et al. (2005) shows that those most likely to *consider* migrating[7] are young males under twenty-five with secondary or vocational educational training, and unemployed. Likelihood to consider migrating is greater in urban than rural areas. Regarding the link between migration and poverty, Castaldo et al. suggest a dual relationship: in rural areas it is the better off who have considered migrating (the poorest cannot afford to emigrate, or do not have the necessary contacts), whereas in urban areas it is the less well off (the migration costs and barriers for the urban poor are less than for the rural poor).

Castaldo et al. model the *intent* to migrate; arguably, this has a tenuous link with *actual* migration. Based on LSMS data on actual migrations from surveyed households, Stampini et al. (2004) present a more complex analysis of migrant selectivity – albeit excluding complete-household migration. They demonstrate that different selection filters operate for different types of emigration (temporary vs. permanent), from different regional origins within Albania, and to different destination countries. Use of the LSMS dataset, with time-specific movements recorded, also sheds light on how migration patterns and migrant characteristics change over time. Tables 3.2, 3.3 and 3.4 synthesise these findings. A primary distinction in all three tables is that between temporary and permanent emigrants.

Table 3.2 compares the characteristics of temporary and permanent emigrants across two time periods, 1990–96 and 1997–2002. This periodisation corresponds to Barjaba's two-stage model of Albanian migration (see Barjaba 2003: 169–179; Barjaba and King 2005: 18–20). Briefly, the first stage of this model consists of mainly male, irregular migration, with migrants taking the lowest-quality jobs in the two main destination countries (Greece and Italy); their undocumented status exacerbates their vulnerability, marginalisation and stigmatisation. In the second stage, large-scale regularisation of undocumented migrants takes place, migrants improve their socioeconomic positions, the structure of the flows 'normalises' with increasing numbers of women and other family members, and new destinations are sought beyond the two neighbouring countries. Table 3.2 reveals contrasts both between temporary and permanent emigrants, and across the two time periods. Permanent migrants tend to be younger (at time of emigration) than first-time temporary migrants, as well as better educated and from less-poor backgrounds. Marked gender differences are observable: only 9 per cent of temporary emigrants are female, but 35 per cent of permanent emigrants are. Regarding the geography of origins and destinations, temporary migrants are more likely to come from the Central and Mountainous regions, whereas permanent emigrants are disproportionately drawn from Tirana and the Coastal region. Temporary migrants go overwhelmingly to Greece; permanent migrants are more evenly spread between Greece,

Table 3.2 Characteristics of temporary and permanent emigrants, by period of emigration, 1990–2002

	Temporary emigrants (first emigration)			Permanent emigrants		
	1990–96 (n=341)	1997–02 (n=324)	1990–02 (n=665)	1990–96 (n=335)	1997–02 (n=767)	1990–02 (n=1,102)
Migrant characteristics:						
Age at migration (years)	28	30	29	26	26	26
Females (%)	6	13	9	33	37	35
Fewer than 8 years' schooling (%)	5	7	6	2	2	2
Higher education (%)	5	4	4	8	8	8
Household consumption per capita, 2002 (Leks)	8,650	7,961	8,314	10,901	9,910	10,213
Region of origin (%):						
Tirana	6	9	7	10	10	10
Coastal	31	29	30	46	41	43
Central	56	48	52	42	42	42
Mountain	6	14	10	1	7	5
Destination country (%):						
Greece	82	76	79	56	37	43
Italy	11	15	13	29	39	36
Other	7	9	8	15	24	21

Source: Authors' re-working of tables in Stampini et al. (2004: 23–24), based in turn on LSMS data.

Table 3.3 Characteristics of temporary and permanent emigrants, by destination country, 1990–2002

	Temporary		Permanent	
	Greece (n=519)	Italy et al. (n=146)	Greece (n=471)	Italy et al. (n=631)
Age at first migration (years)	28	32	26	26
Females (%)	9	10	37	34
Primary education or less (%)	65	48	60	48
Secondary education (%)	31	46	36	41
University education (%)	4	6	4	11
Consumption per capita, 2002 (Leks)	7,944	9,653	9,657	10,635

Source: after Stampini et al. (2004: 24–25), based in turn on LSMS data.

Italy and other countries. The most notable changes over time are an increasing share of females, an involvement of more poorer families (suggesting the early migrants came from better-off households) and a shift of origins from Coastal and Central to the Mountain regions. Also noticeable is the increasing preference for Italy as a destination, especially for permanent emigrants.

Tables 3.3 and 3.4 foreground the contrast between Greece and Italy as destination countries. Emigrants to Greece are younger and have a lower educational standard than those going to Italy; this contrast holds for both temporary and permanent emigrants. Households with migrants in, or having been in, Italy are wealthier than those with migrants in Greece (and non-migrant households). In terms of location of origin (Table 3.4), migrants from Tirana and other urban places are more likely to go to Italy, whereas Greek migration is more intensively drawn from rural and mountain areas.

Table 3.4 Location of origin of temporary and permanent emigrants, by destination country, 1990–2002 (%)

Region of origin	Temporary emigrants		Permanent emigrants	
	Greece	Italy et al.	Greece	Italy et al.
Tirana	51	49	17	83
Coastal urban	79	21	26	74
Coastal rural	76	24	49	51
Central urban	68	32	47	53
Central rural	89	11	55	45
Mountain urban	86	14	14	86
Mountain rural	81	19	48	52
Total	79	21	43	57

Source: after Stampini et al. (2004: 25), based in turn on LSMS data.

Demographic and Spatial Impact of Migration

Here we pick up the discussion on the demographic basis to Albanian migration launched in the previous chapter. We argued in Chapter 2 that demographic factors – above all the rapid growth of population during the communist period – need to be given their rightful place alongside the economic and political factors shaping emigration since 1990. Now we reverse the line of causal analysis and examine the impact of migration on the evolution of the Albanian population since 1990, including its spatial aspects. Reference back to Tables 2.1 and 2.2 reminds us of some of the main trends visible across the 1989–2001 intercensal period: a population decrease for the first time in Albanian history; a halving of natural increase due to markedly decreased fertility rates; and a sharp rise in the share of the population residing in urban areas, due to rapid rural–urban migration. Figure 3.2 superimposes the 1989 and 2001 age–sex pyramids of the Albanian population. From this comparison, we can not only see the demographic impact of a decade of emigration but also muse a little on the likely development of the Albanian population in the future. First, the age–sex selectivity of emigration is very clear: a marked loss of males in the 18–35 age bracket, and a smaller shrinkage of females of the same age range. Second, the size of the age cohort 10–15 years remains intact for 2001, indicating further migration potential over the ensuing decade. And third, the contracted 0–5 cohort for 2001 will lessen pressure for emigration over the longer-term – at least on demographic grounds. This low-birth cohort reflects three interrelated factors: the continuing fertility decline in Albania (TFR having fallen to 2.2 in 2001); the 'unborn' due to the emigration (and hence non-fertility or postponed fertility) of single young adults; and the fact that, where family migration has occurred, these youngest Albanians are resident outside the country.

The demographic situation could change if substantial return migration occurred, which would plug some of the gaps in the 2001 pyramid, especially if foreign-born children were introduced by returning families. At present, large-scale family-based return migration seems unlikely because of the country's ongoing social, political and, above all, economic problems. Our own evidence, presented in the following chapters and especially in Chapter 7, indicates weak propensity to return. Families are tending to see their short- and medium-term futures in Italy, where their children will have better life-chances. Migration to, and return from, Greece has a rather different rhythm because of its shuttle character and because of periodic repatriations by the Greek authorities of undocumented migrants. Nevertheless in Greece, too, an increasing share of Albanian migrants are settling down for the longer term (Fakiolas 2003; Hatziprokopiou 2003; Pratsinakis 2005).

The spatial expression and impact of migration are best examined at the district level of Albania's thirty-six *rrheti*. However, in the published

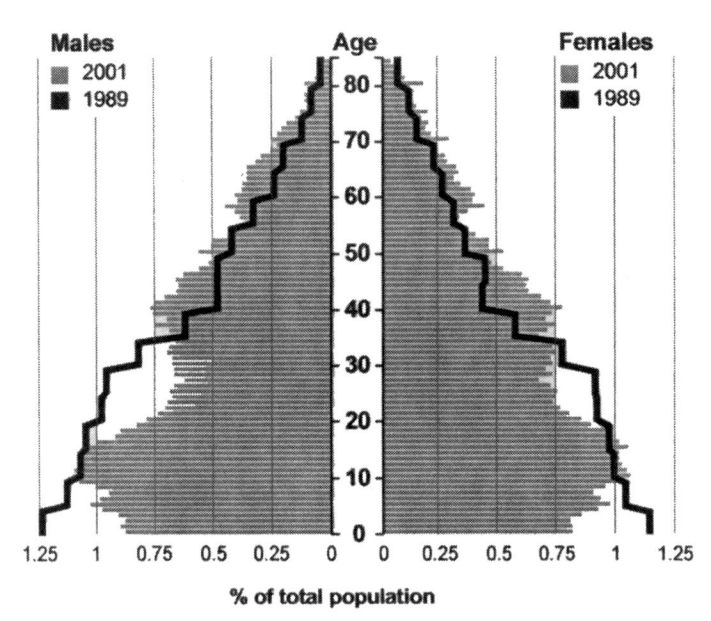

Figure 3.2 Age–sex pyramids, 1989 and 2001
Source: ISTAT (2004: 31).

volumes of the 2001 Census, district-level measurements of international migration are conflated with internal migration. Recently, Carletto et al. (2004) have managed to disaggregate international migration from the other elements of population change at district level, thus enabling separate mappings of internal and international migration.[8] These authors find that almost twice as many individuals migrated internationally (628,319) than changed their district of residence within Albania (355,230) between 1989 and 2001.

Table 3.5 sets out some raw data on migration at the district scale, which are then mapped in Figure 3.3. The first column, total net migration, comprises both internal and international moves, the product being indexed against the 1989 district populations to get a measure of the relative intensity of migration. Note that only Tirana has a positive migratory balance: all other 35 districts experienced net migratory loss during 1989–2001. Five districts – Delvinë, Sarandë and Skrapar in the south, and Tropojë and Pukë in the north – lost half or more of their 1989 populations through net out-migration, and fourteen more districts lost between a quarter and a half of their inhabitants (see Figure 3.3d for location of districts). The third and fourth columns in Table 3.5 give the outflows to internal and international destinations. Clearly, some districts 'specialise' in internal outflows, others in emigration abroad, and yet others are equally involved in both. The final column expresses the ratio between the two types of out-migration for each district. Markedly

Table 3.5 Albania: selected migration statistics by district, 1989–2001

District	Total net migration 1989–01 No.	As % 1989 population	Migration outflow Internal	International	Ratio
Berat	−31,135	−22.8	19,220	16,964	1.13
Bulqizë	−17,759	−35.3	8,427	12,352	0.68
Delvinë	−13,862	−58.3	1,030	13,619	0.08
Devoll	−7,043	−18.5	2,654	5,734	0.46
Dibër	−39,879	−40.1	37,475	3,411	10.99
Durrës	−4,494	−2.7	4,431	50,836	0.09
Elbasan	−28,690	−13.5	10,548	28,510	0.37
Fier	−38,948	−19.1	16,880	36,046	0.47
Gramsh	−16,853	−38.7	11,395	6,277	1.82
Gjirokastër	−17,519	−26.4	2,053	18,065	0.11
Has	−8,593	−39.3	4,412	4,477	0.99
Kavajë	−17,215	−21.2	5,611	16,973	0.33
Kolonjë	−10,167	−41.0	5,304	5,651	0.94
Korçë	−50,116	−28.3	18,494	39,662	0.47
Krujë	−3,053	−5.6	4,814	3,365	1.43
Kuçovë	−9,665	−24.2	2,665	11,596	0.23
Kukës	−36,478	−45.9	33,072	4,567	7.24
Kurbin	−8,371	−15.9	4,333	13,347	0.32
Lezhë	−4,406	−7.1	3,937	11,292	0.35
Librazhd	−15,690	−21.8	12,537	4,786	2.62
Lushnjë	−14,357	−10.7	9,037	19,708	0.46
Malësi e Madhe	−15,010	−34.3	2,842	13,128	0.22
Mallakastër	−8,581	−21.0	5,170	11,807	0.44
Mat	−30,603	−39.9	17,716	14,527	1.22
Mirditë	−22,306	−44.2	14,457	9,097	1.59
Peqin	−4,395	−14.7	3,625	2,178	1.66
Permët	−17,832	−44.8	8,084	10,826	0.75
Pogradec	−12,682	−17.8	7,244	8,880	0.82
Pukë	−25,057	−51.2	17,793	8,034	2.21
Sarandë	−31,847	−49.8	1,523	35,134	0.04
Skrapar	−22,968	−49.4	13,695	10,567	1.30
Shkodër	−37,517	−19.5	7,211	37,197	0.19
Tepelenë	−23,756	−47.7	11,262	13,532	0.83
Tirana	+97,949	+26.6	4,140	57,216	0.07
Tropojë	−25,316	−56.5	16,604	9,462	1.75
Vlorë	−54,105	−30.6	5,535	59,496	0.09
Total	−628,319	−19.7	355,230	628,319	0.57

Sources: Carletto et al. (2004: 18–19); INSTAT (2002: 32).

different ratios are evident. The extreme cases are Dibër in the north-east, which recorded eleven times as many people migrating internally as externally, and Sarandë in the far south, where internal migrants were only 4 per cent of the total outflow.

The geography of these different types of migration becomes readily apparent when we examine Figure 3.3. At the top, the internal and

80 | Out of Albania

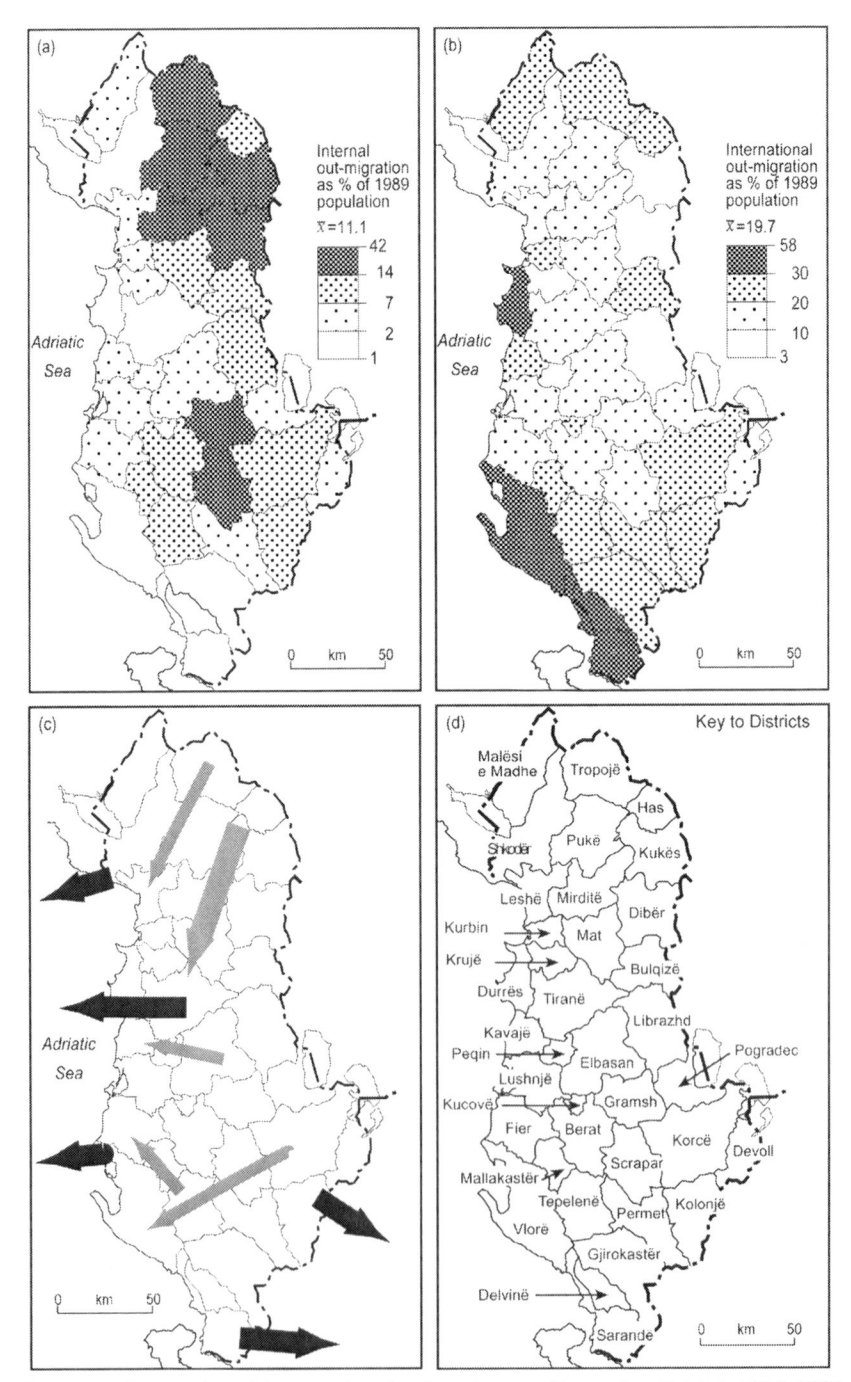

Figure 3.3 Internal and international migration outflows, by district, 1989–2001: (a) internal migration; (b) international migration; (c) main flows; (d) districts
Source: Carletto et al. (2004: 19); Zezza et al. (2005: 187).

international migration outflows (third and fourth columns in Table 3.5) are indexed against 1989 population. For internal migration (Figure 3.3a) there are two main blocks of districts exhibiting high outflow. The main group is in the north-east, especially Kukës, Dibër, Tropojë, Pukë and Mirditë; together these five sparsely populated districts account for one third of total internal migration outflow (Table 3.5). A second, smaller cluster of high internal out-migration focuses around the south-central districts of Gramsh and Skrapar. Particularly low rates of out-migration to other Albanian districts are observed in the far south, in Tirana and Durrës, and in the main northern city of Shkodër. These districts are either involved in *receiving* internal migrants (especially Tirana, Durrës and Shkodër) or, as we shall see below, in 'exporting' international migrants.

The map of international migration (Figure 3.3b) shows a very different spatial pattern from the one for internal movement. All southern districts have above average rates of international migration, culminating in Delvinë, Sarandë and Vlorë, plus the coastal district of Durrës which acts as a bridgehead for emigration to Italy. In terms of absolute totals (Table 3.5), the largest sources of international migrants are the urban districts located at the main coastal and transport gateways to Greece, Italy and beyond. Together the five districts of Tirana, Durrës, Vlorë, Korçë and Shkodër account for 40 per cent of the total. Low rates of international migration are concentrated in northern, central and interior districts, the lowest being Dibër and Kukës, which were the districts of the highest internal out-migration. Finally, there are some districts which have a medium-to-high involvement with *both* types of migration. This includes northern border districts such as Tropojë and Has, and some central-southern districts including Korçë, Skrapar, Kolonjë and Tepelenë. To take one example, Korçë ranks fourth for absolute number of both internal and international migrants (Table 3.5).

Figure 3.3c is a more schematic map of the main migration currents within and out of Albania during 1989–2002. Note that the arrow widths are indicative of, but not directly proportional to, the observed flows. Although migrants to both Italy and Greece come from all parts of Albania, emigration to Greece is particularly strong from the southern districts close to the border. Emigration to Italy, on the other hand, is relatively more common from the more urbanised coastal districts, and from the north. In addition to geographical proximity and communication links, religion and language have some influence on the patterns. The southern districts are where most of the ethnic-Greek, Orthodox minorities live. Albania's Catholic minority – more likely to migrate to Italy – are in the north. And the western districts are where Italian television (and therefore informal language learning) could be most clearly received during the years before and during the post-communist transformation.

As regards internal flows, these are dominated by movements between the rural north and Tirana. The capital is the key destination for all of the five main 'expelling' districts of internal migrants, attracting 70 per cent of the out-migrants from Dibër and Kukës for example (Carletto et al. 2004: 9). Durrës is in most cases the second destination of choice for internal migrants. Whilst Tirana and Durrës receive migrants from all parts of Albania, other cities such as Shkodër, Elbasan, Fier, Vlorë and Korçë receive most of their migrants from neighbouring districts.

Migration and Poverty Revisited

The above examination of the differential spatial patterning of internal vs. external migration takes us back to our earlier discussion on migration and poverty. Table 3.3 suggested that permanent emigrants, especially to Italy, were likely to be more educated and from better-off families than temporary emigrants, especially those going to Greece. The question remains as to whether the higher-than-average household incomes for permanent emigrants and those to Italy are a *causal factor facilitating* such migrations or are a *result of migration* through wealth-enhancing remittances from household members who may have been abroad for many years.

Now, comparison of the poverty map (Figure 3.1) with the maps of internal and international outflow in Figure 3.3 suggests a further, more dichotomised relationship: poorer districts (in the north and north-east) tend to send internal migrants, and relatively better-off districts in the centre and south send mainly international migrants. In Figure 3.4 the poverty headcount (percentage of households below the poverty line) is plotted against first the international migration ratio, and second the internal migration ratio, for each district.[9] For international migration the relationship with the poverty index is upward sloping, whilst for internal migration the relationship is downward sloping (Carletto et al. 2004: 9). In other words, internal migration is *positively* associated with poverty, and international migration is negatively correlated to poverty: note the respective Pearson correlation coefficients of 0.43 and −0.54. So poverty acts as a push factor for internal migration and as a constraining factor for the more costly international migration (Zezza et al. 2005: 184–185, 191).

These multiple distinctions between internal and international migration and, within external moves, between temporary and permanent migration and between Italy and Greece as destinations, advance our understanding of the dynamics of the various types of migration observable in Albania. This is not the whole picture, however, because these binaries do not acknowledge that, within individual households for example, two or more migration types may be engaged in, either sequentially or simultaneously, by various household members. Many of the migrants we interviewed in Italy had previously been in Greece. In a

(a)   r = −0.54

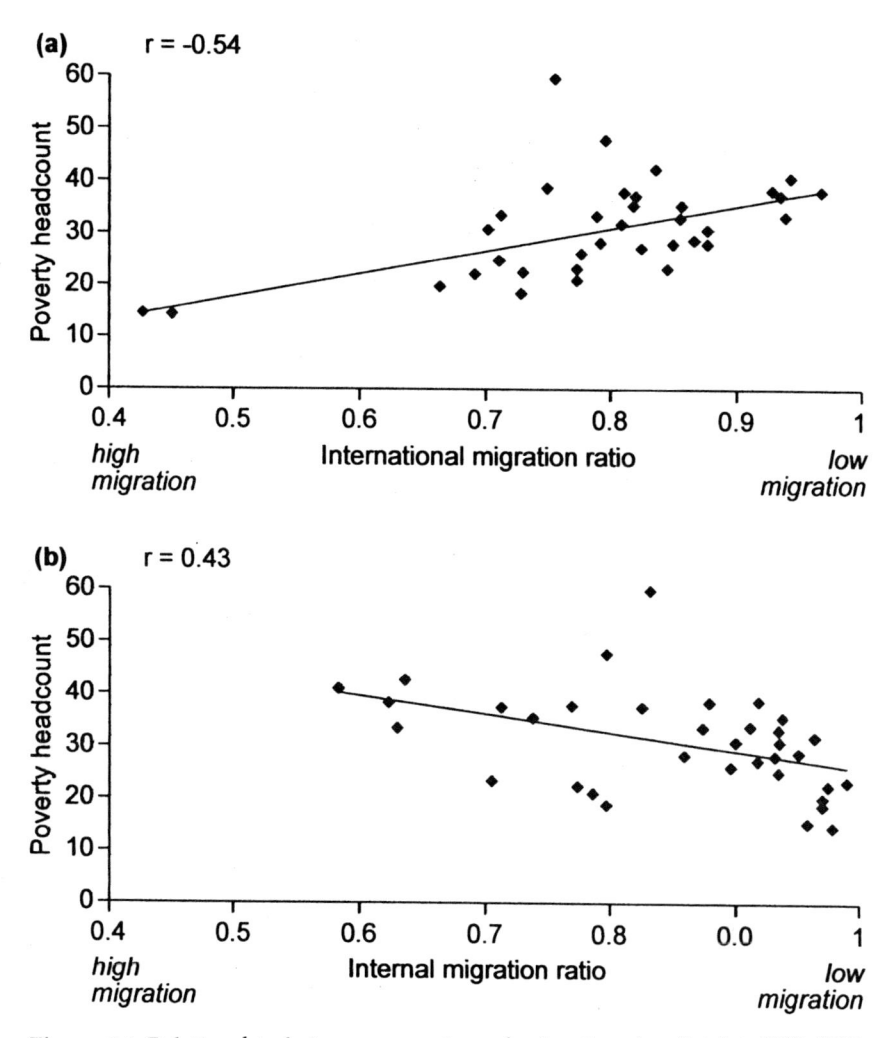

(b)   r = 0.43

Figure 3.4 Relationship between poverty and migration, by district, 1989–2001: (a) international migration; (b) internal migration
Source: Carletto et al. (2004: 27–28); Zezza et al. (2005: 186).

different research project, on Albanian migrants in the London area, we found that most interviewees had been first to Greece and then to Italy, en route for the UK (King et al. 2003: 39–45). Further complications arise when we attempt to disentangle internal from international migration (King 2004). Do migrants tend to move internally prior to emigration? Or is it more common for migrants first to work abroad in order to finance an internal move, perhaps to Tirana, after return? Or are some of these multiple moves occurring simultaneously within the same household – for instance sons and daughters working abroad whilst their parents

84 | Out of Albania

effect an internal relocation prior to a (partial) reunion of the household in a more rational, profitable location in Albania? As we shall see in our final chapter, our own research data do not provide complete and quantifiable answers to these questions, but they do shed light on a number of patterns which are taking shape.

Albanians in Italy

We now move to the other shore of the Adriatic Sea in order to document the development of the Albanian migratory presence in Italy. We begin with a note on data sources, and then deploy the available statistics to trace the evolution of the Albanian presence in Italy from 1990 to 2003. Next, we use the same sources to examine Albanians' social and demographic characteristics and to demonstrate their progressive and rapid 'settling down'. Finally, we portray the migrants' evolving geographical distribution within Italy.

Data Sources

There are two main sources for documenting the year-on-year numbers of Albanians (and other immigrants) legally present in Italy: *permits to stay* and *municipal population registers*. In addition the *census of population* offers a different kind of snapshot every ten years. All three sources have both advantages and disadvantages (Bonifazi 1998: 105–133).

The database on permits to stay – *permessi di soggiorno* – is maintained by the Ministry of the Interior on the basis of permits issued by the *Questure* (police-station offices) in towns and cities the length and breadth of the country. Its main advantages are its continuous updating, and the relatively large number of variables presented – sex, age group, civil status, country of origin, motive for being in Italy, region and province of settlement, length of stay. Its disadvantages are that it does not register minors, who are listed only on the permit of the family head, and delay or failure in cancelling permits when the holder moves from one province to another in Italy, or leaves the country.[10] In addition, it is widely known that there are very many immigrants – including Albanians – living and working in Italy who do not have a permit to stay. These are the so-called *irregolari*.

Despite these problems, the *permessi* database is generally regarded as the most useful of the sources recording the presence of immigrants in Italy, and is the main source used by the very valuable dossiers on Italian immigration statistics published each year by the Caritas organisation. It is the source we use for most of our tables and analysis presented below.

Both the municipal registers and the census – the other two sources – are managed by the national statistics agency, ISTAT. The general opinion is that the municipal registers tend to offer rather poor estimates of the immigrant population. Registration is not compulsory and can only be effected by those with a permit to stay – which leads to underestimation. On the other hand, there is no incentive for migrants who are registered to cancel their registration when they leave – which leads in the direction of over counting (Bonifazi 1998: 112, 130). Only a limited range of demographic variables is available. Two advantages over the permit dataset are the separate recordings of children and the availability of data at the micro level of the *comune* or individual municipality.

The population census, by enumerating the population 'on the ground' on census day, records both legally resident foreigners and *irregolari*. Hence it acts as a useful control to compare with the 2001 records of permit-holders and municipal registers. Its main disadvantage is that it is taken only at ten-year intervals and is therefore only crudely effective in measuring the arrival and settlement of immigrants.

Evolution 1990–2003

Table 3.6 traces the 'stock' of Albanians in Italy according to the permit-to-stay database. The chronological record reflects the key events mentioned earlier: hence the 2,034 permit-holders recorded on 31 December 1990 are 'embassy migrants' admitted by Italy earlier that same year; the 26,381 recorded at the end of 1991 are primarily the 'boat-migrants' who entered Italy in the spring and were given special dispensation under the recently passed Martelli Law; the sharp increase in the late 1990s reflects the 'pyramid emigration' effect, and so on. Clearly the stock of Albanians grew much faster than the immigrant

Table 3.6 Albanians in Italy with 'permits to stay': end-of-year, 1990–2003

Year	No.	Rank	% total	Total immigrants
1990	2,034	65	0.3	781,138
1991	26,381	9	3.1	859,571
1992	28,828	7	3.1	925,172
1993	30,847	7	3.1	987,407
1994	31,926	7	3.5	922,706
1995	34,706	7	3.5	991,419
1996	63,976	2	5.8	1,095,622
1997	83,807	2	6.8	1,240,721
1998	91,537	2	7.3	1,250,214
1999	115,755	2	9.2	1,251,994
2000	142,066	2	10.2	1,388,153
2001	144,120	2	10.6	1,362,630
2002	168,963	2	11.2	1,512,324
2003	233,616	2	10.6	2,193,999

Source: Caritas (1997: 69; 1998: 79; 1999: 119; 2000: 132; 2001: 121; 2002: 96; 2003: 117; 2004: 135).

Table 3.7 Albanians in Italy's regularisation schemes, 1986–2002

Year of scheme	Total applicants	Albanians	Top five countries (%)	
1986	113,349	–	Morocco	18.3
			Sri Lanka	9.9
			Philippines	9.0
			Tunisia	8.4
			Senegal	7.1
1990 'Martelli Law'	234,841	2,471	Morocco	22.9
			Tunisia	11.7
			Senegal	7.8
			Yugoslavia	5.2
			Philippines	4.0
1995 'Dini Decree'	258,761	29,724	Morocco	13.7
			Albania	11.4
			Philippines	7.8
			China	6.2
			Romania	4.6
1998 'Turco-Napolitano Law'	250,747	39,454	Albania	15.7
			Romania	11.1
			Morocco	11.0
			China	7.7
			Senegal	4.9
2002 'Bossi-Fini Law'	704,350	55,038	Romania	20.4
			Ukraine	15.2
			Albania	7.8
			Morocco	7.8
			Egypt	5.2

Source: Caritas (2002: 147; 2004: 135).

population as a whole. For instance, between 1995 and 2003 the total number of foreigners in Italy grew by 2.2 times; Albanians increased their numbers by 6.7 times. Albanians became the second-ranked foreign nationality in 1996, holding that position thereafter; and ever since 2000 Albanians have made up at least one-tenth of the total foreigner population.

Throughout the period 1990–2002, Moroccans were the biggest migratory presence in Italy. Things changed in 2003 as a result of the unexpectedly large scale of the 2002 regularisation. Moroccans became the third largest national community, after Romanians and Albanians. The impact of Italy's periodic regularisations is seen in more detail in Table 3.7. Albanians featured minimally in the first two, but thereafter became prominent in all three recent regularisations, reflecting their desire to 'get papers', become integrated and either settle down in Italy or at least have the legal possibility to 'come and go' as they please. Visits home are facilitated by regular boat connections across the Adriatic and by a range of flight routes from several Italian airports.

Table 3.8 Foreign nationals in Italy: top ten origin countries for regularisation applicants (2002) and total permit-holders (2003)

Applicants for 2002 regularisation			Total permit-holders, 2003		
Country	No.	%	Country	No.	%
Romania	143,947	20.4	Romania	239,426	10.9
Ukraine	106,921	15.2	Albania	233,616	10.6
Albania	55,038	7.8	Morocco	227,940	10.4
Morocco	54,221	7.8	Ukraine	112,802	5.1
Ecuador	36,673	5.2	China	100,109	4.6
China	35,443	5.0	Philippines	73,847	3.4
Poland	34,241	4.9	Poland	65,847	3.0
Moldova	31,217	4.4	Tunisia	60,572	2.8
Peru	17,471	2.5	USA	48,286	2.2
Egypt	16,010	2.3	Senegal	47,762	2.2

Sources: Caritas (2004: 135); CNEL (2004: 47).

Table 3.8 contextualises the scale of the Albanian presence in Italy in comparison with other foreign nationalities. This is done with reference to two sets of statistics – the 2002 regularisation and the permit-holder records from the end of 2003 (which subsume the regularisations). For the 2002 regularisation, the strong impact of East Europeans is clear (unlike earlier regularisations, when 'Third World' immigrants were more dominant – see Table 3.7). From the column showing total permit-holders it can be seen how three nationalities – Romanians, Albanians and Moroccans, each with just over 10 per cent – now stand out above the other main nationalities.

Let us now briefly corroborate the permit data with the other two sources. Bonifazi and Sabatino (2003: 968–970) compare the Albanian permit statistics with the population register data for 1994–2001. There is an approximate correspondence between the two sets, although this is partly an artificial similarity since there are clues that the two sources do not measure exactly the same populations.[11] Albanians in the census were counted at 173,064, higher than both the permit-holders (144,120) and the population register (163,900).[12] The low figure for permit-holders is partly explained by the omission of children. Both the permit and population register sources exclude undocumented immigrants. ISTAT have suggested a 'correction factor' of 21.5 per cent to be added to the population register to account for the undocumented Albanians (Bonifazi and Sabatino 2003: 971). This would imply adding 35,240 to the 2001 register total of 163,900, resulting in a total of slightly under 200,000. This is significantly more than the census figure,[13] but accords with many other estimates, including those of the Albanian authorities. The effect of the 2002 regularisation, adding another 55,000, brings the total to 250,000 or more – in line with the latest estimate from the Albanian government (Government of Albania 2004: 40).

Social and Demographic Characteristics

This is a good place to re-state the main message of our research findings, namely that, despite the recency of Albanians' arrival in Italy, despite their ambiguous reception by the Italian authorities in 1991, and despite the operation of a range of exclusionary measures including fierce stigmatisation, Albanians have rapidly evolved into one of the most successfully settled migrant populations in Italy. Our field evidence for this bold assertion will be spelled out in detail in the next three chapters, in which it will be seen that the notion of successful integration is far from simple and is, instead, multi-faceted. For now, it is useful to preface our fieldwork-based account with some social and demographic indicators which set the profile of Albanians alongside other migrants.

We look first at gender and family dynamics, which suggest a progressive 'normalisation' of Albanians' demographic profile and a stabilisation of their long-term presence in Italy. Three indicators are examined: the female percentage, the proportion of immigrants who are married, and the number of children in the immigrant population.

Table 3.9 sets out the data on the female share of the Albanian population in Italy according to three standard sources, starting in 1994, after the settling-in of the first wave of immigrants, and concluding with 2001, the census year. Although the permit statistics under-record females (probably because permit-holding is strongly linked to work and most Albanian women come to Italy as part of family reunion), the general picture is very clear: females have increased their share of the total population from less than one quarter in 1994 to around 40 per cent by 2001. This is an unmistakeable sign of the rapid stabilisation of the Albanian presence.

Further confirmation of Albanians' rapid family-based settlement is provided in Table 3.10. Data for Albanians are compared to two larger migrant reference groups: the former socialist states of Eastern and Central Europe, and 'countries of strong migratory pressure' – the developing world. This table shows a fast rate of increase in the proportion of Albanian migrants who are married – in fact the male share

Table 3.9 Albanians in Italy: % females according to three sources, 1994–2001

	1994	1995	1996	1997	1998	1999	2000	2001
Permit-holders	22.7	28.3	32.7	27.1	30.7	36.2	34.0	38.3
Population register	24.5	29.1	33.5	32.4	33.7	38.5	39.0	39.4
Census								43.7

Source: partly after Bonifazi and Sabatino (2003: 970).

Table 3.10 Immigrants in Italy: indicators of family structure, Albanians and reference groups, 1992 and 2000

Migrants from:	% males married 1992	2000	% females married 1992	2000	% with children 1992	2000
Albania	22.4	44.8	60.0	72.9	7.1	18.7
Eastern Europe	37.5	47.8	46.4	57.9	9.9	15.2
Developing world	36.9	45.3	42.1	54.8	7.2	13.3

Source: Bonifazi and Sabatino (2003: 979), based on ISTAT data.

doubles between the end of 1992 and 2000. The female share changes less dramatically (by 13 percentage points compared to 22 for males) but is very high anyway, indicating that the female component of Albanian migration to Italy follows a fairly traditional model of behaviour, linked to 'following' men for marriage and family creation. This point has additional force when the data for the comparator groups are examined: here the share of married females is much lower.

The third indicator – percentage of migrants with children – reinforces the picture given by the shares of females and married persons. Compared to the reference groups, Albanians had the lowest share in 1992 but the largest in 2000, again indicating rapid family-based settlement.

Further light on the fast-increasing numbers of Albanian children living in Italy is shed by statistics on pupil enrolments in schools (Table 3.11). From just 1,000 Albanian pupils in the school year 1991–92, the number has grown to 50,000 in 2003–04. The percentage data show that, since 2000–01, Albanians make up 18 per cent of foreign pupils, far above Albanians' overall weight in the foreign population (11 per cent according

Table 3.11 Albanian pupils in Italian schools 1991–92 to 2003–04

Type of school	1991–92	1995–96	2000–01	2003–04
Absolute values				
Nursery	199	802	4,659	9,735
Elementary	532	2,235	15,587	20,930
Intermediate	244	686	7,735	11,538
Secondary	52	418	4,287	7,762
Total	1,027	4,141	32,268	49,965
% total foreign pupils				
Nursery	3.6	7.7	12.7	17.7
Elementary	4.1	9.3	20.3	18.2
Intermediate	4.7	7.2	17.5	17.1
Secondary	1.5	6.5	17.8	17.3
Total	3.8	8.2	17.8	17.7

Sources: Bonifazi and Sabatino (2003: 980); Caritas (2004: 169).

to the permit records, 13 per cent according to the census). Table 3.11 shows that Albanian pupils are now present at a uniform level throughout the school system. In fact Albanians, with 50,000, are the most numerous foreign-origin group in schools, ahead of Moroccans (42,000), Romanians (28,000) and Chinese (16,000). Mention should also be made here of Albanian students in Italian universities. During the academic year 2002–03 there were 6,531 Albanian students enrolled, making up more than 20 per cent of the total of foreign students.[14]

In sum, the trend data in Tables 3.9, 3.10 and 3.11 show that, over less than a decade, Albanian immigration has evolved extraordinarily rapidly, 'revealing a capacity for dynamic change much greater than might have been expected' when those first shiploads of desperate fugitives from communism arrived in 1991 (Bonifazi and Sabatino 2003: 970).

Geographical Distribution

One feature defines the geographical distribution of Albanians in Italy: they are more evenly spread throughout the country than any other immigrant nationality. Whilst some immigrant communities are highly concentrated in one city or region – such as Egyptians in Milan, Bangladeshis in Rome and Tunisians in Sicily – Albanians are present in all regions and are found both in large cities and in small towns and villages. This widespread dispersal might be seen as prima facie evidence for their high level of integration in Italian society, although the precise direction of this possible causal link is not clear (we discuss this point in King and Mai 2002: 172–175). Other hypotheses can also be advanced. One relates to the Italian authorities' policies of dispersal of the refugee-migrants who arrived in March 1991. Useful documentation on this is assembled by dell'Agnese (1996): whilst many arrivals remained in Apulia and adjacent southern regions, significant numbers were resettled in Piedmont, Liguria, Trentino and Friuli, all in northern Italy. Another reason for Albanians' scattered distribution could be their search for work and housing outside of the expensive major cities, taking them into adjacent small towns and rural areas. Or their rather weak ethnic community structures might be a factor hindering their concentration and favouring their dispersion. We examine these hypotheses in later chapters.

As we did for the geography of migrant origins within Albania, we present here both a detailed table and a collage of maps. Table 3.12 contains the regional data, taken from two sources, the 2001 Census, and the permit records for the end of the same year. We set these two sources side by side in order to explore their consistency at the regional level. Interestingly, whilst the two sources record similar totals for the sum of *all* immigrant nationalities (around 1.3 million), the disparity in the figures for Albanians (census 173,000, permits 144,000) strongly suggests that this

Table 3.12 Regional distribution of Albanians in Italy according to the census and permit-to-stay records, 2001

	Census				Permit-holders			
	No.	% total Albanians	% total population	% total immigrants	No.	% total Albanians	% total population	% total immigrants
Piedmont	16,859	9.7	3.9	15.3	13,308	9.2	3.1	13.9
Val d'Aosta	254	0.1	2.1	9.7	261	0.2	2.2	9.6
Lombardy	31,605	18.3	3.5	9.9	24,674	17.1	2.7	7.9
Liguria	5,280	3.2	3.3	14.7	3,578	2.5	2.2	10.9
Trentino-Alto Adige	4,191	2.4	4.4	13.8	4,031	2.8	4.3	12.1
Veneto	16,917	9.8	3.7	11.1	11,547	8.0	2.5	9.1
Friuli-Venezia Giulia	5,686	3.3	4.8	14.9	3,421	2.4	2.8	8.3
Emilia-Romagna	17,138	9.9	4.3	12.7	15,386	10.7	3.8	12.2
Tuscany	22,875	13.2	6.4	21.0	16,824	11.7	4.7	17.8
Umbria	6,400	3.7	7.6	23.5	5,221	3.6	6.2	19.5
Marche	8,528	4.9	5.8	18.7	6,673	4.6	4.5	17.0
Latium	9,917	5.7	1.9	6.5	12,956	9.0	2.4	5.5
Abruzzo	4,970	2.9	3.9	23.2	3,993	2.8	3.1	22.1
Molise	499	0.3	0.6	19.3	533	0.4	0.6	25.0
Campania	3,136	1.8	0.5	7.8	4,154	2.9	0.7	6.5
Apulia	12,698	7.3	3.1	42.1	11,976	8.3	2.9	36.7
Basilicata	1,084	0.6	1.8	31.7	1,132	0.8	1.9	36.1
Calabria	1,673	1.0	0.8	9.3	1,272	0.9	0.6	9.3
Sicily	3,137	1.8	0.6	6.4	2,924	2.0	0.6	6.1
Sardinia	217	0.1	0.1	2.0	256	0.2	0.2	2.3
Italy	173,064	100.0	3.0	13.0	144,120	100.0	2.5	10.6

Source: after Caritas (2002: 62, 443–463), based in turn on the Italian census and Ministry of the Interior permit-to-stay data.

group has high numbers of undocumented migrants and of children, who are omitted from the permit record but likely to be enumerated by the census. Both these hypotheses are supported by evidence already discussed, namely the high numbers of Albanian children in Italian schools, and the 55,000 undocumented Albanians who applied to be regularised in the 2002 amnesty.

Further interesting observations can be made about the regional data. Those regions where the permit totals exceed the census counts of Albanians are all in the south of Italy, plus Latium, the region dominated by Rome. If we sum the percentages of Albanians in the nine southern regions (second column, Latium down to Sardinia), then the contrast becomes even clearer: the south contains 21.5 per cent of the Albanians in the census, but 27.3 per cent of the permit-holding Albanians. How can we explain this difference? The strong likelihood is that many Albanian migrants arrive initially in the south, especially Apulia, where they get their papers and then move to the north where there are higher wages and more employment opportunities. The permit database records them as being in the south, but the census finds them in the north. As other studies have shown (Daly 2001; Schuster 2005), this is a common strategy amongst immigrants in Italy. They find it easier to survive as undocumented migrants in the informal economy and social setting of the southern regions, and they also find it easier to obtain permits in the south, where the bureaucracy operates in a more flexible and discretionary manner. Then, as 'legal' migrants, they move to the better labour markets of the north. We have explored the north/south dimension of Albanians' migratory trajectories in Italy in a separate paper (King and Mai 2004), and further evidence on this will be offered in subsequent chapters of the present book.

Figure 3.5 displays three ways of mapping the regional density of Albanian migrants in Italy, drawing on the percentage data in Table 3.12: (a) their absolute distribution, as a percentage of the total stock of Albanians in Italy; (b) their relative density in relation to the total population of each region; and (c) their percentage share of the total immigrant population in each region. The maps are based on the 2001 census data, which appear to offer a more comprehensive coverage of Albanians than the permit database or the population register.[15]

Figure 3.5a shows that, in terms of absolute numbers, most Albanians are found in a block of northern regions – Piedmont, Lombardy, Veneto, Emilia-Romagna and Tuscany (61 per cent in these five regions). Another 13 per cent are found in two other important regions, Latium and Apulia. However, these figures ignore the fact that all these regions are heavily populated in any case, so we move to Figure 3.5b for a map which relates the density of Albanians to the total population in each region. This shows that Albanians have their greatest relative impact in a belt of three regions stretching across the centre of Italy – Tuscany, Umbria and Marche –

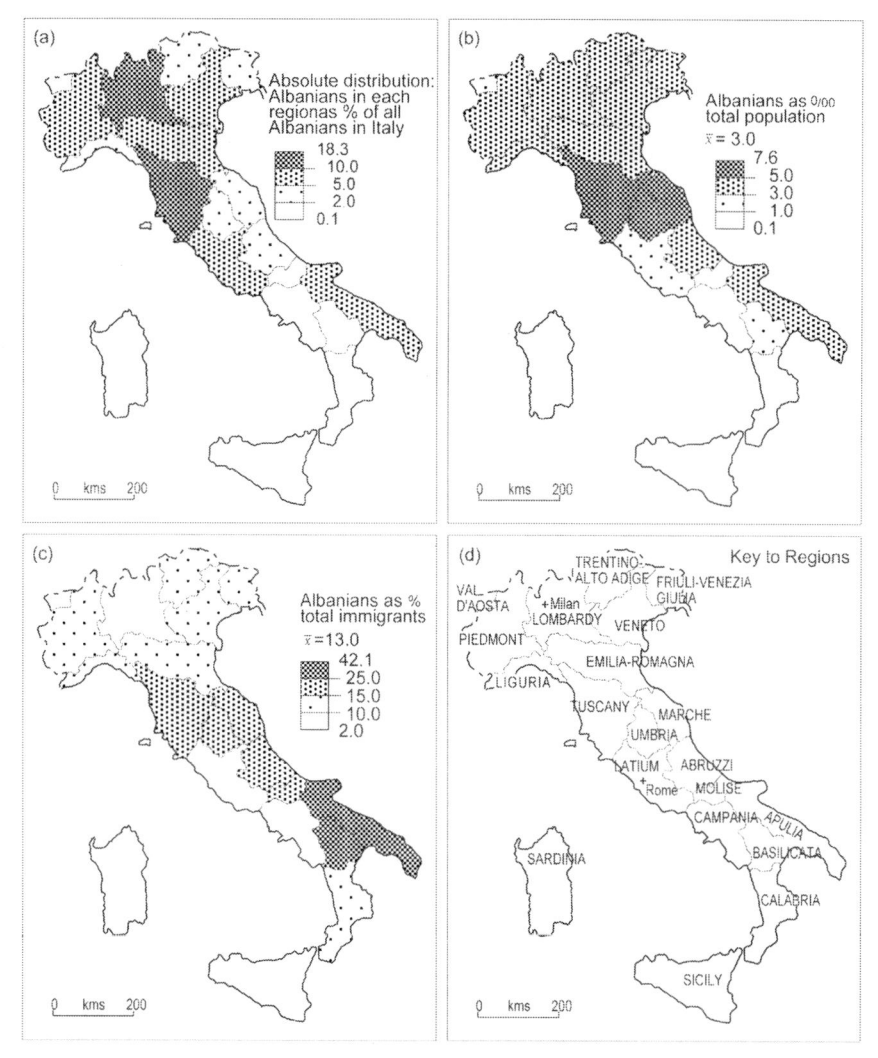

Figure 3.5 Regional distribution of Albanians in Italy, 2001: (a) absolute distribution; (b) relative density; (c) share of total immigrants; (d) regions
Source: Authors' mapping of Italian census data.

where they contribute at least 5 per thousand of the population. Regions of medium–high density are found throughout the north of Italy, and along the Adriatic seaboard.

Figure 3.5c maps the share of Albanians in the total immigrant population of each region. This shows a rather different pattern. The regions of highest density are in the south-east, facing the main route of arrival across the southern Adriatic: in Apulia 42 per cent of the region's immigrants are Albanians, in Basilicata 32 per cent. Albanians also make up fairly large shares (15–25 per cent) of immigrants in a band of regions stretching north along the Adriatic and across to Tuscany, plus Piedmont in the north-west. Regions where Albanians contribute a small share of the immigrant population are of two types: very populous regions (Lombardy, Latium, Campania) where big cities (Milan, Rome, Naples) attract a mix of other nationalities; and peripheral, especially southern regions (Calabria, Sicily, Sardinia) which are relatively unattractive to Albanians and off the track of their main routes of northward migration.

However, the distribution of Albanians, and other migrants, is by no means static. Table 3.13 charts these macro-regional changes, based on permit-to-stay data for 31 December 1995, 1999 and 2003. It must first be borne in mind that the totals out of which the regional shares are calculated have increased significantly over this eight-year period (refer back to Table 3.6): thus all regions saw an absolute increase in both Albanians and all immigrants over the three dates. What Table 3.13 highlights is changing *relative* regional distribution, based on ISTAT's standard five macro-regions of North-West, North-East, Centre, South and Islands. For Albanians and for all immigrants, the North-West and the North-East increase their shares. For the Centre the picture is more confused. This is partly due to the dominating presence of Latium in this macro-region; Latium's migration trends run counter to the other central regimes. Finally, in the South and Islands, the picture is one of general decreasing shares except that, for all immigrants, the mainland South retains stable shares.

The bottom part of Table 3.13 rearranges the division of Italy into two 'halves': North-Centre (minus Latium) and Latium and the South (including the Islands). For both Albanians and all immigrants, this splits the

Table 3.13 Changing macro-regional distribution of Albanians and all immigrants in Italy, 1995–2003 (%)

Macro region	Albanians			All immigrants		
	1995	1999	2003	1995	1999	2003
North-West	26.0	26.2	31.1	30.9	30.7	33.3
North-East	21.0	22.7	24.5	20.3	23.0	24.5
Centre	24.5	28.0	27.9	32.3	29.4	28.0
South	22.9	20.1	14.3	9.9	11.5	10.5
Islands	5.6	3.1	2.2	6.6	5.5	3.7
North-Centre	60.7	68.5	77.0	62.3	65.5	70.8
Latium and South	39.3	31.6	23.0	37.7	34.6	29.2

Source: Permit-to-stay data in Caritas (1996: 76, 325–331; 2000: 137, 362–366; 2004: 471–491).
North-West: Piedmont, Val d'Aosta, Lombardy, Liguria.
North-East: Trentino-Alto Adige, Veneto, Friuli-Venezia Giulia, Emilia-Romagna.
Centre: Tuscany, Umbria, Marche, Latium.
South: Abruzzo, Molise, Campania, Apulia, Basilicata, Calabria.
Islands: Sicily, Sardinia.

country into two clear trend regions: a northern one where immigrants are increasingly congregating, and a southern one, from Rome down, where the relative shares are constantly falling.

The reasoning behind this is as follows. The northern sector contains the economically and socially dynamic regions of Italy where employment prospects, wages and quality of life are highest – although the cost of living is higher too. Above all, this is where most Italian industry is located. The southern part, including Rome and Latium, has a generally weaker economic foundation: services, public administration and agriculture are more important in the regional employment mix (Dunford 2002). Albanians, more so than other migrant nationalities, seem to be unusually sensitive to economic opportunities in different parts of Italy – a theme we will pick up in later chapters with evidence from our own field data. Indeed this diverse geography of migrant settlement and economic opportunity is why we stratified our fieldwork in three locations: Lecce and Apulia, Rome and Latium, and Modena and Emilia-Romagna.

Albanian Emigration to other Countries

Greece

There are several similarities between the flows and experiences of Albanian migrants in Greece and Italy. Both involved migration to geographically and culturally proximate countries where their initial welcome soon turned sour, yet where their survival and progress have been ensured by the demand for their labour in low-status jobs. In both cases their numbers have escalated over the past fifteen years, with a general trend from undocumented to regularised status. And in both cases Albanians have settled throughout the country, in a range of urban and rural settings. But the differences are also noteworthy. Four stand out. First there is the ethnic-Greek factor, which differentiates the experiences of Albanians in Greece according to whether they can claim (or profess to claim) ethnic-Greek origins (Lazaridis 1999). This leads to a range of adaptive and proactive strategies of non-ethnic-Greek Albanians, who have a high propensity to take Greek names, get baptised and convert to Orthodox Christianity in order to lessen the cultural distance between themselves and the hegemonic Greek society – and also to improve their chances of getting a better job and becoming socially integrated (Hatziprokopiou 2003: 1051). Second, Albanians have a much greater numerical dominance in Greece, where they account for about 60 per cent of all foreigners. Baldwin-Edwards points out (2004a: 5) that Greece is unique in the EU in having one immigrant group accounting for more than half of its immigrant population. Third, there is a much higher degree of short-term mobility to Greece. Some Albanians who live in villages close to the border may even go on a daily basis; but there is also much seasonal migration, to coincide with agricultural work or the tourist season. This is linked to the fourth differentiating factor, the much higher incidence of undocumented migrants in Greece. The share of irregular migrants has, however, markedly decreased since regularisations in 1998 and 2001.

Some of the differences noted above – ease of border crossing, higher degree of irregularity, greater engagement in short-term casual work, etc. – are consistent with the findings of Stampini et al. (2004) reported earlier in the chapter, where the rural origins, lower educational levels and poorer backgrounds of Albanians opting for Greece were contrasted with the somewhat more privileged backgrounds of those able to migrate to Italy (see especially Tables 3.3 and 3.4). But, again as noted before, the two migration streams are not as detached as this contrastive analysis would imply. Many migrants move first, on a seasonal or temporary basis, to Greece and then, at a later stage, embark on another migratory career in Italy or further afield.

Available estimates of the scale of the migration to Greece before the 1998 regularisation suffer from extreme vagueness and inaccuracy. Since 1998, two main sources exist for recording the Albanian presence in Greece: regularisation statistics and the 2001 Census. The 1998 regularisation recruited 371,641 applicants for the six-month temporary residence 'white card', 65 per cent of whom (241,561) were Albanians. However, according to Fakiolas (2003: 540), up to 300,000 undocumented immigrants did not apply. Assuming two-thirds of these were Albanians brings the total – regularised and non-regularised – to about 436,000 for 1998. This correlates well with the 2001 Census enumeration of Albanians (443,550) who, moreover, made up 65 per cent of the non-EU, non-ethnic-Greek immigrant population. However, this near-congruence falls apart when we look at the gender split – 18 per cent were females in the regularisation, 41 per cent in the census. Furthermore, the census counted 46,000 Albanian schoolchildren (excluding ethnic-Greek Albanians). As with the Italian case, the Greek census, for all its faults,[16] achieves a more balanced recording of the Albanian population than the residence permit data, which are more orientated to adult working males.

The census also provides useful information about the spatial distribution of Albanians in Greece and their employment characteristics (see Baldwin-Edwards 2004a: 67; 2004b: 54–55). Albanians are found mainly in three types of location: in large urban areas, especially Athens and Thessaloniki; in those rural areas where their labour is utilised in intensive farming; and in the tourist islands. However (as in Italy), they have a widespread distribution and are also found in small towns, in remoter rural and upland areas where they have made an important contribution to rejuvenating rural society, and in some peripheral regions a long distance from Albania, such as Crete. The main sectors of employment of Albanians are construction and agriculture (accounting together for 65 per cent of male employment), industry and tourism (the latter important for both males and females). Females are predominantly employed in domestic service and care-giving jobs.

Immigration of Albanians into Greece has undoubtedly continued since 2001, and there is no evidence of substantial return migration, except for short-term visits. Recent estimates of the Albanian population in Greece suggest 600,000 (Government of Albania 2004: 40). This is consistent with Baldwin-Edwards' (2004a: 4) calculation that the total immigrant population of Greece (excluding homogeneis) approaches 1 million in 2004.

There is now an extensive literature on Albanian migrants in Greece, covering a range of angles including employment and other economic aspects, social exclusion and inclusion, politics and policy on migration, housing, stigmatisation and the relationship to crime – the same themes that we examine for Albanians in Italy. This is not the place to review this literature,[17] but we do wish to spotlight the recent research carried out by Hatziprokopiou (2003, 2004) and Lazaridis (2004), since they used the same interview schedule as we did for our research on Albanians in Italy. Hence, in the chapters which follow, we throw an occasional comparative glance at this Greek-based literature, not least because there are considerable similarities between both the exclusionary treatment of Albanians by the two respective host societies, and the migrants' relative success in overcoming these negative reactions.

Other Countries

By contrast, literature on Albanians in other countries is scarce. Brief reference was made earlier in this chapter to the pre-communist migrations to the United States and elsewhere; the only substantive study is that of Francis Trix (2001) on Albanians in Michigan. More recently, and especially since the late 1990s, Albanians have spread their migratory wings beyond the neighbour countries of Greece and Italy, travelling to other destinations in Europe and to North America: in the words of Kosta Barjaba (2000b), 'from Otranto to Vancouver'. Access to other EU countries has been relatively straightforward via the bridgehead of Italy and the possession of a (genuine or fake) Schengen visa. Loosely structured and fluid communities of Albanians have formed in major cities in France, Belgium, Germany, the Netherlands and, above all in recent years, Britain. Numbers are rather vague since, unlike Italy and Greece, Albanians do not figure amongst the major immigrant nationalities of these countries. Recent Government of Albania (2004: 40) estimates are 15,000 for Germany, 5,000 for Belgium, 2,000 for France, 1,000 for the Netherlands and 50,000 for the UK. This last figure may seem high, but our own recent research on Albanians in the London area (King et al. 2003) suggests it is not unreasonable.

North America is the most desirable desination currently, especially for well-educated migrants. Barjaba (2000a: 58, 2000b: 58) noted the increasing interest in Canada in the late 1990s: 2,000 Albanians legally migrated to Canada during 1996–99. Currently the official estimate is 11,500 Albanians resident in Canada (Government of Albania 2004: 40).[18] The Government of Albania (2004: 40) estimate for Albanians in the US is 150,000; it is impossible to tell to what extent this is inflated by pre-communist migrants and their offspring.[19]

Notes

1 Parts of this chapter draw on papers already published by the authors: see Barjaba and King (2005), King (2003, 2004, 2005b), King and Mai (2002), King and Vullnetari (2003).
2 Estimates of the number of 'embassy migrants' are usually 4,500–5,000, but Barjaba (1997: 13) mentions 7,000.
3 The practice of northern Albanians fraudulently posing as Kosovan-Albanian asylum-seekers undoubtedly took place, but we relegate this piece of information to a footnote in order not to give it undue prominence. Certainly this became a rather common strategy for entry to the UK (Dalipaj 2005).
4 The LSMS data are representative of Albanian geographic and socioeconomic conditions, the sample being divided into four strata: Tirana, Coastal, Central and Mountain regions.
5 Of course, individuals may go abroad intending to stay away only temporarily, but end up staying much longer, eventually becoming 'permanent' migrants; and likewise intending long-term migrants may return quickly due to various unforseen circumstances.
6 UBN criteria are fivefold: inadequate water and sanitation; poor housing; inadequate heating; overcrowding; poor education. Households classed as 'poor' have two or more UBN, 'extreme poor' have three or more (see Albanian Center for Economic Research 2002: 93).
7 Responses to the LSMS question 'Have you ever considered moving abroad, even temporarily?'.
8 International migration is calculated by the residual method, i.e., it is the residual loss resulting from calculations of total population change, natural change (births minus deaths) and net internal migration, for each district. Two caveats about this methodology. First, all calculation errors of total and natural population change and internal migration enter into the determination of the residual. Second, international migration *into* Albania is counted as internal migration to the given district. See Carletto et al. (2004: 7).
9 The international migration ratio is calculated by subtracting the number of international migrants from the 1989 district population, and dividing by the 1989 population; a similar calculation is repeated for internal migrants (Carletto et al. 2004: 9). Note that this method gives a measurement of

international (or internal) migration whereby high scores, e.g., 0.8, indicate *lower* migration than low scores, e.g., 0.5.

10   Thus a migrant moving from one province to another may be double-counted in the permit statistics. Migrants are known to be geographically mobile within Italy (Schuster 2005). Somewhat paradoxically, acquisition of a permit to stay may trigger a return stay in the country of origin. This is because re-entry to Italy is guaranteed if it takes place within the permit's validity. Migrants who are undocumented or 'irregular' are far less likely to make return visits because of the cost, and risk of failure, of re-entry. Periodic 'cleaning' of the permit databases is designed to remove the problem of double-counting and expired permits. Measures are also in train to enumerate more accurately the children of immigrants.

11   To give an example, the closeness of the statistics for 1998 (72,600 Albanian permit-holders, 71,900 on the population register) is a product of the cancelling out of higher numbers of males recorded by the former source (50,300 as against 47,700) and higher numbers of females in the latter source (24,200 against 22,300). Figures from Bonifazi and Sabatino (2003: 970).

12   Interestingly the figures for the *total* foreign population in Italy in 2001 – permit-holders 1,362,600; register 1,465,000; census 1,334,900 – are relatively much closer, indicating particular problems in achieving consistent estimates for Albanians.

13   But it is well-known that immigrants, especially those in a vulnerable or precarious situation, and particularly with regards to their accommodation, are under-recorded in most censuses worldwide (Boyle et al. 1998: 39).

14   Data from the Ministry of Education, Universities and Research, quoted in Caritas (2004: 174). Presumably these students are full-course enrolments, excluding short-term exchange and visiting students.

15   For regional percentages of Albanians according to the population register see Bonifazi and Sabatino (2003: 978). See King (2003: 291) for maps based on the permit data.

16   The main difficulty with the 2001 Greek census, apart from its general under-enumeration of migrants, is its confusing treatment of ethnic-Greek Albanians and other diaspora-born ethnic Greeks. According to Baldwin-Edwards (2004a: 1) ethnic-Greek *homogeneis* (born-abroad) should have been included amongst the immigrants, but he suspects that most census enumerators classified ethnic-Greek Albanians as Greeks, not as immigrants. This introduces a major element of imprecision since, according to one estimate, there were 80,000 Albanians waiting to receive the three-year residence card for ethnic Greeks in 2000 (Barjaba 2000a: 61), and most of these people will not have been counted as Albanians in the census.

17   Amongst the more accessible sources see Baldwin-Edwards (2004b), Droukas (1998), Fakiolas (1999, 2000), Iosifides (1997), Iosifides and King (1998), Kapllani and Mai (2005), Kasimis et al. (2003), King et al. (1998), Konidaris (2005), Lazaridis and Psimmenos (2000), Lianos et al. (1996), Pratsinakis (2005), Psimmenos (2000), Psimmenos and Kasimati (2003).

18   This may well be an underestimate, according to the *Albanian Human Development Report* for 2000, where there is a special discussion of the 'Canada phenomenon' (UNDP 2000b: 42).

19 Particularly as some US-based Albanian sources (Albanian Catholic Bulletin, National Albanian American Council) give even higher figures, rising from 250,000 in the 1980s to 500,000 in 2000, for the 'Albanian-origin' population (quoted in Fischer 2005: 195). The 2000 US Census reported 113,661 Americans of Albanian origin (Orgocka 2005: 140). Albanians have been extremely active participants in the US Diversity Visa Lottery, a scheme whereby the Immigration and Naturalization Service makes available 55,000 green cards every year for countries with low rates of emigration to the US. In some years Albanians have won more of the lottery visas than any other country. Winners have the chance to apply for permanent residence and to bring their spouses and children under twenty-one.

Chapter 4

From Welcome to Stigmatisation

Introduction

The first major act of the recent Albanian migration to Italy was the boat-people flow of March 1991, when both the Italian quaysides and national television screens were filled to overflowing with the faces, clothes and bodies of Albanian people. Day after day, the 'Albanian emergency' was encamped on the front pages of all Italian newspapers (Perrone 1996a: 33). Cynically and simplistically, this could be seen as a kind of 'media rebound': an inversion of the flow of the Italian media's images and narratives which had addressed Albanians in their otherwise isolated homeland throughout the previous two decades, and whose stimulus for migration to Italy we discussed in the latter part of Chapter 2. As former Italian colonial subjects (the colonisation being continued by the invading Italian media during the communist period), Albanian emigrants crossing to Italy in 1991 were a case of 'the empire strikes back' (Centre for Contemporary Cultural Studies 1982), breaking into the Italian mediascape and fully entering the imaginary of the Italian people who, hitherto, had been unaware of their own media's colonisation of the Albanian psyche. During the five months between the two migratory incursions of March and August 1991, Albanians arriving on the southern Italian shores were framed according to an array of competing visual and written narratives. Whereas the first Albanians arriving in Italy in March 1991 were granted asylum as 'deserving' political refugees, those who came after were forcefully repatriated as 'economic', indeed 'illegal' migrants, allegedly deceived by the consumerist and utopian dream provided by Italian television.

Our aim in this chapter is first to portray this shift in representation and immigration policy. This volte-face from welcome to stigmatisation was closely related to how the media treated Albanian migrants and their country of origin; hence the role of the media remains prominent in our discussion throughout this chapter. Second, we demonstrate how the abrupt change was consistent with Italy's need to create for itself an EU-compatible identity, by redefining its perceived moral and cultural boundaries against its 'Albanian frontier'. In other words, Albanian migrants became a strategically-exploited 'constitutive other' within the renegotiation of a viable Italian national identity, which had come under pressure from the conditions posed by the process of European integration and from Italy's political scandals of the early 1990s. Within this perspective, the chapter will analyse the evolution of the discourses through which the Italian media constructed Albanian migrants from their abrupt arrival into the Italian imagination in the early 1990s until the present day. Furthermore, it will try to understand the way in which these discursive practices conditioned the trajectory towards social inclusion of the migrants themselves. But first we need to clarify how the relations between media consumption, the formation of identities and mobility will be conceptualised in the context of our study.

Media, Identity and Migration

Many scholars have emphasised the important influence of the media in everyday life (Brah 1996; Morley 2000; Naficy 1999). This is particularly true for Western societies, where people increasingly rely on media to 'know' the world they inhabit, to develop their individual tastes, to participate in shared events and to create new opportunities for socialisation. Therefore, media consumption increasingly encompasses everyday life and is a key aspect in the formation of common cultural codes (S. Hall 1997). Moreover, it should not be considered as a predominantly individual dynamic but as an inherently social one, since it increasingly frames the emergence of identities by articulating visual and narrative scripts which address us as members of wider groups and communities (Dayan 1998; Morley and Robins 1995). Finally, media consumption plays an important role in the private as well as the public sphere, as it can become a site for the negotiation of roles and values in the family environment (Silverstone 1993) and provide people with common themes and interpretative frameworks (Gillespie 1995). Thus, and continuing our opening discussion of the concept of identity in Chapter 1, media representations are very important in the formation of identity; they begin in the use of a common language and in the circulation and articulation of signs, symbols and values which shape our experience of belonging to and understanding the world we inhabit. However, as Hall emphasises, 'meaning is a dialogue – always only partially understood, always an unequal exchange' (S. Hall 1997: 4).

This last quote is very significant for our later analysis, as it points out that representations can never *determine* identities. The discourses which address us (or migrants) individually or as members of wider social and cultural affiliations are not univocal, but contradictory. Moreover, they get 'metabolised' and made meaning of at a subjective level, thus providing opportunities for negotiation and resistance. However, the process of meaning construction is marked by inequality and conflict, since some social actors can be more powerful than others in exercising power over meaning. So, as a consequence of the emergence of hegemonic interpretations of the complexity of everyday life, some 'archetypal' identities seem more natural and 'correct' than others; people are thereby encouraged to conform to specific and normative models (Butler 1989). Thus, identities should be seen as constantly refashioned and reinforced by competing definitions of sameness, which are deployed against strategically chosen 'others'.

These preliminary remarks are also important with reference to the foundational role of media in engendering and sustaining a sense of *national* identity. Benedict Anderson's understanding of the nation as an 'imagined political community' which is both 'limited and sovereign' is key here. Most importantly, according to Anderson, nations emerged as spaces and places of identification as a consequence of the development of large-scale means of communication – in particular print capitalism but also more recently, of course, televisual media. In Anderson's words, '[P]rint-capitalism ... made it possible for rapidly growing numbers of people to think about themselves and to relate themselves to others, in profoundly new ways' (1983: 46). The advantages in adopting a conceptualisation of national identity in these terms are that it corresponds to a definition of identity in terms of a process of constant and contested redefinition, and that it acknowledges how the spread of media brought new forms of consciousness and belonging.

Not only is identity never complete because it is constantly redefined by different social actors in opposition to a 'constitutive other', but this very process is also continuously challenged by people's mobility beyond already-set boundaries and cultural practices. In late modern times, identities are increasingly sites of contestation and struggle between different understandings and experiences of belonging within, between and across cultures and social actors. This acknowledges the potentially emancipatory role of global media – and its repressive one – in both responding to and eliciting new needs emerging from cultural and social changes (such as mass migration) taking place in local contexts. Following Appadurai, media can provide variegated repertoires of images, narratives and 'ethnoscapes' to viewers throughout the world. These ethnoscapes get disaggregated into complex metaphors by which people constitute narratives of the 'other' as well as 'proto-narratives of possible lives, fantasies which could become prolegomena to the desire for acquisition and movement' (Appadurai 1990: 299).

Returning to the main subject matter of this chapter, the Albanian 'arrival' in Italy, Italian media played a very important role, and in two main respects. Firstly, as we saw in Chapter 2, they acted as *catalysts for social and spatial mobility* by presenting Albanian people with models of personhood, desires and priorities which were alternative to those historically hegemonic within Albanian culture. In this way, Italian television played an important part in fomenting an oppositional stance against Albanian communism, by engaging the needs and aspirations of Albanians in a manner that ultimately led them to conclude that only through overturning the regime could their full identities be expressed. Italian television gave Albanians a detailed (if partial) insight into Italian lifestyles and wealth and taught them familiarity with the Italian language – so that Italians were amazed that the Albanians who landed on the quaysides as refugees from forty-five years of communist isolation actually spoke Italian!

The role of the Italian media in the construction of the migratory project of Albanians can in turn be seen as a dual one. On the one hand by 'visibly' offering alternative material environments, lifestyles and social relationships, Italian media stimulated social change and elicited the migratory flow. On the other hand, Albanians were offered a very simplified and illusionary account of Italian society, privileging the utopia of universal inclusion celebrated by late modern consumer culture over the dynamics of social exclusion and marginalisation at work in advanced capitalist societies. These unexpected, restricting and discriminating practices hit Albanians only after they had reached the other side of the Adriatic.

This last point leads to the second main role played by the Italian media in the Albanian migration to Italy. Media became sources of information about the presence of Albanian migrants within Italian society *for Italians and Albanians alike*. Throughout the 1990s, the representation of Albanian migrants as 'criminals' was probably the main factor fostering their discrimination and marginalisation within Italian society. These concerns have a particular value for the study of social exclusion, as newcomers can unwillingly – and unwittingly – become a host's society's constitutive other. Here, it is useful to refer to the notion of 'moral panic' as a situation in which, within any society:

> a condition, episode, person or group of persons emerges to become defined as a threat to societal values and interests; its nature is presented in a stylised and stereotypical fashion by the mass media; the moral barricades are manned by editors, bishops, politicians and other right-thinking people; socially accredited experts pronounce their diagnosis and solutions; ways of coping are evolved or (more often) resorted to; the condition then disappears, submerges or deteriorates and becomes more visible. (Cohen 1972: 9)

In fact, the Italian media's criminalising and panic-inducing portrayal of Albanians has engendered within both the host and the migrant communities stigmatising prejudices which confined the migrants, especially in the early years, to a condition of illegality and vulnerability. In the rest of this chapter we analyse the Italian media's cultural construction of the Albanian migrant: from a brief and always ambiguous 'welcome' to a deep, intense and long-lasting stigmatisation.

The Securitisation of the Albanian Migratory Flow

The following news account of the first arrivals in March 1991 provides an overture to what was to become much more entrenched in subsequent framings of the Albanian 'emergency'. The account consists of two intercut elements: our description of the images presented on screen by the 8.00 P.M. RAI 1 TV News on 10 March; and (in italics) extracts of dialogue and commentary from the news report.

> On the quayside at the port of Brindisi a young man is carrying his daughter on his shoulders; his wife, who is visibly pregnant, is beside him. All around are a crowd of fellow Albanians, looking exhausted from the recent trip across the Adriatic Sea; also present are ambulances, police and television journalists. When he sees the television troupe the man starts shouting in Italian, full of satisfaction:
>
> *We are free! We are free! I want freedom! My family is here with me ... (indicating his wife's womb) she is waiting for a free child, free! Free! Free! Free! A free child! My daughter is free at last! Thanks Italy for everything! Thank you so much, ciao, ciao, a very big kiss to everybody!*
>
> The report then moves to a scene in which Albanian migrants are trying to reach the shore from an overcrowded boat anchored in the port. The vast majority of the people are exhausted but happy young men. Many try making it to the pier by clinging to the ropes fastening the boat or by jumping into the water and then scrambling up on the pier. A few policemen are trying to stop thousands of Albanian refugees from leaving the boat, but they are soon overwhelmed. While these images of desperation and relief are shown, the voice-over goes like this:
>
> *With the arrival of another boat of desperados the situation here at the port of Brindisi is beyond emergency. We are now facing a real tragedy, as over five thousand refugees have just joined the ten thousand who landed just this morning. There is only a handful of policemen facing a starving and wounded human wall. The refugees are fighting for a piece of bread or a glass of milk and because of the growing tension it is getting increasingly difficult to distribute food to the many children who are still on board. The port of Brindisi is witnessing a very difficult situation, one which is going to deteriorate rapidly in the next few hours. People invoking the intervention of the army are certainly not wrong, while these refugees are facing the ghastly prospect of yet another night without adequate food or health provisions ...*

Although, given the background of political turmoil and economic collapse which was outlined in Chapter 2, the mass flight of Albanians during the early 1990s was perhaps predictable, the 'first wave' of the Albanian boat migrants took the Italian authorities completely by surprise. Within a few days in March 1991, nearly 26,000 Albanians landed on the coast of Apulia. The situation rapidly assumed the character of a disaster, as the Albanians massed on open quaysides without shelter, food or sanitary facilities. After some days of official dithering they were allocated to nearby military and tourist accommodation; repatriation was considered impossible for humanitarian reasons. In order not to contravene the Italian immigration bill in place at the time (the so-called *Legge Martelli*, or Law 39/90), Albanians were given a period of four months to legalise their position by finding a job and a place to stay. Accordingly, the 'first wave' were accepted as refugees; a budget was allocated and they were redistributed to different parts of Italy. In this way the Italian government acted to 'control' the situation, relieving pressure on the cities and region of arrival, and fragmenting the disruptive potential of the migrants themselves (dell'Agnese 1996). The argument was also put by the Italian authorities that a policy of dispersal gave the Albanians the best chance of finding work and accommodation. According to the Italian Ministry of the Interior, at the end of their four-month temporary residence permits (by which time, in order to stay, the Albanians should have found jobs), there were 21,800 still in Italy. Of these, 6,000 had found stable employment, mainly in farming and small industries, 2,000 were in the process of being allocated jobs, 2,000 were undergoing training of various kinds, 2,000 were school pupils and 1,000–2,000 were recorded as having returned to Albania. No records exist for the remainder: either they had returned or had become clandestine immigrants (Barjaba et al. 1992; Pittau and Reggio 1992).

A new crisis arose in August 1991 with the mass-scale arrival of the 'second wave'. The Albanian authorities were unable to prevent the massing of 30,000 desperate people at the ports of Durrës and Vlorë and the subsequent departure of several overloaded ships with 20,000 persons on board. Again the Italian authorities were caught unawares: patrol boats were powerless to stop the flotilla from docking at Bari, above all the *Vlora*, a large merchant ship laden with an estimated 11,000 people who had been at sea for more than two days in terrible conditions. Utter chaos greeted the Albanians who, in sweltering temperatures, were first coralled on the quays for two days and then packed into the city's sports stadium. Like the first wave, the August event received blanket media coverage. Widespread condemnation issued from both the Italian and the international press at the Italian authorities' inhuman treatment of the Albanians; but few European governments voiced their disagreement with the Italian government's decision this time to repatriate. In fact, behind the harsh treatment of the would-be immigrants and the devious method of their repatriation there lay not only the approval of the Albanian government but also the EU's evolving 'fortress Europe' policy of firmly closing the doors to such mass incursions of '*extracomunitari*', non-EU immigrants. Most of the Albanians were sent back by sea; those who refused to go were repatriated by air, duped into thinking they were being flown to another destination in Italy. We interviewed one of these repatriates in Tirana:

> I remember the situation in Bari ... it was terrible – it really made me change my mind about Italy. I had already tried to go [to Italy] in March but I got to Durrës too late, when the police had already blocked access to the port. But going to Italy was a dream to me ... And when we were put in the stadium and treated like that, like animals, I mean worse than animals! Well, then the dream was over for me. I remember at some stage they separated all those who could speak Italian from the rest by saying that we would be taken to Sardinia ... I guess I don't need to tell you where they took us to, eh? Tirana, of course. We were all so angry when we landed, but it was too late. (M30, Tirana)

1991: Testimonies of Arrival, Welcome and Rejection

The different ways in which Albanian migrants were received in the various migratory waves impacted greatly on their trajectory towards social inclusion in Italy. Since the first arrivals were welcomed as political refugees and given a permit to stay, they were able to achieve a much faster socioeconomic integration and were able to start the process of reunification with their families at a much earlier stage, as this interviewee confirms:

> *How did you sort out your documents?*
> Well, we got them automatically, as everybody did who arrived in March 1991.
> *Did you find a job?*
> Yes, almost immediately, I was washing up in a restaurant just days after I arrived and then ... I mean, I changed jobs many times since then. (M50, Lecce)

The situation Albanians met on the Italian shores at the beginning of 1991 was one of extreme confusion and fluidity. The initial lack of a structured cultural construction of Albanians in terms of a threat to Italian identity, and of an adequate response to the migratory crisis, posed both opportunities and predicaments. For instance, if an Albanian migrant arriving on the Apulian coast in March 1991 could enjoy the lack of prejudice and the automatic granting of legal status, s/he could not rely on any network-based form of support, nor on an efficient institutional response. Instead, perhaps, such a person stood a better chance of being helped by a 'guardian angel'. The following accounts need emphasis because they counter the stereotype of the 'anti-Albanian stereotype' pervading both Italian society and much recent academic discussion on the topic.

> Well ... the first day we arrived in Brindisi we met a very special family ... very special for us. After three hours in the port we were tired and I had my family with me: my two daughters, who were fifteen and seventeen...my son, and my

wife of course. I was getting worried as I did not want them to stay there. It was horrible. So we went for a walk into town. There were many people stopping Albanians and asking them if they could help or needed something. Then a Fiat Croma stopped, at around midnight, and the driver said: 'Where are you from?' 'Albania', I said. 'Wait for me' [he said]. To cut a long story short, he arrived back after ten minutes. He arranged for us to stay at the car sales shop he had and then he gave us the use of an apartment. Like I am telling you, incredible. He also found me a job. (M48, Lecce)

When I first arrived in Otranto I was lucky, very lucky to meet a family, they were excellent people and helped me a lot to settle in here. They just came to see whether they could help anyone at the port ... thank God they found me. Initially I worked as a caretaker for them ... they paid me 400,000 lire per month [about €200] and treated me nicely ... they referred to me as their daughter. The head of the house, whom I used to call 'Grandpa', insisted that I should continue at university and helped me very much financially by buying books and also bought me a second-hand car with which I could drive back and forth to university. (F34, Modena)

All those who came after this first 'privileged' group were subjected to very different legal conditions. Later arrivals were not given legal status, and so were forced to access employment and housing as undocumented migrants, thereby becoming exposed to exploitation and marginalisation. On the other hand, many of the later arrivals were able to rely on a progressively stronger and more stable family-based network, which could offer economic and practical support, partially compensating for their lack of legal status. By the late 1990s, most Albanian migrants coming to Italy for the first time could rely on an extensive network of relatives and friends, able to provide them with medium-term accommodation, strategic information and work-related contacts for the further development of their migratory projects. However, as this next interview excerpt proves, sometimes the level of support offered by the family network is very minimal and people have to endure very difficult living conditions, especially in the first months of their stay. The interviewee, still only eighteen years of age, also describes the dangerous circumstances of arriving by night in an illegally-operated speedboat a few years earlier:

Well, my father is back in Albania now; his brother is here in Lecce.
Is this why you came here?
Yes, mainly.
Did he come and pick you up when you arrived?
No, because he lives in San Cataldo and I landed in Otranto. When we arrived we had to jump in and swim, it was dangerous ... we hit some rocks with the speedboat and we had to make it to the shore as fast as possible ... It was very dark and foggy, we stayed wet for four days in the forest, even while sleeping. I arrived on foot in San Cataldo together with some other people. They left then, so I went to my uncle, where after a week I began to work as a shepherd.

How did you get to your uncle, did he come to pick you up?
I went on foot to San Cataldo.
But it is 40 km away!
Yes, we walked at night, so that we would not be seen. When I finally met my uncle he kept me for a week sleeping in his storage room. Then I went to stay with the people who had promised my uncle a job for me, as a shepherd.
So you got the job and a place to stay altogether?
Yes, but it was just another storage room ...
How much did you earn?
500,000 lire (per month), and I used to send 450,000 home – I could do it because I had no expenses in Italy, I had nothing to do but take care of the herd.
It seems like you had a tough experience, for your age.
Well, now I am better ... and at least I was not repatriated like my cousin ... after four years of hard work, with no documents ... they got him one day and the next he was in Albania, where he still is. (M18, Lecce)

After 1991, because of the restrictive visa rules implemented by the Italian authorities, many Albanians resorted to illegal entry, mostly through dangerous rides on speedboats across the Adriatic, from Vlorë to Otranto.[1] The increasing presence of Italian coastguard patrol boats only increased the vulnerability of the migrants involved in this clandestine traffic, who were often forced to 'disembark' in deep waters hundreds of metres from the coast by the speedboat operators, who were fearful of their own arrest. In these cases, sometimes the older people and children could not make it to the shore. On 29 March 1997, as a consequence of a collision between an Italian coastguard vessel and a boat carrying Albanian migrants, eighty-seven people, the majority of them women, children and elderly people, lost their lives. According to the Albanian Human Development Report for 2000, the number of people drowned or lost during 1999 alone totalled more than 340 (UNDP 2000b: 6). A further tragedy occurred on the night of 9 January 2004 when, a few kilometres off the Albanian shore, the engine of a speedboat failed. In rough seas and deteriorating weather, the failure of the Albanian authorities to mount a rescue operation condemned nineteen of the thirty passengers to death by drowning (Dalipaj 2005: 123–5).

Although Albanian migrants coming after 1991 were not given automatic legal status, they could eventually benefit from the various schemes of regularisation mounted by the Italian state (listed in Table 3.7), as well as get help from a more efficient institutional and voluntary-sector infrastructure, especially in the more organised Italian North. On the other hand, the later arrivals found few 'guardian angels' to assist them. Instead what they found was a barrage of negative stereotyping which applied to all Albanian immigrants, whatever their status. The next interview exchange is very interesting in this regard; it is with an Albanian university student in Modena. On the face of it, Albanian students enrolled at Italian universities are well placed: they enter the country with full documentation, they speak good Italian, their social status and social interaction are on a par with their Italian peers. And yet they are still confronted with the same stigma of simply 'being Albanian':

> Well, as soon as you enter Italy you meet that coldness, which is normal in larger cities, but then you meet those prejudices ... 'Where are you from?' 'Albania'. Immediately the eyes turn away, you can just see that the person starts thinking how he might get out of the situation, it's almost as if their brains went dead ... Sometimes you think they are right, you blame it on yourself ...
> *On yourself as a person?*
> No, you blame it on your people ... Because it is not just one person who behaves like that ... it is everybody and you start thinking, 'Why do they feel like that about us? Maybe we actually did something wrong, or are we so different?' I am telling you, every student goes through this in his first year ... every student tries to understand where this hatred might come from ... I think it is because of the media, they have been going on and on about Albanian crimes ...
> *Do you think the role of media is important in all this?*
> Very important. You go home, on the day you got a top mark, you eat a pizza at home with your Italian friends, everything is fine until you switch on the TV and see the news 'Albanians did this and that and that'. Then you have a flashback, you remember those changing faces and feel like changing channel. You suffer. I am telling you, it makes you suffer a lot, the first year is hell, we all wanted to go home. (M22, Modena)

This interview is very revealing about the discursive environment within which Albanian migrants have to articulate their identities. It also gives a clear indication of the higher level of internalisation of stigma which characterises them, compared to other migrant groups. These issues will be dealt with in depth in the next two chapters, which will analyse Albanian migrants' multi-faceted experiences of social exclusion and how these connect to the identity formations which have emerged in the context of emigration.

Explaining the Change of Heart

What factors lay behind the abrupt change of stance of the Italian government in the five months between the first and the second waves? Certainly the interlinked phenomena of the media and public opinion played a key role. Public reaction to the first wave was generally positive: the Albanians were given an heroic label, greeted as 'fellow Europeans oppressed by Communist tyranny' (Millar 1992: 36), as 'Adriatic brethren' (Zinn 1996). In hundreds of hours of television coverage and hundreds of pages of newspaper reportage, the Albanians were 'consumed' by the Italian public, their exoticism patronised by the media, which wrote off fifty years of communist history and homogenised the refugees as 'noble savages' – passive, helpless, lost. In between the two waves a new, more sinister image emerged. Once again, this was manufactured by the media following the lead given by right-wing political ideology and building on pictures of the desperate Albanians cooped up in reception centres. The stereotype was clear: Albanians were incapable of organising themselves; they were work-shy, prone to thieving and violence. Surveys showed such views had quickly become widespread amongst the Italian population (Barjaba et al. 1992); a powerful reconstitution of the Albanians as 'others' had taken place (Zinn 1996).[2]

An early analysis of this 'change of heart' was made by Palomba and Righi (1992) who analysed Italian newspapers' coverage of the two 1991 flows and noted that there was a turnaround in the choice of the key words used to report on the two exoduses, corresponding to a shift in the priorities and initiatives of the Italian political class. Whereas the key verbs and the content of the articles portraying the March flow referred to the necessity to *accommodate* the refugees, and *contain* the flow, the articles dealing with the August exodus focused on issues of *repatriation* and *expulsion*.

This preliminary analysis of the different ways in which the two Albanian exoduses of 1991 were presented by the Italian press serves also to highlight the process of progressive 'securitisation' of the Albanian migratory flow. The invocation of security reasons should be seen as a discursive strategy aimed at legitimising the use of force and at mobilising military resources in order to respond to threats perceived or presented as existential. According to Buzan et al., identity is the main organising concept of societal security, which means that 'societal insecurity exists when communities of whatever kind define a development or potentiality as a threat to their survival as a community' (1998: 119). In this respect, the dramatic shift which occurred in the representation of Albanian migrants between March and August 1991 can be seen as reflecting a parallel repositioning of the *Italian* national identity vis-à-vis the issue of the Albanian migration.

If we interpret the shift in the representation of the Albanian migrants and the way Albanians personified the presence of migrants in the Italian society of the 1990s in this perspective, several questions arise. Firstly, why and in what respects was migration perceived as a threat to Italy's identity? Secondly, why were Albanian migrants identified tout court with the 'migration issue'? Thirdly, what happened between March and August 1991 to explain such a dramatic change in their representation? In order to answer this set of questions, we must bear in mind how the Albanian migration was the most spectacular of a long series of migration-related events which had already been filling Italian newspapers and television screens since the mid 1980s. It is to this already-set genre of migration-related events that we have to turn if we want to understand the specificity of the representation of Albanian migrants.

The Representation of Immigrants in the Italian Media

Although the percentage of foreign people in relation to the Italian population is much lower than it is in traditional immigration countries such as France, Germany or Belgium, the Italian media's representation of foreign migrants in Italy can be seen as having both responded to and engendered anxieties, fostering an interpretation of the phenomenon in terms both of 'moral panic' (Cohen 1972) and of 'social alarm' (Maher 1996: 160). According to Jacqueline Andall (1990), immigration first became a political and media issue in Italy in 1989, when the murder of a black immigrant received wide coverage and a special parliamentary commission was created to prepare a law responding to the various dimensions of migration and integration. In theory, according to Buzan et al., any public issue can be addressed as either *non-politicised*, meaning 'the state does not deal with it and it is not in any other way made an issue of public debate and decision'; *politicised*, meaning 'the issue is part of public policy, requiring government decision and resource allocations'; or *securitised*, meaning 'the issue is presented as an existential threat, requiring emergency measures and justifying actions outside the normal bounds of political procedure' (Buzan et al. 1998: 23). If we combine this interpretive framework with Jessika ter Wal's systematic observations on the Italian media's framing of immigration (2002a, 2002b), it becomes apparent how, from the very beginning, the media were active agents in the politicisation, and then the securitisation, of the issue of migration in public discourse.

The Italian media served as the vehicle through which the main Italian political actors argued that containing and stopping immigration should be the key solution to the structural problems within Italian society. Many studies highlighted the *alleged* or *manufactured interconnection* between the arrival and presence of immigrants and the upsurge in criminal activities, and the legitimation of repressive initiatives from independent public actors and state authorities alike. For instance, Delle Donne (1998) showed how the sensationalistic and criminalising representation of the presence of some Roma settlements on the outskirts of Rome responded to the necessity for the local political actors to justify their decision to 'evacuate' them. Chiodi (1999) analysed the way local newspapers covered the increase of micro-criminality in the Bruciata and Crocetta multi-ethnic areas of Modena by voicing the concerns of ad hoc citizens' committees and local politicians and their unquestioned association of 'immigration' and 'criminality'. In another study carried out in neighbouring Bologna, Quassoli (2004) described the ways in which the police and other social actors blur the distinctions between the administrative and criminal spheres in their dealings with immigrants and crime, leading to new practices of neighbourhood control and social and political scapegoating.

The centrality of the issue of migration in representations of the antagonisms and tensions shaping Italian society in the 1990s was also brought out in a number of content analysis studies. These studies usually denounce the unquestioned association of the arrival and presence of migrants with an increase in criminality, and expose the Italian media's vulnerability to political influence (Maneri 1998; Riccio 2001). During the 1990s the arrival and presence of migrants was undoubtedly subject to a process of progressive politicisation, which meant that the Italian media acted as channels for the expression of pre-digested political interpretations of migration, rather than as properly-documented sources of information for the Italian political class and the general population (Belluati and Grossi 1998; Naldi 2000).

These arguments were corroborated by some important analyses of the Italian media's representation of migration-related events. In 1999 the Italian journal *Studi Emigrazione* published a detailed study based on the analysis of the titles and articles of the most widely circulated newspapers within five Italian regions affected strongly by immigration. The survey covered the years 1991 to 1997. Using both qualitative (discourse and textual) and quantitative (frequency) analysis, the research examined the ways in which the representation of foreign immigrants involved two basic cultural operations: the devaluation of the image (culture, traditions, religion, lifestyle) of the immigrant 'other'; and the construction of a positive image of Italian people (Cotesta 1999a: 393). According to Cotesta (1999b: 469):

> [F]rom this process of symmetric construction and confrontation the Italian 'we' arises as a rational and efficient structure against the degradation, irrationality, disorder and immorality of others. This is only one face of the new Italian identity. The other resurrects the image of the solidarity-oriented Italian, able to bring help in difficult, if not impossible, conditions.

The underlying motto seems to be that 'it is true that Italians cannot make war, but they can give solidarity as efficiently as others make war' (Cotesta 1999a: 393). This consideration is particularly interesting if one considers the unprecedented degree to which, in the last fifteen years, Italy has been involved in international operations, especially in its former colonies of Somalia and Albania. Firstly, as a general response to the Albanian mass exoduses in March and August 1991, the Italian government organised a military-humanitarian mission in Albania, Operation Pelican, which lasted more than two years. Then, in 1997, Italy led Operation Alba, a further mass-scale intervention, with six thousand personnel, aimed at delivering aid and security to the Albanian people at another moment of political and refugee crisis.[3]

Another important and detailed study on the representation of immigrants and ethnic minorities in the Italian media, addressing both television and newspaper coverage of migration-related issues and events, was published by Censis, an Italian social research centre, in 2002. The Censis report underlines how, during the 1990s, the media – especially television – appears to have increasingly acknowledged the 'delicacy' of the issue and to 'make scant use of affirmations and explicit position-taking, preferring implicit messages which are far more capable of influencing opinion formation than explicit ones' (Censis 2002: 24). According to Censis, apparently neutral stylistic trends, such as the identification of a migrant by exclusive reference to his/her nationality, avoidance of use of racial categories and scant in-depth treatment, end up by reinforcing, rather than challenging, existing explicit stereotypes (Censis 2002: 25). This corresponds to ter Wal's distinction (2002b: 53) between 'blatant' and 'subtle' racism in Italian press coverage – the former a characteristic of the right-wing press, the latter more common in mainstream or even left-leaning newspapers. As we shall see in Chapter 6, these considerations are closely reflected in Albanians' experiences of social exclusion: interviewees report that the media's frequent links of the adjective *albanese* to criminal events is a recurrent and oppressive example of 'unfair treatment' and a major source of their stigmatisation in Italy.

Albanophobia

Within the wider context of the Italian media representation of immigrants, Albanians are the group that has been most intensely stereotyped, stigmatised and readily associated with criminality and moral degeneration, with particular reference to trafficking and sexual exploitation. Ever since 1991, the Italian media have given particular prominence, both at national and local level, to crimes committed, even if only supposedly, by Albanian citizens. Jessika ter Wal's analysis of the content of *La Repubblica*, Italy's most widely-read 'progressive' newspaper, shows that in the coverage of the Albanian issue the discourse of official political actors predominated, based on their constant reference to immigrants as a supposed threat to public safety, and as 'unfair players' in a competition over urban space and scarce resources (ter Wal 1999; 2002a: 250–251). In 1997, the controversial portrayal of Albanian refugees by the Italian media was the focus of much criticism, as the Albanian tragedy was represented mainly in terms of a threat to Italian sovereignty, identity and health. Indeed, it is not inappropriate to use the term 'Albanophobia' (Triandafyllidou 2002: 163), which emerged from analyses of the representation of Albanian migrants in Greece (cf. Lazaridis 1996; Lazaridis and Wickens 1999). Analysts of the Italian press (Dal Lago 1999; Maneri 1998; ter Wal 1999) once again blamed the national media for introducing and promoting an unquestioned association between Albanian migrants and potential criminals and for having contributed to a dynamic of stigmatisation fostering social marginalisation and exclusion. Perhaps the most thorough study of the representation of the Albanian migratory flow of 1997 was that coordinated by Enrico Pozzi (1997). Drawing on articles published in six national newspapers, three regional newspapers and three weeklies, Pozzi's study shows how the representation of the Albanian migratory crisis reflected Italy's need to negotiate an acceptable positionality within the process of European identification, by proving itself able to contain and repulse the Albanian 'invasion' of Italian, and therefore European, territory. In this manner, the dramatic events taking place in Albania and the vicissitudes of the Albanian refugee escaping an increasingly desperate situation were filtered only through the needs and priorities of the Italian political class.

This last remark points to another way in which the Italian media were implicated – as mirrors for Albanians about themselves in times of political turmoil (Devole 1998: 122). According to Devole, Albanians watched the crisis triggered by the collapse of the pyramid schemes in 1997 as it unfolded on Italian and other foreign television (and not on Albanian channels) for two main reasons. Firstly, the fact that, in communist times, the Albanian media were distrusted because of their total subservience to the regime meant that, in post-communist times, the Italian media achieved a status of objectivity. This was true especially in the first post-communist years and at times of political crisis. Secondly, Albanian people had no other choice but to watch Italian television because their national television was not functioning regularly and was not considered reliable, due to the state of emergency and political antagonism in the country at the time. And yet, the Italian media were far from objective. By focusing on the most spectacular and exotic events of the crisis (destruction of state properties, children shooting off machine guns, seizure of boats in ports, mass exoduses), by portraying the Albanian crisis in terms of civil war and the total collapse of the state, and not of a political confrontation, and finally in their inability to provide reasonable analytical readings (Devole 1998: 131), the Italian media can be seen as having both anticipated and produced events, and therefore as having played an active part in the way the crisis was shaped.

Returning to the specific representation of Albanian migrants, Jamieson and Silj (1998) carried out interesting research on the actual delinquency rates among Albanians in Italy. Although their study underlines how 'Albanian criminal organisations have undoubtedly gained a solid foot in Italy and are likely to ... expand their activities', it also showed how this could only happen through the cooperation with well-established Italian criminal organisations. As far as the involvement of Albanians in petty crime is concerned, their research stresses how for Albanians, as for other immigrant groups, illegal status contributes significantly to the likelihood of committing such crimes. Indeed, the high percentage of illegal immigrants (83 per cent in 1997) among the total number of non-Italian criminals suggests that immigrant criminality may be more a function of being clandestine than of being an immigrant per se.

Albanians' alleged propensity for criminal activity was further examined by Bonifazi and Sabatino (2003) who reviewed a range of data on arrests and convictions over the period 1991–2000. Criminal justice statistics for 2000 show that Albanians accounted for 10.7 per cent of foreigners reported to the police, 13.8 per cent of those arrested by the police, 11.9 per cent of those charged and 6.3 per cent of those sentenced. The first three figures are close to the Albanian share of the total immigrant population. The fact that the fourth figure (convictions) is half the figures for arrests and charges indicates that Albanians are put under particular pressure, even targeted, by the police, who would seem to make 'presumptions' about Albanians' criminal tendencies. It is true that Albanians do account for half of the foreigners deported (7,543 out of 15,002 in 2000); this reflects their greater involvement in 'illegal' entry compared to other nationalities but also the existence of bilateral repatriation agreements, geographical proximity and the intense patrolling of the Apulian coast (Bonifazi and Sabatino 2003: 988). With regard to other forms of 'criminal specialisation', in 2000 Albanians accounted for 35 per cent of foreigners charged with manslaughter, 34 per cent of those charged for sexual assault, and 51 per cent of those charged with crimes related to prostitution. Again, however, it must be stressed that stereotyping by the police probably accounts for these high rates, at least in part; actual conviction rates are a third to a half lower than these shares. Moreover, it needs to be stressed that the victims of these crimes are mostly other Albanians, not members of the host society.

Erika and Omar and Matteo

Two emblematic cases of Albanophobia and criminal stereotyping occurred in northern Italy in 2001. We describe them here because they recur in the identity-making narratives of the Albanian migrants whom we interviewed in the period shortly after the events took place.

On 21 February 2001 a mother and her twelve-year-old son were found murdered in their home in the quiet provincial town of Novi Ligure, in Piedmont. The first explanations given by both Erika, the seventeen-year-old daughter who first found the butchered bodies, and the Italian police, immediately framed the atrocious murder as a case of attempted burglary carried out by illegal migrants, supposedly Albanians. In the following two days, all of the legal and illegal migrants living and working in the area were arrested, interrogated and released one by one, while a campaign of xenophobic hysteria was mounted by both local and national media. Eventually, a few days later, the Italian police arrested Erika and her boyfriend Omar, and Italian public opinion fell into dismay. Erika and Omar were subsequently sentenced to sixteen and fourteen years respectively for premeditated murder.

On 13 September 2001, Matteo, a fourteen-year-old disabled boy, was found suffocated in his bedroom on the first floor of a villa in the outer suburbs of Modena. His mother had been tied up and thrown in the swimming pool while the father had gone to the local corner shop. The case of Matteo, like that of Erika and Omar, must be contextualised within the high visibility achieved by a spate of so-called 'villa-burglaries' in the representation of migration-related issues in Italy at that moment.[4] In both cases the perpetrators of the crimes tried to instrumentalise the 'villa-burglaries' journalistic genre to cover their own involvement; the first explanations given to the police by Matteo's parents and by Erika and Omar presented the events as a yet another case of burglary, carried out by a ferocious gang of foreigners, 'probably Albanians'. Unlike in Novi Ligure, in Modena the police were careful not to publicise the initial hypothesis and immediately directed their efforts to the family situation. On 18 September 2001, the mother of Matteo was arrested for premeditated murder and was later tried and convicted.

The cases of Erika and Omar and Matteo marked a very important step in the relation between Albanophobia and the negotiation of 'Albanian' identities in the context of emigration, as it exposed the prejudice underpinning the representation of Albanian migrants living in Italy. In Chapter 6, we will analyse the way the infamous case of Erika and Omar sparked a panic-laden debate about the changing nature of what has traditionally been considered the central institution of Italian society: the family. The cases of Novi Ligure and Modena were important occasions for Albanian migrants both to define themselves against the 'degeneration' of Italian family values, and to expose the criminalising and marginalising nature of the Italian media's representation of their presence within Italian society.

The Genealogy of the Albanian Myth and the New Post-1991 Italian National Identity

According to an important book by two Albanian scholars, Vehbiu and Devole (1996), the way the Italian media have framed and described Albanian migration to Italy should be addressed in terms of a *mythical construction*. In their words:

> [A]fter the vanishing of the threat posed by the 'empire of evil' [the communist bloc], the West nearly suddenly faced a new challenge, posed by an uncontrollable migration ... targeting those values that people in the West considered most essential and untouchable: wealth, welfare, work, space, property, ethnic integrity, health. Many countries framed this threat through different myths; in Italy ... Albania was chosen. (Vehbiu and Devole 1996: 9)

George Shöpflin's (1997: 19) definition of a myth is useful here: 'one of the ways in which collectivities establish and determine ... their own systems of morality and values'. The advantage of defining myth in these terms is that it is implicitly harnessed to a conceptualisation of identity which we favoured in our review of this concept in Chapter 1: identity as relational and processual, subject to a continuous historicisation and transformation, rather than immutable and fixed. However, the fact that identities are embedded within 'the narrativisation of the self' and that this is a necessarily 'fictional' process, 'partly constructed in fantasy, or at least within a fantasmatic field', does not undermine their 'discursive, material or political effectivity' (S. Hall 1996: 4). In fact, as we will show in the next two chapters of the book, the Italian media's representation of Albanians (and other migrant groups) has both elicited and engendered stigmatising prejudices which ended up by exacerbating their conditions of social marginality and vulnerability.

Categories of Myth

If we look at the ways in which Albanian migrants have been described by the Italian media, four main discursive sets can be identified:[5]

- Tales of moral depravation.
  Throughout the 1990s and into the 2000s, Albania has been portrayed as a land characterised by a lack of moral boundaries, mainly in relation to Albanian migrants' involvement in the trafficking and sexual exploitation of young women and in drug dealing. The coverage given to Albanian migrants' involvement in criminal activities was not proportional to its magnitude, and was the main factor behind their criminalisation. The way that some aspects of Albanian customary law – which remained in place in a few northern areas during communism – were revived and reinterpreted by some individuals in the post-communist period to respond to new needs and conditions was instrumentally presented as a common practice for Albanian people as a whole (Mai 2001b). Thus, via these 'pseudo-anthropological' explanations (Schwandner-Sievers 2001, 2004), Albanians were presented as a people devoid of any moral scruples, able to exploit even their own young women and children.
- Discourses of demonisation of atheism or essentialisation of religious difference.
  Many Italian journalists found explanations for the re-emergence of criminal behaviour in the Albanian post-communist context in the fact that Albania, from 1967 until the collapse of the communist state, was the only officially declared atheist state in the world, and in the common association of Albania with 'the Muslim world'. Thus, although in Albania both the Roman Catholic and the Albanian and Greek

Christian Orthodox Churches have been present for centuries, 'in the face of the necessity to designate one national religion for Albanians, these have been all transformed into Muslims' (Vehbiu and Devole 1996: 81). Significantly, the first two waves inaugurating the Albanian migratory flow in 1991 happened at the height of the first Gulf War, a period in which Islam came to be intensely associated with the violent subordination of women, fanaticism and fundamentalism. Beyond their contingent instrumentality, these discourses can be seen as mirroring the renewed centrality acquired by the concept of Christianity in the definition of a Western European identity in the post-Gulf War context and after the collapse of the constitutive threat posed by the East European and Soviet communist regimes (Morley and Robins 1993: 22; Zinn 1996: 247)

- Discourses of backwardness, exoticism and isolation.
Throughout the 1990s Albania was portrayed as a country which was both under siege from its own isolation, poverty and backwardness and ready to dissolve into anarchy and uncontrollable migratory flows. From the mythical, exoticising and stereotypical accounts of Italian journalists, Albania is presented as an anti-modern and anti-democratic entity. The function of this myth, according to Vehbiu and Devole, is both to keep alive the potentiality of the threat of invasion and to confirm the superior values of Italianness (1996: 14).

- Narratives of deception and incompetence in relation to the Italian media.
These discourses were particularly strategic in the articulation of an EU-compatible Italian identity in terms of efficiency and capitalist competence. The first accounts of the causes and key factors of the Albanian migration to Italy were characterised by an uncontroversial and widespread assumption about the magnetic role of Italian television in attracting Albanians, 'encouraged by hopes of success, pushed by necessity and drawn into the imaginary world provided by television' (Perrone 1996a: 34). This mythical construction of Albanians as deceived and duped by the wonders of Italian television was articulated in a series of newspaper accounts about Albanian immigrants expecting all Italian cats to eat from silver trays or all Italian women to be like Italian TV female presenters, full of audacious curves and glitter. Interestingly, one of the most frequently recurring narratives in this repertoire was that, because they first got to know Italy by watching Italian television, Albanians expected Italy to be (like) America – Italy's own utopian aspiration. We suggest that these discourses about Albanians' capitalist/democratic incompetence represent the projection onto Albanian migrants of Italians' disillusionment with their own 'American' televisual and neoliberal utopia.

Italy's Search for a New Identity

The intensification of the general phenomenon of international migration to Italy and the sudden appearance of the Albanian migratory flow in the early 1990s ended up by being inextricably interwoven within the post-1989 collapse of the Italian political system. According to Lucio Caracciolo, with the end of the Cold War period, the so-called First Republic, an expression used to refer to the political system and the wider social, cultural and economic context that lasted from the end of the Second World War until the early 1990s, lost its geopolitical *raison d'être*. In the struggle between the two opposed superpowers, Italy had the role of semi-protectorate, allied to the United States. In turn, the shake up of the geopolitical formation which had frozen Italian politics for nearly fifty years coincided with a crisis of internal legitimation of political power (Caracciolo 2001: 29).

The Italian elections of April 1992 are considered the turning point in Italy's transition from the First to the Second Republic (Bufacchi and Burgess 1998: 15); however, the real starting point was 1989. The end of the Cold War undermined the anti-communist cleavage around which much of the Italian political system had been organised, and caused various forms of gross maladministration to be exposed to critical scrutiny by an electorate that had long seemed impervious to them. As a result of an extensive series of investigations into political, administrative and financial corruption carried out by a group of magistrates in Milan (known as the *mani pulite* or 'clean hands'), a political elite dominated by the Christian Democrats, who had been governing Italy without interruption since 1945, was brought down by serious allegations of widespread corruption and connivance with organised crime, burgeoning demands for reform, and the near bankruptcy of the state (Gundle and Parker 1996: 1). The timing of the unravelling of events is particularly significant here. The first sign of the Italian people's dissatisfaction with the established parties came as early as in June 1991, between the first two Albanian migratory waves, when Italians voted massively in favour of the abolition of the electoral multi-preference system, which had been a key instrument of political manipulation and corruption.

It is not our aim to analyse in detail the deep political and cultural significance of the Italian passage to the so-called Second Republic during the 1990s. However, it is important to emphasise the interlocking of contemporaneous events on the two sides of the Adriatic Sea in order to grasp the political and cultural implications of the switch in the way Albanian refugees were perceived and received in Italy (Mai 2003; Perlmutter 1998). The second Albanian exodus came at a period of profound crisis for Italy itself, whose major immediate catalysts were situated in a brief arc of time stretching between the summers of 1991 and

1992; in these few months, Italian history 'acquired an extraordinary fluidity' (Ginsborg 1996: 36).

First, the rearticulation of an Italian identity and national self-esteem was deeply influenced by the economic conditions posed by the ongoing process of integration of Italy into the European Union. In particular, Italy's ability to cope both with the Maastricht Treaty's financial parameters and with the implementation of the immigration control measures set down by the Schengen Agreement became a site of political struggle between Italy and other EU member states. In fact, the Italian economic performance of the early 1990s was far from encouraging, and the national debt rose to exceed 10 per cent of GDP in 1992 (Gundle and Parker 1996: 4). As a consequence of the disastrous budget situation inherited from decades of corruption and irresponsible management, the centre-left government of the early 1990s, led by Giuliano Amato, was forced to introduce drastic budgetary cuts. At the same time, the Italian lira was the target of major international monetary speculations and was withdrawn from the European Monetary Fund because of its financial vulnerability. Furthermore, there was a sharp rise in the unemployment rate. Finally, the dramatic murder in Sicily in summer 1992 of Giovanni Falcone and Paolo Borsellino, two anti-Mafia judges who symbolised the Italian government's commitment to fight organised crime, left Italian citizens in a state of shock and powerlessness.

Because of the convergence of these different factors, Italians' confidence about their entitlement to belong to Europe was shaken, and the old and historically specific cultural construction of Italianness came into crisis. At the same time, a new version, responding to new social and cultural needs, emerged, but this only reproduced many of the symbolic dichotomies and oppositions that had shaped Italian national identity historically: North/South, Europe/Africa, Christian/non-Christian, developed/backward. The enduring resilience of these categories can be seen as a consequence of a 'complex and selective social amnesia of the experience of Italian emigration, of Italian colonialism, of Fascism, the knowledge of the complexity of the Italian society itself' (Maher 1996: 168). Ignoring the hubris of these old dichotomies, especially Italy's own deep emigration history, the effect was to create new boundaries between Italy's *extracomunitari* and the host society.

The construction of an identity through contrapuntal processes of boundary drawing, exclusion and projection onto an imaginary 'other' of potential elements of change and disruption can be seen as a way to cope with problematic issues within any society by 'defensively containing' them (Morley and Robins 1993: 19). However, there is a very problematic implication embedded within this identity strategy. In fact, if any component of any changing identity is projected outwards onto a 'constitutive other' according to a mere logic of negative differentiation, this means that the problem associated with the specific component is never dealt with and remains suspended. The fact that the new articulation of Italian identity of the 1990s emerged in relation to the very same symbolic categories and dichotomies articulating Italianness in the past puts the cultural and political project of the so-called 'Second Republic' in a situation of substantial continuity with the key role played by internal and external colonialism in the process of Italian national identity construction since the country's unification. In fact, within the Italian imaginary of the new times, two symbolic places emerged as poles respectively of 'projective identification' and 'dis-identification' (cf. Morley and Robins 1993: 19–20): Europe, connoting the West, civilisation and modernity; and Albania, symbolising Italy's own rejected past of poverty, backwardness, emigration and totalitarianism.

Why Albanians?

The last question that needs to be explored is the reason why Albanians came to be selected as the *main* constitutive other against which Italy constructed its new articulation of national identity. In order to answer this question, the way foreign immigration was presented as a threat to Italy's moral integrity must be related to the necessity to make meaning of the collapse of both the political system and the moral order of the First Republic.

The advance of federalist and separatist movements such as the *Lega Lombarda* and the mounting intolerance against foreign immigrants in the 1990s can be interpreted as two parallel symptoms of a wider crisis in the relationship of Italian citizens with their country. Although Italian people's reactions to the increasing presence of foreign migrants are not very different from those encountered in other European countries, they can only be fully understood within the context of Italian history since 'the social boundaries set up against foreigners ... resemble those erected between Italians depending on their region of provenance' (Maher 1996: 175). In this context, the symbolic positionality of Southern Italy and of Southern Italians in the historical construction of Italian national identity deserves further analysis. According to Renata Salecl, who has brilliantly analysed the rise of nationalism in the former Yugoslavia, the hatred of the 'other' which sustains nationalism psychologically, is nothing but the outcome of a process of projection onto the (constitutive) other of an aspect of the 'same' which is considered unbearable and unacceptable (Salecl 1993: 105). We believe this line of analysis is interesting because it stresses how '*any given nation and nationality defines itself in relation to differences within it*, to the "vertical" arrangements of such constitutive categories as ethnicity and "race", class and gender' (Allen and Russo 1997: 5, our emphasis). Interestingly, according to a recent study (Sniderman et al. 2000: 85), the discourses sustaining and articulating Northern Italians' prejudice against Southern Italians are not only strikingly similar to those differentiating Italians from immigrants, but 'so far as there is a difference between their judgements of Southern Italians and immigrants, it is the latter, not the former, who are viewed more favourably'. To put it in a nutshell, 'if Northern Italians do not think much of immigrants, they think even less of their compatriots' (Snidermann et al. 2000: 86). This can be related to the specific positionality of Southern Italy within the process of construction of Italian national identity, which is that of a *denied colonial subject*.

At the centre of the imagination of Italy as a unified political subject is the cultural construction of Southern Italy as 'the territorial watershed between Italy as Europeanised (or Americanised) and Italy as African' (Pandolfi 1998: 287). This 'auto-orientalist' construction of a double Italian identity was overcome only for the briefest moment when the Fascist regime proclaimed its agenda of transforming Italy into a late colonial empire and the 'Southern Question' gave way to the rhetorical figure of Italy defined as the direct descendant of Imperial Rome. Only in those interwar years did the entrenched discourse articulating an Italian identity based on the fractured contrast between a 'civilised north' and a 'backward south' give way temporarily to 'an image of Italy as a utopian project, a hazy veil that hid complex differences' (Pandolfi 1998: 287).

There is an obvious interconnection between the Albanian Question and the Southern Question with reference to their positionality as denied colonial subjects within the historical process of definition of an Italian identity (Mai 2003). However, their relations within the Roman Imperial Community were not equal, as the Italian South fared better in racial terms than Albania, which was subject to 'full' Italian imperialism and colonisation. Hence, Albania comes to be a doubly articulated and denied colonial subject of both the Italian imperial project and, within this, Southern Italy's own imperial project. What they share is a position of liminality in relation to the hegemonic Europeanised and North-centric Italian identity and the suppression of their colonial status in the name of an instrumental, racialised and homogeneous national(ist) identity.

In sum, we argue that, in the 1990s, Albanians, because of both their common somatic traits and their common denied colonial status, *were both identified with and substituted for the Italian Southerner as the main constitutive other* against which to articulate a civilised and democratic Italian identity in relation to Italy's aspirational belonging to Europe and the West. Because of their physical and cultural similarity to Italians, and their foreign status, they were perceived as the simultaneous living embodiment both of Italy's primordial 'constitutive other', the Italian Southerner, and of the new constitutive other, the foreign immigrant of the 1990s. Hence, they were criminalised and stigmatised twice: both as disavowed and projected sames and as rejected others.

Conclusion: Hierarchies of Italianness

The mass arrival of Albanians on the Italian coasts and into Italian television sets and newspapers in the 1990s triggered within the Italian imaginary a process of projective dis-identification with a part of Italian history, society and culture that had been strategically separated and rejected. Because of their racial invisibility, Albanians became a mirror reflecting Italy's own unresolved social problems, above all the 'Southern Question' (King and Mai 2002). Emerging dynamics of social antagonism were incorporated into the Italian 'imagined community' according to established hierarchies of Italianness.[6] As we have explained, these emerged out of a disavowal of their own experiences of emigration, internal and external colonisation and racialised discrimination that Italians both endured and enforced since the unification of the country in 1861 (Stella 2002). Italians' own experience of emigration to the United States and Northern Europe was consistent with the internalisation of existing hierarchies of whiteness sustaining racialised cultural constructions of Americanness and Europeanness (Jakobson 1998: 56–62). Through their experience of migration to America and Northern Europe, Italians can be seen as having initially shared with other Third World migrants what Gilroy (1993) calls *double consciousness* – the sense of dual identity which comes from being in, but not of, the West.

By crossing the Adriatic Sea, Albanian migrants were caught in an established category of racialised in-betweenness which mirrored that experienced by Italian migrants in the US. Albanians were presented according to the canons of 'Balkanism' (Todorova 1997). This can be seen as a discursive field which posits the existence of a sociocultural and geopolitical area defined by its 'transitionary status' and 'ambiguity', with the implication that 'because of their indefinable character, persons or phenomena in transitional states, like in marginal ones, are considered dangerous, both being in danger themselves and emanating danger to others' (Todorova 1997: 11, 17). Whereas the Orientalist discourse, which posits an irreconcilable differentiation between the West and the East, produces a polarised racialisation of its constitutive others, the Balkanist discourse can be seen as producing an ambivalent and contradictory racialisation of its subjects. As with the Orientalist discourse, this is based on a large dose of ignorance.

> I remember once something really stupid happened. This neighbour, an old man, asked us where we were from. We told him we were Albanian. He was shocked and told us that he had never seen a white Albanian before! I found it so funny and told him 'Sir you haven't got a clue about Albania. We are all white over there, just like you are.' (F31, Modena)

> Once a woman asked me whether Albania was in Africa. I find Italians ridiculous sometimes because they claim to know so much about Albania and

make bad speculations about Albania all the time, and then they come out with a question like that. (F23, Modena)

Indeed, these quotes, and others which we shall present and analyse in the next two chapters, suggest a further layer of discursive othering – the notion of the 'Albanist' discourse as a 'Chinese box' within the Balkan discourse, or the 'Balkan within the Balkan' (Mai 2003: 91); in other words, an area of the Balkans which is *particularly* unknown, rough and remote, with people to match.

The removal of Italian migrants' own experiences of racialised discrimination is particularly significant when one remembers the centrality of discourses of backwardness in the imagination of Italy and its place in the world of nation states, America being the model against which, increasingly since the end of the Second World War, Italy has measured its performance on the basis of a perceived scale of modernity (Agnew 1997: 24, 39). Here we can reinterpret the insistence with which Albanian migrants were portrayed as duped by Italian media as the outcome of the projection onto Albanians of Italy's deep dissatisfaction with its own American dream. This, as we have shown, was instrumental to the reinforcement of a new national identity in terms of efficiency and (capitalist) competence in times of moral and political crisis.

These considerations are mirrored in the following excerpt from Umberto Eco's appeal to vote against Berlusconi at the political elections in 2001.[7]

> The second category, which we will call the fascinated electorate, certainly the largest one, is made up of people lacking a defined political opinion, but who have founded their value system on the creeping education provided in recent decades by television, and not only those channels owned by Berlusconi. For this group of persons believes in ideals of material well being and shares a mythical vision of life, not different from those whom we may call the Albanian Migrants. The Albanian Migrant would not have thought of coming to Italy if television had shown him exclusively the Italy as portrayed in 'Rome Open City', 'Obsession', 'Paisa' – he would probably have done his best to keep away from this unhappy land. He migrates because he knows an Italy in which a rich and colourful television distributes easy money to people who know that Garibaldi's name was Giuseppe, an Italy of the 'show'.

The way Eco links 'the Albanian migrant' to an undesirable section of the Italian electorate characterised by democratic incompetence exposes the real internal other sustaining the myth of Albanians as duped by Italian television. And if Albanians had been brought up on a diet of Italian neorealist films, for sure they would not have migrated to Italy.

Notes

1 During the mid 1990s, for instance, there were around twenty-five speedboats plying this lucrative trade between Vlorë and Otranto. Each craft carried an average of 16–20 people, and the fare per person was around $60. The agreement between the speedboat operator and the passengers was that if they were sent back by the Italian police within three days, they would get another free ride. These details are from Barjaba and Perrone (1996: 139).

2 This change of heart appeared to be particularly marked in the Salento region of Apulia (roughly coterminous with the province of Lecce), where Albanians moved from being the 'most welcome' immigrant group in the very early 1990s to the 'least welcome' in 1995 (see Perrone 1996b).

3 The recent expansion of Italy's political and economic ambitions into Albania is by no means limited to these two missions. Italy is the most influential foreign country in Albania, as well as the major foreign investor and the largest bilateral aid donor (for details see UNDP 1998: 27). Finally, during the late-1990s Kosovo conflict, the Italian government organised a large-scale fundraising campaign for the 'Rainbow Mission' (Missione Arcobaleno), a vast humanitarian operation for the Albanian refugees from Kosovo, and deployed a significant number of soldiers for the Kosovo peace-keeping military operation.

4 Burglaries of free-standing villas exposed the vulnerability of these properties to theft and symbolised an attack on the privilege and wealth of the northern Italian bourgeoisie, supposedly by immigrants as archetypal 'outsiders' of Italian middle-class society.

5 This section is re-worked from our earlier accounts in King and Mai (2002: 193–4) and Mai (2002b: 83–5).

6 Compare this with Triandafyllidou and Veikou's 'hierarchies of Greekness', also set within the context of Albanian migration (to Greece), including the complicating stratum of ethnic-Greek Albanians (Triandafyllidou and Veikou 2002).

7 In *La Repubblica*, 8 May 2001.

Chapter 5

ALBANIAN MIGRANT LIVES

This is the first of two longer chapters which discuss the social inclusion and exclusion of Albanian migrants living in Italy. Both chapters draw extensively on ethnographic and interview material gathered during our fieldwork. Their aim will be to analyse the narratives and discourses used by Albanian migrants, their employers, and people working in key institutions and NGOs in assessing and 'making meaning' of the dynamics of inclusion and exclusion that migrants are subject to in Italy. These dynamics will be addressed with reference to three main dimensions: work, housing and social life in general. The first two dimensions are dealt with here; the third will be the main topic of Chapter 6. Since our research was carried out in three different socioeconomic contexts, we will also build into our analysis a comparative regional perspective which recognises the different ways in which inclusion and exclusion are encountered in the South, Centre and North of Italy, represented respectively by Lecce, Rome and Modena as our three field sites.[1]

Work

Sectors of Employment

The first general observation is that Albanian migrants tend to be employed in manual or relatively unskilled jobs. Evidence suggests that, in general, immigrants do not compete directly with Italian workers; the two groups occupy complementary sectors of the labour market (Gavosto et al. 1999; Venturini and Villosio 2006). However, as several authors have pointed out (e.g., Melchionda 2003; Reyneri 2001, 2004), the nature of migrants' occupations and the specific working conditions they encounter depend on the productive structures and job opportunities available in the different regional contexts they settle in.

In Modena and in much of northern Italy, Albanian migrants tend to work primarily in the construction sector and in agriculture. They are also involved, but to a lesser extent, in manufacturing (mechanical, food processing) and the service sector, where they are usually employed for manual tasks (Mottura 2001; Mottura and Marra 2003). This pattern of employment is corroborated by the following quote from the representative of the foreign workers' office of one of the trade unions in Modena.

> Well, all migrants were initially employed in humble, unskilled jobs ... then some got to specialise in some jobs rather than in others ... for instance people from Central Africa and Ghana in particular are employed in the mechanical industry ... Albanians are in construction, transportation of goods, removal firms and agriculture.

In Lecce and in the surrounding region, Albanian migrant men tend to be employed in agriculture and construction, which are also the sectors with the highest level of 'irregular', seasonal and informal employment. Many Albanian men get seasonal jobs in agriculture, or get taken on as shepherds (Perrone 2001: 145–146). Women tend to work as cleaners or in the lower-status unregulated strata of the caring industry; they encounter fewer problems in finding employment than men. The city of Lecce, the base for our fieldwork in the South, offered few stable work opportunities for migrants, partly because of its lack of manufacturing industry. Dr P., the head of the *Ufficio Stranieri* in Lecce, replied to our question about Albanians' work patterns as follows:

> They usually get work as unskilled workers ... Women generally are domestic workers, they take care of elderly or ill people ... While men tend to work as night-watchmen, porters, and a bit in agriculture ... although there is not much of that in [the city of] Lecce. I mean, they do a bit of everything, but always at an unskilled level.

On the other hand, outside of Lecce and the other regional and provincial cities (Bari, Brindisi, etc.), there is work available in farming. Molfetta, an agricultural and fishing town further up the Apulian coast, was the site of a few field interviews:

> Albanians work mainly in agriculture and they do all the jobs that Italians don't do. They also work as waiters, house cleaners, gardeners. (M35, Molfetta)

Finally, in Rome, although most male interviewees were working in small mechanical or construction firms, a few were self-employed in those sectors. Others were employed in general manual labour, working as porters, loaders, etc. Younger people, particularly students, were employed on a casual and often part-time basis in the service industries: call centres, restaurants, pubs, bars, deliveries, etc. According to Messia (2003: 222), most jobs done by Albanians in Rome are in the informal or black economy.

Gender differentiation is important in all three sites. Whereas the categories and sectors mentioned above tend to reflect mostly the nature and conditions of male employment, women tend to be employed in the informal service sector, as cleaners or carers of ill or elderly people. As noted above, this is especially true in the South, while in the North and in Rome it is relatively easier for Albanian women to work in the lower ranks of the administrative–clerical sectors.

The above remarks on place and gender demonstrate that employment-wise Albanians are distributed across a wide range of sectors. They do not occupy an 'ethnic employment niche', nor is there anything approaching an 'enclave economy', both of which can be noted for some other migrant groups in Italy, such as the Chinese (in leather goods and clothes), the Filipinos (female domestic and care workers) or the Senegalese (street-hawkers).

Knowledge of Italian society and the language plays an important role in the trajectories of social inclusion of Albanian migrants in all areas, and this is usually reflected in their experience of access to the labour market, as this excerpt from an interview with the CGIL trade union representative in Lecce shows.

> What do Albanians do? They work all the time, that is what they do ... They are usually those with the higher levels of education ... but then they end up doing very manual and unskilled jobs – they work as gardeners or in agriculture, or as guardians. And they are available to do it. They are the ones who best adapt to living in Italy because of the language, they are also familiar with the weather ... the life ... they integrate better ... I think they should be particularly encouraged to come here as it does not take them much to integrate.

In fact, it is the younger women and men – who tend to have a better knowledge of the Italian language – and in particular students, who are usually able to find work more easily. They do so by using a plurality of contacts and sources of information (cf. Messia 2003: 220). They get jobs across a range of sectors, but most often in the service/entertainment industry. The following testimony exemplifies this general pattern and also gives some preliminary evidence on how Albanians make progress in the Italian job market and how they combine different roles, for instance study and work.

> *What kinds of job have you done since you have been in Italy?*
> I have been an interpreter and a translator during commercial fairs ... I sometimes work for the office in charge of them, the Ente Fiere ... they usually look for good-looking girls who can speak Italian and other languages well ... I worked as a waitress in a restaurant ... last year I worked in a pub ... then as a temporary secretary in an office ...
> *Do you think these occupations matched your experience or skills or ...?*
> I think in Bologna it is very difficult to find a good job. However, things could be worse ... I have to be at the University, so I am not in the perfect position to find the ideal job.
> *How did you find these jobs?*

I usually walk around town and knock on doors.
Really?
Well, I usually check newspapers first, but if I don't find anything there, I go by myself to restaurants and bars and ask if they have a job for me.
How have relations with your employers been so far?
Normal, they have been kind, on the whole ... we talk when needed and they usually treated me correctly.
Are you satisfied with your salary? Are you paid like the Italians or there is discrimination?
Yes I am satisfied. If I work more I get more. I am paid like the other Italians who work here. I could also do with a bit more money, but this was not the purpose of me coming here, so I guess I have to live with this situation ... (F23, Bologna)

The last part of this interview is interesting for our analysis later in this chapter. This interviewee did not suffer any particular discrimination or harassment, but she does hint at the fact that many of the jobs she was offered did not really match her skills and experience. This latter point opens up an important issue amongst Albanians (and other immigrants) in Italy: the devaluation of their qualifications by employers.

Deskilling and Under-Valuation of Qualifications

Since most Albanian university certificates are not recognised in Italy, many educated Albanian migrants are faced with a choice: either to sit for the second time more than half of the examinations they had passed in Albania, as required by the Italian university; or to accept being substantially deskilled and hence to work indefinitely in less-qualified, often manual occupations. The difficulty in having degrees and other professional titles recognised and in achieving and maintaining legal status are the main axes shaping the processes of deskilling most Albanian migrants are subject to once they try to access the Italian labour market.[2] Sometimes these two factors reinforce each other, as a person has to have a legal status before he or she can begin to validate or improve their qualifications. The following interview extracts illustrate typical situations:

> In a way I was lucky as I got to work in my field; I was an architect in Albania and I am working for an architect and sometimes as an architect here too. But there is an important difference here. Because my degree cannot be recognised in Italy, thus far I am an 'Albanian architect'. That's the way I am being introduced to people at work and that is the way it is going to be until I get the papers about my degree. I can complete projects, but I cannot sign them. I have the same amount of responsibility as my colleagues, but not the same reward, not only in terms of money ... So until I get my diploma acknowledged, I will always be just an 'Albanian architect' here in Italy and my career will be on hold. (M35, Lecce)

> Since I have been here in Italy I have done all kinds of job, I worked as a cleaner in private houses, as a carer to old people, as a sales assistant in shops. In the meantime I went on with my studies and I got my university degree in Foreign Languages. I worked in an office and then at a call centre and finally at the Italian Chamber of Commerce ... I was in the Commission to recognise Albanian degrees in Italy ... that is quite ironic because I had a lot of trouble in having my own diploma acknowledged. (F27, Rome)

The pressure exerted upon migrants by the economic situation back home is an additional factor in the deskilling and exploitation of migrant labour. This excerpt from an interview with S., who works for the General Confederation of Italian Workers (CGIL) central office in Rome, sets out some of the issues:

> I think it is wrong to create differences and privileges between the Italian unemployed person and the migrant. Because this jeopardises the solidarity between these two individuals. Also, the accusation of [unfair] competition is flawed, as Italian people do not accept the jobs migrants end up by doing. We think it is important that foreign people get an opportunity to choose too. At the moment they cannot as their educational records are not acknowledged. So we try to help by giving information on how to have diplomas and titles recognised ...
> *Is this their most important need?*
> No, hunger is their most important need. They come from poor countries, you don't get Americans coming here and asking for work ... you get people from the Philippines or Albania saying, 'I finished university there, but there is no work, nothing, only hunger ... '. That is what happens. We have lawyers working as domestic helpers. However, I think they should get a chance to integrate according to what they bring with them and the first step is to have their qualifications acknowledged.

Whilst deskilling into manual or low-skilled labour is the general experience for Albanian migrants, our findings also show that nowadays Albanians are no longer (as they were at the beginning of their emigration) exclusively employed as low-status workers.[3] Especially in the North, they are increasingly offered positions of relatively higher responsibility in the clerical-administrative, manufacturing (usually as specialised workers) and catering sectors. In all field-sites, those who succeeded in either converting or completing their studies in Italy, in particular women, were able to find more stimulating and fulfilling working opportunities within the institutional structures and networks dealing with migration-related issues, usually as cultural mediators or interpreters. The area of intercultural mediation was an increasingly important reference point for many younger women, both for training and employment. Often, this choice was motivated by personal experiences of discrimination and hardship, and by the hope of improving the situation of Albanian migrants.

How did you become a cultural mediator?
When I first came to Italy I worked as a cleaner in houses, or caring for elderly ladies. I did these jobs for years. But seeing and living at first hand how Albanians are discriminated against in Italy, the difficulties they face when dealing with services and institutions, and also the way they are treated by the Italian media, only in negative terms, I started dreaming about being able to do something to improve the situation. I first started organising concerts and small cultural events in schools and associations, but when I saw that the *Regione Lazio* was offering a course in cultural mediation I went … I thought it was something that was missing … Later I also found this job [as an educator in a centre for – predominantly Albanian – unaccompanied minors] through a contact I had made while organising concerts. (F35, Rome)

Another area of employment opportunity is interpreting and translating for the police and local law courts. These services actually encourage migrants to market their qualifications, as they acknowledge the 'ethnic' specialisation of their expertise.

Since I got papers, well, I could get normal jobs – if you know what I mean. I worked for a year at an insurance agency, then I started my university degree. I got pregnant at the same time, but still continued studying … After my son was born, I started working as a translator with the local police, because it was 1997 and there was an emergency situation in the area. Since then, my main job is with them, the police and the court, translating and interpreting. My position as an Albanian is quite embarrassing sometimes as most court cases are related to the smuggling of drugs and people and the exploitation of prostitution; only a few are about asylum or appeals against expulsions and stuff like that. (F31, Lecce)

Access to the Job Market

As some of the excerpts cited above partially show, for access to the job market, interviewees tended to rely on informal contacts – in particular on their relatives and on their Albanian and Italian friends and colleagues. This next interview with a representative of the social services in Lecce shows how Albanian migrants are seen as particularly well 'adapted' from the economic point of view. They seem to help each other a lot when looking for work, and this is perhaps their most important area of intra-ethnic solidarity:

What is the level of integration of Albanian migrants, according to your experience?
Well, I think there has been more of an adaptation than an integration. They know very well how to move in the work environment … they are very autonomous from this point of view. They very seldom come here to ask for work opportunities … I think in this respect the Albanian community is quite solid, they tend to help each other quite a lot. So I guess work emerges as a very strong element of integration, more than is the case for other communities, at least here in Lecce. In general, they are doing quite well, compared with other groups.

The overall positive performance of Albanians in comparison with other migrant groups is confirmed by a key-informant interview at the Foreign Citizens Office in Modena:

> From what I can see, I think Albanian migrants encounter fewer problems than others in entering the job or the housing market. Even in cases of particular gravity, where the initial family situation was very difficult from the economic point of view, we did not encounter problems of break-up of the family structure, or in accessing services ... There are other groups which have more problems in these respects.

Reflecting their own rather well-embedded status in Italy, Albanians tend to look for a job by using all of the information and networking resources available. For instance, in urban settings, many interviewees reported having looked for a new employment opportunity by answering newspaper advertisements, contacting private employment agencies or browsing the internet. A typical example:

> Well, my main occupation since I am here in Italy is to help look after elderly people, in residential homes or for private individuals. I found my first jobs through agencies and then built my own network. There are many different agencies, Bologna is very organised in this respect. I usually get between €6 and 8 per hour, off the books. (M23, Bologna)

Albanian associations, particularly in northern Italy and in Rome, are an increasingly important resource when looking for a job. In the North, the social services and NGOs working with immigrants play an important role (Mottura and Marra 2003: 61). The specific role of the Rome-based *Illyria* association is highlighted in this next interview quote.

> Well, apart from my Italian colleagues, who helped me to set up my business and provided me with the necessary guarantees, the Albanian association *Illyria* helped me a lot to solve some difficult bureaucratic problems. I have to say that ethnic associations can act as powerful 'levers' in solving problems of integration and also concrete problems such as work, housing and documents. (M45, Rome).

In the South, and particularly in smaller rural centres, many migrants found work simply by hanging around the main market places and asking local fellow villagers, since this was the most efficient and established way to find a job for migrants and Italians alike. The success of this informal and individualised approach to finding work is confirmed by other research on Albanian migrants in Apulia (Giorgio and Luisi 2001: 91). At the same time hardly any interviewee was unemployed, since at most times of the year there was demand for some kind of casual work. The following interview clip is from Bisceglie, a rural town in Apulia.

What kinds of job have you done in Italy?
I work in agriculture, depending on the seasons, picking fruit, harvesting olives …
How do you find these jobs?
Well, there is a square here in Bisceglie, if you go there in the evening people sit and talk about what has to be done and then you can join in and ask, that is the way everybody does, not only us (Albanians) but Italians too … I remember the first time I did it, I could not speak a word of Italian then … but I still managed to go and pick vegetables the next day. (M23)

However, in many discussions about access to the job market, interviewees felt compelled to raise the insidious role of the media and its campaign of stigmatisation against Albanians, which made it much more difficult for them to get work. Here is one example of how this generalised discrimination resulted in specific exclusionary practices related to the labour market:

Television is the main problem we have – the things they say about us, as if we were all criminals. I will tell you something: once my aunt wanted to change her 24-hours-a-day assistance job as she had to live away from her family, she could not even see her own children and husband anymore. So this eight-hours-per-day assistance job came up. Well, basically there was a sign on the door saying 'We are looking for an assistant for an elderly person … bla bla bla, no Albanians'. I felt very insulted, I was with my aunt, who could not speak Italian very well. When I asked the man offering the job, 'Why don't you want Albanians?', my aunt looked at me and said, 'Leave it, it's his problem, not ours', I mean, although she could not speak Italian well, she had already learnt how to react to this, it must have happened many times. And this happens all the time, also when you look for a place to live, it is very difficult unless you get it from other Albanian families who have to move. (M28, Lecce)

Working Conditions, Discrimination and Legal Status: South, Centre and North

Albanian migrants' working conditions appear to be very different across the three research sites, and need further analysis. The overall degree of inclusion and success of Albanian migrants in each local labour market reflects primarily the level of overall development, diversification and regulation of the economy and society in the three regional settings. Firstly, whereas the majority of interviewees in Modena had a regular work contract, the opposite was true in Lecce and, to a lesser extent, in Rome. In the southern half of Italy, which for this purpose includes Rome, both the size of the informal economy and its role in everyday livelihoods are far greater. As Antonio Messia (2003: 223) writes:

Many small business employers in Rome prefer this 'invisible' type of worker, which guarantees profits and allows the employer himself to evade tax controls. The Albanian worker lives more than other immigrant groups from this 'blackmail' which offers easy access to work, in exchange for risks and uncertainty.

The following excerpt from our interview with G., an Albanian who works for the migrants' information centre in the municipality of Molfetta, in the 'deep South' of Italy, shows how, in this region, Albanian migrants share the same working conditions as local Italian citizens, largely in the informal economy.

> The Albanians in Molfetta ... they all work ... We don't speak about the work in black or white [i.e., in the informal or the formal economy], because we are in Apulia. Here there are all kinds of jobs, especially in the informal economy ... at least at this level there isn't any discrimination because Italians find themselves in the same conditions (laughs).

Secondly, wages tend to be much higher in the North than in Rome and the South (Dunford 2002). Both of these macro-differences can be explained by referring to two factors and their interlinkages: the unequal level of economic development (higher in the North), and the degree of regulation of the labour market (also higher in the North). However, the degree of work regulation varies considerably across different areas of employment, with agriculture and construction being the two sectors most frequently resorting to non-contractual labour in all three sites. A very large degree of irregularity and exploitation was found also in the catering, caring and service sectors, particularly for such jobs as private cleaner, maid and nursing auxiliary.

In all three locations, not only did Albanian migrants tend to be employed in less skilled occupations, but they were often found to be subject to differential treatment. Generally, it was undocumented Albanian men working in construction and agriculture, and both documented and undocumented women working as private maids and nurses, who tended to be more subject to differential payment and treatment. Interviewees reported being paid less than their Italian colleagues, especially in their first occupations. Some women reported being subject to sexual harassment, usually while working as maids or carers in private houses or institutions. The conditions of these women are particularly harsh as they experience labour exploitation, de facto isolation and sexual harassment at the same time. The story of B., 24, now living near Lecce, offers itself as an interesting account of deskilling, abuse, yet determination.

> *What kinds of job have you performed while in Italy?*
> Many ... in the beginning I used to work in a pizzeria, but it was hard for me. I started at 5 P.M. and had to work until 5 A.M., seven days a week, for €125 a week ... Then I found another job, as care-assistant to an elderly man. He was sixty, lived alone and wasn't married. He taught at university. As I graduated

as a nurse in Albania and have experience of working at the hospital in Vlorë, I was trained in how to look after him. He had problems with his ankles, he couldn't do long walks but was self-sufficient. Basically he was fine, he just missed a woman in his life ... All he wanted was for me to wash him ... Then he started molesting me and asked me to be his *'compagnia'* ('to keep him company', so to speak). So he finally told me what he wanted for me ...
How much did you get there?
He used to pay me very well, €25 for two hours. I had to do his medication every day.
And then?
After his 'declaration', I broke off all contact and went to a village nearby; they needed people to pick olives ... That was a very hard job. I had never done a job like this. [In Albania] I always lived in cities.
How much did you get?
€50 per week, six days a week, twelve hours a day.
Were the Italians paid the same?
No, more, about €25–30 a day.
Were all these jobs in the black economy?
Yes, all of them, I have never had a contract since I came to Italy. After the olive job I found a job as a carer, this time with a lady. She was the grandmother of a friend I knew from the church. She gave me €50 per week. They set up a room for me at her house and I had to stay with her during the day because she was afraid of feeling ill. This wasn't good for me because it deprived me of my leisure time. Once we had a discussion about this and she got furious, she could not understand that I needed some time for myself ... So I left ... and after this another friend of mine found me an old couple who were looking for a girl to help them with the cleaning and cooking. They have been very nice to me ... I have been staying there almost three years now ... they give me €300 per month and I have more freedom for myself.

However, cases of harassment also took place in non-domestic jobs.

> I had to leave my first job because the owner kept making sexual remarks all the time ... especially when we were alone. In the end he really exaggerated and began coming closer physically. This made me feel very uncomfortable. I had to leave because of that. It was not such a great job anyway, but it was a very upsetting experience. (F30, Lecce)

Whereas sometimes the differences in payment reported by the interviewees could be justified on the basis of the level of experience of the employees working for the same enterprise, more often the only explanation for the discriminatory pay levels was the economic and legal vulnerability of Albanian migrants. Here is a typical case from the dozens described to us:

> *What kinds of job have you had since you came to Italy?*
> Everything ... you name it, I did it! Cleaning, building, restaurants, distributing adverts ... The only problem was money. Often they paid me for fewer hours than I worked or less money per hour ... I remember I used to work in a

restaurant ... I was supposed to work six hours per day, but I usually worked eight or nine hours, for €400 euro per month. That was every day, I mean, seven days a week.
From your experience, is it common for Albanians to be paid less than Italians? Has it happened to you?
Yes, often. I used to get less. I usually used to get paid a bit more than half ...
Why do you think they paid you less ... I mean how did they justify this difference?
Well, they used to say 'If you want to work, it's like this'. I used to work as a builder for €3.5 euro per hour ...
Did Italians earn more?
Well, I was supposed to earn double that amount. And don't forget that this was all in the black economy. I only accepted because I had to pay my rent somehow ... I had no other choice. (F23, Bologna)

But it was also clear from our field interviews that wage discrimination towards Albanians is not universal. It was much more widespread in the earlier years of the immigration, when most Albanians were undocumented and their lack of knowledge of the system and urgent need to get work to survive constrained them to accept very low wages. Some interviewees, even those who had been in Italy for many years, said they had never been underpaid vis-à-vis Italians. For instance:

None of the jobs I had matched my educational level nor my expectations ... they are the kinds of job one does when needing money to live. I want to finish my studies here in Rome and then try and move to the North, where people say it is easier to find a job, I mean a good job, with papers and all. I used to work as a waiter ... and then for a removal company. At the moment I am working as a cashier in a bar. I used to get €50 a day when I worked at the removal company and I only get €25 now ... the only advantage is that at least it is not a tiring job, it does not strain me physically.
Did they pay you the same as Italians or less?
Wherever I have been I got paid the same amounts as Italians, even when they were much older then me, as it is with the bar, where there are people in their late fifties working for €25 a day ... I think it has got something to do with the individual mentality of each employer – some just want to pay low wages, no matter who you are and where you come from. (M25, Rome)

It also needs to be recognised that there is a substantial differential in wages and living conditions between the North and the South of Italy. Whereas in Lecce an Italian or Albanian young person working in a pub would earn an average of €25 for eight hours of work, in Modena, for the same hours and the same job, they would get €50–60. The situation is more nuanced in Rome, where an average payment for eight hours of work would be in the region of €30–40, depending on the sector. Although many more migrants in Rome were able to have access to regular contracts and acceptable working conditions than was the case in Lecce, situations of differential treatment and irregularity were quite widespread, even when people had an official permit to stay. An example:

> In Rome I worked mainly as a painter or builder. I could not get anything better … the work is very hard, irregular and underpaid too …
> *Is it because of your legal status?*
> No, I do have papers. It is not a big deal in Rome anyway because it is still impossible to find a regular job. My permit to stay has not helped me at all in this respect. When you live in Rome, the permit is only useful if you want to visit your family in Albania …
> *How were your relations with your employers?*
> Well, on the whole they were fine, just like with the Italian people who were working with me … Although once I was not paid by my employer, but since I had no contract there was very little I could do … It is very difficult to get paid what was agreed when you are not regular … It happens to all migrants … we usually get paid weekly and Italians get more money for the same job, normally €75–100 per day, whereas we get €30–40. The payments are the same for all migrants – Polish, Senegalese, Albanians … (M30, Rome)

In general, however, access to documents constitutes a key factor in successful integration. This is especially the case for migrants aiming to set up their own small businesses. The following testimony demonstrates the importance of early arrival, and hence legal status, from the start; it also reminds us of the 'guardian angel' phenomenon which we described in the previous chapter.

> I arrived in Brindisi by boat, the famous boat crammed with thousands of Albanians escaping from the country in March 1991 … I was very lucky as I was sort of adopted by an Italian family living in a small village not far from Rome. They were very kind to me and supported me a lot; I love them as my own family. I performed a lot of different jobs since I came to Italy. Initially, I worked with my adoptive parents in their firm and after having learned the job I started working on my own. I work in construction and painting, mainly for private houses. I currently employ three other people, two Romanians and an Italian. (M38, Rome)

Economic well-being is not only affected by regional differences in wage rates in Italy, it also depends on variations in living costs. The cost of living, which is much higher in the North, partially compensates for the difference in earning, as overall in the North people are offered better living conditions, but at higher costs. The situation is different – and tougher – in Rome, where accommodation prices are more similar to those in the North, when compared to Lecce, while wages are still significantly lower than in the North.

All this means that Albanians, like other migrant groups, find themselves disadvantaged for different reasons in the three areas examined. In the South (and to a lesser extent in Rome), where 'being regular' is an exception for Italians in many areas of work, having to be 'regular' in order to have a permit to stay is actually a disadvantage; hence the paradoxical situation that in some employment sectors

Albanian migrants were the only ones holding a regular work contract, whereas their Italian colleagues could keep on working 'in the black'. Moreover, in order to meet the criteria for the renewal of their work permits, Albanian migrants were often forced to 'buy' a regular contract from their employers and to make voluntary tax payments in order to keep their legal status.

> *How did you regularise your position?*
> I paid. I paid an entrepreneur 3.2 million lire (about €1,600) for a fake contract and then I had problems as we were both questioned by the local labour inspection office ... they wanted to know if I paid or not. We convinced them that the money was for the creation of a partnership, that is how we got out of it. After six months I got my permit. (M28, Lecce)

In the North, on the other hand, being undocumented poses considerable problems, because the degree of regularisation within the large formal labour market is extremely high, and employers either cannot or are much less willing to employ people who do not hold a permit. This means that undocumented migrants in the North are potentially exposed to a higher level of exploitation and differential treatment than they might face in the South, where they can find work in the informal economy more easily. This somewhat ironic situation emerges in the following interview:

> *What kinds of job did you have here in Italy?*
> I mainly worked as a builder, for different firms ... the first time I only stayed in the firm for a month because the employer paid little and exploited me ... I mean we used to work for twelve hours per day, from dawn till dusk, for 80,000 lire ... But the real reason why I left is that I had an accident, I cut my head and one eye ... it was so bad that when we got to hospital even the doctor was traumatised, he said he had never seen anything like it and called two specialists immediately ... they took care of me and I was fine, eventually.
> *Did you used to work in the black economy?*
> Yes.
> *What did your employer do?*
> He came to see me, he could not stop crying and he begged me not to denounce him ... he said: 'Don't worry, I will pay you for all the days off and for the medical treatment' ... but in the end he did not give me anything, I even had to pay for my own medicines. Soon after I recovered, he fired me as well.
> *Where do you work now?*
> I still work in the black economy, in the beginning the new employer was afraid to employ me as I do not have documents ... but then he saw I worked well and decided to keep me. They are very happy with me and the pay is not too bad, I earn about 20,000 lire per hour.
> *Are you paid like your Italian colleagues?*
> Of course not, it is normal ...
> *What do you mean, 'It is normal'? Is it normal because you are Albanian or ...?*
> No, it is normal because I have no documents. Once you have documents you

are paid like an Italian, whether you are Albanian or not, there is no difference, but if you are irregular, well, that is different. (M30, Bologna)

In Apulia, the conditions of general economic vulnerability mentioned above are in part shared by local Italians who, like Albanians living there, are often forced to migrate to the wealthier and more industrialised North in order to secure better living conditions for themselves and their families. More than any other southern region, Apulia functions as a 'bridge or transit area' between Albania and more prosperous and therefore desirable destinations further north (Perrone 2003: 123). In Lecce, many interviewees indicated that they would like to move to the North of Italy. Below, the first interviewee imagines her future in the North, the second had already moved and was interviewed on a return visit to see friends in Lecce.

Where do you imagine your future?
I would like to move to the North. I visited Milan, Turin, Modena, Bologna …
And what was your overall impression?
Well, life is very different. From what I saw, people there work very hard, all day … but they are very secure and that is very important for me, as I have a little daughter. I like the fact that there is more respect for work in the North, I mean why should not I get paid according to the work that I do? (F41, Lecce)

Why did you decide to move to the North?
Because it is better than here, for my daughter and my wife and also for me. My wife was able to find a job in a firm where she can put her qualifications to some use … she was a quality inspector and production manager for a textile factory in Albania.
Who got her this job?
My brother-in-law, he has been living there for over ten years and was able to arrange a job for me too. All of our relatives are there now …
But what is the main difference between here and there?
Many things, first of all the money … then for my children, they can have better chances to get good wages in the future … then education, schools, universities … My daughter has already visited five cities since the beginning of this year and here they only take them on a school outing once a year if they are lucky. (M44, Lecce)

This next excerpt from the interview with G., who works for the municipality of Molfetta, shows how it is usually people with better qualifications and a hope of upward social mobility who move to the North, where they anticipate that they stand a better chance of finding a job according to their qualifications:

How many Albanians live in Molfetta?
There are around six hundred. But their number is down by about 20 per cent because in the last two or three years many have started leaving for the North. They don't find what they seek here because Molfetta doesn't offer much, only

agriculture. Those Albanians who come from the rural areas of Albania continue to stay here, because they feel comfortable here. They are integrated well. The rest, who aspire to more, go north to find something else.

Albanians who have lived both in the South and in the North of Italy are best able to set out the advantages and disadvantages of each location. Typically, these comparative perspectives appreciate the higher level of economic and social security as well as the lower degree of overt discrimination in the North. Two quotes: the first interviewee had worked for a while in Turin, where he had relatives, but then returned to Lecce; the second had moved from Otranto to Modena.

> *How would you compare your experiences in the South and in the North?*
> I think overall in the North I had a better experience, as there I used to work more and earn more, twice as much I am making here. They say that there they are more racist, but to tell you the truth they treated me very well ... They did not think I was Albanian, in fact most thought I was a Sicilian. (M28, Lecce)

> *Did you like it better in Modena or Otranto?*
> In Modena for sure. People work harder and are nicer.
> *What is the most important difference between down there and here?*
> In my opinion, here people don't really refer to you as a foreigner, whereas in Otranto people would refer to you as an 'Albanian' all the time because I had a different accent ... I mean, in Modena too there is racism, but not so much as in Otranto. (F34, Modena)

Trajectories of Inclusion and Exclusion

Summing up, the working environment was found to be an ambivalent arena of socioeconomic inclusion and exclusion. In terms of Heckmann's (2005) four types of integration reviewed in Chapter 1, the labour market is a key component of *structural* integration; Albanians have made significant progress along this dimension, but full parity with host-society workers is some way off. On the other hand there is no major 'enclave economy' effect, nor an abject descent into an unemployed underclass along the lines of the segmented assimilation model, also summarised in Chapter 1. Rather, Albanians enjoy a relatively high level of *interactive* and *identificational* integration, especially through their knowledge of Italian language and culture, and this impacts positively on the social arena of work relatives. Most Albanian migrants we interviewed declared themselves satisfied with the quality of relations with their current bosses and colleagues, whom they often see socially outside the workplace. However, this situation was not a given, but the result of a long and difficult individual trajectory from lower to higher levels of legal entitlement, economic reward and professional acknowledgement. When asked about 'unpleasant' work-related experiences, most interviewees could easily recall instances of unfair treatment by their colleagues and employers in the past. The nature of these experiences of discrimination is extremely varied and usually comprises one or a combination of the following: differential payment, bullying and harassment, unjustified or sudden dismissal, and exploitation. No interviewee reported having been subjected to physical violence. However, many interviewees had only been able to establish respectful relations with their fellow workers after they had endured continuing provocation. Such provocation typically reproduced the stigmatising tropes we mentioned earlier, which have come to frame the anti-Albanian prejudices existing within Italian society at large.

> I think it's so stupid when people unfairly accuse other people of acts that they haven't done. For example, once something went missing in the factory where I work and the manager came straight to me and accused first me and then the rest of the foreigners … he even threatened us that if we don't bring back the things that went missing he was going to sue us. I told him 'You can call the police and let them do the investigation, but it wasn't us'. He later found out that the things were stolen by one of his men who was authorised to do the checking. (M33, Modena)

In other research, interviewees likewise complained that 'my colleagues only know what is said on the television about Albanians'; one observed that his workmates seemed to make a point of discussing in his presence the latest news reports of Albanians involved in crime (Mottura and Marra 2003: 65).

Although experiences of unfair treatment and discrimination at work were encountered in all of the sites in this research, the fact that they were more frequent in the South and in Rome than in the North reflects the much higher levels of discretionality and informality characterising those particular economic and social contexts. But there were examples of good and bad experiences and practices in all three field locations. Generalising, we may identify the key factors conditioning Albanian migrants' process of gradual inclusion as legal status, access to network-based support, and the different socioeconomic and institutional-associative settings encountered in each local context of immigration. Time is another important dimension of 'integration': *ceteris paribus*, the longer a migrant has been in Italy, the greater the chance of achieving regularised status, and the greater the likelihood of progress being made in the job market, as well as in housing, considered next.[4]

Housing

Structural Difficulties in the Housing Market

This second key axis shaping the multi-faceted process of differential inclusion/exclusion of Albanian migrants was the one over which interviewees experienced the most serious episodes of overt discrimination (cf. Romania 2004: 96). Even more so than in the realm of work, most interviewees were only able to find a place to live through the networks of their Italian and more socially established Albanian friends. Whilst the difficulties encountered by Albanian migrants in finding suitable accommodation can be related to their condition as migrants and to the specific prejudice they encounter in Italian society at large, they also reflect the conditions of the housing market for the Italian population as a whole. Current Italian legislation makes it very difficult for a landlord to evict an insolvent or problematic lodger, and this puts a lot of pressure on the renting market. This excerpt from an interview is interesting as it reveals an acute awareness on the part of an Albanian immigrant of the problems facing Italian landlords:

> *Is it easy to find a job here?*
> Well, I would not say easy, but there are plenty ...
> *How about housing?*
> Almost impossible.
> *Is that because you are foreign?*
> Not only, because the same has been true, from what I have heard, for southern Italians as for all other migrants ... Maybe it is a bit worse for Albanians because of their reputation. I spoke to many Italians about this since I arrived. I could not understand why they preferred leaving their flats empty rather than renting them – after all it is a good way to earn money. But after I spoke to them I changed my mind, I understood the risks involved. If I rent a place and I don't pay ... even if you call the police and take me to court ... if I have no money ... what can you do? A civil court case lasts at least five years – which means I can stay in your place without paying for five years! Then I heard that there is another law, which says that you cannot be evicted if you have no money ... So they are right in not renting out their properties ... it is very risky ... I rent it, destroy everything ... don't pay and then leave ... and the owner has to pay. Why? (M32, Modena)

Although the protectionist slant in favour of tenants is undoubtedly a key factor behind the lack of mobility in the renting market, there are important geographical differences in the housing market. Let us look at each regional context in turn.

The availability of more job opportunities and the possibility to enjoy better working conditions have been pull factors attracting many international migrants (and internal workers) to cities in the Emilia-Romagna region in recent decades. Unfortunately, this flow has not been matched by adequate housing policies: as a result, many low- and medium-income households cannot access affordable urban dwellings. According to an official of *Confindustria Modena*, the local employers' association, housing is a problem for everyone in the city, even people born there.

> If you wanted to set up a family tomorrow it would be very difficult for you to find an apartment because prices are very high. You can imagine that things are much worse for a non-EU migrant, because a local person can always count on the support of the family ... contacts ... A migrant coming here will have to live together with other migrants. Many do this, even migrants from the South of Italy ... the living costs are too high here.

Hence, in Emilia-Romagna, and in northern Italian cities in general, it is housing rather than access to employment which marks the main barrier to full socioeconomic inclusion. This finding is corroborated by other research carried out locally (see, for example, Bernardotti 2001; Bernardotti and Mottura 1999). Faced by structural barriers in their access to urban accommodation (shortage of supply, rents way beyond their means, reluctance of landlords to rent to immigrants, etc.), many Albanians (and other immigrants such as Moroccans and Tunisians) are forced to look to rural areas which may be 50km or more from their places of work in the cities (Mottura and Marra 2003: 73). This issue is described in an interview with an officer of the Modena Provincial Authority in the following terms:

> Because of the lack of housing, many foreign workers have found accommodation in rural or mountainous areas. There are villages where the percentage between foreign migrants and locals is fifty–fifty. The kind of housing they find is usually of bad quality ... The important thing to underline is that the demand for housing has changed the distribution of the migrant population in the province ... We have a new type of residential mobility now, with a lot of migrant families living in places we did not think they would live in. This poses a lot of challenges to social and other services targeting them. Modena is still the municipality with the highest [absolute] number of migrants, but there are a lot of 'dormitory' villages nearby or further away.

In fact, in Emilia-Romagna the municipalities with the highest percentage of immigrant residents are formerly depopulated villages in the mountainous areas to the south, where empty, but usually poor-quality accommodation is available at low rents; and villages and small towns to the north, out on the lower Po Plain, where rents are also much lower than in the 'prestigious' cities of Modena, Bologna and Reggio (Mottura and Pinto 2001: 92; Regione Emilia-Romagna 2002: 43, 46).

On top of the structural features of the housing market in Modena and adjacent cities, there is the widespread blanket of anti-Albanian prejudice (Mottura and Marra 2003: 72). One example from our extensive portfolio of evidence on this:

> *Did you encounter any difficulties in renting a property?*
> Yes it was extremely difficult. From my point of view finding a place to live is more difficult than finding a job. They would hire you for a job because they profit out of it, but accommodation is more difficult. They don't really trust us Albanians. When I was looking for accommodation the landlady was sceptical

in the beginning because she didn't even trust the Italians themselves. For example she had this guy from Naples who ran off without paying the rent. (M32, Modena)

The situation is not much better in Rome, because of the same combination of elements: enduring prejudice against migrants, high rents and a very high demand for all forms of accommodation in Italy's capital city. In the words of Simonetta, our interviewee at the Confederazione Generale Italiana del Lavoro (CGIL) trade union:

> The problem migrants encounter in finding a place to live should be understood both as a structural problem and as related to the specific ways in which houses are rented to foreign people ... Here either you have 2 million lire (approximately €1,000) a month or you don't find a flat, which means that both foreign migrants and many Italians have to share flats and this leads to conditions of overcrowding ... If you think that even a university student usually pays at least 400,000 (approximately €200) for a room ... and that a foreign migrant cannot afford more that 250,000 (about €125), you can imagine the kinds of situation this leads to.

In Rome, too, many migrant families are forced to live in small towns and villages well outside the urban area, or in marginal places on the periphery of Rome.

> I live in Bagni di Tivoli ... with my brother ... we rent a flat and pay €360. It is very far from Rome but we had no choice, anything closer was too expensive. Then even when you find something you can afford, it is very difficult to get it ... I had been looking for a flat for one and a half years before finding this one. I looked everywhere, in newspapers, through friends ... but whenever I mentioned I was Albanian they refused to rent me the place. (M28, Rome)

> I live in a hut under a bridge in Magliana [a poor district on the outskirts of Rome] with eight people ... we are all Albanian. We all work, but there is no water or electricity ... it is so difficult to live there. (M31, Rome)

Others were a bit luckier. This mainly involves reliance on Italian or Albanian friends and contacts. Again, two examples:

> I now live in Piazza Bologna, close to the University ... I was lucky as I joined some Albanian friends who already lived there, but it is very difficult to find accommodation in Rome if you are Albanian. When I first got here I managed to find a room in a college run by Catholic nuns and I lived there for four years. I tried to find an apartment during that time but it was impossible. (F30, Rome)

Although the housing market in Apulia and the cost of living in the South seemed to be able to better accommodate Albanian migrants' needs, in the main urban areas such as Lecce or Bari it was very difficult to access affordable accommodation, partly because of pressure from the sizeable student populations of these two cities. Both students and immigrants are looking for inexpensive places to rent and so compete with each other in the same sector of the housing market (Giorgio and Luisi 2001: 92). And here, too, discriminatory behaviour from both private owners and agencies constituted another obstacle, so that interviewees had to rely on the help of their Italian and Albanian friends in order to find accommodation. Andrea, a student at the University of Bari, had actually recorded on his mobile phone a conversation with a potential landlady, which he played back during the interview:

> So here is the message, OK? Listen.
> Landlady: *Albanian? My God. Why didn't you tell me? I thought I had asked you where you came from.*
> Andrea: *I told you I am an Albanian student.*
> Landlady: *Oh, I see ... but ... if you want to see the place ... but to tell you the truth the three other guys living there at the moment are from Foggia and from personal experience I prefer that they stay together, that is all ...*
> Andrea: *OK, I understand.*
> Did you understand too? In other words, she did not want to give me the bedsit because I am Albanian ...

The precise, and 'heavy', meaning associated with the word albanese, 'Albanian', will be further analysed later. From what Andrea says, it clearly carries a deeper layer of discriminatory meaning than more qualified terms such as 'Albanian student' or 'from Albania'.

Despite Andrea's testimony, the view was also expressed by some interviewees that, in Apulia, Albanians faced fewer obstacles to social inclusion than they did in the North, and less resistance from the host society than some other immigrant groups. Field research carried out by Zinn and Rivera (1995) in some small towns in southern Italy found evidence of a lot of help and good relations between Albanian families settled there and their Italian neighbours. A similar interpretation was put to us by a representative of the Lecce Social Services:

> Well, I think gradually they [Albanians] became more autonomous ... economic support is no longer a very significant aspect of our work with the Albanian community ... but the housing problem is an important one, because the situation in Lecce is very difficult ...
> *Is this because there is not enough housing or is it because Lecce people do not want to rent to Albanians ... or to migrants in general ... or both?*
> Mmh ... maybe both. Let us say that there is no available housing – I mean economically available. Then, I don't think that Albanians find a particular difficulty in accessing housing, even private housing. I don't think there is a specific discrimination against them. At least from what I am able to understand from my work. I don't think the city is closed to Albanians; on the contrary, I think that they face less discrimination when compared with some other communities, for example, the Senegalese. More generally people from Africa meet much more resistance.

Local Housing Experiences: Reception Centres, Families and Single People

Despite the common structural features outlined above, individual experiences of housing amongst Albanian migrants were nevertheless very variable. They depended, of course, on many factors, including length of time in the country, legal status, work and income, and household formation. One key finding about the living conditions of Albanian migrants is that very few of them, with the exception of unaccompanied minors, are living in migrants' reception centres[5] or hostels for economically disadvantaged people. Nor do they live in dense concentrations or 'ethnic ghettos'. Rather, they lived in mostly the poor parts of towns and cities, or in smaller villages. The legal necessity for migrants to meet minimum housing prerequisites – notably in regard to space – in order to be entitled to family reunification means that family units live in more-or-less suitable private accommodation. These better-standard living conditions can be economically better sustained by family units as most of their members contribute to the household economy in different ways. One family we interviewed in Modena had even been able to obtain a mortgage to buy their own flat, without any help from Italian neighbours or friends.

Single men encounter the most serious difficulties finding suitable accommodation. They usually share very modest flats with other Albanians. Their economic condition was not the only factor behind their difficulties in finding accommodation; many reported being subject to a much more prejudiced treatment than Albanian families seemed to receive. Students also tend to live in shared flats with other Albanian and, less frequently, Italian fellow students. Albanian single women who are not students tend to live with a family belonging to their extended family-based network. Single women living alone are likely to be associated with the 'Albanian prostitute' stereotype on the part of the host society; and among their own kinship network such independent living might be frowned on because of an assumed loosening of moral behavioural boundaries.[6]

The establishment of a family-based network was one of the most important positive results brought about by the several campaigns of regularisation promoted by the Italian state since the mid 1990s (refer back to Table 3.7). The possibility to rely on a network of friends and relatives has been a very important factor in the dramatic improvement of the experience of social inclusion of Albanian migrants, especially for their housing situation. As our field evidence shows, undocumented Albanian migrants who could not rely on a robust family-based network were the ones facing the most dramatic conditions of social and spatial exclusion; many were forced to sleep rough for long periods or to live in cramped apartments with other Albanians. The following case corroborates these observations.

> *Why did you decide to leave Albania?*
> Well, my father had died and my mother could not make it alone ... she said that going to Italy was the last hope, otherwise we would have to kill ourselves. Thankfully we met this relative of ours by chance once we had arrived in Lecce and he told us where we could stay in the beginning ... We had to live in a small house where there were many other Albanians, There was only one large room and two smaller ones, with a kitchen and a bath. For everybody. We all shared the rent and the food ... it was OK to survive but the place was very dirty ... fifteen people ... all men, and one woman ... Then there were problems, somebody without documents was arrested and we had to move out. Then, thanks to a friend of my mother we met a sister from [name of religious order] ... she really helped us a lot. She found us this apartment and registered us at school.
> *Do you like it? How big is it?*
> Yes, we like it, there are two bedrooms, a kitchen and a bathroom, for the three of us; my brother sleeps in my room. (M17, Lecce)

As was the case with work-related narratives, we found that, for housing, those interviewees who declared themselves to be happy with their current arrangements also recorded an often long series of negative experiences of exclusion from the housing market in the past. However, the points of departure and arrival and the rapidity of progress in housing improvement varied considerably in the three areas under examination. Three main factors frame this regional variation: the degree of state formalisation and organisation, both as regards the phenomenon of immigration and the housing market; the level of socioeconomic development of the area in question; and the local experiences of institutional and social response to migration.

In Apulia, the regional organisations and associations have historically addressed migration as a transitory phenomenon, thereby implicitly considering the region as a '*terra di passaggio*' (transit area) between places of origin and of destination of migrants, rather than as an area of potential settlement. For instance, an official at the *Ufficio Stranieri* (Foreigners' Department) in Lecce told us:

> Well, at the moment there are about 2,300 Albanians legally resident in the province. But many then move to northern Italy. They hold on to the permit to stay we give them, but move north or anywhere they think they will stand better chances of finding work. Most do this after the first two years.

It is indeed true that many Albanian migrants tend to re-migrate to the North of Italy; abundant statistical evidence for this was presented in Chapter 3. But it is equally true that there is a large group of foreign people, especially Albanians, who are the largest group, living and working in Apulia on a stable, regularised basis, whose needs have not been addressed adequately by state institutions and other associations because of the official focus on the *prima accoglienza* reception centres for new arrivals. Other authors have also written of the inadequacy of public sector services for receiving and integrating migrants in Apulia, and of the 'policy' of subcontracting migrant services to private associations which rely on volunteers and epitomise the approach of 'assistentialism' (Giorgio and Luisi 2001: 103; Perrone 2001: 151). The following excerpt from the interview with Lecce Social Services explains the way the Italian migration legislation, which sets aside specific funds for the integration as well as for the 'first welcoming' of migrants, has been interpreted and deployed in this area: by not acknowledging the significant and enduring presence of migrants as an integral part of local society.

> The problem here is that migration is not considered as something that is here to stay. Because of its geographical position, many people think that this is a place through which people transit ... they don't stay ... while the truth is that we have at least two thousand documented migrants in the Lecce area – which means at least as many irregular migrants. This is a factor that never gets taken into account in the allocation of funding ... I can understand why people in institutions start from the number of regularly registered migrants ... but it is not enough.

These points are further corroborated by B., President of the Vëllazerimi Albanian Association in Lecce:

> Well, it is not that the local government has not done anything for Albanians or other migrant groups. But most things are done by voluntary organisations providing services of *prima accoglienza*, not by the local administration. The institutional response to migrants' needs is very slow ... I mean, the reception centres do a great job, but it can't be finished there ... Now most of the Albanians are settled, they have a job, they have a stable future. They are well integrated. Many have their own flats here. Welcoming people is not enough.

The issue of migrants' access to housing in Lecce was at the centre of many local political controversies at the time of our fieldwork there, and reflected a very specific situation. During the 1990s, Mara, a local transgendered sex worker, had made a fortune subletting dilapidated properties to undocumented migrants, becoming the owner of a large section of Lecce's historical city centre. After Mara died in 2001 these properties passed to the local Catholic Church, which had to manage the renewal of contracts with a largely undocumented population, and in a rapidly increasing real-estate market. This excerpt from the interview with Zana, an Albanian female sex worker living in the city centre, shows the problems many migrants had to face after Mara's death.

Mara helped me. Mara was a man who became a woman. I helped her because she wasn't well. She was the owner of this house and had other rooms for rent. I went to the municipality and did all the procedures, but I couldn't get the permit (to stay) because I was expelled once, in 1995. Now I've got the documents, for health reasons.
Have you had problems with housing?
No, I've always lived here. Now they want to get us out. I had a contract with Mara ... Now that she is dead, it all depends on the nuns, who inherited everything. The contract is for another two years, maybe after that I will move away. Who knows?
Are you satisfied with the place you have?
It's OK, only the two of us live here ... It is small. Mara died before she could formalise anything because she suffered a stroke and died without having enough time. Here it is small for two persons. Do you want to see it? Come! I went to the nuns and they told me to go away because they weren't interested in what I had arranged with Mara. I can't leave the house now. I might when the lease runs out. If they ask more, I will try to pay, I can't live on the streets. I am alone. I've never been married. I've no children. I live with a person but we're not married. (F35, Lecce)

The legacy of Mara was one, rather unique, aspect of the migrant housing situation in Lecce. Another was the way in which the local municipal office responded (or rather, did not respond) to migrants' needs. Yet another was the role of the voluntary sector. In general, the voluntary associations were adept at adapting their services to the evolving needs of the foreign population, but they did so in a politically charged scenario which we will return to in the next chapter when we consider the role of Albanian associations.

The housing policy situation is better in Modena, where migration was acknowledged as a permanent feature of the 'receiving' socioeconomic context by both local associations and state institutions; the problem is one of high property costs and rents. The political scenario in Emilia-Romagna is rather cohesive compared to the one in Apulia. The former region has historically been characterised by the hegemony of the Left at all levels of local and regional administration. Moreover, regional and local administrations have traditionally been both very efficient and particularly sensitive to issues of social exclusion, and were able to develop a more comprehensive set of initiatives responding to the specificity of migrant needs (housing support, job centres, etc.).[7] In 1997, 150 Albanians sent to Modena by the Italian authorities after their arrival on the Apulian coastline were dealt with by a network of initiatives of solidarity and social intervention supervised by the Foreign Citizens Office (*Ufficio Stranieri*). Most of these families were helped to access the labour and housing markets and were self-supporting by the time our fieldwork in Modena took place, as this excerpt from the interview with

N., who helped the Albanians on behalf of the *Ufficio Stranieri* back in 1997, shows:

> Once those 150 people arrived we managed everyday life in the camp ... Children, family problems, food, health, everything. They were all families, except two singles. It was not easy, the moment the Prodi decree was issued basically those who matched the prerequisites could stay, those who did not had to leave. This was quite a dramatic moment. Luckily most people did not stay in the camp waiting and had already arranged a contract.

The implementation of the so-called Prodi decree, which granted leave to remain in Italy only to those migrants who had a regular job and a housing contract at the time of its enforcement, triggered a chain of solidarity amongst associations and many ordinary citizens in Modena, in order to help the Albanian migrants to meet the criteria. Although this 'solidarity chain' had a very positive general outcome, as the migrant testimony below indicates, nevertheless forty people were deported to Albania overnight as they failed to meet the criteria of the decree.

> The people of the *Ufficio Stranieri* at the Modena Council found our first flat for us. They helped us a lot, especially in the beginning, they paid for our rent for a while, then as soon as we could we started looking for a flat in the private market, now we are thinking of buying it, although it is so expensive ... I got this flat through friends and personal links, it is the only way to get around in Italy, with houses and jobs you have to go through friends. (F30, Modena)

As we mentioned above, the housing market for migrants in Rome is characterised by an extreme shortage of affordable accommodation, except outside the city. In Rome itself rents are very high. Most interviewees had to rely on the assistance of Italian and Albanian friends and acquaintances to find a place to live; almost none reported seeking help from an Italian or Albanian association.

As well as being Italy's capital and largest city, Rome is also one of the world's favourite tourist destinations and an important transit point for international and intercontinental travel. In this respect Rome must be considered as an important place of both transit and settlement for migrants. There is a parallel to be noted here with the situation in Lecce – also a city of transit and settlement, if on a rather different scale and with respect to different avenues of arrival. The combination of these two elements poses a challenge for the people helping migrants in Rome, because of the constant inflow and outflow of migrants, and the variety of their needs. In the words of S., of CGIL:

> Rome is a very diverse city because it is not only a place where people live and stay, it is also both a transit and an entry point ... There is Fiumicino Airport ... A lot of people arrive in Rome as their first entry into Italy or Europe. Then it is also a tourist place ... and this attracts many people, who then stay on. Many

people from poor countries end by staying ... In Rome, usually, most Albanians are in transit ... They are looking around to see where else in the country they might want to settle more permanently. Usually they head north, especially those without any prospect of settlement here. At the same time there are around ten thousand Albanian residents, I mean regularly resident. If we include undocumented people then the overall number could go up to fifteen thousand people ... I mean, there is an important element of transit, but also a sizeable community.

In comparing the different individual trajectories from an initial situation of exclusion from the housing market towards better housing and living conditions, some common threads emerge. In Apulia there is a profound contrast between the inefficiency and lack of coordination of the institutional response to migrants' needs, and the generosity and availability of many private citizens (Da Molin 2001: 13). This was true especially in the early stages of Albanians' migration, although accounts of solidarity and kindness can also be found in much more recent times. Albanian migrants' life-histories of settlement and improvement of living conditions in this region contain many anecdotes of Italian 'guardian angels' adopting Albanian families or individuals and actively sustaining their process of social inclusion for years. Overall, southern Italians are perceived by many Albanians as being 'warmer' and 'friendlier' and more generous than Italians in the North.[8] This interviewee had lived in the southern region of Calabria before moving to Modena:

> *If you make a comparison between the South and here what would you say?*
> The people down south are more sensitive and warm ... they are more similar to us ... whereas here people mind their own business and are more reserved.
> *Having said that, why do you still prefer to stay here?*
> Because we sort of got settled here and I had friends here. In fact, I really like Modena. We feel more comfortable. Even when I go home to Albania, I miss Modena very much and I feel like home when I come here. (M35, Modena)

Indeed, despite these discourses of cultural proximity to southern Italians, we find that most of the migrants who have lived both in the North and in the South of the country actually prefer settling long-term in the North, where they find better living and working conditions, and sometimes less racism.

Summing up, Albanian migrants' variable but often intense experiences of social inclusion and exclusion must be seen as located at the encounter between the specific conditions of the employment and housing markets in the three study areas, the locally-based agents of integration and social intervention, and finally the locally-manifested character of generalised stigmatising discourses of Albanians as 'rough' people, prone to violence, criminality and prostitution. The interlocking of these three dimensions is mirrored in the reasons why Albanian migrants seek help from social services and voluntary bodies in the different locations. In Lecce and in Rome, Albanians resort to services in relation to problems they encounter in getting access to work and regularisation opportunities, whereas in Modena they go to social services mainly to obtain help in accessing the housing market and health facilities.

The Interplay between Regularisation and Access to Housing and Work

At the time we carried out our Italian fieldwork, between October 2001 and July 2002, Italian migration legislation was under review from the then right-wing government. The new bill, the so-called Bossi–Fini decree, which amended the existing Turco–Napolitano law, was approved on 11 July 2002 and became operative after 9 September of the same year. However, long before its approval, the decision of the Berlusconi government to modify the existing legislation by increasing control over both the presence of existing undocumented migrants and the arrival of new clandestine migrants had long been at the centre of the Italian political and wider public debate. In fact, the Bossi–Fini law itself originated out of the political need of the centre-right coalition to respond to promises it had made during an electoral campaign which had been very much orchestrated around the supposed association between the growing presence of migrants, the poor performance of the Italian economy and an upsurge in crime.

The Bossi–Fini decree was not an autonomous piece of legislation, but an attempt at a more restrictive amendment of the previous Turco–Napolitano law. More than anything, the Bossi–Fini law was a political statement of the new right-wing coalition on the role of migration, on the regulation of labour and on their complex relations. Actually the changes implemented under the new decree did not correspond to the xenophobic and extremist declarations which accompanied its preparation. As Giovanna Zincone has pointed out, there was 'a very strong discrepancy between public rhetoric and public action regarding illegal immigration' and in the end 'the main difference between centre-left and centre-right in Italy relates far more to proclaimed strategies and values than to legislation' (Zincone 2006: 348). The Turco–Napolitano law was the product of the geopolitical order and priorities of the 1990s, which were shaped by Italy's negotiation of its full membership of the European Schengen club and its perceived (and real) ability to contain the inflows of illegal migrants, as we noted in Chapter 4. On the one hand the Turco–Napolitano law introduced many provisions which can be seen as a progressive step forward towards equality and justice of treatment for migrants within Italian society. Unlike previous laws and policies, it acknowledged that migration had become a structural aspect of Italian society in many different ways:

- by allowing legal immigrants to enjoy the same social rights as Italian citizens;
- by abolishing the necessity to establish that an Italian or EU worker was not available before hiring a non-EU migrant for the same position;
- by facilitating family reunification (the children and spouses of immigrants holding a one-year permit to stay were authorised to join them immediately and, if adults, were allowed to work);
- by funding the training and employment of cultural mediators and creating a budget for multicultural activities;
- by making the annual migrant entry quota decree compulsory;
- by introducing the possibility for a new migrant to stay in Italy for one year in order to search for work, under the guarantee of an Italian citizen or a regular migrant – this was the so-called 'sponsor' or 'job search' visa.

On the other hand, the Turco–Napolitano law also introduced many of the repressive measures which were to be 'toughened up' by the Bossi–Fini decree, such as the setting up of temporary detention centres to manage the deportation of undocumented migrants, and the possibility of deporting illegal immigrants who had committed crimes. In this respect, key aspects of the Bossi–Fini decree are the following:

- *Housing*: an employer wanting to employ a foreign citizen will have to guarantee the availability of a dwelling, which has to be in conformity with the minimum standards required by public housing.
- *Deportations*: as foreseen by the Turco–Napolitano law, the foreign citizen who is found on Italian territory without a permit to stay will be subject to deportation as an administrative sanction and accompanied to the border. A foreign citizen not in possession of valid documents will be detained in a 'centre for migrants' (*centro di permanenza*) for sixty days (previously thirty), during which the authorities will try to identify her/him. Should this be impossible, the foreign citizen will be required to leave Italy within three days (previously fifteen). Any subsequent attempt to re-enter Italian territory is considered a *criminal offence*.
- *Quota*: the decree determining the number of non-EU migrants allowed to enter Italy each year becomes optional and not compulsory.
- *Visa*: the possibility of migrating to Italy to search for work, 'sponsored' by an Italian citizen or a legally-resident migrant, which was one of the main innovations introduced by the Turco–Napolitano law, is cancelled.
- *Permit to stay*: according to the Bossi–Fini decree, the permit is only to be issued to foreign citizens who already have a work contract, and has

a duration of two years (previously four). This new permit to stay is called 'contract to stay' (*contratto di soggiorno*) and has to be reviewed each time the foreign worker changes job during its duration. If, by the end of the two years, the foreign citizen loses his or her job, s/he will have six months to find another one. Failing this, s/he will have to return to the country of origin. Not to do so means becoming an 'illegal immigrant'. Moreover, the employer has to cover the expenses for the repatriation of the non-EU foreign employer at the end of his or her contract. Anyone employing an undocumented non-EU foreign citizen risks a prison sentence of up to one year and a fine of up to €5,000 for each irregular worker. Non-EU foreign citizens can only be employed when no Italian or EU citizens are available to take the position. The maximum duration of a permit to stay for seasonal workers is lowered to nine months. Finally, all permits to stay have to be renewed ninety days (previously thirty) before their expiry.

- *Control and prevention of illegal migration*: more powers are given to the Italian navy to block the boats bringing migrants to Italy while they are still offshore. In addition to this, the Italian Home Office will have the power to send police to inspect embassies and consulates.
- *Family reunification*: the non-EU foreign citizen who is in possession of a 'contract to stay' can ask to be joined by his/her partner, his minor-age children and his adult children if these are proven not to be able to provide for their own economic survival. As for parents, they can join their children only if they are older than sixty-five and if no other member of the family can provide for them in the country of origin.
- *Administration of migration-related issues*: each provincial administration should create a unified office for the management of migration-related issues, which will also be responsible for the employment of foreign migrants.

Within the political environment of the time, the proponents of the Bossi–Fini law presented it as a measure fostering the integration of migrants by making their permit to stay conditional on their ability to remain in contract-based employment and find adequate accommodation. People on the left of the political scenario, however, have strongly criticised these provisions. They stress that migrants have become even more dependent on their employers and landlords in order to 'keep legal', and are thus more, rather than less, vulnerable to falling into situations of illegality and exploitation. In other words, they pointed out that the law, by making legal status more inaccessible, would systematically lead to an increase, rather than a decrease, in the social exclusion and exploitation of migrants.

However, the way the Bossi–Fini decree was actually applied in practice did not reflect the tone and content of the political rhetoric which had accompanied its elaboration. Thus, paradoxically, the centre-left coalition parties and leftist political organisations found themselves attacking the Berlusconi government for having diluted the very restrictive measures already implemented by the immigration law which had been passed by the centre-left government! In the end, many of the more drastic and 'propagandistic' provisions initially foreseen and fed to the media during the period of preparation of the Bossi–Fini decree were not included or implemented. For example:

> [T]he residence period for family reunification was reduced from three years (according to the old Bossi–Berlusconi Bill) to one year, and then eliminated. The crime of clandestine immigration was not introduced, and arrest on remand was only allowed when the immigrant was found in a flagrantly illegal position for the second time … The new tools of repression were attenuated partly for reasons of cost; trials and deportations are expensive, and cannot be used for every single overstayer. Some tools already existed: the Turco–Napolitano Act provided for illegal immigrants to be escorted to the frontier in some cases at the discretion of the court, without any trial or right to defence. The Bossi–Fini Act extended this provision, which originally only applied in a limited number of cases, to all persistent offenders. The proposal of adding fingerprints to residence permits issued to foreigners with a visa exceeding three months, which caused scandal and protests from left-wing circles, was postponed … The proposal of using weapons to combat clandestine immigration was immediately mitigated by embedding their use in the framework of 'compliance with legality and international law'. (Zincone 2006: 363)

Moreover, notwithstanding the xenophobic and hard-line tones of the rhetoric of the centre-right coalition, or maybe exactly because of it, the Bossi–Fini decree coincided with the largest regularisation in Italian history. Although initially targeting exclusively undocumented migrants working in the care industry, the so-called *'badanti'*, in the end the regularisation allowed more than 630,000 undocumented migrants (out of 704,000 applicants) to obtain documentation, albeit on the precarious conditions spelt out by the Bossi–Fini decree.

Far from being a paradox, *the regularisation was an integral part of a political project which had at its heart the further flexibilisation of the Italian labour market*. In this respect, the mix of xenophobic rhetoric and actual pragmatism characterising the Bossi–Fini decree can be seen as responding to three of the main political and economic strands sustaining the centre-right coalition: the drive towards the liberalisation and flexibilisation of the labour market (*Forza Italia*), the xenophobic fear of miscegenation (*Lega Nord*), and the perceived necessity to defend a national(istic) identity under threat (*Alleanza Nazionale*).[9] Indeed, the juxtaposition of xenophobia and practicality inherent in the coalition's policy towards migration seems to correspond to the old Italian expression *'chi disprezza compera'*, meaning that the one who despises something or somebody in public is usually the one who is privately interested in obtaining it, and at a lesser price.

The interview material we gathered mirrors the debates which surrounded the drafting and approval of the Bossi–Fini decree as they were reproduced and challenged by actors who were very differently positioned within the migration scenario: migrants, the ethnic associations representing them, students, trade unions, local and national institutions, non-governmental associations, etc. The implementation of the law was preceded by a series of decrees from the Ministry of Labour and the Home Office, which set new restrictive parameters for the granting of permits to stay. Not only did these directives change established procedures and practices, but they were not implemented coherently by the provincial *Questure* (the police bureaux), which were responsible for granting permits to stay to foreigners (Triandafyllidou 2003). Furthermore, in many cases the *Questure* arbitrarily anticipated some of the restrictive measures to be foreseen by the forthcoming law in advance of its actual endorsement. Let us now see how these provisions, and the way they were administered, impacted on the lives of Albanian migrants and on the various social initiatives designed to help them.

The 'Contract to Stay' and the Increasingly Precarious Nature of Working Conditions

Probably the most innovative element of the Bossi–Fini decree was the introduction of the *contratto di soggiorno* (contract to stay). According to this, a non-EU citizen is entitled to stay on Italian territory only if an employer secures him or her a regular work contract, provides suitable accommodation and guarantees to cover the travel for the return of the migrant to their home country at the end of the contact. These provisions, which represent an anachronistic return to a depersonalised understanding of migration in terms of labour supply, as with the European guestworker schemes of the 1950s and 1960s, have two different sets of implications. Firstly, they make the non-EU citizen completely dependent on his or her employer, who is now responsible both for the economic life and for the accommodation of migrants, thus increasing the potential levers of exploitation. Secondly, the enforcement of these measures involves considerable extra paperwork, an increase in administrative costs, and further delays in the process of issuing contracts, visas, etc. By making the employment of migrant labour and the acquisition of legal papers more difficult, these provisions can be seen in terms of encouraging a resort to illegal practices, such as the employment of undocumented migrants without a regular contract and the 'purchase' of contracts by non-EU migrants in order for them to 'stay legal'. The following excerpt from our interview with V., president of an Albanian association in Rome, corroborates this view:

> Even when the migrant actually gets the contract, the way contracts happen in Italy, you must know about that, right? Anyway, even when they get the

contract, they have to accept many compromises. I mean, most people actually buy the contract. Even when you have papers, it does not matter. You are subject to blackmail because you are foreign. This is the way they address you: 'Look, I am already doing you a favour now, so I can fire you whenever I want.' From the very beginning this implicit blackmail is there. You can do what you want, take them to court, anything. But you still need to survive the moment he fires you. If you go to the police for the renewal of papers and tell them you are in dispute regarding your firing, they do not renew the permit to stay. They say: 'Where is the contract?' So you need to get another job, then you get it, but you are still waiting for the outcome for the trial ... so basically, you then end up by losing the permit to stay and they kick you out.

As we argued above, the Bossi–Fini decree should be seen as an integral part of the political project of the Berlusconi government, which had the 'flexibilisation' of the labour market as one of its main priorities, and which had the effect of interrupting or 'dis-integrating' the process of stable migrant settlement in Italy. The following excerpt from an interview with the national representative of CGIL, the most left-leaning of the three main Italian trade unions, maps out some of the interconnections between the Bossi–Fini decree and the wider politics of the Berlusconi government, and draws attention again to the increasing precariousness and vulnerability of migrant workers under the Bossi–Fini 'regime'.

So, you know that the pillar of the Bossi–Fini is the 'contract to stay'. But you cannot analyse the Bossi–Fini in isolation. You have to put all of the decrees and laws of this government together to see the overall plan and the effects. Now, they want to extend the right to fire without a just cause to enterprises with fewer than fifteen employees ... this is the famous Article 18 issue ... About 65 per cent of migrant workers are employed in this kind of enterprise. If an entrepreneur knows he can fire somebody without having to prove anything and that your permit to stay is dependent on the contract ... you can be blackmailed twice ... This is what happens: I know that your contract finishes in two months and that your permit is tied to that. I call you and tell you: 'Look, I don't need you anymore because you are too expensive ... you don't work enough ... I could fire you just like that ... Unless you are willing to work for half of what I used to give you before, and I need you to do ten hours rather than eight ... '. Non-EU foreign migrants are forced to accept these conditions because, if they lose the permit, they lose everything.

All the entrepreneurs we interviewed were managing small and medium enterprises (SMEs) in the three fieldwork sites. When we asked them what they thought about the restrictive measures implemented or foreseen by the Bossi–Fini decree, most complained about delays in the regularisation of migrants or in issuing visas. Although these bureaucratic obstacles were already seen as problematic before the introduction of the new decree, the situation worsened considerably around the time the interviews were made. Many employers were also very critical of the decision to abolish the 'sponsoring visa', which they saw as the only way they could get to know *in person* the worker whom they were potentially about to employ – something they all thought was very important. From both the migrant and the entrepreneur interviews we discovered that the key mechanism of migration management introduced by the Turco–Napolitano and Bossi–Fini laws, which is based on the selection of people to be employed before they enter Italian territory, can only be made to work through a cumbersome subterfuge. All the entrepreneurs and migrants who engaged in the process of regularisation covered by the legislative arrangements of the time did so according to the following sequence. In all cases the migrant was already in Italy, usually as an undocumented worker, and was introduced to the employer by a relative or an Italian or Albanian friend. After an interview and usually a period of probation, the contract was issued and the migrant had to return to Albania, where he could then apply for a visa according to the quota system. So, the theoretical basis of the Bossi–Fini system is problematic for a number of reasons. Firstly, it fails to acknowledge that entrepreneurs, especially those directing SMEs, are not willing to employ people they have not met in person. Secondly, the current system of managed migration has not eradicated the danger of personalistic exploitation; rather it has made the personal links and liaisons between the entrepreneur and the migrant more important and strategic. Thirdly, the current system 'pretends not to know' that the majority of migrants who are being regularised are already in Italy, and forces them to return to the country of origin. This increases the costs and risks of regularisation considerably, and is only really viable for neighbouring countries such as Albania, but not for more distant countries. The following excerpts from interviews with entrepreneurs expand on these points:

> I think the current system is absurd ... regularising an irregular migrant means forcing him to return to Albania and come back here, which is not always possible ... they are usually very scared of all the risks involved. Because if they go and their application is rejected, then they have to come on a speedboat for a second time, and that is very dangerous and expensive. I think that people who are already in Italy and find a job here ... we should integrate them. Perhaps we should repatriate only people who are found without papers and a job. But those who are working ... they should just get papers here in Italy and stay. (Firm of market traders, Molfetta)

> *How did you begin having foreign workers?*
> Well, they just started coming here directly – the first ones – then it was word of mouth. There are also employment services and training centres contacting us. But word of mouth is key. Black people are all brothers; Arabs are all cousins!
> *And Albanians?*
> They are all friends or relatives (laughs).
> *What kinds of difficulty have you encountered in employing them?*

> Well, the way papers are issued nowadays is a real waste of time. They make you go round and round between offices. I went there to follow the application of an employee of mine – it took us two years! Also, now if you find somebody to regularise, you can't. You are supposed to employ people you don't know and I am not prepared to do that. I like to look people I employ in the eye, this is a small firm after all. (Plumbing firm, Modena)

The Bossi–Fini decree also determines a minimum number of square metres per person living in the same dwelling as one of the main criteria for the renewal of the permit to stay and, even more significantly, for granting requests for family reunification. Although this rule was already foreseen by the preceding legislation and is aimed at improving the living conditions of migrants, the modifications introduced by the Bossi–Fini decree made these criteria more binding. The introduction of stricter criteria can end up by fostering further marginalisation and vulnerability of immigrants, especially if there are no complementary measures of economic support to bridge the gap between the housing market and the wages of the migrant population. Many employers were very aware of this problem:

> Albanians do not have more problems than others in finding a place to live ... which does not mean that they have no problems! We have had to help so many migrants to find a house ... they don't get it without a word from us. I think there should be special provisions for this, that the state should buy housing from private landlords and give accommodation to migrants ... but authorities are never interested in helping entrepreneurs in Italy. (Metal-working firm, Modena)

Furthermore, by restricting the rules regulating visas for family unification, the Bossi–Fini contradicts Italian entrepreneurs' opinions that migrants with families are more trustworthy than single people.

> *Why do you prefer employing people who live with their family?*
> Because they tend to be calmer and more settled, they see work as a resource for the family, not only for themselves. They are already integrated, more stable. The new directives limiting family reunification are very negative for us. When Albanians have a family, they are better behaved, better workers ... When they have a family, they sort of have to [integrate], I mean children go to school and that in itself makes a lot of difference. (Heating firm, Modena)

The inability of the Bossi–Fini legislation to respond to the 'real' needs of the Italian labour market leads to widespread practices of manipulation and circumvention of the legislation. As many interviewees put it, this was the only way 'to get things going'. These strategies of resistance against an inefficient and discriminatory legislation took two main forms. The first was a manipulative alliance between the employer and the employee to allow family unification to happen.

> *How is the demographic composition of the Albanian community? I am interested in particular in the processes of family unification. Is it on the increase or not?*
> Definitely. Although I should not be able to tell you this as we are supposed to know only about work-related cases. Anyway, there is something I can tell you ... If we look at the overall number of work-related applications for regularisation, there is a very significant increase. If you look carefully at the certification attached to the form, you can see that usually there is a relative involved ... already employed by the same firm. Very frequently, you can notice that two entrepreneurs request the husband and the wife, respectively. What happens is that people need to renew their permit to stay, but because the direct avenues of the family unification visa are closed, they manage to get a work visa instead, as it is the only possible way now. (Interview, Ufficio Provinciale del Lavoro, Lecce)

The second practice, which can be called the 'get the papers and run' strategy, is usually more unilateral and sees the Albanian migrants instrumentalise current legislation to get papers and then disappear into the grey economy in the local area or move to where they can enjoy better conditions within the formal economy, usually in the North. For these reasons, the phenomenon of getting papers and then 'moving on' was much more frequent in the South than in the North.

> Molfetta was the first to receive Albanian migrants back in 1990. We witnessed the very first arrivals, and were able to integrate over sixty immigrants. They had no experience of working in the sea, but they settled down. And after two or three months, once they got the permit to stay, they abandoned us. Therefore we decided to contact the Italian embassy in Tirana and request fishermen, specifically. This was also a negative experience. They all had the right CV and papers but I am not really sure where they got those papers from. Some stayed, most got the permit to stay and moved to another sector. There is a lot of pressure to migrate in Albania and many people are taking advantage of the opportunities to leave. We began working with a recruitment agency in Tirana and we discovered that the director was charging people a lot of money to get them to come here. He even arranged contracts by which he was entitled to 6 per cent of the Italian wage. When we decided to stop this contact we were even threatened by these people. (Fishing cooperative, Molfetta)

> At the moment, people enter Italy within quotas and with contracts with people who could benefit from that scheme ... but then after two days they go and work for another firm, where they are really needed. I think the only way is to allow for a high degree of flexibility ... people arrive at the border, they are issued with a permit to stay and a reasonable amount of time to stay in Italy and find a job and a place to live. (Interview, *Ufficio Provinciale del Lavoro*, Modena)

This last remark introduces the next section, which deals more specifically with the way in which Italian migration legislation, by focusing on a very restrictive interpretation of 'managed migration', fails to respond to the reality and complexity of the needs of the Italian labour market, and of society in general.

Mismanaged Migration: The Politicisation of Migrant Quotas

From the above, it is clear that the Bossi–Fini law, and Italian migration legislation in general, fail to address the reality of Italian society and economy. In an essay written in 1997, Umberto Eco problematises the difference between migration and immigration, claiming that 'we only have immigration when the immigrants (admitted according to political decisions) accept most of the customs of the country into which they have immigrated, while migration occurs when the migrants (whom no one can stop at the frontiers) radically transform the culture of the territory they have migrated to'. These definitions allow Eco to claim that 'what Europe is still trying to tackle as immigration is instead migration' and to underline that 'Europe will become a multiracial continent…whether you like it or not' (Eco 1997: 98–99).

A key implication of Eco's argument is the necessity to accept the scale and magnitude of the phenomenon we are dealing with when we talk about 'migration'. Whilst the quantitative magnitude is often exaggerated in the public perception, migration is a deeply and continuously historical phenomenon which is bound to transform the texture of European societies in the same ways in which European colonialism transformed non-European ones or the arrival of new 'barbarian' populations transformed the Roman Empire. This historical reality check enables us to see that current Italian migration legislation is based on three misplaced and utopian assumptions:

- that the mobility of entire populations and the geopolitical, economic and social transformations encompassing migration can be managed through a quota system selecting people before they enter the territory of a country (i.e., Italy);
- that an electronic interface could substitute the existing, largely informal, practices shaping employment in Italy;
- that it is possible to consider migration as a work-related phenomenon, without taking into consideration the fact that the arrival of new populations will, sooner or later, radically transform Italian society.

As far as the first of these assumptions is concerned, the Bossi–Fini law can be seen as further radicalising the founding belief of the Turco–Napolitano law – that migration can actually be contained and managed within set immigration quotas – by abolishing what was perhaps its most advanced measure: the possibility to enter Italy to seek work through the warrant of a sponsor. Although this latter measure was criticised by the Bossi–Fini advocates for implicitly legitimising personalistic relations, in fact it acknowledged the way relationships of trust and solidarity actually work in Italian society (and amongst migrant groups), offering migrants the concrete possibility to search for work and find adequate solutions for their economic survival within one year. Many entrepreneurs and representatives of economic sectors were very critical of the impossibility of regularising migrants already in Italy. They suggested that only more flexible solutions – accepting the arrival of migrants as a structural feature of Italian society – are the answer. This interview exchange, with an employer of migrant workers in a metallurgy firm in Modena, is typical (but unusually cogent) of many we recorded on this topic:

> *What do you think about the current changes in the legislation regulating migration?*
> Well, it is a very bad moment. They don't really want to help us. All of the changes introduced are not making things easy for employers or workers. All of these rules put us in great difficulty. Before, there was more flexibility and support for small and medium enterprises. There are so many people who are working here without documents. Why not give them the possibility to regularise first? If they are already working, well, what is the problem? It is not a big deal. After all our country will always face irregular migration. We can try to limit it but it will never work. Italy is for Albanians what America was for us. The difference is that the United States always had migration and never stopped it; we, since we have been one of the last countries to have a big flow of emigrants, still need to learn how to manage immigration.

The rigidity of the quota system as the only way to regulate migration to Italy further exacerbates the condition of social exclusion and the potential for exploitation Albanian migrants are subject to. The dramatic decrease in the number of illegal passages across the Otranto Strait, celebrated as an uncontroversial success of the 'toughening' of the Italian position on migration by the propaganda of the Berlusconi government, did not correspond to an improvement of living conditions in Albania, even less so with a decrease of the migratory pressure from Albania to Italy. As a result, prices for illegal passages and forged documents increased. Migrants had to find even more money to be able to access Italy, thus becoming even more vulnerable to exploitation by traffickers and abuse in the labour market once in Italy.

As far as the second utopian assumption listed above is concerned, during the period of fieldwork, the Italian Ministry of Labour and Social Policy agreed to carry out a project, with financial aid from the European Social Fund and logistical support from the International Organization for Migration (IOM), to identify and promote initiatives in Italy for the vocational training and insertion in the labour market of migrant workers from the Balkan region and North Africa. Albania, Morocco and Tunisia were the three main target countries. Another objective of the project was to improve and develop the Computerised Database of non-EU Workers (*Anagrafe Informatizzata dei Lavoratori Extracomunitari*, or AILE), a database which promotes the matching of supply and demand within the (migrant) labour market. At the end of the project, in September 2001, IOM had selected a total of 5,038 Albanian workers, who were 'potentially employable by Italian entrepreneurs through AILE' (IOM 2001: 7) amongst over 26,000 candidates.

Although the main aim of the project was to provide technical assistance to the Italian government in setting up 'an innovative mechanism for the management of labour migration' (IOM 2001: 13), the IOM report does not indicate whether the database was actually used by Italian firms for the recruitment and employment of migrant workers. However, from our interviews with U., who was in charge of the training section of the programme at IOM's Rome office, it appears that during the phase of selection of potential participants there was a dramatic decrease in illegal passages to Italy. In his words:

> At the time, data about the number of people entering Italy illegally indicated that illegal crossings from Albania had almost stopped, which shows that whenever legal ways of entry are available, people tend to choose the legal way. And it is logical, since it is safer and cheaper ... The problem here is that our country had a schizophrenic behaviour in this respect because the range of measures introduced just a few years ago, like the sponsor visa or the visa for work search, which was basically a self-sponsor visa, they are going to be scrapped now. Now the only instrument seems to be the database, but it is difficult to see how this will work. It is difficult to believe that it is possible to select and appoint somebody exclusively through a database ... Perhaps it can work with manual or very unskilled jobs ... but definitely not for qualified staff. This is a very important limit of this scheme. The computer cannot allow you to have enough information to make that choice. And not all Italian entrepreneurs are familiar with this method or with information technology yet. The only way is the combination of the database with other measures which proved successful in the past, which for Albania was the visa for work search.

These considerations were further corroborated by A., an Albanian employee who, at the time, was managing the selection process of Albanian migrants and their entry into the AILE database. According to him, the idea of using a database as the sole interface between migrants and their employers was not successful in its main purpose:

> Technically speaking it went well. We were supposed to select and train people to be inserted into the AILE database ... and that is what we did, and I think that part of the project was well thought out and well implemented. However, the most important aspect of the project was to get these people to come to Italy. This is what did not work. I think that the whole idea of the use of the database presupposes a level of organisation of the Italian labour market which does not correspond to reality. Also, the database was too complicated for most Italian entrepreneurs. And the whole system was linked to the quota system, which seriously underestimates the number of migrants that are needed by the Italian labour market ... The AILE database never worked; it is not enough to create an instrument without promoting it thoroughly. The AILE was only networked with maybe five provincial centres. We did not have the possibility

to investigate what happened at the ministerial level, but the AILE database definitely did not work in enabling labour demand and supply to meet.
From our own interviews with entrepreneurs it is very clear that they would not consider employing somebody through a database and would only employ somebody they either meet directly or who is introduced by somebody they trust ...
Well, I understand that; I remember once we were in Padua and there entrepreneurs were looking for specialised welders ... there was a strong demand, but they did not even want to hear about the database.
How many people were selected and how many found work through the AILE?
Well, at the end of the last year we were able to select more than five thousand, of whom I think two thousand were able to get to Italy, some with us, some individually ... We cannot know how many of these were actually selected through AILE ... I mean technically speaking the AILE is up and running and any entrepreneur can search for profiles and use it ... but there is no way to verify that it is working.

Finally, regarding the third of our list of 'unrealistic' assumptions set out above, questions concerning the family linkages and responsibilities of worker migrants were not even mentioned, let alone there being any acknowledgement of the need to integrate foreign workers and their accompanying or joining family members. This only compounded the myth of being able to plan the Italian labour market's demand for migrant workers without reference to the specific characteristics of the Italian economy, especially its 'informal' nature in many sectors. Even before the restrictive measures foreseen by the Bossi–Fini law, the system of managed migration envisaged by the pre-existing legislation was entirely dependent on the ability to read and interpret the needs of the Italian labour market. Whereas the first quota decree of February 2001 authorised the entry of a maximum of 50,000 non-EU workers and of 13,000 non-EU seasonal workers, the definitive quota decree of 18 May 2001 added 20,000 more seasonal workers, thus making 33,000 seasonal migrants authorised for 2001. Interim quotas for the following year specified 33,000 seasonal migrants for the Centre-North, supplemented by 6,400 for the South. Beyond these quantitative fluctuations, the qualitatively most relevant aspect of the quota decree, for the purpose of our research, was the political interpretation of the role of migration in Italian society, and its relation with the unemployment rate nationally and in different Italian regions. As far as the first aspect is concerned, the 2001 decree distinguishes for the first time between seasonal and non-seasonal workers and allocates more quotas to seasonal workers, compared to the 2000 decree. As far as the second aspect is concerned, the quota decree for 2001 mainly allocates migrants to the Centre-North of Italy, in consideration of the high number of Italian unemployed people in the South in comparison with the rest of the country. These political considerations had, in turn, very pragmatic repercussions on the criteria according to which quotas were allocated, and thereby on the lived experiences of the Albanian migrants we interviewed. This was backed up by testimonies from three categories of interviewee: migrants themselves, Albanian association spokespersons, and representatives of key Italian institutions. A good example of the last category is the following conversation with the Modena-based representative of the Italian Confederation of Agriculture (CIA), which had to deal with the consequences of a substantial underestimation of the quotas for 2002, and of delays in the release of the ministerial directives.

> *Do you think the way quotas are managed responds to the needs of the agricultural sector?*
> Absolutely not ... I mean, perhaps the idea is good, but the number is completely underestimated and badly distributed. As CIA, we sit at the table where these quotas are negotiated ... Now, talking about the famous 33,000 seasonal workers for this year ... we were only allocated 450 people, and this is one of the provinces of Italy with the lowest unemployment rate ... Then, different places need people at different times, depending on the type of agriculture. The arrangements in place nowadays are too slow and we cannot provide farmers with the labour they need in time. I mean the labour is here already, but we cannot employ it because they have no papers. This year the situation was very confusing. In mid March there was a disposition authorising more seasonal workers, because in the South too they need people. Many of the people who are already here are actually registered as unemployed in the South and they get here or anywhere where there is work ... they are not unemployed, they are simply registered with the employment office. So, those who were authorised in March all went to the South ... and we did not have enough workers. Around half the requests were not met in Emilia-Romagna ...
> *So what happens with the people who are already here?*
> We need them but we can't do anything because they are not authorised to work. They approach entrepreneurs, usually. Then the employer comes here and asks me to regularise the worker within the quota system. When I get the authorisation, I give it to the person who, naturally, is here; he then needs to go home and get the papers in order to enter legally!
> *It seems quite an ordeal for everybody ...*
> What can I say? I accept that there needs to be some form of control, but limiting people's entry so harshly is not right. We could not even meet half of the requests ... they were all regular requests, which would have enabled many people to work and many employers to solve a problem. They were complete with the offer to provide accommodation and everything. Why don't they approve them all? Why don't they let them all come? After all these are not renewable permits ... so after nine months they would have to leave ...
> *Well, I guess the fear is that they will not go back ...*
> Look, this is a false problem because, as a matter of fact, they are already here!

People working in Albanian associations and in institutions dealing with the entry of migrants into the labour market reported many instances of preventive and arbitrary implementation of some of the measures associated with the Bossi–Fini law. Some of these problems impacted on Albanian migrants quite negatively, as the following excerpts show.

> My permit to stay will expire next year and I am getting worried as the new immigration law is already making everything more difficult. I have always worked like mad since I came here, but never with a contract ... it is very unfair because, although I have been working twenty-four hours a day, I will not be able to keep my papers with this law. I do not have a regular job ... who has in Italy anyway? The difference is that I need to have one in order to stay. (M28, Rome)

> The main problem here [in the South] is the size of the irregular economy. I mean, if you want the permit to stay you must have a contract ... and nobody here has a contract, not even the Italians! Now things are getting worse as they are not giving permits to stay for one or even five years, as it used to be. Now even if you buy a contract for a permanent position, as many migrants have to do, they only give you a permit for, say, five months. This is really a problem for migrants, especially those working in agriculture, because if your contract finishes in November, which is a dead period here, what are you going to do – people don't make new contracts in November and then you become irregular. (Interview, Employment Office, Bisceglie)

The policy of prioritising seasonal over permanent workers and of allocating seasonal quotas to the regions with the lowest unemployment rate rests on two key assumptions, both false. The first is that, in conditions of high unemployment, migrants 'steal our jobs', occupying positions that would be sought by Italians. This was refuted right at the beginning of this chapter, citing Gavosto et al. (1999) and Venturini and Villosio (2006). The second is that the more than 220,000 non-EU migrants registered at Italian employment offices at the end of 2000 are actually unemployed. As far as this assumption is concerned, Emilio Reyneri (2004: 83), a noted expert on the Italian labour market, writes that, in the South, 'those registered as unemployed are in fact part-time, in transit from one short-term contract to the next, or irregularly employed'. Our research corroborates this argument. Take, for example, this excerpt from an interview at the provincial employment office in Modena:

> To be honest, it is very difficult to understand what this new law requires ... As I have heard, one of the main ideas is that before non-EU migrants access a work possibility here in Italy we should make sure that there is no availability of Italian workers for that position. Well, I think such an idea is unrealistic – they should really provide employment offices with the necessary infrastructure to enable verification of the employment status of those who are registered. As things are at the moment, it is very difficult to do this with registered Italians or migrants ... can you imagine with those who are not registered, who are a lot? ... Can I make a provocative suggestion? I would give the permit to stay to everybody, because that is the only way you can actually monitor them, help them, make sure they are not involved in illegal activities.

These remarks are very much in tune with those of the Lecce representative of the Ministry of Labour, who stressed how the relation between migration and the official unemployment rate must be contextualised within the relative weighting between local formal and informal economies.

> There is a contradiction: on the one hand there are many people registered and looking for work; on the other there are many employers looking for people in agriculture and other manual jobs ... and a high level of unemployment. Why? Let us say how things are ... [Italian] people who are unemployed ... they all have good education ... a university degree ... they are not really available for manual jobs. That is why there is a demand for foreign manual labour, Italian people are no longer available to fill those positions. This is the reality. Then, another contradiction. Once non-EU workers get to Italy, they register with the employment centres and stay there for a long time. Then, when the fruit-picking season arrives, employers come here and look for non-EU workers, but find none. The reason is this. There are people who entered Italy with a permit to stay for work, they needed a job to enter and then they abandoned it, maybe because the work relationship did not work out or because they wanted to move to a different and better occupation. They then register with us, otherwise they risk being sent home, as the law requires them to be registered. That is why the situation is as it is.
> *How about Albanians?*
> Well, we have many of them and they fit the bill perfectly. What entrepreneurs say is that they tend to change jobs often, that their mentality pushes them to do so.

The Reality of Migrants and the Informal Economy

How true is the last statement in the previous quote – that Albanians are somehow predisposed to change their jobs more often than other workers? In fact, many employers and (non-Albanian) key informants semed to subscribe to this view. But evidence we collected from dozens of Albanian migrant workers revealed that there was no inherent resistance to commit to a long-term occupation; particularly in the South, their only route to a legal status was to move from one casual job to another, and wait for an opportunity to regularise to come up. In synthesis, the job-hopping nature of Albanians' working behaviour should be seen as the consequence of:

- the irregular pattern of employment in agriculture and construction, which are their main sectors of employment;
- the fact that, as they strive towards settlement and integration, they usually stop wherever acceptable living and working conditions are met;
- the inefficiency of migration legislation in responding to the basic needs of migrants, such as family reunification, or the need to circulate between Italy and Albania as a way to maximise the economic benefit

of migration, i.e., by earning in Italy and living as much as possible in low-cost Albania.

Clearly, in relation to the last point, allowing a circular or to-and-fro pattern of migration is only possible if migrants have access to legal documentation. Moreover, this regime of mobility would allow Italy, and not only Albania, to maximise common benefit from the encounter between the needs of the Italian labour market and Albanian labour supply. It is difficult to see how the rigid tying of the permit to stay to contracted work would increase the level of social inclusion and decrease the vulnerability of many migrants.

In order for the links between migration and the Italian labour market to be regulated in a way which would benefit all involved, the system needs to start by acknowledging, or at least tolerating, what is already working. More specifically, any attempt to regulate migratory flows should be based on a realistic assessment of the important role of the informal economy in the economic performance of Italy as a whole. Of course it is true that the informal economy is the background for higher levels of exploitation and inequality, but it is also true that 'coming clean' is not economically sustainable for all entrepreneurs and in all sectors. This interview with a key informant who works for the CGIL trade union in Lecce, shows how the issue of the regularisation of migrants is tightly linked to the size of the informal economy and the general economic situation of southern Italy.

> *How can a trade union like the one you are working for help non-EU migrants?*
> They mainly work in the black economy ... and this has got many implications for their integration, because a regular job is the only key to have a permit to stay and to move towards citizenship. This is how we can help them, helping them negotiate regularisation with their employers ... Which also means explaining to employers all of this; why it is important to offer migrants the opportunity of regularisation. But migrants are even more afraid than employers, because they are afraid of losing their job ... the possibility to take care of themselves ... to stay here ... everything. But the phenomenon of the informal economy is very complex, it is a structural aspect of this society. We are trying to help firms 'come clean' through programmes facilitating their gradual emergence out of the informal economy ... These programmes were quite successful with the textile firms. They are in a vulnerable position because they are subcontractors working for other firms ... they work in a condition of very strong competition. I am talking of very small firms ... textile workshops, that decide to open their own firm in the basement. Their contractual power is also very low, vis-à-vis the people commissioning work, who are usually in the North ... So, what happens is that they cannot afford to pay the whole of the national contract ... so at the end they collapse, they close down ... Then there are firms which do not even try to emerge ... because they are not in a position to offer the full contract ... The culture of working in the black economy is very rooted here.

In Lecce, we also interviewed a key representative of the provincial employment office who had been involved in a Ministry of Labour research project on the relationship between immigration and unemployment. The following excerpt from the interview offers an analysis of the interconnection between migration and the local informal labour market in this province:

> We got estimates of the unemployment rate reaching 29 per cent! This is ridiculous … we would have riots in the street if that was the case. The real issue here is the habit of working in the black economy … and this is the same with Italians and with foreigners. So the ministry in Rome says: 'Why should we authorise the entry of more workers from outside the EU, when people from the EU who are currently unemployed could be employed instead?' This is a misunderstanding, and I will explain why … Look, these are the letters we sent to non-EU people who were registered here as unemployed. We sent out more than 1,000 forms and only 297 were filled in and sent back. The rest were returned to us by the post office.
> *How do you explain this?*
> Well, many things. Firstly, these people are not here – Lecce is an area of transit. Or they have a fake employer … a fake address … because they need this to get papers … but they are not here. The problem here is that they are now trying to stop authorising new entries for seasonal work on the basis of the official unemployment rate. This is a very big misunderstanding because even when we mail registered Italian people … they don't turn up … if the job is manual or the pay is very low. I am convinced that a non-EU worker will never be in the position of stealing a job from an Italian. They occupy all of the segments of the labour market that Italians refuse … They [the Italians] will never do it because whether they do that job or not will not alter the living standard they already enjoy.

Although references to the presence of irregular employment and of 'lavoro nero' were more common and open in the South and in Rome, entrepreneurs in Modena mentioned that employment in the informal economy was still taking place. To quote one of them: '[T]he cultural habit to work in the black economy still exists because it is convenient for both the employer and the employee … there is a convergence of interests and this is what makes it happen'.

Conclusion

The housing and work narratives presented in this chapter clearly demonstrate two things. First, they reveal complex patterns of structural integration and differential inclusion/exclusion according to the model we introduced in Chapter 1. Second, they show how the migration experiences of Albanians have been shaped by their encounter with the structural problems and dynamics within Italian society. These dynamics range from the economic to the political and cultural, and are expressed at both national and regional/local levels. The most important are:

- the delay with which Italian society acknowledges that the 'migration turnaround' of the late twentieth century – from emigration to immigration – corresponds to a fundamental and irreversible economic, social and cultural transformation;
- the irresponsibility of the Italian media in their representation of migration-related issues;
- the lack of affordable housing for migrants and the constraints posed by current protectionist legislation in the rental market;
- the size of the Italian informal economy and its complex relation on the one hand to global competition and on the other to regional production systems;
- the existence of key (usually unskilled) sectors of the Italian labour market which are no longer filled by Italian workers and which can only be met by migrant labour;
- the difficulty in managing migration exclusively through an impersonal *a priori* selection of migrant workers in relation to the presumed needs of the Italian labour market based on misleading unemployment rates.

Whilst this chapter has analysed the implications of these structural dynamics in relation to Albanians' experiences of accessing work and accommodation, in the next we explore the ways in which they have negotiated their identities in the wider social sphere.

Notes

1. The broad analytical framework of Chapters 5 and 6 follows that sketched out in an earlier paper on Lecce and Modena (King and Mai 2004). Our account in this book develops the earlier analysis in several ways: it adds a third field location (Rome); it uses different interview materials; and it goes into considerably more analytical depth and detail.
2. For a study which provides a lot of detail on Albanian migrants' generally high levels of educational experience and language skills see Da Molin and Carbone (2001: 34–40). Based on surveys of migrants arriving in Apulia during the 1990s, these authors found that 10 per cent were graduates, another 53 per cent had high-school diplomas, and only 6 per cent had not progressed beyond elementary school. Two-thirds of the 376 migrants surveyed knew Italian, and a quarter knew English; significant numbers (5–10 per cent) also knew Greek, French and Russian.
3. Amongst studies which document the generally rapid upward occupational mobility of Albanians in Italy, see the useful volume edited by Ugo Melchionda (2003); especially useful, in terms of comparative perspectives with our own research, are the regional chapters on Apulia (Perrone 2003),

Latium (Messia 2003) and Emilia-Romagna (Mottura and Marra 2003). A rather more negative impression of Albanians' occupational mobility is given by Kosic and Triandafyllidou (2004), based on a comparison with Polish immigrants.
4 Much the same conclusion can be applied to the experience of Albanians in Greece. Indeed the similarities between the labour-market experiences of Albanians in the two countries are remarkable. Almost identical stories of exploitation, abuse and under-payment are recorded in Athens by Lazaridis (2004) and in Thessaloniki by Hatziprokopiou (2003, 2004). Likewise there is much evidence for occupational advancement over time; as we found in Italy, a crucial turning point is the acquisition of legal status, which in Greece only occurred after 1998.
5 We are referring here to the so-called *centri di prima accoglienza*, or 'centres of first shelter'. These were (and are) emergency accommodation centres for migrants when they first arrive in Italy and have no possibility of accessing 'proper' housing. Such reception centres are intended as temporary solutions, with the idea that migrants will move out after a few weeks or months, but may end up by staying much longer because of the lack of feasible housing alternatives. Many of these centres are made up of temporary, prefabricated huts, rather like soldiers' barracks. For a powerful descriptive analysis of one such centre, inhabited by Moroccan migrants in Bologna, see Però (2001: 171–176).
6 Vincenzo Romania (2004: 62–63) elaborates on the 'young Albanian women = prostitute' stereotype with the revealing story of Francesca, who arrived in Italy on a legal tourist visa. She came from a well-to-do Albanian family and had just graduated in Law from Tirana University. Her aim was to enrol at Venice University and develop a career in Italy. Staying temporarily with her cousin in nearby Padua, she suffered a serious fall whilst doing some cleaning work on a balcony. The police and hospital authorities refused to believe her account, convinced instead that she was a prostitute who had been beaten up by her pimp.
7 See Aurighi (1997). However, this 'model' of left-oriented solidarity and efficiency towards migrants has been exposed as something of a myth, at least as far as the region's capital city Bologna is concerned, by Però (1999, 2001, 2002); see also Grassilli (2002).
8 The same comparison was found in Daly's (2001) study of Tunisian migrants in Modena and Sicily.
9 At the time of our fieldwork the government in power was the *Casa delle Libertà* coalition led by Silvio Berlusconi, media tycoon and the richest man in Italy. The context for the emergence of this right-wing coalition was the collapse of the corrupt and discredited Christian Democrat dynasty in the early 1990s. Of the three main components of the new coalition, *Forza Italia*, the creation of Berlusconi, had an ambivalent ideology vaguely inspired by neoliberalism (except when it came to protecting the many personal interests of its leader); its members were an amalgam of ex-Christian Democrats, ex-Liberals and ex-Socialists. The *Alleanza Nazionale*, fronted by Gianfranco Fini, brought together post-Fascist elements and the more conservative ex-Christian Democrats; its political programme emphasises Italy's Catholic heritage and celebrates Italians' entitlement to security and their national(ist)

identity, with particular reference to the 'threat' posed by immigrants. The *Lega Nord* is a federation of regionalist parties geared to greater autonomy (sometimes bordering on secession) for Northern Italy. Its leader was Umberto Bossi until serious illness removed his vulgar charisma from the political stage. The Northern League's political programme and propaganda are marked by an overtly racist attitude towards immigrants.

Chapter 6

SOCIAL EXCLUSION AND INTEGRATION

The same ambivalences and contradictions experienced by Albanian migrants when accessing the job and housing markets were encountered in their narrated experiences of broader social inclusion and exclusion. Following once again Heckmann's (2005) fourfold typology, whereas in the prior chapter we concentrated on *structural* integration, here we follow the three remaining dimensions – *cultural*, *interactive* and *identificational*. This chapter will explore these wider *spaces of social interaction and identification* in several realms: Albanian migrants' relationship with Italian state institutions and associations, with fellow Albanians and with the Italian population at large. Our analysis sees these social negotiations as positioned between, on the one hand, the narratives of criminalisation circulated by the Italian media and, on the other side, specific Albanian cultural, social and historical settings.

What Do You Do in Your Free Time?

The View from Albania

Answers to our question about how Albanian migrants spend their time out of work and family commitments reflected the plurality of lifestyles which emerged out of the sociocultural monotone of the communist years, but also the tough conditions of being a migrant worker – a member of a vilified minority – in an often racist Italian society. Earlier research by one of the authors (Mai 2002a) shows that the spectrum of lifestyle choices in contemporary Albania is characterised by the conflictive juxtaposition of three main lifestyle-related discourses: the *normal* lifestyle, the *family* lifestyle and the *modern* lifestyle. First, then, we return to the set of interviews with *prospective* migrants in Albania – young people who were contemplating their future migration trajectories in the context of their dissatisfaction with life in late-communist and early post-communist Albania. Here are two typical examples of the discourse about normality and how such a 'normal' way of life is seen as most, or only, achievable by going abroad:

> *How would you define your lifestyle?*
> Normal.
> *What does this mean?*
> Just live life as it comes ...
> *Where do you think you can best follow this lifestyle?*
> There is no question: abroad, Italy, maybe more in the UK. (M18, Durrës)

> I don't tend to have a particular way of life ... I like to be always just myself – normal. I would like to be a journalist, I mean a good journalist ... I don't think I will be able to achieve this in Albania ... not at all. (M25, Durrës)

The other lifestyle most interviewees referred to was the 'modern' one, which was often very ambivalently disguised within the 'normal' lifestyle discourse, as in the following example:

> My preferred lifestyle ... would be to live quietly in this world ... to live normally, a normal life ... it is difficult here ... But it is normal to want to live according to your desires ... I mean, to live in a modern way ... to do what you want ... that is exactly what young people want nowadays ... to work during the day and have fun at night, even after 10 p.m. To go out and have fun with girls. (M20, Tirana)

However, a modern lifestyle was also seen as something different from a normal one. Following a modern lifestyle is associated with a more radical critique of the family-centred model of life and of the patriarchal gender roles which are hegemonic in Albania. In particular, younger people associate a modern lifestyle with the freedom to go out at night, to be completely independent from parents and from a conservative mentality and, most of all, to live together with their partner without marrying:

> A modern lifestyle is the only way life is now – not like here. To have fun, to go to the disco with friends, to kiss in the streets, to wear what you want without being discriminated against. (M16, Durrës)

> A modern lifestyle for me would be to have a beautiful place, a life ... Well, to tell you the truth, I think that the best example of what a modern lifestyle would be here in Albania is the possibility to live with a partner without being married. I don't think my parents or relatives would ever tolerate something like this. Once I spoke to my aunt, quietly, not to shock her ... I told her 'I want to go and live with my boyfriend ... without marrying'. She just could not believe it. I pretended to joke, but in reality I meant it. (F17, Tirana)

Many interviewees considered the desire or the possibility to lead a modern lifestyle as a key factor in the development of their migratory project; they spontaneously made the link between the search for alternative lifestyles, migration and foreign media consumption. They saw migration to the 'West' as the only way to follow both a modern and a normal lifestyle: to 'be' who they want and to 'develop' themselves.

> I think a modern lifestyle here in Albania is a very important concept for young people, who want to live their life like other Europeans. The possibility to follow a modern life is the main reason for the emigration of young people because life here is very repressed ... and very passive, while life outside is more active. Young people nowadays have in their blood the desire to do something different ... I mean, media have changed our culture ... about the way you see life ... we do not see it anymore from inside the four walls of our places ... but in relation to activities ... we give a lot of importance to our education ... the possibility to have an interesting job and to develop ourselves. (F17, Durrës)

The third discursive set is the reference to a 'family' lifestyle, employed almost exclusively by older interviewees in Albania. These usually criticise and dismiss the 'alternative' character of the modern lifestyle in the name of a 'family' lifestyle which is seen as allowing people to be truer to their selves.

> I have no particular lifestyle ... I think that building and taking care of my family is my lifestyle ... This modern lifestyle is not for me. Young people think that wearing new clothes is modern ... they think that by following that lifestyle they are somebody ... but in fact they become nobody. But having said that, the possibility to enjoy this so-called modern lifestyle has been a very important factor for Albanian young people's desire to migrate abroad. (M29, Durrës)

> Personally, I don't like this modern way of life at all. I am a bit conservative ... I see myself within my family and that is about it. I don't like being surrounded by too many people or having too many acquaintances ... not to mention those discos ... I like to lead a simple life, in the evening going out for a pizza with my wife, going back to work ... maybe during the weekend going to the beach, without having to create such a sensation. This is my way of life. (M28, Tirana)

The View from Italy

The diversity of answers to our question about the way Albanian migrants in Italy spent their free time partially mirrored the scenarios we have just outlined. Actually, the majority of migrants stated that they had very little free time left to enjoy – their lives were subsumed by work and/or study. However, if one looks more closely at the actual activities Albanian migrants engage in when free from work, one finds that, as with all social groups, consumption and leisure patterns vary considerably across the spectrum of age, gender and education-related differences (Perrone 2001: 151).

In general, people who are married tend to refer to a 'family lifestyle' when describing the activities they usually engage in. They spend their free time meeting other Albanian families, often in their own flats, and tend to go out for a meal on special occasions.

> We have Italian friends but mainly Albanians. They come and visit us fairly often and we do the same. Family-wise we go to the park together with the children. (M33, Modena)

> I like Italy a lot because it is very quiet. It's not like Albania where there are so many problems. I'm here only to work. I go to work from home and then go back. That's the only route I cover. It's difficult to meet other people if you have this kind of life.
> *Do you socialise mainly with people from your own country, with Italians, or with other migrants?*
> More with Albanians because I work with them.
> *What do you like doing together with other Albanians?*
> I do not go out with my Albanian friends because I prefer to save money in order to support my family in Albania and buy a home here in Italy for the time they will come to settle here. My family is in Albania. (M34, Rome)

As these excerpts indicate, the economic condition of the migrant and his/her commitment to the family are key factors shaping lifestyle choices. Within the 'family' lifestyle framework, Albanian men may go out for a meal or a drink with their Italian male work colleagues, but the level of involvement in socialising is heavily conditioned by linguistic competence and the amount of money they have to spend. Therefore, undocumented migrants, or those whose life trajectory is shaped by the need to support their families at home in Albania, have very different experiences of leisure and consumption. They tend to have less contact with fellow Albanians, and even less with Italian people (see also Perrone 2001: 151).

At the other extreme of the leisure and socialisation scenario are students, who can rely on networks of friendship and informal socialising offered by the educational setting. Although there may be some initial settling-in problems, which were noted in the previous chapter, in general their lifestyle does not differ much from that of their Italian fellow students. Here are two examples of student interviews:

> *Do you socialise mainly with people from your own country, with Italians, or with other migrants?*
> It's indifferent for me. I usually go out with Albanians and Italians.
> *How are your relations with Italians?*
> Sometimes good, especially with students. At first, it is quite difficult to socialise with Italians at work or in the university but, after some time, the relationship improves.
> *What do you like doing together with other Albanians? Is it different from what you like doing with Italians?*
> Normally I go out for a drink or to the cinema, both with Italians and Albanians. (M23, Rome)

What do you do in your free time?
At the weekend I go out with some friends. I stay with friends or I watch TV here at the student residence ... In this hall of residence there are about forty Albanian students.
And how are the relations between Albanians and Italians here?
The relations are very good, there are never conflicts. In fact, I have a lot of Albanian and Italian friends and I get along very well with both. (F21, Bari)

However, many younger interviewees differentiated in that they usually shared more home-based and 'traditional' activities with fellow Albanians, and engaged in more non-home (and expensive) forms of entertainment with their Italian friends:

What do you do here in Italy in your free time?
In the beginning I used to go to the gym because I didn't have many friends then. Later on, through my cousin, I got to know some girls and boys.
Were they Italians?
Some of them were Italians but many Albanians as well ... With the Albanians we do things we used to do just like in Albania, going to coffee shops, chatting at home, etc. Whereas with the Italians we go to clubs, bars and have a different type of entertainment. (M21, Lecce)

The level of stigmatisation Albanian migrants are subject to is an important background factor behind the choice of their lifestyle and in the establishment of friendships. Significantly, the circulation of criminalising narratives about Albanian migrants creates a prejudice against fellow Albanians which does not encourage interethnic relations and pushes some Albanian migrants instead to relate mainly to their Italian peers.[1]

Do you socialise mainly with people from your own country, with Italians, or ... ?
I socialise with Italians. The only Albanians I socialise with are my family.
Why?
I feel a bit different towards Albanians now.
Do you mean different from when you were in Albania or from when you first arrived in Italy?
From both I would say. Now I see things in a different perspective and things are for sure different here.
...
Are you proud to be Albanian?
About some issues, yes ... but on another level, no ... I am affected by what some Albanians do. I feel bad for the bad things that Albanians do here in Italy. They do things that other immigrants don't do ...
How does that affect you?
I lose my trust and respect for them. (F30, Modena)

Have you been helped by other Albanians here or by Italians?
I have led a rather reserved life. Especially since ... because of the work I do [interpreter for the police] I don't trust Albanians. For the fault of some stupid people, even honest workers and people have to pay. But the fact is that I only

trust some [Albanian] people. For all the others, often I don't even want to make it clear that I'm Albanian. (F31, Lecce)

It is on the basis of these relations of aspired proximity, friendship, inclusion and rejection that similarities and differences are identified between Albanians and Italians. Typically, within these narratives of sameness and otherness, Italians are criticised for not keeping their word and for being unwelcoming hosts; the counterpoint is frequent reference to the Albanian traditions of *'besa'* (the honour associated with keeping one's word) and *'mikpritie'* (hospitality).[2]

> *What do you like and dislike about Italians?*
> I like the fact that they are hard workers. Italy is also very beautiful. I don't like the fact of not keeping their promises. They just talk ... but it means nothing.
> *Are they different from you in this?*
> Yes, we promise when we know our ability [to deliver]. The given word is the given word [referring to besa]. According to the Kanun I must kill even my son to keep the given word. (F31, Lecce)

> *Are there any particular aspects of the Albanian way of life which contrast with the Italian way of life?*
> To keep one's word. This is an important value for Albanians that is superficially observed by the Italians. Italians are not able to keep the promises they make. This is the first impression I had when I first came to Italy and that still persists. (M29, Rome)

Gender and the Family

Other differences perceived between Albanians and Italians related to family values and respect for parents and the elderly. These differences influenced, to some extent, the degree of social contact between the two nationalities, including prospective marriage partners.

> *What do you like about Albania? Are there values that you stress particularly?*
> I like the way we respect older people. We treat them better. Here it does not make any difference whether people are young or old. I was raised by my grandmother who lived and died in my house. In the family of my fiancé [who is Italian] I get worried about these things ... in spite of their big houses and servants his friends have put their aged parents into homes and abandoned them there. (F27, Lecce)

> *What Albanian elements would you like your children to maintain?*
> I want them to respect their families and create families with Albanian traditions. I think Italians are a bit wrong in the freedom they give women. They think we mistreat Albanian women. But I wouldn't agree with what some of the women do here. For example a woman going out on a Friday with her friends (both females and males) while she is married and has family commitments. (M33, Modena)

Gender was also a significant area of comparison between Albania and Italy.[3] Albanian migrant women generally praised Italian culture for the greater equality it allowed women to enjoy, but male interviewees expressed unease about this aspect. Let us first listen to a selection of female voices.

> *Are there aspects of Italian culture that you don't like and which are in contrast with your culture?*
> No, because here in the Mediterranean the cultures are nearly the same. There are a lot of Albanian values and expressions that are the same in Italy. I find the same things.
> *But where is the difference?*
> Well, the family for example. My parents always lived with my brother even after he got married. And then women ... In Tirana it is different from other parts of Albania; they have their space, but in other areas they are very oppressed. A very good thing about Italy is that women have more space than the men, even if they still take more responsibility [more than men] for the children and the house.
> *What do you like or dislike about Italian people?*
> They talk a lot and do not keep their word.
> *And what do you like?*
> They are softer, more gentle ... Albanians are very strict ... particularly men, while Italian men behave much better with women. (F46, Lecce)

Although most women had positive views of gender relations in Italy, some were critical of the way that gender equality seemed to undermine the authority of men and the performance of the parental function within families. The following quote represents this view:

> Well, I think that in Italian families there is too much freedom. Sometimes it is difficult to understand who is who ... fathers, mothers, children. This is negative because there is no communication, everybody on his own ... Maybe it is because men and women have achieved a very high level of equality here in Italy.
> *You make it sound as if it was a bad thing ...*
> Well, it is not positive. I am not patriarchal but I think men should be respected as men and women as women. Men should take the responsibility for the family; it is his burden ... and the woman must help him. She should be at the same level, as far as dialogue and exchange of opinions are concerned, but not in terms of responsibility. (F32, Lecce)

Although many younger interviewees already had an Italian partner, or did not preclude this possibility in principle, the field of love between Albanians and Italians seemed to be the one ridden with most difficulties, for both women and men. Key factors explaining this tension included the prejudices existing in Italian families, the difference in the level of control exerted by Albanian families on young daughters, and the economic inequality between Albanian and Italian young people. An example:

Have you ever had an Italian boyfriend?
Yes.
What is the main difference between having an Italian or an Albanian boyfriend?
Well, the difference is that an Italian man ... he will never be able to understand some things. For example, what happens in a family or if you speak about Albania ... Even if he tries, he can't.
Can you give me an example?
Well, for instance that you can't go out, or that you have to be back by a certain time ... they don't understand. (F21, Lecce)

Meanwhile, Albanian men tended to complain about the level of emotional and economic investment required by having a relationship with an Italian woman. However, the main problems Albanian men seem to face are peer competition from the Albanian side and the family pressure and prejudice on the Italian side: a difficult combination to manage.

> I tried to go out with an Italian girl but it was too difficult. They need so much time to dedicate to them, which I don't really have. I work as well as go to university so I can't manage a relationship like this ...
> *What is the difference between an Italian girlfriend and an Albanian girlfriend?*
> I would prefer having an Albanian girlfriend.
> *Why is that?*
> Because I want an Albanian wife.
> *Why not an Italian?*
> I think it's purely because Italian girls are fond of entertainment and for them that is top priority, whereas an Albanian girl would see things a bit differently.
> *Isn't it because Italian girls are very independent?*
> Yes, for this reason as well. (M24, Lecce)

> I have had a lot of Italian girlfriends but all of these relationships finished ... In most cases I was the one to decide to end it as I could not take it any more. Often, girls were influenced by their parents, who were ready to judge me without knowing me well ... just because I am Albanian. On the other hand, my Albanian friends gave me a hard time because they were jealous of the fact that I kept going out with Italian girls. (M30, Molfetta)

Access to Institutions and Social Services

In analysing the way in which Albanian migrants managed and rated their entitlement to various public services and valued the quality of their participation in society in general, two key aspects stand out. Firstly – at least at the time the interviews were carried out – Albanians appeared to be the migrant group making the least use of the facilities and services offered – as was the case with state employment services, noted in the previous chapter. Secondly, service providers and employers reported having been confronted with unusual pressures and demands when working with Albanians, who were often portrayed as aggressive and ungrateful when they felt they were entitled to rights, benefits and services. We will deal with these two issues one by one.

A Low Profile, and a Record of Unfair Treatment

As regards the lower 'visibility' of Albanian migrants in social and health support institutions, this could well reflect the increasing efficiency and importance of family-based networks in granting support and advice. This hypothesis is corroborated by the fact that most interviewees indicated that it was usually their families and friends who provided them with the support and advice they needed. Moreover, this matches the way Albanians tend to rely on friends and family for access to the labour and housing markets, as we pointed out in Chapter 5.

> Well, I think they are particularly well integrated ... the only thing they did not know anything about was the employment office. They did not even know it existed, but they knew very well how to find work through friends and family, by word of mouth. (Interview, employment training centre, Bisceglie)

> Albanians tend to refer to friends and family when they need something ... they are not used to go to the state for help ... They always find an Italian friend who tries to help them when they are in need. (Interview, Albanian Democratic Association, Bologna)

This last excerpt underlines another potential explanation for Albanians' relative autonomy from systems and initiatives of social intervention, when compared with other groups – their experience of the state as a problem rather than a response to their needs. This makes them more inclined to rely on 'privatised' family and friendship-centred networks of solidarity (Perrone 2001: 150).

Our interview material revealed very few cases reported of unfair treatment in relation to Albanians' access to health, education and social services. However, especially in Rome and in the South, some instances of inappropriate behaviour from the police were mentioned, such as this typical example:

> Once we [the interviewee and other Albanian friends] had an argument with some Roma [football club] supporters and the police came. When the policeman came to me he was quite relaxed but when he realised I was Albanian he asked me for my documents immediately and began to be arrogant – he changed his attitude when he realised where I was from. This was by no means the first time ... It happened frequently that public officers became much rougher towards me after they realised I was Albanian. (M44, Rome)

Leaving such cases of overt discrimination aside, people interviewed both in the North and in the South complained about the lack of information and the level of discretionality practised by the various foreign citizens' departments (*Uffici Stranieri*) of the Italian police. This, too, is confirmed by other research (Kosic and Triandafyllidou 2004; Triandafyllidou 2003). Here is a typical example from our file of interviewees.

> In general there are lots of problems for us with the police. They delay applications for working and residence permits a lot … The bureaucracy … it's the second most important thing (the first being media stigmatisation) for the migrant living here in Italy … I am here since 1991 and I have seen the numbers [of Albanians] grow … especially here in Apulia … The office is the same as it was ten years ago, it doesn't change, at least the reception office. They receive people as if they were animals … that is the way they treat them … Sometimes they say 'Shut up or else we'll send you back to Albania … '. Just like that, openly. Policemen have their difficult days – probably also because of Albanian criminals – and they vent it on us … They keep you going there for six months for something that should take a week, telling you, 'Come back tomorrow', a thousand times. And you waste your time, don't go to work, you miss lessons at school, just because they want you to wait in a queue … Often they are not even aware of important changes in the law and we have to get information somewhere else and tell them, because otherwise they will keep finding excuses to send us back and drag things out even longer. (M49, Lecce)

The most interesting and by far the most common answer to the question about experiences of discrimination when accessing services or in public situations points to the pervasiveness of the stigma towards Albanians in everyday attitudes amongst Italians. The following are just two examples of this experience.

> Yes, once it happened that there were two old ladies talking about Albanians in the bus and saying that they never pay for the ticket, etc … But she wasn't aware that we were listening … I felt really bad listening to them talking like that. (F25, Bologna)

> … the expression 'shitty Albanians' … You hear it everywhere. … Once we were at the marketplace and a lady shouted: 'Today we have great savings, take advantage of it now because, after the shitty Albanians come, there will be nothing left!' She said it two or three times. (F55, Lecce)

We will deal with the capillary nature of the *albanophobic* discourse in the next main section of this chapter, where we will focus our analysis on the specifically Albanian experience of Italian racism. Returning now to the main focus of the present section, we pick up the second issue flagged up earlier.

An Over-Assertive Attitude?

Many Italian public servants and employers reported being confronted with a rather demanding and sometimes impulsive behaviour when dealing with Albanian migrants. Whether this perceived 'attitude problem' is purely a reaction against the discriminatory treatment mentioned above is a moot point, for it could also reflect some deeper sociocultural traits of Albanians in the context of their dual experience of life under communism and the chaotic exit from the strictures – but also the certainties and guarantees – of 'the regime' (Mottura and Marra 2003: 62). Before we explore this question, we present a selection of voices from Italian public servants and employers about Albanians' attitudes and behaviours, as they see them:

> Well, there can be problems … and sometimes the cultural mediation can be very useful to understand some specific aspect of their behaviour …
> *Can you give me an example?*
> Well, in many Albanian families we noticed a very strict definition of gender roles, with women in a very submissive role … Then there was a very pressing request from Albanian families to access health services and the housing services. Albanians tend to expect a lot from us, they expect to receive everything and if they don't [get what they want] they react in a very violent way and start making accusations through newspapers. (Interview, *Ufficio Stranieri*, Modena)

> Albanians have integrated very well. I think Italians took their clothes off for Albanians and that cannot be denied … It's just that Albanians seemed to think that they were owed these things. They used to go to Caritas and say … 'You must find work for me'. Hold on a minute, I am here to help you get some rights, but I don't really have to give you work, money, houses. This is a great problem because Albanians have developed quite a reputation for being difficult … for demanding too much … and of course for their involvement in criminal activities, which some of them do. (Priest, Greek Church, Lecce)

> In comparison to other migrants, Albanians tend to be less sociable, more confrontational. If a colleague intervenes to explain something or to solve a problem, they react negatively. They only accept orders from the boss … they do not accept that there are managers for different sectors. We had the same problems with southern Italians when they first started to come here to work … Then they got used to different systems and it was OK. (Entrepreneur, Modena)

How can we interpret this Italian discourse about Albanians' aggressive behaviour? On the one hand, the representation of Albanians as impulsive and violent fits the canons of *albanophobia* we analysed in Chapter 4, and can be seen as consistent with an overall representation of Albanian migrants as the embodiment of backwardness and lack of civilisation. If one follows this line of analysis, it is possible to argue that it is because of their higher level of understanding and integration within Italian society that Albanians can afford to be confrontational and 'raise their stakes' instead of subserviently accepting their subaltern condition and complying with the constraints and injustices imposed by the system.

The following passage might explain the way Albanians' aggressive and demanding approach can be seen as part of the success story of their dynamic integration in Italy, which is jeopardised by their 'bad reputation', disseminated by the Italian media. This interviewee also supports the finding of Mottura and Marra (2003: 63) and Perrone (2003: 149) that Albanians are apt to challenge authority more readily than other groups because of their higher level of 'union' or 'rights' culture, and their overall political competence.

> *Are there differences in relation to how migrants adapt to local society? How about Albanians?*
> Their integration is very easy because, thank God, Albanians know how to speak Italian when they come ... However, compared to Tunisians and the Senegalese, Albanians are more isolated.
> *Do you think that the bad reputation they have is a problem for their integration?*
> Yes, it influences it a lot, but direct negative experiences reinforce the lack of trust this population enjoys. Once they are integrated, they expect much more than other migrants. They also tend to be more trade-unionised than Italians.
> (Interview, fishing cooperative, Molfetta)

But this is only part of the explanation. On a wider historical scale, the way that some Albanian migrants are perceived (rightly or wrongly) as rather aggressive when dealing with Italian institutions and employers must be seen as reflecting a complex process of social and economic transformation, not an essentialised, shared 'cultural' trait. Albanians' difficulty (but also success) in dealing with conflict, inequality and entitlement in Italy is just a minor detail of the overall process of post-communist transformation, characterised by the exit from a social environment marked by the celebration – and ultimately the frustration – of universal entitlement. We described this painful process of transformation in some detail in Chapter 2.

One final point. The perception of Albanian migrants as aggressive when demanding access to services might be exacerbated by Italian people's cultural construction and experience of 'help' and 'charity' in relation to their understanding of migrants' position in Italian society (Perrone 2003: 151). Many interviewees pointed out how Italians' racism towards them was sometimes expressed not overtly, but via paternalistic and condescending attitudes and episodes. Here are two eloquent examples of this which move us towards a more extended discussion of racism.

> *Do you think Albanians are treated fairly in Italy?*
> I think they are not treated fairly, because, except those who deserved it, like pimps, thieves, criminals, the rest of the population did not get what they deserved ... There is a continuing refusal to accept that an Albanian can be an intellectual ... that an Albanian can be a doctor with the same level of competence, and not only from the legal point of view ... This is a very difficult

thing to accept, believe me. I have the impression that Italians can help you and very generously too ... but when you reach your objective, they are not very happy about that. They are happy about having helped you, but maybe not so much that you got that far. (M23, Bologna)

So many people were surprised that I was aiming very high, this somehow bothered them. I was studying a lot and I did not want to get 28, but 30 [the top mark in the Italian university system]. I always wanted and expected the maximum from and for myself. I am a perfectionist by nature. People who see you exclusively as a subject of their charity cannot accept that you might aim for something more or different. I was surprised, but not really upset by these episodes. They were telling me that I was too ambitious, that humility wasn't part of me ... this is true, I am not humble and I started realising that 'charitable' people liked more submissive kinds of people. I wasn't their cup of tea ... I am very proud, I mean, all Albanians are proud, they do not want to be pitied at all, they'd rather not eat than accept to be treated like a *poverino* (poor wretch). Your concept of charity is very different from ours ... Many times people came to me with very run-down and worn-out things and asked (she now uses an ironically compassionate voice), 'Do you need these, dear?' I mean in Albania nobody would give you this kind of thing as a gift ... and since these charitable people are not used to taking no for an answer, when you thank them and say, 'No', they think, 'How dare she not take these things? Who does she thinks she is?' I mean, first of all, I always thank people and then ... Why do you have to do it in front of twenty other people? Do you really want them to see you how 'good' you are or do you want to help me? I think for this kind of people I was 'too much', but I think these people do not know what it means to really respect people. (F31, Lecce)

The Specificity of Racism towards Albanians

I once heard a mother trying to scare her child by telling him: 'Stop it because the Albanians will come and get you if you behave like this!'. (F25, Bologna)

As we have already seen, Albanian migrants' overall experience of social inclusion and exclusion in Italy has been continuously filtered through of a thick veil of prejudice affecting all spaces and moments of social interaction. Although many Albanian interviewees did consider Italians' attitude towards them as openly 'racist', the majority felt the need to point to the 'indirect' nature of Italian racism – referring to it as 'light' or 'gentle', as something which is experienced 'in the air' rather than in a direct or confrontational way. The following three interview clips with Albanians in various parts of Italy reveal some of the ways in which this subtle (and sometimes not so subtle) 'cultural racism' manifests itself.

I was never insulted directly but I have sensed it very often, it is in the air. Even in the place I work in, I mean, it is a very official and educated environment, but I feel I always have to fight and to prove that what they think about

Albanians is wrong. This is very tiring ... I am really sorry to hear or to see that Albanians are objects of contempt, I feel sorry but I am also very fed up. (F31, Lecce)

What do you think about the treatment of Albanians in Italy?
We are considered in a particular way. We are Albanians and that's enough. If you start talking with a person and you say you are from Albania the conversation usually turns towards specific arguments such as prostitution and criminal affairs. You can never establish a normal conversation on these occasions. I never met a person who started talking about food or culture with me after having known I was Albanian; the conversation immediately turned to the problems I just mentioned. This bothers me a lot. (F30, Rome)

Remember that story of the girl who said the Albanians killed the family, which was not true ... Or for example when that lady was blaming the Albanians for the stealing that went on in her home. She later found out that it was her nephew who wanted to buy drugs and kept stealing her stuff. I heard somebody say that there were twenty million Albanians in Italy! I told him that are only three million people in Albania ... how can there be twenty million in Italy? (F25, Bologna)

The Albanian 'Monstre'

Practically all interviewees, independent of their educational level, class, gender and age, referred to the direct responsibility of the Italian media for creating a stereotypical construction of the Albanian migrant as the embodiment of all the features characterising 'uncivilisation'. Many of the narrated experiences of negotiation of Albanian migrants' social identities that we collected demonstrated how, in its current use, the term *'albanese'* has lost its simple denotative function and is now used as an insult between Italians, as the following interview clips show.[4]

Coward like an Albanian ... you are dressed like an Albanian ... Albanian basically is the adjective, Albanian is the adjective Italian people use when they show their contempt for something. (F31, Lecce)

I read in the Zingarelli Italian dictionary that the sentence *'fare l'Albanese'* (behaving as an Albanian) is translated with the concept of behaving in a criminal way. That explains a lot of things. Of course this adjective is wrong. I remember an interview with an Italian girl in the United States regarding the concept of mafia. She was asked whether she felt like a mafiosa. There was a strong reaction in Italy to this interview: the media criminalised the interviewer. (M20, Rome)

Many Albanian people reported feeling associated with the stereotypical 'image' of a *golem* interposed between themselves and whatever they wanted to do in Italy. Whenever they try to get a better job, look for a flat, establish professional relations at work, or make friends at school or university, they encounter this cultural construction every time they are asked where they are from. The most common experience of prejudice, as noted in several earlier quotes, was an almost imperceptible change in their Italian interlocutors' expression and body language on hearing the answer, 'I am Albanian'. The cultural construction of the Albanian migrant as a de-humanised *non-person* (Dal Lago 1999) was reflected in the way many interviewees related being told by Italians that they actually 'did not look like Albanians'. The following are two examples of this syndrome:

> So what happens when you say that you are Albanian, what do people say?
> Ah, really?! That is amazing, you don't look like one!
> And how do you respond to that?
> Well, I usually say that we don't have three eyes or four ears ... and start laughing! (F21, Lecce)

> How do people react when they learn that you come from Albania?
> They don't react well. They say 'Ah ... ' and then maybe, 'You do not look like an Albanian'. Which stands for, 'You're so nice that you do not seem to belong to that people'. I'm really bothered about that because often people presuming these things do not know Albanians at all. I am fed up with telling people that I'm Albanian because I do not want to see their disappointment. I normally become red when they realise that I'm Albanian. Once I said I was Greek to an Italian who asked me where I was from, but when he replied that not many Greek girls are as nice as me, I admitted I was Albanian ... I did not want people to think that Greek girls are nicer than Albanian girls! (F30, Rome)

The Experience of Students and Younger People

It is younger people, and students in particular, who, by being much more reliant on their relations with their Italian peers in their everyday lives, seem to be more ambivalent in their strategies of self-definition. A very large proportion of interviewees were highly conscious of the specific connotation of the term *albanese* in Italian and tried to avoid it by saying that they were 'from' Albania or from a specific town in Albania, rather than declaring themselves 'Albanian'. M., a student in Lecce, recounted the following episode:

> The first time I realised there is something wrong with the word 'Albanian' in Italy was when I had my first Italian boyfriend. He was from a village near here ... maybe it is better here in Lecce, but out in the villages there is a lot of prejudice. Well, what happened is that when he introduced me to his parents he felt like he had to explain my accent; he said, 'Tell them you are Italian, from the north, don't tell them you are Albanian'. I could not accept this and asked him, 'And what is the reason?'. 'Nothing', he said, 'I will explain later ... here if they know that you are with an Albanian girl they worry ... it is not so much about the Albanian girl, but since the girl is Albanian we don't want our son to

get into some strange game.' So I guess the name 'Albanian' means something to keep away from, something dangerous ... a strange game.

This area of sentimental relations was one of the most complex arenas for the negotiation of Albanianness in Italy and the one in which the majority of episodes of identity dissimulation were encountered. It was not infrequent to hear single Albanian men and women being forced to pass as Greeks or other less stigmatised nationalities in order to emancipate themselves from the prejudice they were subject to from their peers and acquaintances (cf. Romania 2004: 92). Many, especially men, reported being left by their partners once they 'came out' to them as Albanians. Here are two examples, one where the relationship survived the revelation, one where it did not:

Have ever had an Italian girlfriend?
Yes ...
And how did it go? Were there any problems to do with the fact that you are Albanian?
In the beginning there were no problems because I decided not to tell her that I was Albanian. After knowing her better and understanding that she valued me as a person, I decided to tell the truth.
And what happened?
She was a bit shocked at first, for the lie more than anything ... But her parents ... they didn't expect to find an Albanian like me and they were very surprised. They kept apologising for the things they had said sometimes ... They knew me very well by then, I mean that was OK ... they didn't go mad ... they were only very surprised. (M23, Modena)

Once I met this Italian girl at university. She approached me herself. I was sitting on my own in the canteen and she asked what degree I was doing and other general questions ... She didn't ask where I was from but I was determined to tell her at some point if I was to see her again because I didn't want any confrontation with her later on. So one night she invites me to her place ... We were having fun and enjoying ourselves and I really wanted to tell her about my life and such things. But at that moment her flatmates came in so we left. She then kept text-messaging me and telling me how much she was attracted to me and other stuff. One day I couldn't hold back and had to tell her so I blurted it out. I never thought I could have seen anybody as stunned as she was. It was unbelievable. She didn't know what to say. She withdrew her hand from around my neck and I asked her whether she was feeling all right. I suddenly realised that my nationality disappointed her so much. I thought that was so ridiculous. I now see her just randomly and she greets me with this guilty conscience for having left me so unfairly. (M24, Lecce)

Widening the Discourse of 'Albanianness'

One of the most interesting aspects of this semantic transformation is that Italians have started using the term *'albanese'* to signify a difference *between themselves,* according to unspoken, but interiorised hierarchies of

Italianness. These racialised hierarchies were historically laid down by the fundamental opposition between a cultural construction of a Northern Italian identity in terms of efficiency, honesty and industriousness, and its Southern symmetrical opposite, connoting lack of organisation, criminality, dishonesty and laziness. Before the arrival of Albanians on the scene, Italian identity was frequently positioned against the construction of a semi-colonial internal other, the '*terrone*', the peasant, the Southerner, an embodiment of all of the undesirable features to be ascribed to an idealised national character (Mai 2003). The following participant-observation event helps to illustrate the different ways in which these labels are articulated and reflect on Albanian migrants' experience of Italian society.[5]

A group of Albanian students studying at the University of Lecce went to watch a football match where the local team, Lecce, was playing Lazio, one of the two Rome-based soccer teams. During the game, Lazio supporters started insulting Lecce supporters by calling them *albanesi di merda* – shitty Albanians. Lecce supporters replied by shouting back, '*No, albanesi di merda siete voi*' – 'No, it's you who are shitty Albanians'. The Albanian students found themselves encompassed by symbolic and discursive fields within which the adjective used to denote their own nationality, *albanese*, was associated with a doubly articulated cultural construction of the Albanian migrant.

This event can be interpreted in various ways. On the one hand the current use Italians make of the term *albanese* refers to the way in which Albanian migrants in the 1990s became the new symbolic embodiment of non-Italianness. On the other, this term only partially complemented and overlapped with already established subaltern and constitutive others, such as the Italian *terrone*, the primitive rural Southerner. Both of these dimensions have complex implications for the nature of the process of social inclusion, both in the North and in the South of the country, and deserve further exploration.

In fact, like their varied experiences of work, the identity positionality offered to Albanian migrants in Italy differed considerably between the North and the South. This became clear in the narratives of interviewees who had an experience of emigration both in Apulia and in the North of Italy. In both places, Albanian migrants found themselves trapped within a pre-existing discursive field hierarchically ordered according to culturally constructed shades of Italianness. Unlike most Albanian migrants who, if they move internally within Italy, relocate from South to North, D. had spent some time in the northern city of Brescia before moving south to Lecce:

> In the beginning, in Brescia, my Italian neighbours were very worried when I told them I had decided to move to Lecce. They advised me to be very careful with the people there. They warned me against them. When I used to live in

> Brescia I had to take the Trieste–Durrës ferry to go to Albania. In those days there was a cousin of mine studying at the university in Padua. She lived with some friends. I stayed for a night there and there was a girl from Lecce. I said to myself, 'This poor girl is going to Lecce … '. I should have never said that. And then I came here myself. I had this image of the South of Italy. Now I have changed it completely. (F30, Lecce)

However, at a national level, Albanians came to be subliminally associated with Italian southerners, both in their everyday lives and symbolically. Albanian migrants living in the South of Italy often shared the same living and working conditions as local southern Italian workers and interpreted their prejudice and diffidence as a means by which these Italian southerners could feel 'more Italian'. Many interviewees used the *terrone* discourse to fight back against these dynamics of exclusion and marginalisation.

> Once I went to repair something in a house urgently because my colleague had forgotten to go. I am sure I had taken the order correctly, but the lady kept asking my boss, 'Why didn't you come earlier? I was waiting for you!' I don't know what he replied but at some stage I heard her say, 'But I told that Albanian on the phone'. I decided to keep on working but, as the dispute was getting worse, I went downstairs and asked her, 'What is your name?' She said her name, to which I replied, 'Do you know I have a name too?' I continued, 'I heard you call me "Albanian", so how do I have to call you?'. And she repeated her name. I continued and told her, 'Tell me where you come from, because that is the way you called me'. She said, 'Ostuni, I am from Ostuni' [a small town in Apulia]. As she kept on talking in dialect, I told her, 'Tell me in Italian, or do I have to call you "*terrone*"?'. She was very offended that I called her '*terrone*', so I told her, 'Next time I come round remember I have a name and a surname. And if you call me "Albanian", I will call you "*terrone*"' … I was so angry that day. (M51, Lecce)

Countering the 'Monstre'

The students we interviewed seemed particularly affected by the stigma attached to Albanian migrants in Italy. We suggest this is for a contradictory set of reasons. On the one hand, because of their excellent knowledge of the Italian language, their legal status and their access to the many occasions of socialisation provided by the educational system, their life trajectories and social status are most similar to their Italian peers; hence they experience particularly rapid and successful inclusion, both work-wise and in the broader social context. However, the initial period, when they are first confronted with the intense stigma attached to Albanian migrants, is particularly hard for them too. Moreover, as students, they are better able to offer a more intellectual critique of the host-society stereotyping of Albanians.

We learned from our interview with the Cultural Attaché of the Italian Embassy in Tirana that Albanian students studying in Italy achieve exceptionally good results when compared to their Italian and other foreign peers. This judgement is confirmed by our many colleagues who teach at Italian universities. Of course, this can be seen as a positive influence on their work-related inclusion strategies as it encourages them to achieve and obtain more; but it also exerts considerable stress in their daily lives. Some students who were interviewed reported feeling under a lot of pressure to prove themselves to be the best in their class, and felt very distressed when they failed to conform to this role.

> *Did you ever feel unfairly treated at school?*
> Yes, in the beginning ... When I was at junior school, my classmates said that, since I was Albanian, I might infect them with some strange illness ... they always kept away from me ... I did not say anything to my mother, she was always so tired and did not need any more problems ... I mean, I used to play with them anyway, we were kids after all, but there were always these remarks and they never took me seriously ... it went on like this for three years. Once I remember there was a chess tournament and I won it just because I wanted to prove that I was also good at something ... not so much to win, but to prove them wrong, that I could be good at something too. As an Albanian.
> *Was it also positive or just stressful?*
> I think it was positive, overall. Then when I went to high school I learnt how to defend myself, because I was bigger than they were, so I showed my muscles and said, 'Have you got a problem?' and they shut up.
> *What did they used to say to you?*
> They insulted me, calling me 'Albanian' and I used to be furious about this, especially because I felt they used that word as an insult. (M17, Lecce)

When prompted about examples of the unfair way in which the Italian media have criminalised Albanian migrants, many interviewees referred to the infamous case of Erika and Omar, which we have already mentioned in Chapter 4. The following excerpts are just two in a very long repertoire of references to that (in)famous case.

> *How about when they (the Italian media) talk about Albanians, do you think it is a fair representation?*
> Of course not. We are talking about a population, about a nation. Why use the word 'presumably' to refer to Albanians whenever there is a criminal episode in this country. That's not fair at all because you can't criminalise a country and its people by always presuming that a murder was committed by an Albanian. Most of the time it happens that the true culprit was another: a husband after killing his wife and her lover put the blame on Albanian thieves ... The same happened with Erika and Omar. (M29, Rome)

> *What do you think about the way the Italian media portrays Albanians?*
> Albanians did horrible things in Italy and we are very ashamed for this ... but Italian media made no distinction and described all Albanians as criminals.

Even with this recent case, with Erika and Omar ... Now, even the worst Albanian criminal, they would never kill their brothers or their mothers. That has never happened to us ... It is not an Albanian problem and they should not say 'It was an Albanian' if they are not sure. (F55, Lecce)

As these quotes show, the case of Erika and Omar represented a very important occasion for Albanian migrants living in Italy to reposition their identities against the media's stigmatisation. Firstly, the case enabled them to expose the instrumental and biased nature of Italian media's representation of Albanian migrants. Secondly, the fact that the murder took place within a family setting, and more specifically that the traditional roles of parental authority were somehow subverted by this horrific murder, were important factors enabling Albanian migrants to carry out two counter-operations:

- to define themselves in positive terms against the 'degeneration' of Italian family values; and
- to recognise, in the resilience of family values and institutions within Albanian culture, positive aspects of identification in the context of their diasporic experience in Italy.

However, their relative powerlessness in relation to the narratives of criminalisation circulated by the Italian media means that their individual and family-based efforts can never completely overcome exclusionary practices and attitudes enforced in the wider public sphere. This limitation is important because it links to the emergence of an Albanian diasporic identity formation. In turn, this expresses itself both at an individual level, through the cultivation of interpersonal relations and family-based networks, and at a collective level, through the emergence of a broader response to stigmatisation and discrimination by the creation of Albanian 'ethnic' associations – the topic of the next section.

Albanian Associations

Reasons for their Development

In each of the Italian field settings where this research was undertaken, there were several Albanian associations, between them offering a range of initiatives and forms of support to different groups of people and needs within the Albanian community.[6] While some of these catered for specific sectors of the Albanian population, such as students, most associations had the generalised aim of supporting the needs of people establishing their families in Italy. And unlike other migrant nationalities, which often founded their associations at a very early stage of their settlement in Italy, partly as a vehicle to help them 'settle in', Albanian associations have developed rather slowly. Many were established in order to counter the consequences of remorseless stigmatising of Albanians by the media. The following extract from our interview with R., the director of *Bota Shqiptare*, an Albanian newspaper printed in Rome and available nationwide,[7] is particularly significant in this respect. His *a posteriori* reconstruction of the aims of the newspaper effectively condense those of the several Albanian associations we contacted during the research:

> There was definitely a need we were faced with … Albanians here have faced the dreadful attack of the media and things like that … So, in the beginning, we had to unmask these cases and tell the truth, that what most Italian papers had written was not right. Even when they wrote lies in big letters, nobody thought of denying it. Secondly, we also thought of keeping in touch with Albania as well, because the internet was not very well established in Italian society [in 1998 when the newspaper was founded]. So we wanted to provide Albanians with a bridge of information as well with Albania. It was also to promote the Albanian activities that happened here, the different associations, even in their small activities, it was a way of promoting and giving them space that they would never have.

These next two quotations, from the interviews with E. and B., the directors of the Albanian associations *Drita* and *Vëllazerimi*, in Bologna and Lecce respectively, enlarge further on these considerations.

> The name of our association is '*Drita*'. It was established in 1996 to help the Albanian community in Bologna. In the beginning the principal objective was to help women, as they were in a more vulnerable position in the community, especially when it came to finding a job and because they play a key role in the life of the family and in raising children. This meant addressing the problem of the representation of Albanian women and trying to show the other side of the coin.
> *Why? What was on the first side of the coin?*
> The prostitute, the woman who doesn't know anything, who hasn't got any intellectual abilities, who has no control over her life …
> *Where was this woman?*
> I kept meeting her everywhere, on Mediaset channels, in newspapers, most importantly in the mentality of Italians. I found this image almost everywhere.

> *Vëllazerimi* was born step by step … There had already been other efforts to form it ten years ago when we first arrived. But it did not last long because it lacked organisation … Now conditions have changed, most Albanians have stable jobs … The moment has come to create something. Living here, even if we are able to have many of the things we wanted, we can never forget that we are Albanians. When we saw the way television kept exaggerating things we felt we had to do something about it … in order to show that not all Albanians are like that. That is why we created this association, to build a positive image and show the real face of emigration to both Italians and Albanians, and for the future of our children.

This last remark points to yet another important aim of Albanian associations: to provide alternative, positive elements of identification for

Italians and Albanians alike, but especially for the sake of Albanian children who were born in Italy or were taken there at a very young age, who face very high levels of marginalisation, stigmatisation and isolation, especially in the context of education. As a response to the cultural construction of Albania as a place and a society lacking moral values, and to the campaign of de-humanisation of Albanian migrants waged by the Italian media, Albanian associations celebrate respect for the elderly and other family-related values of Albanian culture as positive aspects of differentiation from Italian culture and society.

Furthermore, new occasions for the celebration of Albanian identity established themselves as important initiatives for creating a feeling of belonging to a community. For example, most Albanian associations have revitalised national anniversaries such as 'Albanian flag day' on 28 November, which has become an opportunity for migrants to meet and talk about the varied experiences of 'being Albanian' in Italy, and simply to have fun together.

> Well, the association [*Vëllazerimi*] was born because we wanted to let the voice of Albanians be heard, particularly hearing the newspapers and TV speaking so badly. And then there was a precedent ... I have organised the celebration of Independence Day every 28 November. This is the sixth year that I do it.
> *But in Albania, did you celebrate it?*
> Everybody celebrates it.
> *What do you usually do on this day?*
> We invite everyone who wants to come, take our flag and kiss it. After that we recite Albanian patriotic poems, sing our national hymn, eat together, dance and sing. It is more an Albanian thing, but we also invite Italians ...
> *Do you enjoy more celebrating it here or in Albania?*
> I think more here ... I feel more about national pride here. (F46, Lecce)

However, migrants who arrived more recently, and in particular students, seemed to be far less interested in the celebration of family values offered by Albanian associations; instead they appreciated the greater level of freedom available to young people in Italy.

> *Are you a member of any Albanian associations?*
> No, I am not. I don't trust these cultural associations. It's not that I don't care but I don't go in general.
> *Do you like Italy?*
> It depends. There are things I like and I dislike.
> *For example?*
> I like it that I am much freer than in Albania. Those [Albanians] who are here live with the same mentality as in Albania, even my parents. (F21, Lecce)

The final reason for creating an Albanian association was in order to resolve specific issues Albanian migrants encountered in their everyday lives, such as access to regular status, housing and the labour market. The

Albanian association *Illyria* in Rome was particularly oriented towards problem solving rather than the celebration of a shared cultural identity. Unlike most 'culturally oriented' associations, *Illyria* had quite a clear left-wing political agenda. It was particularly focused on issues of legalisation, which it claimed as having facilitated for Albanian migrants though the organisation of regular public protests.

> *What is the main aim of this association?*
> Defending the rights and representing the problems of migrants. We aim at doing that by providing information. We do not want to take the place of people in solving their own problems, just enabling them to do it themselves.
> *And what kind of problems do Albanian migrants encounter in Italy?*
> The main problem is regularisation ... we try to offer migrants an opportunity to be regularised.
> *What results have you achieved so far?*
> I think our association played an important role in decreasing the number of undocumented Albanians in Rome ... I am basing this on a comparison with other Italian regions. Before we started protesting, there were more expulsions in Rome than in the rest of the country; now it is the contrary ... This is a political result, which we achieved through protests – they understood that Albanians can be united. And they gave in. They authorised the quotas for the regularisation in 1998. If we had not protested, we would not have achieved this. (V., *Illyria*, Rome)

Political Relations

Establishing the actual impact of the public protests organised in Rome by *Illyria* on the awareness of statutory bodies such as the *Questure* towards the problems of the regularisation of Albanian migrants would be impossible. However, the example of *Illyria* remains unmatched in Italy and points to the difficulty Albanian associations have in finding a space and a voice within local settings that are politically charged. Although there are now several Albanian associations in Italy, they are usually highly competitive, fragmented and therefore vulnerable to being instrumentalised by Italian social and political actors. This is what happened in Lecce, where *Vëllazerimi* got caught up in a game of local power-politics around the housing issue. The city's centre-right administration subcontracted many of its 'duties' towards migrants to *Lecce Accoglie* ('Lecce Welcomes'), an ideologically leftist organisation and information centre working for the cultural and economic integration of immigrants. Whilst *Vëllazerimi* tried to work with the 'official' powers in the town hall, the director of *Lecce Accoglie*, who wanted to portray Lecce as a racist city which closes its doors to migrants, voiced the following sharp critique about the Albanian association:

> The problem with the Albanian association is that it does not represent the Albanian population. I know for sure that the vast majority of the Albanians

> who are here do not know this association ... This is an association made up of very presumptuous people, with a much higher level of education than the rest of the community. They are very defensive and unwilling to cooperate and show some respect for people who have been working in the social field for such a long time ... They came here with such arrogance, telling me all about integration and how to use my money ... When I first heard that there was an Albanian association I was very happy because I think that their bad reputation derives from a very pronounced individualism – the inability of two people to say the same thing ... I am saying two because they always come in pairs; I have never seen more than three Albanians together.

This strategy of patronising delegitimation, stressing the lack of representativeness, was countered by B., on behalf of *Vëllazerimi*, in this description of the way that his association's attempts to collaborate with local bodies have been based on a broad quest for democratic consultation and transparency:

> We organised a public demonstration together with the Municipality of Lecce, which was very popular. Then we cooperated with the Province, by contributing to the drafting of a document which suggested ways to improve policies involving migrants ... We did it all together, with other members of the provincial consulting body. The document was later approved by the provincial assembly and we were very happy about that. In general, I think we did well. Because a voice defending the interests of Albanians was established out of nothing. Now people know that there is an association defending the rights of Albanian migrants. And then there are all the parties we organise, training for migrants, the leaflets ... We are known, not only to Albanians but to Italian bodies as well. That is where we wanted to get – some form of unity. We are trying to do things in a transparent way. We collect signatures before showing any idea to the authorities, to make them understand that it isn't just an initiative of a group who wants to be more visible.
> *How do you divide work within the association?*
> There is a director, then we discuss with all the members. I am the legal representative. The vice-president is a woman. She is also responsible for women's issues. Then there is another person who is in charge of legal matters ... Another who knows more about employment ... We have done a lot to be where we are and we want to be here for a long time.

The problem of relating to the political context of Italian migration-related initiatives, resources and institutions was very prominent in the life of Albanian associations. Whereas *Vëllazerimi* in Lecce 'chose' to take sides with the municipality and the province within a very polarised local scenario, in Rome *Illyria* chose the autarchic route, by not making any binding alliance with any large Italian organisation in order to safeguard its autonomy as much as possible – the Enverist way!

> We try to keep away from just helping people ... because that is the best way to lose your autonomy. What we do is provide information and apply political

pressure. The moment you start providing assistance to migrants, you are forced to cooperate with institutions in a different way. I would rather not depend on people paying for services, and be autonomous. At the moment the association lives through personal subscriptions. Maybe in the future we will cooperate more with Italian organisations like trade unions ... But not now. (V., *Illyria*, Rome)

The View from the Italian Side

On the Italian front, most interviewees, when asked about their knowledge of Albanian associations, emphasised their ephemeral and competitive nature. Key interviewees underlined how relations between Albanian migrants in general were characterised by a higher degree of diffidence and mistrust than existed in most other migrant groups. On the other hand, when there are direct interpersonal relations of friendship or family affiliation involved, Albanians showed high levels of kinship solidarity.

> There are two associations here in Modena that sometimes are on good terms and sometimes not ...
> *What problems do they encounter?*
> Well ... I think it is a general problem of mutual trust. They seem to have a sceptical attitude towards institutions, but also amongst themselves. At the same time, there is a lot of solidarity when it comes down to people who have a personal relationship, friends and in particular members of the family. Otherwise, if there is no previous contact there is no feeling of solidarity. From what I have been able to see, it is a bit early to talk about an Albanian community, although there are groups that get together, through family affiliation. (Director, *Ufficio Stranieri*, Modena)

> The Albanian community is not very cohesive. It is different from others, as far as we can understand ... In general, they don't seem to like helping each other here in Italy ... there is a sort of closure when it comes down to dealing with problems and difficulties ... There is a diffidence towards institutions in general, and if you combine this with the lack of solidarity within the community ... You can see that it is not simple working with Albanians ... Many young people, when I ask them if they go out with people from their own country, the classical answer is 'I am not going with Albanians'. They would rather be with Italians than other Albanians. (Interview, Social Services, Lecce)

These considerations seem to be yet another discursive strand of the Italian cultural construction of Albanians as the embodiment of 'uncivilisation', according to which this time they are somehow culturally unable to form communities, associate and act collectively. The alleged incapability of Albanian migrants to take collective action and create organisations is mirrored in the parallel discourse about their inability to express interethnic solidarity, except when they are bound by privatised liaisons such as family affiliation and pre-existing close friendship

(Romania 2004: 10). The following excerpt from an article published in *Limes*, a well-known Italian geopolitics journal, on the Albanian 'non-community' in Rome, is more an exercise in the *albanist* discursive repertoire (see Mai 2003) than an attempt to explore the complexity beneath the myth.

> The Albanian community in Rome does not exist. Not in the sense that there are no Albanian migrants in the capital city. On the contrary, but the Albanians living in our capital have almost no relations with each other, they do not have a community ... Those arriving fresh from Albania can only find a friend or a relative to help, host and feed them for the first months. As for the rest, very limited contacts exist with fellow nationals. Not only is there no reference point, but there is also no meeting point. Albanians living in Rome are ... in villages of the hinterland or in outer areas of the capital city, but never next to one another. They often choose the same area, the same street, but they don't live close [as neighbours]. They don't go to the same bar, nor the same square. They stay amongst themselves, mostly in a family setting ... The only cohesive groups ... are the Albanian criminals, running the prostitution racket in Rome. (De Bonis 2001: 273–275)

Given the racist undertone of these observations, whose basic message is that the only interest bringing together Albanians is criminal behaviour, their hesitation in forming collective associations hardly comes as a surprise. This is all the more important when one thinks that this article was published in an otherwise relatively progressive and informed journal. Not only is this article part of the myth-making industry that acts as a self-fulfilling prophecy, it also implicitly refers to unspoken and internalised hierarchies of civilisation, according to which 'civilised', 'modern' and 'Western' social groups are allowed to be cosmopolitan and individualistic, while others are supposed to form 'communities' and enjoy their own traditions. In fact, if one substitutes 'Albanian' with 'Italian', and 'Rome' with 'New York', and travels back in time to the 1920s, the relation between the hierarchies of civilisation and the process of strategic differentiation structuring the argument of this article become very clear. Interestingly, many interviewees made the association between Italians' emigration to the United States and their own experience of stigmatisation by Italian media.

> People only get to see the bad side of Albania ... Albanians are represented very badly and this is quite surprising because the Italians in America went through similar things, so people should understand. (M30, Lecce)

> But think, for example, when Italians went to America for the first time. What did the Italians do? Things like the mafia, drugs ... It's the same thing, identical. Italians should not speak like this because they have had the same experiences. If it was unfair for them then it should be unfair for us too, no? But that is not the way it is ... I don't understand. (F22, Lecce)

Thus, some of the considerations articulated above can be seen as fitting perfectly with the process of 'de-civilisation' that Albanian migrants are subject to in Italy, and as consistent with the *projective disidentification* of Italians' own supposed 'amoral familism' (cf. Banfield 1958) on the Albanian semi-colonial other. Alongside the evidence presented in the rest of this study, the following quotes seem to knowingly resist and challenge this stereotypical and demeaning representation of Albanians as incapable of interethnic solidarity. These voices present a much more nuanced, complex and therefore credible interpretation.

> *Do Albanians support one another in Italy?*
> Yes. They do help each other in Italy, as they do in Albania. The nature of Albanians pushes them to help their compatriots, though adaptation to Italian society may change their character a bit. (M29, Rome)
>
> *Do Albanians help each other here?*
> Yes.
> *More than in Albania?*
> I think more.
> *Did they ever help you?*
> Almost everybody. After my brother died ... everybody helped me. Economically and spiritually. Not only me, but also my mother and my family, and it is still like that. (M30, Lecce)
>
> *Do Albanians support one another in Italy?*
> Yes absolutely. For example if my cousin were to come here I wouldn't let him stay in the street or with no place to sleep. (M30, Modena)

The above interview clips counter the Italian stereotype of Albanians as an 'atomised' group of migrants lacking community cohesion. Many interviewees do indeed confirm the family-based and interpersonal nature of solidarity and social relations amongst Albanians. But others reflect an attitude of widespread diffidence towards 'unknown' fellow Albanians. They point out that one of the reasons why Albanians are careful in establishing relations with other Albanians is the need to undertake a form of selection, according to criteria of personal compatibility, but also to avoid jeopardising their efforts toward social inclusion by getting entangled with the 'wrong kind' of Albanian. The following excerpts express similar takes on the issue of Albanian migrants' diffidence.

> *How are Albanians behaving here, I mean how do they relate to other Albanians?*
> They are a bit diffident, because you try to get somewhere and you are afraid that by knowing other Albanians all your efforts will be sabotaged. (F31, Lecce)
>
> *How about Albanians, do they help each other here in Italy?*
> Well, yes, but not like other communities.

> *Why is that?*
> Here you don't have your friends or neighbours like in Albania, you have the Albanians you found here ... your friends are scattered all over the world. Most of my friends are now abroad, some in Italy, some in America, some in Greece. The Albanian people I got to know here I met through my [Albanian] girlfriend, who had already selected them ... I mean, Albanians here help each other, but they all have their own problems to take care of. However, they help each other less than other communities such as the Chinese or the Moroccans. I don't know why, maybe it's got to do with the experience of communism, which made us very diffident. (M30, Lecce)

From our earlier discussions, the issue of Albanian diffidence towards other Albanians can be seen as the result of the partial internalisation of the Italian discursive construction of the Albanian *golem*, i.e., of Albanians as the epitome of non-civilisation and immorality. However, the readiness with which this internalisation has framed Albanians' self-perception in collective terms can only be fully explained by engaging once again with their specific history and culture, and the way in which these were transformed across the exit from communism.

Searching for an Albanian Identity

The complex ways in which Albanian national culture had been articulated and appropriated by the pre-1991 communist state mean that it is difficult for Albanians in Italy to find positive elements of national identification with which to confront stigmatisation at a collective level. Moreover, the new individualised nature of Albanian identities, which stems from the rejection of the communist experience of enforced and abusive collectivism, is a very important obstacle hampering the establishment of Albanian associations and undermining a collective response to stigma. This is a first key factor behind the fragility and fragmentation of Albanian associations. It is not by chance that it is usually the younger people, whose 'migratory projects' are often different from the family-based life trajectories, and who oppose the authoritarian and repressive values which are hegemonic in Albania, who are the least interested in associating under the 'Albanian' banner, as these two interview extracts demonstrate:

> *Why do you think Albanians seem to encounter more problems in creating associations?*
> I think there is a refusal, a rejection of the very idea of belonging to an association ... [In communist times] associating was presented as a way for the individual to participate in the group, but in the end it was the contrary ... the individual aspect was lost. I think that, more than a rejection of nationalism, there is a rebuttal of associations, of collectivism and collectivisation in general. (M26, Modena)

Are you a member of any Albanian association?
No.
Would you like to be?
I don't know ... because I think in these matters it is better never to trust [Albanian] people who are older than thirty. They have that old 1970s idea of the youth movement. I know the way they see it and I don't want to be associated with them. Their vocabulary ... their behaviour ... makes me realise that they will never understand certain things ... They think that, just because they are older, they are better ... the very idea annoys me! (M22, Modena)

Secondly, the contradictory coexistence between the post-communist rejection of authoritarian collectivism and the survival of a personalistic interpretation of power relations within migrant associations undermines their development, leading to fragmentation, conflict and disillusionment. The next two interview excerpts highlight the way the individualistic nature of Albanian post-communist migratory identities, the resilience of authoritarian forms of power management, and the historical role of the family as the hegemonic institution structuring social life, can be seen as frustrating any collective response to the dynamics of social exclusion that Albanian migrants are subject to:

I think one problem is that, in some cases, associations are created by just a few people who want to establish themselves, more than to respond to the needs of the Albanian community ... Then there is a lack of coordination. In Bologna there are three associations ... the problem is that they cannot cooperate. It is the Albanian lifestyle [in which] everyone follows a separate individual path. And this is not something Albanians do because they are in Italy. It has its roots in the situation of chaos Albania is in. Albanian people cannot act as a group when they have a problem and this is a great disadvantage for them. (J., Albanian Democratic Association, Bologna)

This is not an association that gathers [people together] ... instead there are just volunteers taking charge of issues to help fellow Albanians. Sometimes people come here to drink a coffee, to ask us how we are. But that is it. Perhaps Albanians lack this kind of organisation. Maybe for political reasons ... because they don't want to have anybody over their head ... And there is a lot of diffidence ... But then again ... Albanians have always been autonomous ... even in Albania. If you look at people from Senegal, they tend to live in communities back in Senegal while we only have the patriarchal family. (E., *Drita*, Bologna)

Finally, the high level of stigmatisation of *albanesi* in Italy has also acted as a very powerful deterrent against the emergence of associations that might want to appropriate that term in politically, socially and culturally emancipatory terms (Messia 2003: 223). Some interviewees admitted that they had to overcome a feeling of diffidence towards other Albanians, which is usually blamed on the negative portrayal circulated by the Italian media.

> One of the most important aims of the association is that we meet up, we talk and get to know each other better ... To be honest, from what we heard from the TV about the crimes presented at first as done by Albanians, although it often came out later that they were not actually responsible, we became very reserved and didn't want to make friendships with other Albanians. When this friend of mine ... whom I met in the park while I was there with my grandson, invited me for dinner, my daughter told me to stay away from her; we didn't know who she was. However I went and I saw that they were all good people. It is a pity that we don't communicate more with each other. (F55, Lecce)

Signs of Improvement

During our research in Italy we participated in many social and cultural activities organised by Albanian associations. We could see how they had gradually achieved more visibility at a local level. Notwithstanding their efforts, the various local events promoted by Albanian migrant associations could not possibly erode the power and 'everyday' nature of the stigma built up by the Italian media. Interestingly, the only nationwide project countering the Italian media's stereotypical criminalisation of Albanian migrants was promoted by the IOM (International Organization for Migration) office in Rome, which is also in charge of managing the entry quotas described in the previous chapter. The project, which was funded under the European Union's EQUAL programme,[8] was very effective in identifying the media as a key element of Albanians' exclusion. Many events and activities were organised, including the setting up of a news agency run by migrants and the printing of documentation about the 'other side' of the Albanian migration coin.

Towards the end of our fieldwork in Italy, some interviewees started commenting that perhaps the high tide of 'Albanophobia' had passed, due to the switch of the media's focus onto dramatic international events and Muslim migrant groups after the tragedy of 9/11.

> Well, the media need to survive, and in order to do that when they find an oportunity they do exploit it by exaggerating the news. For example, there are good and bad Albanians, and as regards the latter, they normally tend to exaggerate the phenomenon. This also depends on timing. For instance, at the moment, due to international terrorism, the media are now portraying Tunisians, Moroccans and Algerians in a bad way and they are leaving us alone a bit. What can I say, given the situation, I can only wish that Osama Bin Laden keeps dominating the news, so (laughing) Forza Osama! (M44, Rome)

In addition, many interviewees mentioned the recent success story of Kledi Kadiu, an Albanian ballet dancer in a popular television show produced by Mediaset.[9] This was grasped as a very important – but all too rare – example of positive representation.

How about when they talk about Albanians on the TV, what do you think of that?
They give an extremely negative imagine of the Albanians. I think it is not fair at all.
Can you provide me with any specific example?
Erika and Omar: they accused the Albanians in order to avoid jail! I leave them in the hands of God: He will take care of them. At the same time, it is very good for us that Maurizio Costanzo invites Kledi to his show, that's great for us because he is a good dancer and represents us in a good way. I think Costanzo is doing good for us – something against discrimination. (F29, Rome)

Although recent studies indicate that there is a common perception of improvement in the media representation of Albanian migrants (see, e.g., Chiodi and Devole 2005), this is not so much a result of a much-needed improvement of Italian media practices with regard to the representation of migration-related events. More likely, this perceived improvement has more to do with the switch of the Italian media's stigmatising furore onto new constitutive others, such as Islamic terrorists, who suddenly became more strategic in relation to Italy's own positioning and self-perception within the Western world.

What Does it Mean to be Albanian in Italy?

The most characteristic aspect of Albanian migrants' experience of negotiation of their individual and collective identities in Italy is ambivalence. As we have seen, on the one hand nearly all of the interviewees declared themselves proud to be Albanian and mentioned instances in which they strenuously defended the worth of their own 'Albanianness' at an individual and interpersonal level. On the other hand, when asked about their attitude towards fellow Albanians in Italy, many reported experiencing a feeling of diffidence.

From our interviews and detailed observations in various parts of Italy, it appears that Albanians have exhibited a rather extraordinary ability to bridge the gap between social inclusion and exclusion, especially on an *individual basis*. On the other hand, at a *collective level*, at least at the time the interviews were carried out, Albanians were still the most heavily stigmatised and criminalised migrant group in Italy, and this had many implications for the nature and rapidity of their trajectories from a condition of social exclusion to one now increasingly of inclusion. These two dimensions of social interaction can be seen as disconnected axes of identity negotiation in relation to which they have different entitlement, power and possibilities to intervene. In edging towards their new 'diasporic' consciousness, Albanian migrants have to negotiate compromises between their troubled pasts, both under 'the regime' in Albania and during the chaotic post-communist transformation, and as migrants who were initially (but very briefly) welcomed and then brutally rejected (King and Mai 2004: 473–474; see also Mai 2005).

We have also seen that the partial interiorisation of (self-)stigmatising narratives was evidenced in the way in which many migrants, during interviews, made a point of 'being different' from other 'Albanians', thereby implicitly accepting the criminalising connotation associated with the term *albanese*. Therefore, on the Albanian side, the discursive mantra that seems to sum up the regime of partial and ambivalent internalisation of the host society's criminalising discourse is one whereby 'it is true that some Albanians are bad, but I am good'. This can be seen as mirroring the discourses of differential inclusion and exclusion that Albanian migrants experience in Italian society at large (cf. Castles 1995). In fact, a very similar version of the same process of ambivalent acceptance of media criminalisation was found in our interviews with Italian entrepreneurs who employed Albanians, most of whom insisted that 'their' Albanian employee was not like the others, since 'he was good'. However, as J., of the Albanian Democratic Association in Bologna, cleverly points out,

> It is quite paradoxical that Italians keep claiming that the Albanian they know is OK, but all others are not … because according to this rule then all Albanians are OK!

One of the most interesting implications of Albanians' ambivalence vis-à-vis their feelings of allegiance to their Albanianness was the evidence we found of instances of dissimulation in order to escape the burden of stigmatisation. Here is one more example to reinforce this point, related to us by another of our key interviewees, R., of *Bota Shqiptare*:

> Once an Albanian friend of mine was sitting in a train with another person who was talking on the phone in Albanian, and then there was an Italian as well there in the same compartment. At the end when he finished talking in Albanian, the Italian asked the guy: 'Where are you from?' And he said … 'Well, I'm … Romanian … '.

This anecdote is taken to a deeper analytical level by the Arbëresh priest of the Greek Orthodox Church in Lecce. The priest was asked about the importance of Albanians' 'reputation' for their integration in Italy. He replied:

> Very important! At all levels. Sometimes, people who are very well integrated deny being Albanian. They even refuse to speak Albanian. I know people who refused to speak in Albanian with me when they meet me in public because they don't want people to know that they are Albanian … Not everyone is doing that of course … but some do … And I am sorry about their children because they are completely Italian, they are losing the use of the Albanian language … They have an inferiority complex compared to everything Italian that is quite damaging …

Do you think Albanians are more or less integrated than other migrant groups?
Well, I think they are more integrated than others, but maybe not very proud ... For example somebody I know used to brag about the fact that Italians did not recognise him as Albanian. This bothers me a lot ... So, yes, Albanians integrate easily ... they want to be exactly like Italians!

This last interview quote points us to what is undoubtedly the key aspect of Albanian diasporic identities in Italy, which is the coexistence of specific conditions of vulnerability with a strong drive towards assimilation. The self-propelled assimilation is sometimes so successful that Italians often do not realise that the person they are talking to is an Albanian. In a country where strong currents of internal migration produce a mixing of accents at the local level, the sound of slightly-accented Italian in the mouths of long-resident Albanians or young people who have spent much of their lives in Italy is often taken as 'just another accent' – perhaps from Sardinia, as one of our interviewees said. Dorothy Zinn's research in schools in Basilicata, the adjacent region to Apulia, shows that Albanian children appear to have little desire or incentive to preserve their mother tongue, and parents likewise do not give much encouragement (Zinn 2005). Seeing their children's future as being in Italy, parents see little value in maintaining Albanian as one of their children's languages (given that they also learn more 'useful' languages, such as English, at school); moreover, Albanian children's continued use of Albanian in public settings such as the street or the playground would serve only to mark them out as 'Albanian' and therefore open to discriminatory or racist reactions by other children (Romania 2004: 71).

Italians' *albanophobic* reactions are inversely mirrored by Albanians' italophilia, which in turn reflects, as we have noted quite extensively earlier in this chapter as well as in Chapter 2, the key role played by Italian television in the emergence of alternative individual and collective identities during the passage to post-communism. Because of the constant presence of 'subversive' Italian television within everyday family life, Italy was the imagined space on to which Albanians first mapped their hopes and desires. Italy enjoyed the status of the country most likely to provide an 'answer' to local needs, to offer a refuge from the growing disappointment and disillusionment with Albania's own dim prospects. In the process of this idealised projection, Italy has been configured as not only culturally closer to Albania than other Western nations, but as a more advanced version of local culture (Mai 2002a).

In this respect, Albanian contemporary society can be seen as a 'diaspora space' (Brah 1996) where both those who 'leave' and those who 'stay put' experiment with multiple, both old and new, subject positions, values and social practices. What is particularly interesting about the concept of 'diaspora space' is that it implicitly acknowledges the key role played by imagination in the elaboration of migratory life-trajectories across economic, gender, moral and other boundaries, whether this happens 'abroad' or 'at home'. If we conceptualise migration not only in terms of physical displacement, but as a condition of *subjective displacement*, as a disembedding of subjectivity from the social and cultural sites which have previously anchored it, then it is possible to argue that Italian television watching emerged as a practice within which new Albanian diasporic identity formations were, and continue to be, articulated.

These observations also help us to explain how Albanians' unusual vulnerability to the interiorisation of the stigmatising portrayals disseminated by Italian television was exacerbated by the Italian media's diasporic function in the emergence of post-communist collective and individual identities. Interestingly, virtually no Albanian household of those we contacted in the course of our Italian fieldwork had access to satellite television. In fact, virtually none of the people who were interviewed were interested in watching Albanian television in Italy, and only a dozen or so interviewees were aware of the existence of Albanian newspapers published in Italy. In reality, all the interviewees watched Italian television regularly. Thus, Italian television was a key cultural formation in Albanian migrants' everyday life, and an important reference point for Albanian people's understanding of their role, presence and identity in relation to Italian society. So, along the conventional channels of cultural integration – language, food, behavioural norms, 'cultural knowledge' of the host society – Albanians score highly; but there is no reciprocal acculturation on the part of Italians, who have no respect for Albanian culture at all.

We have knowingly avoided the use of the term 'mimicry', which has been used by other scholars with reference to the issue of Albanians' integration in Italy (notably Romania 2004), because the concept it describes can be seen as implicitly reinforcing, rather than questioning, imagined hierarchies of civilisation structured around the superiority of the original (Western) culture versus the mimetic (non-Western) others (Bhabha 1994: 85–92). Rather than focusing exclusively on the way Albanians mimic Italians in order to 'pass' and escape discrimination, we believe that the relationship between Albanianness and Italianness can be captured in its full complexity only if it is seen as structured by interlinked hierarchies of internal diversification at work within each of the two identity formations involved (Mai 2003). This means that Albanians and Italians should be seen as equally mimetic and strategic in presenting their selves according to internalised hierarchies of modernity and civilisation. It is within this symbolic network and its stratified hierarchies that the strategies of identity positioning take place. On the one hand, as we have seen, Italians distance themselves from Albanians in order to feel more 'civilised' in relation to their perceived backwardness, with particular reference to the Southern question and its role in defining

Italianness for internal and external 'consumption'. On the other, Albanians reject their association with a stigmatised portrayal of themselves by selectively disavowing aspects of their cultural background they perceive to be detrimental to their aspired inclusion into a common symbolic and social space.

The readiness with which interviewees of Muslim background were keen to minimise their attachment to their faith is a further indication of the way dissimulation emerges at the encounter of the hierarchies of Westernness structuring Albanian and Italian national identities and the colonial undertone characterising their relationship. The following interchange is revealing in this respect:

> *Where are you from?*
> I am from Shkodra [the main town in the 'Catholic North' of Albania].
> *Are you Catholic?*
> No, I am Muslim. So to speak, because I entered a mosque twice in my life.
> *Is religion important for Albanians?*
> No, it isn't important.
> *Is it a problem for Italians that most Albanians are Muslim?*
> No, we have never had any problem on that score. Albanians are very tolerant about religion. We are the only country in Europe where three religions live peacefully together. Look, here the Albanians don't practice it much, because they aren't that religious. (M35, Molfetta)

The role that the downgrading of religion played in the construction of an Albanian national identity deserves further attention. In comparison with other experiences of nationalism in the Balkans, Albanian nationalism started several decades later and in another historical context. Lubonja (2002: 91–92) emphasises how Albanian nationalism did not emerge out of the process of liberation from Ottoman domination, as was the case of Greek and Serb nationalism; instead, Albanian nationalism started at the time of the Russian–Turkish war (1878), which brought independence to Serbs. With the gradual disintegration of the Ottoman Empire, it became necessary to save the regions inhabited by the Albanians from the threat of being divided up and claimed by the Serbs and the Greeks; at the same time, there was a perceived need to differentiate Albanians from Turkish identity. This historical context has greatly influenced the development of romantic myths of Albanian nationalism and is a key moment in the creation of the mythology which has since dominated Albanian collective memory and culture.

Although it is beyond our remit in this book to analyse these myths in detail,[10] we do want to stress how they can be seen as instrumental in defining 'Albanianness' against competing neighbouring forces, in relation to its ascribed belonging to the West, and against the remnants of its deep Ottoman experience. Emerging from a history of cultural marginality, fragmentation and isolation within the Ottoman Empire, and from a condition of cultural vulnerability due to the absence of any 'national' religious threshold of identification, 'the doctrine of national unity, which must be seen as a reaction to prevalent insecurities, became central ... during the communist period' (Misha 2002). This Albanian synergy of nationalism and communism has many implications for the way current 'discourses of belonging' in relation to the West, the East and Albania are central to Albanian people's migratory projects and shifting identities.

Thus, returning to our interview material, whilst it is true that religious affiliation has been downplayed, even purged, throughout the history of Albanian national(ist) identity, it is also true that Albanian migrants of Christian faith have been very ready to emphasise their religious affiliation, and those of Muslim background are even willing to 'convert' to Catholicism in order to facilitate an easier life in Italy. An entrepreneur in Molfetta who employed several Albanians spoke in the following terms about their integration:

> Their integration is very easy because, thank God, Albanians know how to speak in Italian when they come ... you really can see what television did ... They integrate easily and they know about Italy but you have the impression sometimes that they make things up ... For instance, sometimes they pretended to be Catholic and then it comes out that they were not ... They are afraid to show who they are because obviously somebody must have suggested to them that was the way to do it ... particularly Muslims ... Catholics tend to open up immediately ... they already feel integrated.

Not only were many Muslim interviewees more likely to relativise the attachment to their faith, but many saw the conversion to Christianity of their children as helpful to their integration into Italian society. Although many interviewees underlined how Italian society was much more open and tolerant in relation to religious diversity when compared to Greece,[11] where many had worked before coming to Italy, Albanians' flexibility in adapting to what they perceive would facilitate their inclusion into Italian society is indicative of the kind of pressure they are subject to in Italy (Perrone 2001: 144). In the following quote a representative of the social services in Lecce points out the similarity between Albanian and Roma families in this respect. This similarity is not coincidental, since the Roma are, along with the Albanians, the most stigmatised social group in Italy (cf. Sciortino 2003: 162; Sniderman et al. 2000: 85).

> I think Albanians adapt more easily ... An example is their attitude to religion. They don't care at all. And this is a more general attitude, not only about religion. There is a tendency to adapt to situations in a positively instrumental way. I think this is very helpful, really. They seem to have a very pragmatic attitude most of the time and they are able to adjust very easily. It is very different with Moroccans, for whom religion is very important for their sense of belonging. Albanians have the same attitude as Roma people. We run a

programme of education targeting Roma children and we asked their parents to indicate their religion, specifying that it was only important in order to see whether we needed to arrange the weekly religion teaching hour ... They all decided to avail themselves of the religion hour because they thought it would help their children to fit in.

The combined process of selective dissimulation and emphasis of features perceived as undesirable or desirable in relation to the subject's imagined life-trajectory is a structural feature of the articulation of individual and collective identities. But Albanians in Italy are by no means unique in this regard. Thus, an Albanian migrant minimising his or her affiliation to Islam; the southern Italian saying to a northern Italian, 'I was born in Palermo, but I lived in Verona for many years'; and the Italian migrant in the UK saying 'I am Italian, but I have a PhD from the US': all are trying to position themselves according to the same symbolic maze of 'Westernness', 'modernity' and 'civilisation', but with very unequal access to symbolic, economic, cultural and social capital.

We conclude this chapter with a further example of the interconnection between the symbolic and other layers of Albanians' experience of social inclusion and exclusion within Italian society. Together with the earlier-noted success of the ballet dancer Kledi Kadiu, the participation of the Albanian singer Elsa Lila in the Sanremo Italian national song context in 2003 was celebrated by many interviewees as the most evident sign of improvement in the overall condition of Albanians in Italy. 'Sanremo' is perhaps the most popular show on Italian television – its iconic importance to television watching in pre-1990s Albania was noted in Chapter 2. Although everything about Elsa Lila, from her looks to her voice and singing style, could be seen as entirely within the repertoire of Italian pop music, her successful performance was considered a great success for Albanians; she proved the international viability of Albanians as successful and 'normal' within the Italian social imaginary. At least symbolically, Elsa's achievement was a sign of Albanians' complete integration into the Italian mediascape, if not into Italian society as a whole.

Notes

1 This detachment from co-nationals is commented on at some length by Romania (2004: 70–71), who describes both a general process of passing themselves off as Italians in order to avoid contact with other Albanians, and the specific practice of parents instructing their children not to make friends with Albanian children at school.
2 Along with *kanun*, which was briefly dealt with in Chapter 2, *besa* and *mikpritie* are crucial within the genealogy of Albanian identity. But, as with *kanun*, there are regional variations within Albania. Whilst the tradition of

hospitality is widespread throughout Albania, *besa*, as a spoken term, is mainly used in the north; it is rarely used in the south where it is more an implicit behavioural notion rather than a formally uttered concept. For details see Doll (2003: 147–148).

3 For a similar comparison between Albania and the UK concerning gender roles, see King et al. (2006).
4 We give other examples of this in King and Mai (2004: 469–474) and Mai (2005: 552–555).
5 For a more detailed recounting and interpretation of this episode see Mai (2005: 555–557).
6 For an overview of the phenomenon of Albanian associationism at a national level, see Chiodi and Devole (2005).
7 In English 'The Albanian World'; see http://www.botashqiptare.net/
8 For more information about the 'Segni Particolari Albanese' project see http://www.immagineimmigratitalia.it/Rapporto%20progetto%20Equal%20Azione%203.htm (Italian) or https://equal.cec.eu.int/equal/jsp/dpMonitoringComplete.jsp?cip=IT&national=IT-S-MDL-288&year=2003&validation=false (English and Italian).
9 Kledi Kadiu was often quoted as an example of the way Albanians 'were not all bad' and contributed 'something positive' to Italian (and Albanian) culture. His face filled the front page of *Sorrisi e Canzoni*, a mainstream TV magazine, in its 5 April 2003 issue. In a feature article inside the magazine (pp. 44–51), the 'Albanian most loved by Italians' recounts his arrival on one of the 1991 ships, clad only in shorts and flip-flops.
10 According to Lubonja (2002), there are three main constitutive myths at work within Albanian nationalism. Firstly, those exalting the antiquity of the Albanian people and language as the oldest in the Balkans. These were instrumental in distinguishing Albanians from Greeks and Serbs and in establishing their entitlement to territorial sovereignty in the name of their autochthonous status. Secondly, the myth of Skanderbeg. 'In the absence of a medieval kingdom or empire the Albanian nationalists chose as their symbol the figure of Skanderbeg' which 'became a mixture of historical facts, truths, half truths, invention, and folklore' (Misha 2002: 43). Although his action had never involved all Albanians – neither Kosovo nor most parts of the south were ever included – Skanderbeg was made a national hero. In reality Skanderbeg is a very ambivalent figure. Despite having a Turkish name and title, he was instrumental in defining 'Albanianness' against the experience of Ottoman islamisation and in relation to Albania's ascribed belonging to the West. Thirdly, Albanianism as the only religion of Albanians. Albanian nationalism had to develop in competition with religion, often even assuming an anticlerical character. With the intention of unifying the Albanian people who were divided into three religions, to underplay the threat of fragmentation posed by the interference of the Serb and Greek Orthodox churches, and to sever Albania's links with the Ottoman experience, Vaso Pasha, a Catholic who had served the Ottoman Empire, wrote in one of his most famous poems that 'the religion of Albanians is Albanianism' (quoted in Lubonja 2002: 92). This is particularly significant if one keeps in mind that the Ottoman Empire used to divide the population into administrative units (millets) on religious criteria, according to which 'the Albanian muslims

would be in the same millet as the Bosnians and the Turks, while their Orthodox compatriots belonged to the same millet as the Greeks and the Serbs' (Misha 2002: 34).

11   For analyses of strategies of dissimulation adopted by Albanian migrants in Greece, which include name-changing, religious conversion, baptism and professing ethnic-Greek identity, see Hatziprokopiou (2003); Lazaridis (1999, 2004); Pratsinakis (2005).

Chapter 7

RETURN TO ALBANIA?

Introduction

After three chapters with the migrants in Italy, in this final chapter we redirect our gaze back to Albania. We pick up a number of topics and questions signalled in the first three chapters of the book. Having examined, in Chapters 2 and 3, the background to, and evolution of, Albanian emigration to Italy and elsewhere, this chapter looks at the reverse process – the impacts of migration on Albania. This breaks down into three tangible aspects, which structure the next three sections of the chapter:

- what happens when migrants leave – the effects of emigration on the family members and communities left behind;
- the impact of emigrant remittances on Albanian households – how remittances are received and utilised;
- return migration – who returns, why, for how long, and with what effects?

In the fourth and final part of the chapter we broaden the discussion to consider what the future holds for a country which has been, and continues to be, so reliant on migration. As we shall see, this is both an economic question and an existential one. From an economic point of view, the critical challenge is for migration, remittances, return and wise investment to regrow the Albanian economic structure, and divert the country from its slide into depopulation and economic and social abandonment. On a more existential plane, we want to conclude the book with a discussion on the meaning of migration for the Albanian collective psyche. Set against what Nicholas van Hear (1998: 217) has called the *diasporisation* of the Albanian population, with more and more Albanians settling abroad in an ever-widening circle of countries, what is the notion of *home* for Albanians living both in Albania and in Italy (and elsewhere), given the disruptive events in Albania since 1990, and given the ambiguous memories of the communist era?

Our fieldwork in Albania had to be selective in location because of the virtual absence of public transport and car-hire facilities in the country, and our dependence on borrowed vehicles, lifts, and the scarce accommodation available outside a few major towns. The main regional settings for fieldwork were threefold:

- the far north – Shkodër and Kukës districts;
- the urbanised centre – Tirana and Durrës and their peri-urban surroundings;
- the south – Vlorë and Sarandë districts.

These three areas were strategically chosen for their broad representation of the various migration and economic dynamics which emerged in our discussion of the spatial differentiation of migration types in Chapter 3. However, these three regional foci did not comprise all of our fieldwork and interviewing. As we travelled around other parts of the country we naturally did interviews as and when opportunities arose. So small numbers of interviews also took place in a variety of other locations, including Burrel (centre-north), Lushnjë and Berat (centre-south) and Korçë (south-east).

Interviews were of three main types:

- key informants – academics, government officials, NGO personnel, etc., who were mainly interviewed in Tirana and from whom we derived expert testimonies on the evolution and nature of Albanian migration, its relation to wider economic and social processes, and questions of policy;
- returnees – some had returned permanently or semi-permanently to Albania, others were just visiting from abroad;
- 'residual households' – typically these were middle-aged or older people whose adult children were working abroad.

These interviews – seventy-three in all – are the main databank of material for this chapter. We asked returnees about the circumstances of their return, their resettlement, investments, and plans for the future, including staying or re-emigrating. In the 'residual household' interviews we mainly posed questions about remittances, household survival and poverty alleviation, family separation, plans for the future and the likely return of émigré family members. Alongside our own primary data, we also refer to the results of other surveys carried out in Albania which shed light on the key themes of migration, remittances and return (especially Arrehag et al. 2005; De Soto et al. 2002; de Zwager et al. 2005; Gedeshi et al. 2003; Kule et al. 2002; Labrianidis and Lyberaki 2004; Labrianidis and Hatziprokopiou 2005).

What Happens when Migrants Leave?

This book is basically about Albanian migrants: as emigrants, as immigrants in Italy, and as returnees in Albania. However, it is important, when telling the 'story' of migration, not to overlook those who do *not* migrate. They are the flip side of migration and they are, in some ways, as profoundly affected by migration as the migrants themselves.

Undoubtedly, emigration brings economic rewards: to the migrants and their families, and to the Albanian state in terms of foreign-exchange remittances to help shore up the national balance of payments. These economic benefits incur considerable social and human costs, however. As economic migrants, Albanians' lives in Italy (and elsewhere) are filled with work and not much else. They suffer discrimination and stigmatisation, as we have seen. But as mass emigration of the young drains Albania of its vital elements, the impacts on the 'home' population are, if anything, even more socially disadvantageous. Especially in rural areas, the selectivity of emigration – mainly young adult or teenage males – leaves village populations correspondingly distorted, and the rural economy veers towards a state of collapse.

Effects on the Landscape and Village Life

Sivignon (1995) has described the abandonment of agricultural land in southern Albania resulting from the mass departures of the early 1990s. This is a process of land degradation which involves not only the withdrawal of labour from the fields but also the progressive collapse, through lack of maintenance, of terrace and irrigation systems and other elements of the physical infrastructure of farming. Depopulation in the southern hills and mountains is merely a catalyst for further emigration as it potentially undermines the survival of village communities in demographic, economic and cultural terms. Ten years after Sivignon's paper, our own field observations in southern Albania reveal little attenuation of the process of land abandonment. Between Vlorë and Sarandë, the fertile agricultural land surrounding the villages which dot this spectacular coastal scenery, which in communist times used to produce enough lemons and oranges for the whole country, remains largely unused as most young people have left to work in Greece and Italy. Some land is re-utilised by internal migrants from the poorer north of Albania, but overall it is difficult to see a productive future for Albanian farming in the upland areas which cover the majority of the national territory.

The following interview with a bar owner in southern Albania illustrates a typical situation. As the owner of the only recreational facility in the village, he was well informed of the whereabouts of its inhabitants.

> Our village used to have 1,500 people. Of these, five hundred, at least, are in Greece, another five hundred must be in Italy, now only old people, some wives and children are left here ... and I might have to close my business soon – who comes here any more? This bar used to be the canteen of a huge

agricultural cooperative which employed the whole village ... Now the village is abroad and the few people still living here will be forced to leave soon.
Why did they leave?
What kind of question is that? There is no work here any more. All of those who are able to work are working abroad, all of them.
And who works the land here?
Nobody, elderly people only cultivate what they need for themselves; nobody is cultivating in order to sell and make a profit.

Vulnerability Effects

In terms of the differential impact of emigration on various elements of the population, women, children and older people have generally been negatively affected by the predominance of younger males in the migration stream. As the Albanian migration process matures, family reunion migration lessens the problem of family separation; but not all are able, or want, to reunite with husbands and fathers working abroad. Meanwhile, children's education in rural regions is threatened by the closure of schools, emigration of teachers, and non-availability of transport to get them to whichever schools are functioning.

Several studies of women and children, as both victims and protagonists of migration, have been made since the mid 1990s, mostly by international organisations and NGOs (Orgocka 2006; UNDP 2005; UNICEF 1998). In a society which is still very patriarchal, women's freedom of movement and action – for instance to migrate independently – is severely constrained and, particularly in the north, is replaced by concerns over their security and safety (Lawson and Saltmarshe 2000: 139–140); as a result of these concerns, some parents keep girls out of school. This father, from Lezhë in northern Albania, recounted his particular experience:

> Young people are unsafe when they walk to school. My own daughter was kidnapped while walking to school. She managed to free herself. I identified the kidnappers but the police told me they were powerless to do anything about it. (Quoted in World Bank 1999: 18)

This increased vulnerability is the result of the interaction of the two dominant processes reshaping, and fragmenting, Albanian society over the last fifteen years: mass migration and the post-communist transformation. Albania's post-communist trajectory was characterised on the one hand by the disappearance of social provisions addressed to vulnerable groups and individuals, while on the other hand the free-market 'utopia' has produced an increasing gap between classes and genders; these effects are exacerbated by demographically-selective migration streams which rupture established family structures. In general, the disintegration, or recomposition in new forms, of the traditional nuclear and extended family structures is intensifying conflict within the family environment. In such a situation it is easy to understand how women, especially, tend to become increasingly vulnerable.

According to the World Bank's vulnerability report on Albania (1999: v, 23–25), women constitute the largest group 'at risk' through the two processes noted above. They fall into two subcategories:

- *Adult women without male 'protectors'*: this occurs because of the migration of husbands and other male relatives, often compounded by divorce. In cases of divorce and abandonment, most women cannot return to their families, where they would be considered an economic burden. Women who have to, or want to, live independently, without the control or protection of men, are isolated and rejected, and become vulnerable to violence and depression.
- *Young women at risk of prostitution*: initiation into prostitution occurs mainly through relatives, close friends and boyfriends who may be linked to criminal gangs. Extreme poverty and rigid gender roles, which are most accentuated in rural areas of north Albania but are also widespread in more attenuated forms throughout the country, increase the risks involved. Poor parents of young girls seek early promises of marriage as a way out of poverty. Although violence and kidnapping of young girls may be involved, in many cases families are complicit in their departure, according to a re-introduction from the pre-communist period of a distorted betrothal tradition, combined with the permanent migration abroad of young men.

The trafficking of young Albanians – principally young girls in their teens, but also young boys – is a topic of enormous sensitivity. Undoubtedly tragic, it also contains the potential for distortion and exaggeration by the media and even by the agencies concerned. Indeed, even those involved (or not, as the case may be) can conceivably have an interest in inflating the scale of the phenomenon: for instance, parents who prefer to say that their daughter was kidnapped rather than admit she has simply run off with her boyfriend, or young women who say they have been trafficked in order to enlist official or NGO assistance. We have not given the trafficking issue undue prominence in this book because we did not want to contribute to its spectacularisation: there may indeed be several thousand Albanian sex-workers in Italy (Campani 2000), but they are a very small percentage of the quarter-million Albanians legally resident in the country.

Social Abandonment of Older People

More important for our analysis of the impact of large-scale emigration on the residual society, including its household and family structures, is the issue of the social abandonment of older people – 'orphan pensioners', as they have been called (King and Vullnetari 2006). Their problems are most severe in upland areas of Albania where the population lives in scattered villages and hamlets and where out-migration has been heaviest. In mountain areas of the far north and far south, many places are snowbound during the harsh winters. This makes these locations peripheral even without migration, so the emigration of the younger generations only increases the social and physical isolation experienced by older people in the highlands. In the words of a 70-year-old interviewee in Vullnetari's recent study of the impact of migration on older persons in a village in south-east Albania, 'the elderly have been left like stones in the middle of the road' (Vullnetari 2004: 11).

According to both the World Bank's (1999) vulnerability study and the UNDP's latest Human Development Report on Albania (2005), elderly people are considered to be one of the most vulnerable groups in the country, suffering from social isolation, poverty and insufficient access to basic health services. There is strong evidence of increasing numbers of old people living alone and in dire conditions, and a large unsatisfied demand for institutional care. Pensions – derived from work done during the communist period – are very low, as is supplementary economic assistance (*Ndihme Ekonomike*) paid to needy people and the unemployed. According to De Soto et al. (2002: 35–38), the economic assistance payments are patchy and subject to political party favouritism; moreover, many households cannot reach one of the thirty-six district offices to request payment. Similar problems apply to the health service, which is of particular interest to older people; especially outside of the capital, health facilities have deteriorated since the end of the regime, with many rural health centres closing (De Soto et al. 2002: 67–73).

Our own field studies support these general findings reported above, and provide often emotive accounts of the feelings, frustrations and sadness suffered by older people who must live with their children far away.

First, an interview with an elderly couple living near Tirana in one of the disordered, peri-urban squatter zones which lie outside the capital. The interview first confirms the scale of emigration – even in this urban fringe area to which there has been a lot of internal migration from other parts of the country – and then gives the slightly different perspectives of the old man and his wife on the future: the man feels fatalistic about his children's return, whereas the wife has a plan for the return of their youngest son who, according to Albanian custom, bears the ultimate responsibility of caring for the parents of the family in their old age.[1]

> How do I feel about the fact that my kids have all gone away? How can I feel, but sad. But then I look around me and see that 80 per cent of the people who live here are in the same situation; only old people, women and kids live here. *Did you ever ask your children to come back?*

> Well, how can we do that? What possibilities can we offer them here?
> Wife: All you need is a bit of cooperation and organisation ... We decided all together that the son who is in Greece will return with his family for a couple of years, until the younger one returns from Italy. We won't be alone. He will come and stay with us with his wife and kids until the other one returns. What else can we do? We are old ... we cannot go and live abroad at our age.

This couple regard themselves as too old to contemplate following their children abroad. For others, this is more of a distinct possibility, as we shall see in a little while. The above interview also hints at another feature of Albanian migration: that it is common for different members of the family to be spread in different countries. Greece and Italy are the main destinations, but migrants from the same family may well be in other European countries or elsewhere in the world. Furthermore the same migrant (usually a son) may progress through a sequence of destinations, usually starting with Greece, then to Italy, and perhaps elsewhere. The following interview with a middle-aged man in Lushnjë reflects this multi-destination sequence. It confirms Greece as the usual 'first destination', reveals the hazardous and expensive nature of clandestine entry to Italy (and, even more so, to the UK) and sheds light on the characteristic reliance on kin and friends along the way.

> He [26-year-old son] used to live in Greece where there is a lot of work in agriculture ... then with the money he made there he went to Italy with a friend. He went from Vlorë, by speedboat – he paid $300 for the trip. Once there he worked, staying with a cousin in the south of Italy, and saved the money for the trip to the UK in a lorry. It was very exhausting, he had to stay inside the lorry for five days because the French police stopped it for some reason ... but they did not get caught and eventually they got to the UK. There were three of them ... close friends ... all they had was a bottle of water. (Father, Lushnjë)

But the theme which resonated the most strongly through the interviews with residual households was that of loneliness and separation from children and grandchildren. During the long era of communism, the family remained the cornerstone of Albanian society: exalted by the regime, it was also the private space of passive resistance, for it was only within the walls of the household that a more personalised lifestyle could be expressed. Middle-aged people looked forward to a calm old age, with guaranteed state welfare, surrounded by their families, especially their grandchildren. This expectation has been rather suddenly denied as a result of the mass departure of so many young men and women since the early 1990s. For nearly all elderly Albanians, family and grandchildren are their very *raison d'être*; not to be able to share such everyday pleasures and duties within a family context has been a bitter blow, and an unanticipated consequence of the democratic transition. Expressions of social isolation were accompanied by great uncertainty about whether children would eventually return, and if so, where to. Most parents expressed their desire for the return of their migrant children, but at the same time their awareness of the lack of economic and social preconditions for this actually to happen.

> I have fourteen family members abroad and ... I cannot complain about them. Of course, if you asked me, I would like them to come and live here. But here you can't work, there's nothing to eat, and the house is not finished yet. Where is the father who doesn't want his children close by? But what do I want my children here for, if they only wander around on the street, without a job and a proper place to live? It's best for them if they stay where they are. (M60s, north Albania)

The fact that so many Albanian migrants are working abroad without proper documents makes it difficult, if not impossible, for them to return: their irregular status would be discovered at the border and it would be expensive to pay to smuggle themselves back to their destination country. This is a major obstacle to the partial normalisation of family relations through regular visits.

> If you would listen to my heart, I wish to God that he [his son who is an 'illegal immigrant' in England] be caught and sent back here, so that I can see my son with my own eyes. I don't wish this for him, but I wish it for me, because I know it's not good for him to come back to Albania in such circumstances. I am going crazy not so much for the love of my son, but for the love of my grandchildren (at their mention, he starts to cry). Why those bastard governments are not giving us permission to see our sons abroad? You have left us, fathers and mothers, in tears ... There is no word to describe my pain when I hear my grandchildren call me Grandfather [on the 'phone] and I haven't even seen them yet ... (M50s, north Albania)

Here, then, we confront a major problem of international and EU migration politics: the obsession with preventing immigration of third-country nationals means controlling virtually all aspects of their mobility; this denies families which are split by migration their human right to a normal family life, in this case the ability to visit each other, even at times of significant family events such as births, weddings and funerals. From our fieldwork in both Italy and Albania, we found many instances of emigrants who cannot return to Albania because they are not properly documented, and of older people who, despite being physically capable of travel, are denied entry visas or put off by the cost and bureaucracy involved.

However, for those migrants whose residence permits are in order – and we saw from Chapter 3 the rapid increase in 'regularised' Albanians in Italy (and Greece) – visits back and forth are now more feasible. Regular ferry services link Durrës and Vlorë with a range of Italian Adriatic ports, and air services connect Tirana to an increasing number of

Italian cities. Moreover, another option presents itself – that the migrant's parents (or perhaps just one parent) can join him or her abroad, either under an official family reunion arrangement, or on a visitor's visa followed by overstaying. Evidence on the emigration of older Albanians, especially women, is beginning to accumulate. Analysis of the results of the 2002 Living Standards Measurement Survey by Reilly et al. (2005) reveals that, whilst men are almost twice as likely as women to consider migrating abroad, older women (those aged fifty-six and above) are more likely to consider migration than older men. This trend is backed up by evidence from the 2001 census which reveals that there are 10 per cent more males than females in the 60–69 age cohort – an unusual result given that male life expectancy is less than that for females (INSTAT 2002: 28–30). This is consistent with a recently observed phenomenon in Albania known as 'migrating grannies', whereby older women follow their sons and daughters abroad to look after the grandchildren so that both parents can work and maximise their income-earning potential. Furthermore, such migration is an important element in conveying Albanian culture and the language to the youngest generation, living abroad (King and Vullnetari 2006). It also makes grandparents feel useful and appreciated, giving them an active role in transnational, trans-generational care.

However, this option is not widely available, and brings its own problems and dilemmas (see King and Vullnetari 2006; Vullnetari 2004). Quite apart from legalistic problems of access and visas, 'follow-the-children migration' is really only attractive to the 'young old' rather than the 'old old'; the latter are likely to be less robust in health, and more attached to their village homes. Further problems arise because of linguistic isolation and adaptation to the way of life in their children's country of immigration. Grandchildren have difficulty in seeing the relevance of being taught their ancestral language and 'traditional culture' by their grandparents. Finally, by joining one of their children abroad, grandparents risk losing touch with their other children, who might be in other countries, or be internal migrants living elsewhere in Albania.

Remittances: Albania's Saviour?

Economics views remittances as the repayment to migrant-sending countries for lending its human resources to another country via international migration. For sure, remittances have long attracted the attention of migration researchers as a kind of adjunct to their study of the migration process, but recently there has been growing interest in their developmental potential. Remittances lie at the heart of the so-called migration–development nexus (van Hear and Nyberg Sørensen 2003) and have become the focus for a burgeoning literature on the part of academic researchers, both migration specialists and development economists, as well as international organisations and government bodies. It is useful to summarise some key elements of the debate in order to set the Albanian experience in context.

The 'Great Debate' on Remittances

Remittances are widely seen as the litmus test of the benefits of emigration for the migrant-sending countries (IOM 2005: 179). World Bank figures show a global remittance flow to poor countries of $93 billion in 2003. This figure is subject to at least two qualifications. First, it ignores 'reverse remittances' – financial resources sent to migrants by their families at home, to support their education for instance, or to pay agents to arrange clandestine border crossings. One estimate suggests that this reduces the net remittance transfer to developing countries to $50 million (IOM 2005: 279). Second, remittances recorded by official sources such as banks and balance-of-payments statistics are only part of the total. The quantity of remittances conveyed by informal channels is unknown, but one study (Puri and Ritzema 1999) estimated that unofficial transfers may contribute around 36 per cent of total flows, which would inflate the earlier quoted global figure of $93 billion to around $140 billion. Some estimates suggest total remittances to poor countries may be as high as $200 billion (Sander 2003: 6). Either way, remittances have now become the second largest global capital flow after foreign direct investment (FDI) and ahead of Overseas Development Assistance (ODA).

Despite the recent 'remittance turn' (Kapur 2004; Ramamurthy 2003), the debate on migration and development remains polarised. The *positive or optimistic scenario* stresses that remittances are a stable financial flow to poor countries, that they can have a counter-cyclical effect in times of economic hardship, and that they are widely disseminated across the migrant sending countries, including the poorest regions whence many migrants originate. In contrast to prestigious foreign-aid projects, remittances are person-to-person, targeted at the needs of the recipients. Decisions about the sending and utilisation of remittances are taken at the individual or household level, negotiated between the sender and the recipient, who are usually members of the same kin group. Remittances can enhance long-term economic growth, especially if they are used to finance children's education and improvements in diet and health. Even in situations (as in Albania) where they are mainly used for consumption and building houses, they can have positive multiplier effects in the local economy by stimulating demand, increasing money circulation and creating employment. At a macro level, substantial remittances constitute a vital source of foreign income, helping to pay for imports, repaying foreign debts and improving creditworthiness (IOM 2005: 273). At the micro level it is argued that remittances can be invested in farming and small-scale businesses such as food processing, light industrial workshops or service outlets, all of which help to grow the local economy. Social development may also be enhanced where remittances are donated or pooled into community facilities such as village halls, health centres, road improvements etc.

The *negative interpretation* of remittances highlights the following issues. Remittances are not an adequate compensation for the export of human capital that migration involves, nor do they atone for the harsh life of a migrant worker – poorly paid, overworked and subject to racism and discrimination. Secondly, emigration rarely involves the 'poorest of the poor' but, rather, implies a selectivity whereby only those who can afford it actually migrate. This has two consequences which work against the notion of migration as an equalising process. First, brain and skill drains impact negatively on the sending country, whose most talented individuals are hoovered up by wealthy countries in a kind of 'development aid in reverse'. Second, remittances increase inequality in the migrants' home country, since it is the richer families who can afford to send members abroad, and who therefore receive the payments sent back. Further doubts surround the effectiveness of remittances as an exogenous stimulus to development. It is often alleged that most remittance capital is spent on 'unproductive' outlets such as housing, the conspicuous purchase of consumer durables, and lavish social occasions, rather than on 'productive' investments in farming, industry and business development. Migrants' lack of business and investment acumen hampers their utilisation of remittances in a way that would maximise economic development potential. Meanwhile, remittances spent on imported goods negatively affects the balance of payments. Undue reliance on remittances opens up emigration countries' vulnerability to unforeseen external shocks, such as unemployment or repatriation. Remittances are in danger of creating a culture of dependency: migrants' relatives do less work on the assumption they can live off remittances and children assume they will go to work abroad (IOM 2005: 192). Finally there is the issue of the extent to which remittances act to 'patch over' economic difficulties and hence to defer fundamental structural changes (for instance in education, politics, the labour market) which are essential for longer-term poverty eradication and development (Ellerman 2003).

In recent years the balance has swung towards an appreciation of the positive impacts of migration and remittances, which are thought to outweigh the potential drawbacks. Nevertheless, questions remain about the extent to which remittances reduce poverty and inequality (IOM 2005: 179). Adams and Page (2003) analysed data from seventy-four low and middle-income countries and found a positive relationship with poverty alleviation, both in terms of reducing the absolute numbers of poor people, and the severity of poverty. On the other hand, the relationship to inequality is inconclusive, and is dependent on the social/income classes from which migrants were drawn in the first place. Where the poorest migrate, remittances should have an equalising effect; where the poor are too poor to migrate, the impact will tend towards increasing inequality. However, these are not simple issues: amongst the complicating factors are how inequality is measured, and the possibility that different trends can operate at different stages of the evolution of migration from a given country. For Mexico, Jones (1998) found that income inequalities at first increase, and then decrease, as the migration stream matures; at whatever stage, however, rural incomes improve relative to urban ones since remittances flow disproportionately to the rural areas of migrant origin.

The final element of the debate concerns the *policy dimension*. How can the effectiveness of remittances' development impact be maximised? Again, this involves issues at a variety of scales. At the international scale, remittances are effective to the extent that there are real wage differentials between the origin and destination countries, and ease of entry into the labour markets of the latter. Liberalising policies on entry will therefore have the effect not only of increasing remittance flows but also of improving the 'human' quality of the migration experience – removing the necessity of being an 'illegal' immigrant working at exploitative wage rates in the black economy, and allowing the migrant to make frequent return visits to sustain family and other social relationships in the home country. Paradoxically, relaxing entry restrictions may well lessen the pressures for permanent settlement, since migrants can come and go as they please and not be trapped into a binary decision of settling for good or not migrating at all (Harris 2002).

Remittances and the Albanian Economy

Undoubtedly, remittances have become one, if not *the*, major factor in the economic survival of Albania over the past fifteen years. Based on Bank of Albania estimates,[2] annual remittances to Albania have grown from $150 million in 1992 to more than $1 billion in 2004 (Table 7.1), including $310m from Italy through what has been termed the 'Italy–Albania remittance corridor' (Hernández-Coss and De Luna Martínez 2006). Measured in per capita terms (total remittances divided by the population in Albania), the figure has grown from $100 in the early-mid 1990s to $200 in 2001 and to $300 in 2004. The only interruption to this upward trajectory occurred in 1997 when the pyramids crisis shook the entire national economy, as was noted in Chapter 2. Investment in the pyramids had been largely fuelled by remittances; the schemes' collapse bankrupted many migrant households and frightened off investment in Albania. Several of our interviewees has lost money in the pyramids. A typical example:

We invested a lot of money in those bloody firms and lost everything [nervous laugh] ... I wanted to open a business [in Albania] and needed more capital, so I thought this was a way ... but I left it too long, and it all went, four years of my life, of work ... myself and my two brothers. (M30s, southern Albania)

Table 7.1 also shows the proportion of remittances sent through informal channels, i.e., outside the formal banking system and money transfer companies such as Money Gram and Western Union. Although the informal route – which includes money carried by migrants themselves on their return visits or sent via relatives and friends or paid private couriers – has been decreasing as a share of total remittances over the years, it still accounts for more than half by value. Survey data (712 emigrants in Greece, Italy and the UK) collected by de Zwager et al. (2005: 25–36) show that informal channels are used by most migrants, including more than three-quarters of those questioned in Italy ($n = 223$), but for smaller amounts than are sent via the formal system. Given the difficulties of estimating informal remittances, the overall estimates listed in Table 7.1 must be regarded as approximate. Finally, remittances-in-kind have to be recognised. These are mainly consumer goods bought by emigrants abroad and sent or carried back to Albania.[3] According to some surveys these account for 13–17 per cent of total remittances (de Zwager et al. 2005: 21).

Table 7.1 shows a strongly rising profile of remittances in recent years. What of the future? It seems inevitable that remittances are destined eventually to fall, and perhaps quite soon. Two factors point to this conclusion. First, since the mid 1990s the Albanian migration stream has entered a period of maturation whereby the emigration of young single males (including married men leaving their families behind) gives way to

Table 7.1 Remittances to Albania, 1992–2004

Year	Total remittances in US $ million	% sent via informal channels	Remittances as % GDP
1992	150	–	–
1993	275	–	22.3
1994	378	92.5	19.4
1995	385	84.5	15.5
1996	500	88.0	18.6
1997	267	68.7	11.6
1998	452	74.9	14.8
1999	368	75.8	10.0
2000	531	58.3	14.3
2001	615	60.3	15.2
2002	632	55.3	13.9
2003	778	60.1	11.4
2004	1,028	54.3	13.7

Source: Bank of Albania estimates in de Zwager et al. (2005: 21).

a more demographically balanced émigré population composed increasingly of nuclear families with women and children. As family reunification takes place abroad, and as new families are formed and enlarged abroad with the foreign birth of children, so the money available for remittances will be less, and there will be fewer family members in Albania to remit to. This trend is backed up by our own interview evidence and other survey data (e.g., de Zwager et al. 2005: 51; Maroukis 2005: 220–221).[4]

Second, the statistical evidence of other countries shows a fall-off in remittances some years after the main wave of emigration has ended. The comparison with Greece is rather instructive here (Nikas and King 2005). Greece's postwar emigration, which was mainly to West Germany, peaked in the mid 1960s and fell away dramatically after 1970. The profile of total remittances to Greece peaked in the early-mid 1980s; the flow from Germany peaked in the late 1970s. This suggests a 'remittance cycle' of around fifteen or at most twenty years after the onset of mass emigration. Thus, remittances to Albania may start to decline before the end of the present decade.

On the other hand, there are two factors which point towards the continuation of a high remittance flow rather than its decline. One is the improving economic situation of Albanian emigrants in their host countries – as we have seen from the Italian field evidence. This means that incomes rise, potentially leaving a greater surplus to be saved or remitted. According to de Zwager et al. (2005: vi) Albanian emigrant households living abroad save an average of €5,390 per year. The second factor is the low rate of return migration to Albania. We say more about this later in the chapter. But the comparison with Greece is again interesting. Here the fall-off in remittances, especially from Germany, from the late 1970s was matched with high rates of return migration. Available statistics suggest that between a third and a half of the Greeks in Germany returned to their home country after the early 1970s (Fakiolas and King 1996: 174). This reduces the overall stock of remitters in the emigration country. For Albania, the stock of emigrants residing and working abroad is likely to remain high in the medium term; therefore the flow of remittances may well be assured, at least until 2010 (de Zwager et al. 2005: 53).

Remittances and Household Survival

As we noted in Chapter 3, conventional wisdom in Albania holds that emigration has been the most effective means to ensure economic survival and an improved quality of life since the early 1990s. It must be stressed, however, that, especially in the early years of emigration, it was seen as a strategy to combat poverty and insecure and difficult economic conditions, rather than as a route to wealth and prosperity. According to

IMF's Albania Country Report for 2005, 'for many families ... access to a migration network, family exposure to migration ... [and] the remittances that follow ... [are] one of the most viable means to escape poverty' (quoted in de Zwager et al. 2005: 39). Likewise, the World Bank study of Albanian poverty concluded that remittances were the main factor distinguishing non-poor from poor families: living conditions of rural families not receiving remittances are generally very bad (De Soto et al. 2002: 121).[5] According to data from the Albanian Living Standards Measurement Survey for 2002, remittances accounted for 47 per cent of total household income of those households receiving remittances; a very similar figure (43 per cent) was recorded by de Zwager et al. (2005: 39–40) based on a survey of 897 households receiving remittances in 2004. The latter survey recorded an average annual value of €2,619 for remittances received by Albania-based families with members working abroad (de Zwager et al. 2005: 42). As our own field research indicated, such figures, as averages, cover a range of individual circumstances: in some cases, residual households may be totally dependent on remittances as their only source of income; in others, remittances contribute a much smaller fraction of total household income, which may also be made up of pensions, sale of agricultural produce, other paid work done by resident household members, profit from a small business etc. Two interview extracts illustrate this contrast. The first tells how remittances alone enabled the family to survive and to improve its living conditions:

> I went to Greece at first, as we all did back then, to help the economic situation of my family. I worked from morning till night ... I used to send all the money I earned, as my family needed everything. My parents used all the money to survive, for food ... Later they bought the TV and fixed the roof, they also improved the windows and the heating, for the winter. The house was not as you see it today. (M39, Sarandë)

In other cases, remittances are integrated with other sources of income, as in the second interview quote, from a return migrant in a more affluent family. This interviewee left later, during the 1997 civil disturbances, fleeing on a fishing boat to Italy. After staying with friends and relatives in different places, he settled in Rome, where he worked in the pastry and bread-making trade, which enabled him to get regularised. When asked if he sent money home, he replied:

> Well, it depends. Life is expensive in Italy and I also wanted to live my own life ... Luckily my parents did not need money, so I could save some in the bank. I only sent small amounts in the beginning, but my parents kept insisting that I kept some money for my future, so that is how it went. (M28, Durrës)

The dominance of the 'survival function' of remittances is backed up by survey data. The results of two recent large-scale questionnaire-based

Table 7.2 Use and investment of remittances to Albania according to two recent surveys

Kule et al. (2002) ($n = 700$)	% by value
Consumption (both daily consumption and consumer goods)	52.7
Saved in bank	16.0
Invested in a financial institution	7.0
Invested in property	7.0
Invested in a commercial concern	5.2
Invested in a productive business	1.3
Invested in agriculture	1.0
Other	9.9

Gedeshi et al. (2003) ($n = 1,180$)	% of respondents making investment
Daily needs of household	69.7
Repair or furnish dwelling	29.9
Investment in property (buy or build)	18.0
Make investment in Albania	9.4
Savings in a bank	6.4
Other	4.0

Source: Kule et al. (2002: 235); Gedeshi et al. (2003: 54).

surveys on remittance spending are given in Table 7.2. Kule et al. (2002) surveyed seven hundred respondent households involved in transmitting remittances in 1998, the sample being spread over many parts of Albania. More than half the money sent by emigrants was used for consumption by recipients, and 16 per cent was saved; only 7.5 per cent was invested in 'productive' enterprises, such as commerce, workshops or farming. Broadly similar findings resulted from a 2002–03 survey administered to 1,180 migrants as they re-entered the country at Rinas international airport, the seaports of Durrës and Vlorë, and the two main road crossings on the Greek border (Gedeshi et al. 2003). Here the results set out in Table 7.2 refer to the percentage of total respondents stating that they had engaged in a particular type of remittance spending or investment; hence the column total exceeds 100. From this survey, seven out of ten respondents had used remittances to satisfy the daily needs of the household in Albania, another three out of ten had spent remittances on improving the living conditions in their Albanian dwelling, and another two in ten had invested in building or buying a new dwelling in Albania. As in the previous survey, fewer than one in ten had diverted remittances to 'productive' investment in Albania.

The general picture, then, is clear and confirms that the majority of emigrants see the primary objective of their remittances as supporting the daily needs of their family members in Albania. Expanding, upgrading and furnishing the home comes second, followed by investment in property and, at some distance, investment in economic activities such as farming or some other enterprise. The Albanian case supports the model of Nyberg Sørensen et al. (2003: 13) who suggest that the typology of remittance use evolves over three stages: first, on family maintenance and improvement of living conditions; second, on conspicuous consumption; and third, on productive activities such as land improvements and small firms. Moreover, our own more qualitative research reveals other categories of spending not listed in Table 7.2, such as the purchase of a car (often seen as a prestige symbol), investment in education (common for remittances sent to urban families), or the use of remittances to maintain significant cultural and life-cycle events such as weddings and funerals (important in the maintenance of the moral authority and survival of the extended family based in Albania).

Sending, Receiving and Gendering Remittances

In this section we use our field data to answer a series of questions about the mechanics of remitting:

- How are remittances sent, with what frequency, and what are the sums involved?
- How are remittances spent or invested?
- Who makes the key decisions in sending and utilising remittances?

As we shall see, there is a strong gender dimension to all these questions, especially the last one. This reflects still-entrenched gender mentalities and behaviour in Albanian society. If anything, gender divisions have been sharpened and reconstituted by the uncertainties of the post-communist transformation; and by the way in which emigration itself provides different opportunities and constraints which are often articulated along gender lines. According to INSTAT (2002: 27), males accounted for more than two-thirds of total emigration between 1989 and 2001. Moreover, whilst most males emigrated either before marriage or, if married, on their own, 86 per cent of Albanian migrating women were married. As far as remittances are concerned, the most important consequence of this situation is that, once they leave their own parental families upon marriage, they enter the families of their husbands and can therefore only contribute to the economy of the new family they become part of.

Returning to the three questions posed above, we did not collect systematic quantitative data on amounts and frequency of remittances. This was partly for ethical reasons – we did not want to pry too much into such matters and run the risk of damaging the atmosphere of the interview and of jeopardising the rest of the information sought – and partly because the macro-data and survey results reviewed in earlier subsections of the chapter gave us some idea of the scale of remittances sent. Our data, although unsystematic and sometimes impressionistic, do nevertheless reinforce these general trends, as well as showing how variable remittance experiences are. Given that many interviewees had also migrated to Greece as well as Italy, we are able to use these multiple migration experiences to make comparisons; moreover, our parallel survey data on Albanian migration and remittance behaviour in the UK (King et al. 2003) offer additional comparative perspectives.

From these combined insights we find that:

- most Albanians do not remit constant sums every month; rather the amounts depend on availability of income through often irregular work, and respond also to the fluctuating needs of the family back home in Albania;
- generally remittances are high in the early years of migration, when the need to support family members and improve their living conditions back home is most urgent;
- in general, single young men supporting parents and siblings in Albania, and married men who emigrated on their own, leaving family members behind, are the ones who send the largest amount; the life trajectories of these migrants are still anchored in Albania, whereas those who have their families with them abroad are focused on a more permanent stay and have fewer family members to remit to;
- remittances are higher from Italy than from Greece, but often higher still from migrants in the UK;
- most migrants send remittances by informal means rather than through formal banking channels.

Some quotes from interviews add a little detail to these generalisations:

> Yes, I help my family [his parents, etc.] at home – I send them money so they don't have to worry about anything ... I do not use banks, I mainly use cash ... I don't care what they use it for, the most important thing is that my family is OK. So, every two months or so I send about £2,000. (M23, London)

> My eldest son, who was in Greece and is now in Italy, wanted to build a place for himself and his family, so he only sent us small amounts of money, especially when he was in Greece ... My other son is still in Greece. The eldest is in America; he sends us lots of money, and with his money and that from Greece we were able to buy this house and build the petrol station. (M57, Durrës)

> Our situation changed a lot when my three sons went to live in Italy. They were not married then and could send all the spare money they had ... Before, when they had been in Greece, they could send very little, because the pay is so low there ... With the money from Italy we set up this business; I rented this place from the state and little by little turned it into a hotel ... Now we are all living from this activity, so I guess it was a good investment. (M60s, Dhermi, southern Albania)

Dominant over all are narratives which stress the role of remittances in ensuring the survival of family members back home; upon their survival can be built some modest improvements in living standards. For those with higher capital inflows, mainly from higher-wage economies in London, northern Italy or North America, investments can be made in new houses and new economic activities such as shops or hotels.

With relatively few exceptions, decisions on sending and deploying remittances remain in the hands of male household members – both those abroad and those in Albania (King et al. 2006). This reflects both the traditional gendering of Albanian society and the fact that males have been the main protagonists of Albanian migration. Although it is true that increasing numbers of females have been emigrating, most of them do so as 'followers' or 'accompaniers' of primary male work migration. Where independent female migration does take place (except for university study or professional careers abroad), it is overlain with negative moral judgements.

In our interview discussions on remittances we found a range of reactions ranging from 'hard-line' male dominance to some accommodation to alternative situations. We start with an uncompromisingly traditionalist stance. The respondent is a man in his 50s, originally from the north, but interviewed in Bathore, outside Tirana.

> What do you mean, who decides? I decide.
> *And your wife?*
> She hasn't got a problem ... there's no difference between us in the way we see things.

The second excerpt, from an interview with a middle-aged couple near Durrës, reveals a slightly more flexible attitude, but also makes the point that, when life is hard and income scarce, there is not much discussion to be had.

> Husband: In this family it is me who decides how the money is spent ... Over there, they can do what they want. They decide everything about their own places, I mean the ones they build here. We opened two separate accounts so they find it (their remitted income) when they come back. If I need money I just phone them and it is here in ten minutes, through Western Union.
> *What about your wife, what if she needs something different? Does she phone and ask them for money in the same way?*
> Husband: No, I phone. A couple of times she phoned, but we had agreed on what to ask first.
> Wife: We don't disagree on these matters. It's just the two of us here and look around, what can we want [to disagree about]?

Although it was nearly always the men who took financial decisions in the household, in most cases this seemed to be more of a *de jure* arrangement, whereas *de facto* decisions – to the extent that these need to be made – tended to be through the active consultation of all family members, as is apparent from this next excerpt:

> Well, of course it is my husband who decides in the end, but normally we take decisions together, even the little children, if they understand! [laughter]. When we decided to buy the land in Shkodër there was some disagreement between our two sons – the one living in Italy wants to return and live there, while the other one living in England would prefer we all stayed here in this place. In the end we bought it, because it was the best choice for all of us. (Family interview, rural north Albania, wife speaking)

Where negotiation over the destination of remittances takes place between migrant spouses, some jealousy and disagreement can result, as this example from our London fieldwork illustrates:

> We have supported both our families, although more my husband's. The money was used to build the new house and to buy new furniture. My husband is paying monthly for the education of his brother. He is also sending money to his sister who is completing a university degree. However, they are never content with what we send … they always ask for more. They think that it is easy to make money here … We sent a lot in the beginning, £2,500 per year, but not any longer … Sometimes I argue with my husband because he always agrees to give them money … and they decide how to use it as well … All they do is ask my husband for money and he gives it to them. (F24, London)

The gender–power dynamics inherent in the Albanian virilocal marriage system, whereby a daughter passes into the family of her husband and hence has no further economic responsibility towards her parents, throws up severe financial imbalances in the migration context of remittance flows. Although some renegotiation can take place, as shown in the previous quote, migrant daughters are generally only allowed to help their parents in special circumstances, often under the guise of sending occasional 'presents' rather than regular remittances (King et al. 2003: 56). From the point of view of emigrant households in Albania, those with more sons are clearly more financially favoured than those with daughters. When we asked a middle-aged father of five daughters (and no sons) in central Albania whether his daughter who is abroad sent him any money, his answer was swift but rueful:

> No, of course not! She has got no responsibility for this family now, she is part of her husband's family and must contribute to its well-being. This is the tradition here … I have four more daughters, can you imagine?! Two are already married, and two are getting married soon … but there is no money coming into this household. Only expenses. I have invested a fortune in their education … but the moment they leave this house, not one penny comes back!

Return: Myth or Reality?

In Albania, great uncertainly surrounds the question of return migration. Amongst migrants there is much talk of return – but also of not returning. Amongst migrants' kin in Albania the return of their emigrant relatives is also much discussed – but tempered by a dawning realisation that perhaps their family members will not return. This is especially hard on elderly parents who fear a lonely old age, as we saw earlier in this chapter. Amongst government officials, NGO commentators and academics there is likewise a growing swell of debate – about how much return movement is actually taking place, about return trends in the future, and about the potential of returning migrants to invest in, and hence stimulate, the Albanian economy. Lacking in all this debate is hard information. Who are the returnees, where are they relocating to, and how do they survive in a country which they previously fled because it held no future for them? We first review the types of return that are thought to be taking place; this is based on a few key interviews, and on government, NGO and academic reports – also few in number. We then present our own fieldwork findings, drawn mainly from interviews carried out in Albania with returnees and residual migrant household members. We describe what interviewees have done since returning from abroad, and we discuss what changes would have to take place in Albania in order for more migrants who are currently abroad to return.

Types of Return

In Chapter 3 we mapped and tabulated the spatial pattern of both emigration and internal migration in Albania, covering the intercensal period 1989–2001. Unfortunately there are no data to map the geography of return migration. What we have instead is a series of more intuitively observed types of return based on 'common knowledge' of the phenomenon of Albanian migration and return, especially the insights shared with us by key interviewees. To some extent these types of return interface logically with the broad types of emigration, also discussed in Chapter 3. Thus temporary migration implies temporary return, overseas settlement in North America or Australia implies no return, clandestine emigration leads to involuntary repatriation, and so on.

- *Repatriation – 'return as failure'*. Forced return – the most common form is repatriation as an 'illegal' immigrant – is regarded as a return of failure, since the enterprise of emigration has been curtailed, with all the personal and economic implications this has. Often, the intention of the forced returnee is to emigrate again as soon as possible in order to revive the migration project.

- *Family and holiday returns.* Such returns are part and parcel of 'normal' emigration and are expressions of living transnationally. For Albanians in Italy and Greece who have legal status, such returns are unproblematic since there are relatively cheap bus, ferry and air connections which have grown in response to migrants' needs. However, as we have already noted, visits home for migrants who do not have the requisite residence permits may be impossible, thereby creating splits in families and displacement from 'home'.
- *Seasonal return.* This type of return occurs as a function of employment opportunities, especially in Greece, where work in agriculture, tourism and construction has a seasonal pattern. Such returns may also converge with migrant workers' wishes to maintain a family base or connection to Albania, rather than become full-time emigrants.
- *Open-ended return.* In this scenario return takes place without, necessarily, a long-term intention to resettle for good. The idea is to 'see how it goes' over the short to medium term. Amongst the factors which might contribute to the decision to remain in Albania permanently or re-emigrate are finding satisfactory employment, income levels, the success of a business, and personal and family circumstances. If the return involves bringing back children, their ability to (re)settle may be a key element in future migration planning too.
- *Return for good.* This is likely to be the case for returnees who are able to build a successful future for themselves in Albania, perhaps by setting up a viable business. More negatively, individuals who view their emigration as a disappointing or disillusioning experience may also be back for good. Older returnees are more likely to return permanently, especially as they approach retirement age.

Surveys on Albanians' intentions to return rarely ask about these different types and conceptualisations of return. Respondents' answers may not be very comparable because of this lack of consistency in the *meaning* of return. This problem should be borne in mind in the following survey data.

- In the first large-scale sociological analysis of Albanian migration, carried out via interviews with migrants in Italy and Greece in the early 1990s ($n = 1,148$), Barjaba and Perrone (1996: 150) found that nearly half of the interviewees (45 per cent) did not know whether they would return to Albania or not. Only 28 per cent thought that they would return to Albania for good.
- A late-1990s survey by Paterno and Toigo (2004) of three immigrant groups in Italy – Moroccans ($n = 105$), Tunisians ($n = 80$) and Albanians ($n = 145$) – found that Albanians were the most likely to have plans to return home (respectively 30.5, 49.4 and 53.8 per cent had such plans). Curiously, the same survey also found that Albanians were the most

likely to intend to stay in Italy for good (respectively 21.2, 20.5 and 30.3 per cent said so).[6]
- A 2002/3 survey of legal emigrants entering Albania over the Christmas/New Year holidays (brief questionnaire administered at ports of entry, $n = 1,200$) found that 66 per cent would like to return home, 20 per cent had no intention of returning, whilst the rest were adopting a 'wait and see' attitude (Gedeshi et al. 2003: 61). The 'return' orientation was much higher for emigrants in Greece (79 per cent) than for those in Italy (52 per cent) or further afield (Canada 27 per cent, USA 17 per cent).
- The most recent survey, carried out in April–May 2005 by de Zwager et al. (2005: 56–60), interviewed 712 emigrants, mainly in Greece (405), Italy (218) and the UK (60). Overall, 55 per cent stated they would like to return, 21 per cent said they definitely did not want to return, and 24 per cent were undecided. This time the propensity to return was only slightly higher for Albanians in Greece (58 per cent) compared to Italy (54 per cent).

What do these surveys reveal? On the face of it, two things. First, decisions about return tend to become more clear-cut as time passes – witness the much higher 'undecided' share in the first survey. Second, it would appear that at least half of Albanian emigrants would like to return. But this begs a further question: what is the relationship between a wish to return and the likelihood of the return actually happening? A migrant may want to return but know full well that this is impossible because of economic conditions. As with emigration (cf. Carling 2002), there is a difference between *aspiration* and *reality* of return. So, a wish to return may not eventuate a return; indeed, the wish to return might well be fuelled by the inability to do so.

In other words, return to Albania remains in a deeply ambiguous state. This comes out in our interview data, and is also reflected in statistics and the literature on Albanian migration. The title of Kosta Barjaba's (2000c) collection of essays on Albanian emigration – *Ondate senza Ritorno* ('Waves without Return') – reveals his view that most emigrant Albanians will not return. A few years later Labrianidis and Hatziprokopiou (2005) wrote that 'Albanians were returning to their country after all'. Despite the fact that some return *has* taken place, most authorities – key informants and our own field observations – confirm a weak propensity for Albanian migrants in Italy and elsewhere to return. Above all, this is because the current state of the Albanian economy offers little encouragement to do so.

Experiences of Return

During our Albanian fieldwork we interviewed several returnees who had returned under a variety of circumstances. Rather few said they had returned for good; for most, the return was provisional; and for some it had been an involuntary return. We also encountered migrants who were back home on family or holiday visits, and we voice some of their testimonies too.

At base, the scale of return has to do with the balance between push and pull factors operating in reverse – i.e., push factors from the destination country, and pulls from Albania. For the most part both these forces are relatively weak, hence limited stimulus for return is generated. In Italy, as we have seen in foregoing chapters, integration has been relatively rapid: employment has been found, accommodation has been secured, savings have been accumulated, friendships have been forged, the language has been learnt, and so on. Despite their continuing stigmatisation by Italians, Albanians have come to identify with Italy and Italian popular culture, and increasingly see their future – and that of their children – there rather than back in Albania. Much the same story of reasonably successful integration, especially since the post-1998 regularisations, is found for Albanians in Greece (Hatziprokopiou 2003; Lazaridis 2004; Lyberaki and Maroukis 2005; Pratsinakis 2005).

On the Albanian side, the pull factors attracting returnees are weak. Of course there are family pressures to return, but there are many other elements which repulse potential returnees. These include a still-backward economy, extremely low wages and incomes, lack of infrastructure, a general climate of political venality and civic corruption, and a sense of pessimism about possible change. Above all, it seems, Albanians do not 'trust' their country; in the wake of the collapse of communism, there is very little by way of civic culture (Maroukis 2005: 219). At an existential level, too, Albanians are unsure as to what kind of Albania they are looking to return to, or where they would see themselves 'fitting in'. They reject the old, harsh Albania of 'the regime' (although now and again some elements of nostalgia resurface), but they are disoriented and discouraged by the post-1990 transformation, where everything seems chaotic and people are pitted against each other, unprotected by legal safeguards or a sense of security, economic or otherwise.

Let us explore some of these issues through the direct testimonials of migrants, both those living abroad and returnees. Some cross-generational aspects of return were mentioned earlier, when we discussed the obligation – now fading – of adult children, especially youngest sons, to look after ageing parents. The following account describes a different type of return, of a husband and father for whom family separation proved to be impossible because of the fact that he had no legal status abroad:

> I had to come back because of my family. My wife and my children could not carry on without me. It was very difficult ... they were crying every time I phoned ... My wife in particular wanted me to return ... she said it was too

much for her on her own ... I would have stayed two more years to secure a better future for my family ... but it would have been better if they gave me a permit to stay instead, so that I could get better wages. Because I had no documents I had to work off the books ... and the money was not that great ... I could not send home much, just enough to fix the place up a bit ... If I had had a permit to stay I could have stayed abroad a bit longer and come home and see my family every three months or so. (M31, Breglumasi, near Tirana)

Where undocumented migrants had been repatriated by the authorities – as was happening quite a lot from the UK during the fieldwork in Albania – the intention was usually to go abroad again as soon as possible, depending on the contacts and resources required for this.

They repatriated two young guys from our family recently. They stayed here for a month and then left for Italy. They said it immediately – I cannot live here anymore, I'm not staying here, I have to go back. (M50s, Rinia, near Durrës)

Migrants who return on holidays or for short visits are often struck by the poverty, squalor and poor facilities in Albania, after having become used to better living conditions abroad.

When my two sons came back ... they could not believe what they saw here ... After two days they couldn't stand it any more ... they didn't say anything, of course, but it was plain to see. (M48, Bathore, near Tirana)

Infrastructure is certainly a major obstacle to return, not just in terms of personal inconvenience, but also because it hampers attempts to set up functioning businesses, which need guaranteed supplies of power and water, and decent road connections. An interviewee in the World Bank study (De Soto et al. 2002: 8) summed up this barrier to return:

Infrastructure is a big problem ... There aren't enough roads. We need to have water ... but now we don't any more. Power is low and interrupted all the time ... we cannot use domestic appliances. If the state improves infrastructure, people will come back from emigration and invest. Otherwise no-one will come back here to live. (Interview, near Sarandë)

Our interview data, and the results of other surveys, do indicate a business orientation on the part of many Albanian migrants who are wanting to return. In a study of Albanians in Apulia, Giorgio and Luisi (2001: 98) found that a quarter of their subjects wanted to start a business on their return to Albania. Of them ($n=116$), most were oriented to commerce (28 per cent), small industries and crafts (26 per cent) and tourism (18 per cent); only 8 per cent thought of investing in agriculture. Likewise, many of the 'residual families' – usually the emigrants' parents – we talked to expected their children to return and perhaps open a business. To what extent this expectation was founded on reality or hope was hard to tell. Two fathers talk about their sons:

> My son ... wants to come back here to live. He told me recently that he just wants to make some more money over there and then open his own construction firm here ... to be a builder here.

> When they get married they will come back here and open a business. They want to open their own restaurant, or a shop, they want to be self-employed.

But there are many objective difficulties to an economically successful return. The above two interviews took place in the new settlements springing up around Durrës and Tirana respectively. These two cities are the economic heart of Albania and the only region where the population is growing, above all by internal migration. Elsewhere, opportunities for returnees are not so good.

> What kind of activity could we open here? There are no roads, no water supply, it's not up to us to build these things. (M40s, north Albania)

Those who have returned confirm the scale of these infrastructural problems, which are especially a barrier to business development. Two examples from our returnee interviews:

> Here there is no proper electricity, we only have it four hours a day. How am I supposed to work in these conditions? I considered buying a generator, but it would be too expensive, because the machinery in the factory is very powerful ... So we can only work at night ... we are paralysed without electricity, it is our main problem. (M40s, owner of a paint firm, Gjirokastër)

> I decided to open the bar here whilst I was working abroad – to start an enterprise that would employ and support the whole family. Altogether I invested more than 1 million Lek that I saved during five years of hard work in Greece. I bought the premises, a generator and all the things to make the business work ... Here you sometimes don't have electricity until the evening ... and water is a problem too. So I built a well for the water and bought a generator for electricity. Here you have to solve even the most basic problems for yourself, the state does nothing for you. (M40s, bar owner, Shkodër)

In areas away from the main towns, business prospects of returnee enterprises are limited by a shrinking market due to further migration and depopulation. South of Vlorë, and all the way down to Sarandë, stretches the most beautiful coastal scenery in Albania, one of the northern Mediterranean's last undeveloped coastal landscapes. Some embryonic tourist enterprises are springing up, yet the area continues to be affected by depopulation and seasonal migration to Greece. Passing through the villages of Dhermi and Vuno in winter, we found most of the houses deserted and the land uncultivated. In the streets of these villages only a few elderly people could be seen. At Himarë, the largest settlement along this coast, with a population of 3,200 according to the 2001 census, we stopped for lunch at a restaurant run by two returnees. They explained how the shrinking of the local population was affecting their small business:

> I am sorry that half the things on the menu are not available, but we keep very few things in stock in winter as very few people come here to eat ... Everybody from this area is in Greece. We were also there, we came back a couple of years ago, to build this restaurant, but this is the last winter we spend here ... There is no tourism in winter, it's not worth it, there are very few people left here. In the summer it is different, many migrants come here with their families, they even come from Kosovo and business then is good.

As we saw in Chapter 3, the district of Vlorë has been affected by emigration to a greater extent than most other parts of Albania, and this has both positive and negative implications for its future development. On the one hand, high remittance inflows have played a key role in keeping poverty at bay, so that people here are better off than in other rural areas in Albania. But emigration has undermined the demographic and cultural survival of many communities, nowadays inhabited mostly by older people. With family abandoned, the only activity offering possibilities for socioeconomic development and employment is summer tourism. During the summer season the villages are temporarily flooded by their enlarged and returning families, by Albanian emigrants from other parts of the country who come here on holiday, and by the holiday visits of the local and international elites from Tirana. International tourism to Albania has yet to take hold (D. Hall 2000).

Missing infrastructure, poor market demand and seasonality are not the only obstacles to returnee enterprise. Business plans may also be frustrated by the lack of personal security, shortage of credit and general political instability. This returnee described his various attempts to set up a small business and the difficulties he had faced:

> Of course I would like to start a new business ... but it's not just a question of money ... it's also got to do with security. If I had the financial resources I would start my own wholesale business. I actually tried to open a dairy once, because my father used to be a dairyman. With the money I had earned in Greece I bought all the tanks and stuff, but just as I was returning home to resettle, the troubles began [referring to the pyramids], it seemed as if a civil war would break out ... there were roadblocks and people were getting robbed ... I got afraid and decided to sell everything ... However, when I did come back [a little later] I built a cowshed to start producing milk and meat, but we had to close it down; in order to make money, it needed more investment ... So I decided to open a petrol station, which is not going very well because the road here is in a terrible state and there is not much passing traffic ... If only the government could guarantee some security, and offer some credit to build

new economic activities … I mean long-term credit, not a few months but 10–20 years. (M35, central Albania)

Our final example of migrant business development comes from an agricultural setting in the district of Lushnjë in south-central Albania. This is a rather rare example of a successful family-farm enterprise, boosted by remittances and savings from family members abroad – sons in Italy and the UK. One son remains abroad with his own young family, the other works on the farm. The interviewee, in his early 50s, had been an agronomist during the communist period. The farm is a self-standing economic enterprise. Glasshouses have been built, and the farmer has diversified income sources by opening a farm-based retail outlet for agricultural supplies to local farmers.

> Now we are fine, I mean we are normal. My son is not sending anything now because he has to take care of his own affairs and his own family over there … In the beginning he used to send us 200 or 300 dollars every month, through Western Union … now he has his own responsibilities over there.

When asked about the possibilities for returnees to develop new enterprises and whether there was any financial help from banks or the state, the interviewee replied:

> Well, nothing really … The state is so poor and disorganised that we must help it, not the other way round! The thing is, you either have a son abroad who can help you, or you just stay where you are. Private banks can give money only to people who already own something … You see, we own but we don't own – do you get it? There is nobody here who can tell you what you own [because of the chaotic land privatisation] and so banks cannot help you at all … They can only offer you short-term loans at very high interest rates, more than 20 per cent – who can afford that? All the people who have started businesses have done so through the help of their relatives abroad. But only a few decide to invest, because the country is still very unstable. Do you remember 1997 and all those troubles? Well, people lost their trust and so just use money to survive, to eat. They would rather keep it under the bed because they do not trust the government, the politicians … The memory of the pyramid schemes is still vivid … It is not that people don't have money, they do. But they keep it in a vase because they are afraid to lose it. Not to mention the taxes … they are so high … because nobody pays them and those who do pay have to pay for everybody else.

The success of this enterprise was mainly due to the interlocking of the sons' earning capacity as emigrants abroad and the father's expertise as a trained agronomist. This example demonstrates that success in the migration–development nexus in Albania can often depend on the pooling of family resources and expertise, rather than on the individualised behaviour of the returnee acting on his (or her) own.

Albania and Migration: What Future?

The last decade and a half has seen a profound political, economic and sociocultural transformation in Albania. The depth and range of this multifaceted change have been such as to defy both prediction and classification: a turbulent and chaotic transformation unprecedented in the history of Albania, with few parallels elsewhere (UNDP 2002: 17). The most obvious similarities are with the other post-communist countries of Europe. But what distinguished Albania was its very different point of departure – the poorest, most rural, isolated and introverted country of the continent, ruled by an ultra-orthodox communist autarchy which rejected even those reforms which had been implemented in other communist states. Most Albanians were naively prepared for their sudden engagement with the wider world, and the country all too easily fell prey to the polarising and partly-destructive effects of an abrupt switch to a neoliberal economy spearheaded by the predatory instincts of Western capitalism.

Communism's collapse was replaced by a desire to *become a country like the rest of Europe* as soon as possible. 'We want Albania to be like the rest of Europe' was the slogan of the democratic movement in 1991, as it fought off the last vestiges of the 'late-communist' regime. Albanian aspirations were laced with simplistic visions of political democracy, constitutional reform, and the privatisation of almost everything. Economic development was viewed as unlimited external assistance and foreign investment (UNDP 2002: 17). For its part, Europe, both in the form of the EU and, individually, from Albania's closest Western neighbours, Italy and Greece, has been complicit in fostering the 'European destiny' of Albania. It must not be forgotten that the Albanian political, economic and migration drama unfolded alongside the break-up of the former Yugoslavia, Albania's 'other' neighbour which all but encircled the country to the east. For sure, the Western powers did not want Albania to complicate an already messy Balkan unravelling. Hence the trade-off: EU, and especially Italian, investment and humanitarian aid in return for a neoliberal regime and the control of external migration. The EU has identified Albania as one of its top-priority third countries for the control of irregular migration, and the issue of migration management has emerged as a vital element of the so-called 'Stabilisation and Association Process'. Since the end of 2004, when the *National Strategy on Migration* was published (Government of Albania 2004), Albania has a five-year national action-plan on this key issue. Some progress has already been made. On 18 February 2006, the EU President Jose Manuel Barroso addressed the Albanian Parliament with the following words: 'Albania has made much progress over the past year. As a consequence, we now plan to take Albania's relationship with the European Union to the next level.'[7]

If the EU has instrumentalised migration in its developing relationship with Albania, this ignores, to some extent, the depth of meaning – both economic and psychological – for Albania itself. We consider each of these dimensions in turn.

Migration, Development and Sociospatial Inequality

Evidence on the economic significance of migration for Albania and its people has been presented throughout this book, especially in Chapters 3, 5 and earlier in this chapter. Within the context of the new opportunities and risks posed by Albania's post-communist transformation, migration (both external and internal) emerged as the main strategy of survival for a large number of households in all regions of the country. Therefore it should be seen as a coping mechanism rather than a route to prosperity and riches. Our own field observations, and most other surveys too (e.g., De Soto et al. 2002: 39–41; de Zwager et al. 2005; Kule et al. 2002), confirm that migration and remittances do determine to a large extent the economic status of Albanian families. Although all the 'residual households' we interviewed lived in modest dwellings, the difference between those who received remittances and those who did not was clearly apparent. And it was also clear that some households – in particular those with many sons abroad – did better than those with fewer emigrant members.

Other survey data presented in this book confirm the essential characteristics of the Albanian emigration: its demographic selectivity (younger adult males predominating, but less so over time); its human capital endowment (two-thirds of emigrants having completed at least secondary education); and its spatial incidence (originating from all parts of Albania, but especially from southern, central and coastal districts). From Chapter 3 we learnt that, although Albanian migration has been essentially poverty-driven, the poverty–migration nexus is by no means straightforward. In the north of Albania, poverty is certainly the main factor stimulating *internal* out-migration; but *severe* poverty constrains the ability to emigrate abroad, except perhaps for short-term casual work in Greece. Although emigration to Italy has occurred from all parts of Albania, there are selection filters at work: emigration to this country has been mainly from the more urbanised, coastal districts, and with a predominance of better-educated, better-off family origins (Carletto et al. 2004; Zezza et al. 2005). However, Stampini et al. (2004) show that, as time passes, emigration – including that to Italy – spreads to less-educated people and to poorer areas of the country.

From the other side of the migration equation (destination and return), complementary findings emerge from recent survey research by Lois Labrianidis and his colleagues. This shows that Albanian migrants in Italy, as well as being from less-poor backgrounds than those in Greece, also earn and remit more, but are less likely to be able to reintegrate back to Albania in the event of return migration (Labrianidis and Lyberaki 2004; Labrianidis and Hatziprokopiou 2005; see also de Zwager et al. 2005). Once again, this confirms the contrast between the back-and-forth nature of much Albanian migration to Greece, and its more permanent character in Italy. This in turn reinforces the strong impression gained from our Italian fieldwork that Albanians are transforming themselves into a stable minority of the Italian population. Indeed, on many objective criteria Albanians are the immigrants who are the most similar to the Italians themselves, even if most Italians are unwilling to admit this fact. The irony of Italians' rejection and ambivalence towards their Adriatic neighbours, who were once their colonial subjects, and who have been subjected more recently to the neocolonialism of both Italian media penetration and Italian military–humanitarian missions, should not go unnoticed. Albanians' assimilation is thus asymmetrical: all the progress is on the Albanian side, but it is met with resistance by Italian society.

Back in Albania, the potentially beneficial economic impact of external migration has been seized on by the government, which sets out a blueprint for capitalising on migration as a development stimulus in its *National Strategy on Migration* (Government of Albania 2004).[8] Covering the five-year period 2005–10, the National Strategy on Migration (NSM) aims to provide Albania with a more comprehensive and integrated policy on migration – moving from a series of ad hoc measures designed mainly to combat irregular migration to a more holistic policy based on migration management. More specifically, the NSM covers the following policy domains:

- protection of the rights of Albanian emigrants abroad;
- linking up and strengthening the identity of Albanian communities abroad;
- channelling migrants' remittances into economically productive business investments;
- designing a better labour migration policy, in cooperation with destination countries, for instance in working out quotas of temporary or seasonal migrants destined for key sections of labour demand;
- encouraging return migration, especially of skilled migrants;
- facilitating the travel abroad of Albanian nationals on short-term visas;
- developing an appropriate legal and institutional framework for managing emigration and return.

Within the current five-year strategy, and for some time thereafter, Albania is likely to remain a country of emigration; however, over the longer term the NSM optimistically sees Albania as a country of immigration, following the now-established trend of other Southern European countries. More immediately, the NSM complements two other strategy documents approved earlier – measures to combat trafficking in human beings (2001) and the integrated border management strategy (2003).

In the rest of this subsection, we critically re-examine four dimensions of the economics of Albanian migration: remittances, human resource implications, impact on political and civic culture, and sociospatial polarisation. Where relevant, we introduce the NSM's perspectives on these issues.

The main economic impact of emigration on Albania is the inflow of remittances, dealt with at length earlier in the chapter. The official policy of the NSM is to 'drive remittances to investment into businesses' (Government of Albania 2004: 43). This is to be achieved by two means: increasing the share of remittances transferred through formal banking channels, so that banks have a stock of capital to lend for business development; and shifting the 'usage model' away from immediate consumption (on food, clothing, household goods, construction of new homes, etc.) into business investment outlets. This accurately reflects the mantra of 'remittances-for-development' rhetoric worldwide (e.g. IOM 2005: 269–274). In Albania an alternative view, more cynical, but probably realistic, sees any attempt to 'manage' remittances in this way as unlikely to succeed because it would be resisted by the migrants as just another attempt to interfere with their individually-earned economic resources geared towards personal survival and the development of their own private schemes. Along with the wider project of migration, these 'private schemes', some of which may shade into illegal activities, are the people's response to the collapsing collective context, widely perceived as corrupt and untrustworthy. With the memory of the pyramids fiasco less than a decade old, why should migrants listen to government entreaties to invest their hard-won remittances this way or that?

This leads into a wider debate, which we have generally not seen as part of this book's remit but which should at least be mentioned, concerning the emergence of violence, criminality and trafficking as strategies of survival by different social actors in the context of the post-communist transformation. Undoubtedly, illegal activities – ranging from individual acts of banditry to widespread and endemic political corruption – have become embedded into the wider dynamics of change in Albania in the last decade and a half (Schwandner-Sievers 2001). Organised crime has grown steadily more sophisticated as it consolidates links between closely-knit Albanian diaspora clans and the wider criminal world. The government has responded with a series of highly-publicised anti-trafficking measures. However, while the authorities acknowledge the existence of organised crime in Albania, they appear not to have accepted the full extent of its ties to individuals in top state offices, the police and politics. In many areas the traffickers work with the complicity of police and customs officers and enjoy the protection of high-ranking politicians. Key interviews with individuals close to the phenomenon strongly suggest that a fair share of remittances finds its way into fuelling illegal activities, above all trafficking of would-be migrants and smuggling of contraband. Of course the illicit nature of these activities means it is impossible to estimate the share of migrant earnings 'diverted' in this way. Furthermore, the booming construction industry benefits from the large amount of illegally earned money that is laundered through the building of hotels, bars, restaurants and blocks of flats. As one interviewee said to us, pointing to a large block nearing completion, 'How could he have built it with his own sweat?'.

The second major impact of emigration is on Albania's human resources. One obvious repercussion is the removal of unemployment, either directly (when the unemployed emigrate) or indirectly (when emigrants vacate jobs which are filled by unemployed persons). According to the NSM, which wants to project an optimistic interpretation of the potential benefits of emigration, 'the work of Albanian emigrants in the advanced economies of the host countries has provided them with familiarity and know-how of management style, work ethics, new sectors of economy, techniques and technology that is new to Albania. Hence the return of such migrants could contribute to the transfer of (these) skills to Albania' (Government of Albania 2004: 8). However, most emigrants do not work in jobs where such skills are acquired. They are denied access to these jobs by three barriers which act either singly or in combination: their confinement to casual, low-status jobs in the informal economy; anti-immigrant or anti-Albanian discrimination in the labour market; and non-recognition of their Albanian qualifications. Evidence of these barriers was presented in Chapter 5.

Given the absence of statistics on return migration, its scale, nature and impact are the subject of considerable debate and differences of interpretation, again as noted above. Whilst some authors are cautious about the size of the return flow, and hence its developmental impact (e.g., King 2005b; King and Vullnetari 2003), others are more optimistic. The most forceful proponent of return-led development in Albania is Beryl Nicholson who, based on village studies in southern Albania, argues that returning migrants are 'agents of development' who deliver 'cost-effective development' (Nicholson 2004a: 94) through their establishment of micro-enterprises which serve local needs – examples are 'the tractor, the shop and the filling-station' (Nicholson 2004b). In another paper Nicholson (2002) points out that returned emigrants not only contribute to grass-roots development in Albania but also continue to benefit their respective host countries after return. She gives examples of returnees from Italy and Greece who have set up businesses importing and selling their former employers' products in Albania. Nicholson's return-as-development thesis is given further support by Kule et al. (2002) who, based on more extensive survey data (interviews with 1,500 migrants and non-migrants and with 200 employers), find some evidence that emigration increases the chances of employment for returnees, when compared to job-seekers who have not emigrated.

Another human resources aspect of emigration from Albania is its manifestation as a brain drain. According to Gedeshi et al. (1999), half of Albania's scientists and academics left the country during the 1990s; departure rates were highest for the most highly-qualified and senior intellectuals. Whilst much of this emigration was economically motivated – above all to attain higher salaries than the precarious stipends paid by Albania's universities and academies – many people left for political and cultural reasons. The political nature of appointments to government, civil-service and some academic posts in an environment which was (and remains) polarised between the two dominant parties meant that those belonging to the faction not in power have had to leave the country or suffer ostracisation and humiliation.

Opportunities for emigration have also presented themselves to increasing numbers of Albanian students, many of whom have been well-placed to take up grant and bursary schemes offered by international foundations and foreign governments. Nearby Italy has been a prime destination for these students, given the fact that so many young Albanians speak Italian. Currently five thousand are studying at Italian universities. Low university fees and easy travel access are further attractions for Albanians to enrol at Italian universities. A small quota of university students were amongst our interviewees in Rome, Modena and Lecce, and we heard their experiences of living, studying and working in Italy in the prior three chapters.

The key question with brain drain is, of course, return: is there a 'brain regain' which may benefit the source country, especially if young, highly-educated people return with their human capital enhanced by further qualifications and experience? Some highly-educated individuals do return after their studies abroad; others no doubt consider it but do not act on it, at least for the time being. As the political parties wax and wane in governmental power, those whose jobs depend on political patronage emigrate or return in little waves. The recent switch back to the Democrats in the 2005 election saw a significant number of foreign-educated young professionals and technocrats incorporated into the new government at various levels. But opportunities for all those university-educated Albanians who are currently abroad are woefully insufficient. Given the Albanian political and economic situation – low salaries and a prevailing culture of bureaucracy, indifference and mediocrity in public administration – there is little to encourage them to come back and help solve the very real problems of the country (UNDP 2000b: 42).

Thirdly, emigration also has an impact on political and civic culture. The great majority of Albanian emigrants live and work in countries with liberal democracies; although many emigrants say they are too busy with work to familiarise themselves or engage with host-country politics, nevertheless some familiarity with more 'open' democratic principles rubs off. But it is uncertain whether emigrants wish or are able to engage with Albanian politics back home. Most Albanian emigrants left at least partly out of a sense of rejection of the political system in Albania. For many, this represented a double rejection: both of the communist regime and of the clique-ridden political system that succeeded it. Albanian migrants are not so much apathetic towards home-country politics; rather they are profoundly disappointed in a corrupt political system which remains trapped in a duel between two hegemonic parties and their respective behemoths.

Thanos Maroukis (2005) argues that part of the answer to the question of how Albania's political and civil-society renewal is to take place lies in the hands of the migrant community, and in particular in the social-capital-rich informal networks of relatives, friends and co-villagers, not in formally constituted Albanian migrant associations, which remain weakly developed. Such bottom-up civic improvement can only be successful if supported by appropriately robust state frameworks, for 'legality is the decisive springboard for economic development and social advancement of Albania today' (Maroukis 2005: 219). As things stand, the Democrat and Socialist Parties cannot guarantee the full democratisation and transparency of Albania's political landscape and civil society. Such a top-down reform needs external agents such as the EU, World Bank and the NGO sector in Albania. What should result, in the view of Maroukis, is a synergy whereby beneficial and externally managed top-down reforms are complemented by grass-roots measures aimed at enhanced citizen participation and consensus building (2005: 226).

Three flaws can be identified in Maroukis' vision of an Albanian transnational civil society based on its evolving diaspora. The first is that most Albanian emigrants abstain from any kind of political or civil-society engagement with the homeland beyond sending remittances to their families. Their sense of abandonment by the Albanian state and of hopelessness for improvement estranges them from Albania, the more so as time passes. Second, the two main countries where Albanians have settled, Italy and Greece, are hardly paeans of political and civil-society virtue, so the trust-enhancing learning process becomes limited. And third, the top-down approach of introducing improved civil-society values into Albania via externally financed NGO projects generates its own circles of parallel social formations, enclaves and intrigue, as Steven Sampson (1996) has devastatingly portrayed in his essay on 'the social life of projects'.

Finally, in this overview of Albanian migration–development dynamics, we highlight the relationship to social and spatial inequality. This is a complex story, involving an interweaving of international and internal migration, the progressive polarisation of the Albanian space economy, and the rise of new market-oriented business and professional classes alongside the post-communist political elites. Although this polarisation does have a pronounced geographical expression – above all the contrast between the new burgeoning urban, almost cosmopolitan, world of Tirana and the peripheral highland regions of traditional views, ongoing poverty and economic marginalisation – its true manifestation is much more complex and is based on the juxtaposition of various elements – 'modern' and 'traditional', poverty and material wealth, introversion and extroversion – sometimes even in the same family or household. The following extract from one of the Human Development Reports for Albania captures the coexistence of various social, economic and cultural forms within families and small village communities or urban neighbourhoods:

> Albanian families are going through a multifaceted transformation so profound as to defy the traditional system of classification. Whereas [before 1990] the sole source of income was a totally predictable wage from a state institution, [today there are] ... multiple sources of income: income from work, income from the sale or rental of privatized property, remittances from emigrants, interest on savings deposits ... The new Albanian economy offers a wide variety of activities, from traditional, poorly-paid but secure state jobs to modern, well-paid and highly demanding jobs with private firms or foreign organizations, from temporary opportunities to permanent positions, all within the same area ... If we look outside the main urban centers, it is not rare to find large families, the members of which do very different kinds of work. Thus we see the coexistence of the typically rural with the typically urban, of the traditional with the contemporary, and of physical labour with intellectual work. Especially in the suburbs of urban areas and in villages near them, different members of the same family may be engaged in herding, agriculture or trade. In these families, one or two young men may be working in Italy or Greece; someone else may have found employment in the service sector in a nearby city, as a waiter, cook or postal worker ... [Another] characteristic of Albanian families is the strong heterogeneity of living conditions, in that people often seem to enjoy an advanced standard of living in one sense but to be lacking basic necessities in another. Especially in cities, but also in certain villages, it is not rare to find a household with a remote-control colour television but little or no running water. The owner of a Mercedes may keep it in a muddy yard enclosed by dilapidated walls. Youths sporting jeans may be accompanied by their mothers dressed in traditional garb. In cities, horse-drawn wagons weave in between luxury automobiles. Thousands of cramped, modest apartments stand in stark contrast to hundreds of newly built houses with ample space and light. (UNDP 1996: 18)

This lengthy quote offers everyday examples of a set of interlinked phenomena – migration, globalisation, post-communism, poverty, the 'patchwork economy' – which are articulated in a specific way in the Albanian context, as Natalia Ribas Mateos has recently shown in her imaginative ethnography of Tirana–Durrës as a Mediterranean/Balkan 'border city' (2005: 276–339). Ribas Mateos' study shows that, although on a macro scale there are clear economic and demographic contrasts between the core of Tirana–Durrës and the peripheral regions of Albania, even within the core there are extreme contrasts. Ongoing migration, particularly that between the poverty-stricken north and the shantytowns in the interstices of the Tirana–Durrës corridor, spawns new microscale spatial expressions of centre–periphery. The peri-urban squatter settlements outside these two cities are a kind of inner periphery where, often, living conditions are little better than those left behind. But such places are, at least, 'slums of hope' rather than remote rural fastnesses of isolation and despair. For the rural–urban migrants, the new peri-urban dwelling offers a chance of work and income in the city, perhaps in the informal economy, or a launch-pad for emigration abroad and, ultimately, a platform on which to build something better on return.

If internal migration brings the 'periphery' to the 'core', then the periphery itself is far from homogenous. Regional towns and cities act as foci for local rural–urban migration. Some places, such as Korçë, show a certain dynamism due to a combination of their inherited prosperity (always relative, in the Albanian context), and their new role as receptors for local migration, returnees from abroad and small business development. Other places – Bajram Curri in the far north, Bilisht in the southwest – mushroom because of their strategic location on key routes to the nearby border. Yet others start to display a touristic future, notably Sarandë with its pleasant promenade, new hotels and extensive archaeological remains at nearby Butrint.

Onto this constantly shifting map of sociospatial polarisation has been projected elements of foreign culture, above all that of Italy. The fundamental cause of this xenophilia is rejection of a disavowed communist past combined with extreme uncertainty about the current state of the nation and what 'being Albanian' stands for. According to Becker and Engelberg (2004: 111) 'an Italian–Albanian symbiosis ... seems to pervade the whole country'. The mechanisms for this derive from Italian television's neocolonisation of Albania – a process which started well before the collapse of communism as we saw in Chapter 2 – and migration to and return from Italy. Italian culture has therefore acquired a particular status within Albania: for Albanians there seems to be Albania, Italy and then the rest of the world. Italy is seen as culturally closer, not really foreign – a more advanced version of local culture. Albanian young people, in particular, seem to feel differently about Italy than they do about other foreign countries: they seek and find similarities between Albanian and Italian culture in the name of a 'Mediterranean' identity. This does not imply that Albanian young people still prefer Italy as a potential migration destination; nowadays most prefer the idea of migrating to the UK, the US or Canada, even if a move to North America is unrealistic for all but a privileged and lucky few. What Italy represents is a nearby culture that functions as a complement to Albanian culture, compensating for those areas of Albanian culture that are seen as lacking, namely consumption, luxury, beauty, sexuality, fun. But, contrary to what Becker and Engelberg imply in their quote above, this layer of Italian culture is not spread evenly across Albania. It is most strongly felt in the urban areas and coastal districts: areas closest to Italy and where Italian TV transmissions were originally most clearly received. And there is also an age-related effect, most intensely felt by younger generations up to the age of thirty-five or thereabouts; these are the groups the most affected by watching Italian TV in their formative years, and thus able to speak Italian. Many will have visited Italy or have siblings or other family members living there.

A Diaspora in the Making?

For Albanians the meaning of emigration is not just about economic survival and coping with poverty. The ability to travel abroad is important within the context of the country's communist past. Albania's history of extreme isolation has left a scar on the collective memory of the people who draw a direct connection between democratisation and the freedom to go abroad. But nowadays restrictions on freedom of travel derive not directly from Albania's own government, but from the denial of visa-free movement on the part of so many countries. The Albanian gulag, previously clamped from the inside by Hoxha's repressive mechanisms of ultra-control, has now been recreated from the outside by the EU's rejection of third-country nationals and by increasingly rigorous surveillance of border areas. The Albanian government has been drawn into compliance with this repressive regime of migration control as its price for closer economic and political ties to Europe.

But, to a large extent, the genie is out of the bottle. Now, one in four Albanians is an emigrant, and relatively few are likely to return, at least for the short to medium term. The scale of the migration that has occurred from Albania since 1990 is without precedent in Europe in recent years; it is unique both because of its relative scale and because of its concentration almost exclusively on two neighbouring countries.

Such a massive and recent emigration localised to adjacent countries hardly fits the conventional definition of a diaspora, which implies deep historical roots, a wide scattering of destinations and a measure of forced exile (Cohen 1997). And yet, viewed in a broader historical and geographical sweep, we can indeed talk about an Albanian diaspora or about the *diasporisation* of Albanian migration (cf. van Hear 1998: 216–217). The exile of the Arbëresh constitutes its first historical moment, resulting in a scattering of Albanians into some fifty villages and small towns in southern Italy and Sicily. Retrenchment of the borders round the new Albanian state in the early twentieth century created a 'close diaspora' in Kosovo, Macedonia and Montenegro where, today, as many ethnic Albanians live as are in Albania itself. Long-distance emigration of southern Albanians in the pre-communist twentieth century produced diasporic communities in the United States and Australia, as we recounted in Chapter 3. Then, during the 1960s and 1970s, ethnic Albanians from the former Yugoslavia migrated as *gastarbeiter* to Germany, Austria and Switzerland, evolving from their guestworker status into settled communities where, however, their Albanian ethnic or regional origin (as Kosovans, Macedonians, etc.) was often subsumed under another identity (Blumi 2003). The 1990s' exodus of Albanians to Greece and Italy was the next – and most dramatic – moment in this variegated migration history, creating another geographical layer of diaspora in nearby countries. At the end of the decade the Kosovan strife saw the scattering of ethnic Albanian refugees to several European countries, followed by the return of most of them after a relatively short time. Meanwhile Albanian migrants moved on from Italy and Greece to spread to other European countries such as France, Belgium, Germany and the UK, as well as to the US and Canada.

The use of the term 'diaspora' has become commonplace now in Albania, at least in official circles. There is an extensive reference to the Albanian diaspora in the National Strategy on Migration (Government of Albania 2004: 41–42, 69, 71), and an 'Institute for Albanian Diaspora' has recently been set up within the Ministry of Foreign Affairs. Amongst the Institute's specified tasks are: to assemble a complete inventory of information on the Albanian diaspora through the preparation of a geographical and demographic atlas; to provide networks of contacts linking the various parts of the diaspora, especially including links to the homeland; and to target university-educated Albanians currently living and studying abroad (Government of Albania 2004: 69). A clear distinction emerges here between the rank-and-file members of Albania's mass migration of low-status workers on the one hand, and the implied conceptualisation of the diaspora as a more elite grouping of individuals, who may make significant contributions to Albania's economic, political and cultural development, on the other. This was confirmed in 2006 when the UNDP funded the appointment of a Programme Manager for a project 'facilitating greater engagement of the diaspora in Albania's socio-economic development'. This post was to realise many of the economic objectives set out by the NSM for the diaspora, including industrial investment in Albania, bringing innovative ideas and international best practice to Albania, a 'brain-gain' incentive to attract highly-qualified returning migrants to public-sector employment, and the transfer of scientific and research knowledge via visits of foreign-based Albanian academics to lecture at Albanian universities.

Although emigration from Albania is likely to continue for some time, due above all to the still-strong economic and demographic push pressures, as well as migration network factors which structure the channels of migration in an ever-expanding web in time and space, its character has been changing in recent years, and these changes will continue. Peaks of emigration recorded in the early 1990s and around the pyramids' collapse in 1997 are unlikely to be repeated. Indeed in recent years there seems to have been a continuous decrease in the rate of emigration, due to several factors: increased effectiveness of border control; the campaign against human trafficking; improvements in both economic conditions and political stability in Albania; and the fact that so many people have already emigrated (Government of Albania 2004: 7). In destination countries, especially Italy, Albanian immigrants have become more settled and integrated, aided both by their own efforts and by periodic regularisation schemes. Family reunification consolidates communities abroad, in a way that was not possible in the early and mid 1990s, when most Albanian emigration was irregular. Labour migration and family reunion are increasingly complemented by young Albanians going abroad to study.

As the map of Albanian migration unfolds, with new destinations, new types of migration, and new expressions of Albanian transnational and diasporic identity, so the need arises for new studies of this 'moving picture'. This book has been about migration to one key destination country across the past decade and a half. Whilst providing an in-depth case-study which aspires to have some exemplary value, it has also taught us how any form of migration, to one place at one moment in time, is historically and geographically embedded in wider mobility schemes. Above all, Albanians have been adept at seeking out new destinations and new opportunities. The field is thus open for further study of one of Europe's most fascinating and emblematic recent migrant groups.

Notes

1. This is a strong custom in Albanian rural society which is still virilocal – the newly-married wife automatically switching to become part of her husband's family, and part of that family's system of honour and economic support. Traditionally, middle-aged and older parents live with one of their sons, usually the youngest, and his wife. The youngest son is referred to as *djali i pleqërisë* – 'the son of old age' – whose role it is to care for his parents in their later years. See King and Vullnetari (2006) for more details on this.
2. The Bank of Albania estimates remittances as the difference between foreign currency coming in and that going out. This is clearly a rather crude measure and does not exclude income from activities such as illegal smuggling. World Bank and IMF estimates of Albanian remittances are somewhat lower, although derived partially from Bank of Albania data (de Zwager et al. 2005: 21).
3. One indelible image from our fieldwork is the memory of a small middle-aged Albanian man staggering under the weight of an enormous TV set which he was carrying between the Greek and Albanian checkpoints on one of the roads connecting the two countries.

4   Not all these interview survey data are consistent, however. For instance, when de Zwager et al. interviewed Albanian emigrants abroad the balance of opinion was towards declining remittances in future years. When the same team surveyed remittance-receivers in Albania the majority expected remittances to increase, or at least to remain constant, in future (de Zwager et al. 2005: 51, 55).
5   There is one study, however, which questions the crucial nature of remittances in alleviating poverty and in distinguishing the non-poor from the poor. Arrehag et al. (2005) draw on returns from a survey of 1,315 households in the Korçë district of south-east Albania to show that there is surprisingly little difference in living standards between remittance-receiving and non-receiving households.
6   As with rather a lot of the research done on migrants by Italian scholars, there are doubts over the robustness of the field methodology. Only a few methodological considerations are given (Barsotti 2004: 20–22). It appears that the samples were not standardised by basic sociodemographic characteristics (nearly all the North Africans interviewed were men, whilst a quarter of the Albanians were women); methods of selection and interviewing varied; and, rather importantly, the three groups were interviewed in different regions of Italy – Moroccans in Tuscany, Tunisians in Ancona (Marche) and Albanians in Bari. Given the importance of the regional economic context to the nature of the immigrant experience in Italy, this is a serious flaw in the comparative analysis.
7   See J.M. Barroso: 'Building for the future: making a success of the Stabilisation and Association Agreement'. Parliament of Albania, speech 06/103, Tirana, 18 February 2006.
8   The National Strategy on Migration is financed by the European Community under the CARDS programme ('Community Assistance for Reconstruction, Development and Stabilisation') and has been supported technically by, and with co-funding from, the International Organization for Migration (IOM) in Tirana.

Bibliography

Abrahams, F. 1996. *Human Rights in Post-Communist Albania*. London: Human Rights Watch.
Adams, R.H. and J. Page. 2003. *International Migration, Remittances and Poverty in Developing Countries*. Washington DC: World Bank Policy Research Working Paper 3179.
Agnew, J. 1997. 'The myth of backward Italy in modern Europe', in B. Allen and M. Russo (eds), *Revisioning Italy: National Identity and Global Culture*. Minneapolis: University of Minnesota Press, pp. 23–42.
Albanian Center for Economic Research. 2002. *Common Country Assessment: Albania*. Tirana: ACER for the UN System in Albania.
Alia, R. 1988. *Our Enver*. Tirana: 8 Nëntori.
Allen, B. and M. Russo. 1997. 'Introduction', in B. Allen and M. Russo (eds), *Revisioning Italy: National Identity and Global Culture*. Minneapolis: University of Minnesota Press, pp. 1–19.
Andall, J. 1990. 'New migrants, old conflicts: the recent immigration into Italy', *The Italianist* 10: 151–174.
Anderson, B. 1983. *Imagined Communities*. London: Verso.
Anthias, F. 1990. 'Race and class revisted – conceptualising race and racisms', *Sociological Review* 38(1): 19–42.
Anthias, F. and G. Lazaridis (eds). 1999. *Into the Margins: Migration and Social Exclusion in Southern Europe*. Aldershot: Ashgate.
Anthias, F. and N. Yuval-Davis. 1993. *Racialised Boundaries*. London: Routledge.
Appadurai, A. 1990. 'Difference in the global cultural economy', in M. Featherstone (ed.), *Global Culture*. London: Sage, pp. 295–310.
Arrehag, L., O. Sjöberg and M. Sjöblom. 2005. 'Cross-border migration and remittances in a post-communist society: return flows of money and goods in the Korçë district, Albania', *South Eastern Europe Journal of Economics* 3(1): 9–40.
Aurighi, S. 1997. *Strada Facendo 1987–1997. Il modello di accoglienza modenese nel decennio della grande immigrazione extracomunitaria*. Rome: Edizioni Lavoro.
Baldwin-Edwards, M. 2004a. *Statistical Data on Immigrants in Greece: Final Report*. Athens: Mediterranean Migration Observatory, Panteion University.
—. 2004b. 'Albanian emigration and the Greek labour market: economic symbiosis and social ambiguity', *South-East Europe Review* 7(1): 51–66.
Baldwin-Edwards, M. and J. Arango (eds). 1999. *Immigrants and the Informal Economy in Southern Europe*. London: Frank Cass.
Balibar, E. and I. Wallerstein (eds). 1991. *Race, Nation, Class: Ambiguous Identities*. London: Verso.

Banfield, E.C. 1958. *The Moral Basis of a Backward Society*. Glencoe: The Free Press.
Barjaba, K. (1997) 'Tipologie comportamentali dell'emigrazione albanese', in *Albania: Oltre l'Emigrazione*. Turin: Ires, pp. 11–17.
Barjaba, K. 2000a. 'Contemporary patterns in Albanian migration', *South-East Europe Review* 3(2): 57–64.
—. 2000b. 'Da Otranto a Vancouver. L'emigrazione nel nuovo contesto sociopolitico albanese', in C. Lanni (ed.), *Albania, un Paese d'Europa. Il Fattore Migrazione*. Turin: Edizioni Gruppo Abele, pp. 47–66.
—. 2000c. *Ondate senza Ritorno*. Rome: International Organization for Migration.
—. 2003. *Shqiptaret, Keta Ikes te Medhenj*. Tirana: Korbi.
Barjaba, K. and R. King. 2005. 'Introducing and theorising Albanian migration', in R. King, N. Mai and S. Schwandner-Sievers (eds), *The New Albanian Migration*. Brighton: Sussex Academic Press, pp. 1–28.
Barjaba, K. and L. Perrone. 1996. 'Forme e grado di adattamento dei migranti di cultura Albanese in Europa (Italia, Grecia, Germania), 1992–1995', in K. Barjaba, G. Lapassade and L. Perrone, *Naufragi Albanesi: Studi, Ricerche e Riflessioni sull'Albania*. Rome: Sensibili alle Foglie, pp. 123–162.
Barjaba, K., Z. Dérvishi and L. Perrone. 1992. 'L'emigrazione albanese: spazi, tempi e cause', *Studi Emigrazione* 29(107): 513–538.
Barsotti, O. 2004. 'Le rimesse: aspetti teorici e linee della ricerca', in O. Barsotti and E. Moretti (eds), *Rimesse e Cooperazione allo Sviluppo*. Milan: Franco Angeli, pp. 11–23.
Becker, J. and A. Engelberg. 2004. 'The land of extremities – an Albanian time journey', *South-East Europe Review* 7(1): 111–120.
Belluati, M. and G. Grossi. 1995. *Mass Media e Società Multietnica*. Milan: Anabasi.
Berghman, J. 1995. 'Social exclusion in Europe: policy context and analytical framework', in G. Room (ed.), *Beyond the Threshold: The Measurement and Analysis of Social Exclusion*. Bristol: Policy Press, pp. 10–28.
Bernardotti, M.A. (ed.). 2001. *Con la Valigia Accanto al Letto. Immgrati e Casa a Bologna*. Milan: Franco Angeli.
Bernardotti, M.A. and G. Mottura. 1999. *Il Gioco delle Tre Case. Immigrazione e Politica Abitativa a Bologna dal 1990 al 1999*. Turin: L'Harmattan Italia.
Bërxholi, A. 2003. *Atlasi Geografik i Popullsisë së Shqipërisë*. Tirana: Akademia e Shkencave e Shqipërisë.
Bhabha, H. 1994. *The Location of Culture*. London: Routledge.
Biberaj, E. 1998. *Albania in Transition*. Boulder: Westview Press.
Blumi, I. 2003. 'Defining social spaces by way of deletion: the untold story of Albanian migration in the postwar period', *Journal of Ethnic and Migration Studies* 29(6): 949–965.
Bonifazi, C. 1998. *L'Immigrazione Straniera in Italia*. Bologna: Il Mulino.
Bonifazi, C. and D. Sabatino. 2003. 'Albanian migration to Italy: what official data and survey results can reveal', *Journal of Ethnic and Migration Studies* 29(6): 967–995.
Boyle, P., K. Halfacree and V. Robinson. 1998. *Exploring Contemporary Migration*. London: Longman.
Brah, A. 1996. *Cartographies of Diaspora*. London: Routledge.
Brah, A., M. Hickman and M. Mac an Ghaill (eds). 1999. *Thinking Identities: Ethnicities, Racisms and Culture*. Basingstoke: Macmillan.

Buda, A. 1985. 'Some questions about the history of the formation of the Albanian people and of their language and culture', in Academy of Sciences of the People's Socialist Republic of Albania, *The Albanians and their Territories*. Tirana: 8 Nëntori, pp. 5–32.
Bufacchi, V. and S. Burgess. 1998. *Italy Since 1989: Events and Interpretations*. London: Macmillan.
Bulmer, M. and J. Solomos (eds). 1999. *Racism*. Oxford: Oxford University Press.
Butler, J. 1989. *Gender Trouble: Feminism and the Subversion of Identity*. London: Routledge.
Buzan, B., O. Waever and J. de Wilde. 1998. *Security: A New Framework for Analysis*. Boulder and London: Lynne Reiner Publishers.
Byrne, D. 1999. *Social Exclusion*. Buckingham: Open University Press.
Campani, G. 1993. 'Immigration and racism in Southern Europe: the case of Italy', *Ethnic and Racial Studies* 16(3): 507–535.
Campani, G. 2000. 'Immigrant women in Southern Europe: social exclusion, domestic work and prostitution in Italy', in R. King, G. Lazaridis and C. Tsardanidis (eds), *Eldorado or Fortress? Migration in Southern Europe*. Basingstoke: Macmillan, pp. 145–169.
Caracciolo, L. 2001. *Terra Incognita: Le Radici Geopolitiche della Crisi Italiana*. Bari: Laterza.
Caritas. 1996. *Immigrazione Dossier Statistico* 1996. Rome: Anterem.
—. 1997. *Immigrazione Dossier Statistico* 1997. Rome: Anterem.
—. 1998. *Immigrazione Dossier Statistico* 1998. Rome: Anterem.
—. 1999. *Immigrazione Dossier Statistico* 1999. Rome: Anterem.
—. 2000. *Immigrazione Dossier Statistico* 2000. Rome: Anterem.
—. 2001. *Immigrazione Dossier Statistico* 2001. Rome: Anterem.
—. 2002. *Immigrazione Dossier Statistico* 2002 Rome: Anterem.
—. 2003. *Immigrazione Dossier Statistico* 2003. Rome: Anterem.
—. 2004. *Immigrazione Dossier Statistico* 2004. Rome: IDOS.
Carletto, G., B. Davis, M. Stampini and A. Zezza. 2004. *Internal Mobility and International Migration in Albania*. Rome: FAO, ESA Working Paper 04–13.
Carling, J. 2002. 'Migration in the age of involuntary mobility: theoretical reflections and Cape Verdean experiences', *Journal of Ethnic and Migration Studies* 28(1): 5–42.
Carter, F.W. 1986. 'Tirana', *Cities* 3(4): 270–281.
Castaldo, A., J. Litchfield and B. Reilly. 2005 'Migration and poverty in Albania: what factors are associated with an individual's predisposition to migrate?', *Journal of Southern Europe and the Balkans* 7(2): 157–173.
Castles, S. 1995. 'How nation-states respond to immigration and ethnic diversity', *New Community* 21(3): 293–308.
—. 1998. 'Globalization and migration: some pressing contradictions', *International Social Science Journal* 156: 179–186.
—. 2000. *Ethnicity and Globalisation*. London: Sage.
Castles, S. and M.J. Miller. 2003. *The Age of Migration*, 3rd ed. Basingstoke: Palgrave Macmillan.
Censis. 2002. *Tuning into Diversity. The Representation of Immigrants and Ethnic Minorities in Italian Mass Media*. Rome: Censis.
Centre for Contemporary Cultural Studies. 1982. *The Empire Strikes Back*. London: Hutchinson.

Chambers, I. 1994. *Migrancy, Culture, Identity*. London: Routledge.
Chiodi, L. and R. Devole. 2005. 'Albanian migrants in Italy and the struggle for recognition in the transnational public sphere', in L. Chiodi (ed.), *The Borders of the Polity. Migration and Security across the EU and the Balkans*. Ravenna: Longo, pp. 169–188.
Chiodi, M. 1999. 'Immigrazione, devianza e percezione d'insecurezza', *Dei Delitti e Delle Pene* 6(3): 115–140.
Chossudovsky, M. 2000. 'The criminalisation of Albania', in T. Ali (ed.), *Masters of the Universe? NATO's Balkan Crusade*. London: Verso, pp. 286–316.
Clunies-Ross, A. and P. Sudar (eds). 1998. *Albania's Economy in Transition and Turmoil*. Aldershot: Ashgate.
CNEL. 2004. *Indici di Inserimento Territoriale degli Immigrati in Italia*. Rome: Consiglio Nazionale dell'Economia e del Lavoro, Documenti 44.
Cohen, R. (ed.). 1995. *The Cambridge Survey of World Migration*. Cambridge: Cambridge University Press.
—. 1997. *Global Diasporas: An Introduction*. London: UCL Press.
Cohen, S. 1972. *Folk Devils and Moral Panics*. Oxford: Martin Robertson.
Cole, J. 1995. *The New Racism in Europe. A Sicilian Ethnography*. Cambridge: Cambridge University Press.
Cotesta, V. 1999a. 'Mass media, conflitti etnici e immigrazione', *Studi Emigrazione* 36(135): 387–394.
—.1999b. 'Mass media, conflitti etnici e identità degli italiani', *Studi Emigrazione* 36(135): 443–471.
Da Molin, G. (ed.). 2001. *L'Immigrazione Albanese in Puglia*. Bari: Cacucci.
Da Molin, G. and A. Carbone. 2001. 'Caratteristiche demografiche e sociali degli albanesi immigrati in Puglia negli anni novanta', in G. Da Molin (ed.), *L'Immigrazione Albanese in Puglia*. Bari: Cacucci, pp. 21–60.
Dal Lago, A. 1999. *Non Persone*. Milan: Feltrinelli.
Dalipaj, M. 2005. Albanian Migration to the United Kingdom: A Hidden Migration? Brighton: University of Sussex, MPhil thesis in Migration Studies.
Daly, F. 1999. 'Tunisian migrants and their experience of racism in Modena', *Modern Italy* 4(2): 173–190.
—. 2001. 'The double passage: Tunisian migration to the South and North of Italy', in R. King (ed.), *The Mediterranean Passage: Migration and New Cultural Encounters in Southern Europe*. Liverpool: Liverpool University Press, pp. 186–205.
Dayan, D. 1998. 'Particularistic media and diasporic communications', in T. Liebes and J. Curran (eds), *Media, Ritual and Identity*. London: Routledge, pp. 103–113.
De Bonis, M. 2001. 'La non-comunità albanese', *Limes: Rivista Italiana di Geopolitica* 2/2001: 273–276.
De Rapper, G. 2005. 'Better than Muslims, not as good as Greeks: emigration as experienced and imagined by the Albanian Christians of Lunxhëri', in R. King, N. Mai and S. Schwandner-Sievers (eds), *The New Albanian Migration*. Brighton: Sussex Academic Press, pp. 173–194.
De Soto, H., P. Gordon, I. Gedeshi and Z. Sinoimeri. 2002. *Poverty in Albania: A Qualitative Assessment*. Washington DC: World Bank Technical Paper 520.
De Zwager, N., I. Gedeshi, E. Germenji and C. Nikas. 2005. *Competing for Remittances*. Tirana: International Organization for Migration.

Del Re, E.C. 2000. 'Società albanese in evoluzione: il fattore migrazione', in C. Lanni (ed.), *Albania, un Paese d'Europa. Il Fattore Migrazione*. Turin: Edizioni Gruppo Abele, pp. 9–44.

dell'Agnese, E. 1996. 'Profughi politici e rifugiati "economici" in Italia: il doppio esodo albanese del 1991', in M.L. Gentileschi and R. King (eds), *Questioni di Popolazione in Europa: una prospettiva geografica*. Bologna: Pàtron, pp. 69–81.

Delle Donne, M. 1998. 'Il cuore è uno zingaro... Pregiudizi e strategie della esclusione', in M. Delle Donne (ed.), *Relazioni Etniche: Stereotipi, Pregiudizi, Fenomeno Migratorio ed Esclusione Sociale*. Rome: Edup, pp. 15–41.

Derhemi, E. 2003. 'New Albanian immigrants in the old Albanian diaspora: Piana degli Albanesi', *Journal of Ethnic and Migration Studies* 29(6): 1015–1032.

Devole, R. 1998. *Albania: Fenomeni e Rappresentazioni*. Rome: Agrilavoro.

Doll, B. 2003. 'The relationship between the clan system and other institutions in northern Albania', *Southeast European and Black Sea Studies* 3(2): 147–162.

Donald, J. and A. Rattansi (eds). 1992. *Race, Culture and Difference*. London: Sage.

Dorfles, P. 1991. *Guardando all'Italia: Influenza delle TV e delle Radio Italiane sull'Esodo degli Albanesi*. Rome: RAI–VQPT.

Droukas, E. 1998. 'Albanians in the Greek informal economy', *Journal of Ethnic and Migration Studies* 24(2): 347–365.

Dunford, M. 2002. 'Italian regional evolutions', *Environment and Planning A* 34(4): 657–694.

Eco, U. 1997. 'Le migrazioni, la tolleranza e l'intollerabile', in U. Eco, *Cinque Scritti Morali*. Milan: Bompiani, pp. 93–113.

Edensor, T. 2002. *National Identity, Popular Culture and Everyday Life*. Oxford: Berg.

Ellerman, D. 2003. *Policy Research on Migration and Development*. Washington DC: World Bank Working Paper 3117.

Eriksen, T.H. 2002. *Ethnicity and Nationalism*, 2nd ed. London: Pluto Press.

Essed, P. 1991. *Understanding Everyday Racism*. London: Sage.

European Commission. 1992. *Towards a Europe of Solidarity: Intensifying the Fight Against Social Exclusion*. Brussels: COM(52) 542, 23 December 1992.

Fakiolas, R. 1999. 'Socio-economic effects of immigration in Greece', *Journal of European Social Policy* 9(3): 211–229.

Fakiolas, R. 2000. 'Migration and unregistered labour in the Greek economy', in R. King, G. Lazaridis and C. Tsardanidis (eds), *Eldorado or Fortress? Migration in Southern Europe*. London: Macmillan, pp. 57–78.

Fakiolas, R. 2003. 'Regularising undocumented immigrants in Greece: procedures and effects', *Journal of Ethnic and Migration Studies* 29(3): 535–561.

Fakiolas, R. and R. King. 1996. 'Emigration, return, immigration: a review and evaluation of Greece's postwar experience of international migration', *International Journal of Population Geography* 2(2): 171–190.

Fassman, H. and R. Münz (eds). 1994. *European Migration in the Late Twentieth Century*. Aldershot: Edward Elgar.

Fischer, B.J. 2005. 'Albanian refugees seeking political asylum in the United States: process and problems', *Journal of Ethnic and Migration Studies* 31(1): 193–208.

Fonseca, M.L. and J. Malheiros. 2005. *Social Integration and Mobility: Education, Housing and Health*. Lisbon: Universidade de Lisboa, Centro de Estudos Geográficos, Estudos para o Planeamento Regional e Urbano 67.

Foot, J. 1995. 'The logic of contradiction: migration control in Italy and France, 1980–93', in R. Miles and D. Thränhardt (eds), *Migration and European*

Integration: The Dynamics of Inclusion and Exclusion. London: Pinter Publishers, pp. 132–158.

Freud, S. 1958. *Formulations of the Two Principles of Mental Functioning*. London: The Hogarth Press.

Fuga, A. 1998. *L'Albanie entre la Pensée Totalitaire et la Raison Fragmentaire*. Paris: L'Harmattan.

Fuga, A. 2000. *Identités Périphériques en Albanie*. Paris: L'Harmattan.

Gavosto, A., A. Venturini and C. Villosio. 1999. 'Do immigrants compete with natives', *Labour* 13(3): 603–622.

Geddes, A. 2000. *Immigration and European Integration: Towards Fortress Europe?* Manchester: Manchester University Press.

Gedeshi, I., H. Mara and X. Preni. 2003. *The Encouragement of Social-Economic Development in Relation to the Growth of the Role of Remittances*. Tirana: Centre for Economic and Social Studies, Research Report for UNDP and Soros Foundation.

Gedeshi, I., H. Mara, R. Dhimitri and K. Krisafi. 1999. *Egrimi i Elitës Intelektuale nga Shqipëria gjatë Periudhës së Tranzicionit*. Tirana: Luardsi.

Gillespie, M. 1995. *Television, Ethnicity and Cultural Change*. London: Routledge.

Gilroy, P. 1993. *Small Acts: Thoughts on the Politics of Black Cultures*. London: Routledge.

Ginsborg, P. 1996. 'Explaining Italy's crisis', in S. Gundle and S. Parker (eds), *The New Italian Republic: From the Fall of the Berlin Wall to Berlusconi*. London: Routledge, pp. 19–39.

Giorgio, A.G. and G. Luisi. 2001. 'L'immigrazione albanese in provincia di Bari: determinanti e impatto socioeconomico sul territorio', in G. Da Molin (ed.), *L'Immigrazione Albanese in Puglia*. Bari: Cacucci, pp. 79–120.

Gjonça, A., C. Wilson and J. Falkingham. 1997. 'Paradoxes of health transition in Europe's poorest country: Albania 1950–90', *Population and Development Review* 23(3): 585–609.

Goldberg, D.T. (ed.). 1990. *Anatomy of Racism*. Minneapolis: University of Minnesota Press.

Goldberg, D.T. 1993. *Racist Culture*. Oxford: Blackwell.

Government of Albania. 2004. *National Strategy on Migration*. Tirana: Albanian Government in cooperation with the International Organization for Migration.

Grassilli, M. 2002. '*Gabibbo* and the squatters: who speaks for whom? Alternative and official representation of immigration in Bologna', in R. Grillo and J. Pratt (eds), *The Politics of Recognizing Difference: Multiculturalism Italian-Style*. Aldershot: Ashgate, pp. 115–137.

Gundle, S. and S. Parker (eds). 1996. *The New Italian Republic: From the Fall of the Berlin Wall to Berlusconi*. London: Routledge.

Hall, D. 1994. *Albania and the Albanians*. London: Pinter.

—. 1996. 'Recent developments in Greek–Albanian relations', in R. Gillespie (ed.), *Mediterranean Politics, Vol. 2*. London: Pinter, pp. 82–104.

—. 2000. 'Tourism as sustainable development? The Albanian experience', *International Journal of Tourism Research* 2(1): 31–46.

Hall, S. 1996. 'Who needs identity?', in S. Hall and P. Du Gay (eds), *Questions of Cultural Identity*. London: Sage, pp. 1–17.

Hall, S. (ed.). 1997. *Representation: Cultural Representations and Signifying Practices*. London: Sage.

Harris, N. 2002. *Thinking the Unthinkable: The Immigration Myth Exposed*. London: I.B. Tauris.
Hatziprokopiou, P. 2003. 'Albanian immigrants in Thessaloniki, Greece: processes of economic and social incorporation', *Journal of Ethnic and Migration Studies* 29(6): 1033–1057.
——. 2004. 'Balkan immigrants in the Greek city of Thessaloniki: local processes of incorporation in an international perspective', *European Urban and Regional Studies* 11(4): 321–338.
Heckmann, F. 2005. *Integration and Integration Policies*. Bamberg: European Forum for Migration Studies.
Heckmann, F. and D. Schnapper (eds). 2003. *The Integration of Immigrants in European Societies*. Hamburg: Lucius and Lucius.
Hernández-Coss, R. and J. De Luna Martínez. 2006. 'The Italy–Albania Remittance Corridor. Shifting from the Physical Transfer of Cash to a Formal Money Transfer System'. Document for Discussion presented at the conference on 'Remittances: An Opportunity for Growth', Bari, 3–4 March 2006.
Hill, S. 1992. 'Byzantium and the emergence of Albania', in T. Winnifrith (ed.), *Perspectives on Albania*. Basingstoke: Macmillan, pp. 40–57.
Hollifield, J.F. 1997. 'Immigration and integration in Western Europe: a comparative analysis', in E.M. Uçarer and D.J. Puchala (eds), *Immigration into Western Societies: Problems and Policies*. London: Pinter, pp. 28–69.
Hoxha, E. 1973. 'Intensifying the ideological struggle against alien manifestations and liberal attitudes towards them', in *Selected Works*. Tirana: 8 Nentori, pp. 812–849.
INSTAT. 2001. *Social Indicators Yearbook*. Tirana: Instituti i Statistikës.
——. 2002. *The Population of Albania in 2001. Main Results of the Population and Housing Census*. Tirana: INSTAT.
——. 2004. *Migration in Albania*. Tirana: INSTAT.
IOM. 2001. *Selective Migration Flows from Albania to Italy: Final Report*. Rome: International Organization for Migration.
——. 2005. *World Migration 2005*. Geneva: United Nations and International Organization for Migration.
Iosifides, T. 1997. 'Immigrants in the Athens labour market: a comparativge study of Albanians, Egyptians and Filipinos', in R. King and R. Black (eds), *Southern Europe and the New Immigrations*. Brighton: Sussex Academic Press, pp. 26–50.
Iosifides, T. and R. King. 1996. 'Recent immigration to southern Europe: the socio-economic and labour market contexts', *Journal of Area Studies* 9: 70–94.
——. 1998. 'Socio-spatial dynamics and exclusion of three immigrant groups in the Athens conurbation', *South European Society and Politics* 3(3): 205–229.
Jakobson, M.F. 1998. *Whiteness of a Different Color: European Immigrants and the Alchemy of Race*. Cambridge MA: Harvard University Press.
Jamieson, A. and A. Silj. 1998. *Migration and Criminality*. Rome: Ethnobarometer Working Paper No. 1.
Jones, R.C. 1998. 'Remittances and inequality: a question of migration stage and scale', *Economic Geography* 74(1): 8–25.
Kapllani, G. and N. Mai. 2005. '"Greece belongs to the Greeks!" The case of the Greek flag in the hands of an Albanian student', in R King, N. Mai and S. Schwandner-Sievers (eds), *The New Albanian Migration*. Brighton: Sussex Academic Press, pp. 153–172.

Kapur, D. 2004. *Remittances: The New Development Mantra?* Geneva: UNCTAD and Intergovernmental Group of Twenty-Four, G–24 Discussion Paper 29.

Kasimis, C., A.G. Papadopoulos and E. Zacopoulou. 2003. 'Migrants in rural Greece', *Sociologia Ruralis* 43(2): 167–184.

King, R. 1987. *Italy*. London: Harper and Row.

—. 2003. 'Across the sea and over the mountains: documenting Albanian migration', *Scottish Geographical Journal* 119(3): 283–309.

—. 2004. 'Albania: interrelationships between population, poverty, development, internal and international migration', *Méditerranée* 103(3–4): 37–47.

King, R. (ed.). 2005a. 'New Perspectives on Albanian Migration and Development', special issue of *Journal of Southern Europe and the Balkans* 7(2): 131–277.

—. 2005b. 'Albania as a laboratory for the study of migration and development', *Journal of Southern Europe and the Balkans* 7(2): 133–155.

King, R. and N. Mai. 2002. 'Of myths and mirrors: interpretations of Albanian migration to Italy', *Studi Emigrazione* 39(145): 161–199.

—. 2004. 'Albanian immigrants in Lecce and Modena: narratives of rejection, survival and integration', *Population, Space and Place* 10(6): 455–477.

King, R. and J. Vullnetari. 2003. *Migration and Development in Albania*. Brighton: University of Sussex, Development Research Centre on Migration, Globalisation and Poverty, Working Paper C5.

—. 2006. 'Orphan pensioners and migrating grandparents: the impact of mass migration on older people in rural Albania', *Ageing and Society* 26(5): 783–816.

King, R., J. Connell and P. White (eds). 1995. *Writing Across Worlds. Literature and Migration*. London: Routledge.

King, R., M. Dalipaj and N. Mai. 2006. 'Gendering migration and remittances: evidence from London and northern Albania', *Population, Space and Place* 12(6): 409–434.

King, R., T. Iosifides and L. Myrivili. 1998. 'A migrant's story: from Albania to Athens', *Journal of Ethnic and Migration Studies* 24(1): 159–175.

King, R., N. Mai and M. Dalipaj. 2003. *Exploding the Migration Myths*. London: Oxfam and The Fabian Society.

King, R., N. Mai and S. Schwandner-Sievers (eds). 2005. *The New Albanian Migration*. Brighton: Sussex Academic Press.

Konidaris, G. 2005. 'Examining policy responses to immigration in the light of interstate relations and foreign policy objectives: Greece and Albania', in R. King, N. Mai and S. Schwandner-Sievers (eds), *The New Albanian Migration*. Brighton: Sussex Academic Press, pp. 64–92.

Korovilas, J.P. 1998. *The Albanian Economy in Transition: The Role of Remittances and Pyramid Investment Schemes*. Bristol: University of the West of England, Working Papers in Economics 28.

Kosic, A. and A. Triandafyllidou. 2004. 'Albanian and Polish migration to Italy: the micro-processes of policy implementation and immigrant survival strategies', *International Migration Review* 38(4): 1413–1446.

Kressing, F. 2002. 'General remarks on Albania and the Albanians', in F. Kressing and K. Kaser (eds), *Albania – A Country in Transition*. Baden-Baden: Nomos, pp. 11–24.

Kressing, F. and K. Kaser (eds). 2002. *Albania – A Country in Transition*. Baden-Baden: Nomos.

Kule, D., A. Mançellari, H. Papapanagos, S. Qirici and P. Sanfey. 2002. 'The causes and consequences of Albanian emigration during transition: evidence from micro data', *International Migration Review* 36(1): 229–239.

Labrianidis, L. and P. Hatziprokopiou. 2005. 'The Albanian migration cycle: migrants tend to return to their country of origin after all', in R. King, N. Mai and S. Schwander-Sievers (eds), *The New Albanian Migration*. Brighton: Sussex Academic Press, pp. 93–117.

Labrianidis, L. and A. Lyberaki. 2004. 'Back and forth and in-between: Albanian return-migrants from Greece and Italy', *Journal of International Migration and Integration* 5(1): 77–106.

Lawson, C. and D. Saltmarshe. 2000. 'Security and economic transition: evidence from north Albania', *Europe–Asia Studies* 52(1): 133–148.

Layard, R., O. Blanchard, R. Dornbusch and P. Krugman. 1992. *East–West Migration: The Alternatives*. London: MIT Press.

Lazaridis, G. 1996. 'Immigration to Greece: a critical evaluation of Greek policy', *New Community* 22(2): 335–348.

—. 1999. 'The helots of the new millennium: ethnic-Greek Albanians and "other" Albanians in Greece', in F. Anthias and G. Lazaridis (eds), *Into the Margins: Migration and Exclusion in Southern Europe*. Aldershot: Ashgate, pp. 105–121.

—. 2004. 'Albanian migration into Greece: various forms, degrees and mechanisms of (in)exclusion', in M.I. Baganha and M.L. Fonseca (eds), *New Waves: Migration from Eastern to Southern Europe*. Lisbon: Luso-American Foundation, pp. 71–90.

Lazaridis, G. and M. Koumandraki. 2001. 'Deconstructing naturalism: the racialisation of ethnic minorities in Greece', in R. King (ed.), *The Mediterranean Passage: Migration and New Cultural Encounters in Southern Europe*. Liverpool: Liverpool University Press, pp. 279–301.

Lazaridis, G. and I. Psimmenos. 2000. 'Migrant flows from Albania to Greece: economic, spatial and social exclusion', in R. King, G. Lazaridis and C. Tsardanidis (eds), *Eldorado or Fortress? Migration in Southern Europe*. London: Macmillan, pp. 170–185.

Lazaridis, G. and E. Wickens. 1999. '"Us" and the "Others": ethnic minorities in Greece', *Annals of Tourism Research* 26(3): 632–655.

Lianos, T., L. Katseli and A. Sarris. 1996. 'Illegal immigration and local labour markets: the case of northern Greece', *International Migration* 34(3): 449–484.

Logoreci, A. 1977. *The Albanians*. London: Gollancz.

Lubonja, F. 1997. 'For a critical spirit', in F. Lubonja and J. Hodgson (eds), *Perpjekja/Endeavour: Writings from Albania's Critical Quarterly*. Tirana: Perpjekja, pp. 25–31.

—. 2002. 'Between the glory of a virtual world and the misery of a real world', in S. Schwandner-Sievers and B.J. Fischer (eds), *Albanian Identities: Myth and History*. London: Hurst, pp. 91–103.

Lyberaki, A. and T. Maroukis. 2005. 'Albanian immigrants in Athens: new survey evidence on employment and integration', *Southeast European and Black Sea Studies* 5(1): 21–48.

Mac an Ghaill, M. 1999. *Contemporary Racisms and Ethnicities*. Buckingham: Oxford University Press.

Maher, V. 1996. 'Immigration and social identities', in D. Forgacs and R. Lumley (eds), *Italian Cultural Studies*. Oxford: Oxford University Press, pp. 160–177.

Mai, N. 2001a. '"Italy is beautiful": the role of Italian television in the Albanian migratory flow to Italy', in R. King and N. Wood (eds), *Media and Migration: Constructions of Mobility and Difference*. London: Routledge, pp. 95–109.

—. 2001b. 'Transforming traditions: a critical analysis of the trafficking and exploitation of young Albanian girls in Italy', in R. King (ed.), *The Mediterranean Passage: Migration and New Cultural Encounters in Southern Europe*. Liverpool: Liverpool University Press, pp. 258–278.

—. 2002a. 'Between Losing and Finding Oneself: The Role of Italian Television in the Albanian Migration to Italy'. DPhil thesis in Media and Cultural Studies. Brighton: University of Sussex.

—. 2002b. 'Myths and moral panics: Italian identity and the media representation of Albanian immigration', in R. Grillo and J. Pratt (eds), *The Politics of Recognizing Difference: Multiculturalism Italian-Style*. Aldershot: Ashgate, pp. 77–94.

—. 2003. 'The cultural construction of Italy in Albania and vice versa: migration dynamics, strategies of resistance and politics of mutual self-definition across colonialism and post-colonialism', *Modern Italy* 8(1): 77–93.

—. 2005. 'The Albanian diaspora-in-the-making: media, migration and social exclusion', *Journal of Ethnic and Migration Studies* 31(3): 543–561.

Mai, N. and S. Schwandner-Sievers (eds). 2003. 'Albanian Migration and New Transnationalisms', *Journal of Ethnic and Migration Studies* 29(6): 937–1096.

Maneri, M. 1998. 'Lo statuto del'extracomunitario nella stampa quotidiana', in M. Delle Donne (ed.), *Relazioni Etniche: Stereotipi, Pregiudizi, Fenomeno Migratorio ed Esclusione Sociale*. Rome: Edup, pp. 479–489.

Marmullaku, R. 1975. *Albania and the Albanians*. London: Hurst.

Maroukis, T. 2005. 'Albanian migrants in Greece: transcending "borders" in development', *Journal of Southern Europe and the Balkans* 7(2): 213–233.

Martelli, F. 1998. *Capire Albania*. Bologna: Il Mulino.

Martin, C. 1996. 'The debate in France over "social exclusion"', *Social Policy and Administration* 30(4): 382–392.

Meksi, E. and P. Iaquinta. 1991. 'Aspects d'évolution démographique en RPS d'Albanie', *Population* 46(3): 679–693.

Melchionda, U. (ed.). 2003. *Gli Albanesi in Italia: Inserimento Lavorativo e Sociale*. Milan: Franco Angeli.

Messia, A. 2003. 'Oltre l'esclusione: l'inserimento sociale e lavorativo degli albanesi a Roma e nel Lazio', in U. Melchionda (ed.), *Gli Albanesi in Italia: Inserimento Lavorativo e Sociale*. Milan: Franco Angeli, pp. 205–227.

Miles, R. 1989. *Racism*. London: Routledge.

—. 1993. *Racism After 'Race Relations'*. London: Routledge.

Miles, R. and D. Thränhardt (eds). 1995. *Migration and European Integration: The Dynamics of Inclusion and Exclusion*. London: Pinter Publishers.

Millar, P. 1992. 'Road to nowhere', *Sunday Times Magazine*, 13 September, pp. 30–40.

Mingione, E. and F. Quassoli. 2000. 'The participation of immigrants in the underground economy in Italy', in R. King, G. Lazaridis and C. Tsardanidis (eds), *Eldorado or Fortress? Migration in Southern Europe*. London: Macmillan, pp. 29–56.

Misha, P. 2002. 'Invention of a nationalism: myth and amnesia', in S. Schwandner-Sievers and B.J. Fischer (eds), *Albanian Identities: Myth and History*. London: Hurst, pp. 33–48.
Misja, V. and Y. Vejsiu. 1982. 'De l'accroissement démographique en RPS d'Albanie', *Studia Albanica* 19(1): 3–30.
—. 1984. *Shndërrimet demografike të familjes në RPSSH*. Tirana: Universiteti i Tiranës, Fakulteti i Ekonomisë.
Misja, V., Y. Vejsiu and A. Bërxholi. 1987. *Popullsia e Shqipërisë (Studim demografik)*. Tirana: Universiteti i Tiranës 'Enver Hoxha'.
Morley, D. 2000. *Media Territories: Media, Mobility and Identity*. London and New York: Routledge.
Morley, D. and K. Robins. 1993. 'No place like *Heimat*: images of home(land) in European culture', in E. Carter, J. Donald and J. Squires (eds), *Space and Place: Theories of Identity and Location*. London: Lawrence and Wishart, pp. 3–32.
—. 1995. *Spaces of Identity: Global Media, Electronic Landscapes and Cultural Boundaries*. London: Routledge.
Morozzo della Rocca, R. 1997. *Albania: le radici della crisi*. Milan: Guerini.
Mottura, G. 2001. *Lavoro e Percorsi di Inserimento Sociale degli Immigrati Stranieri in Emilia-Romagna*. Bologna: IRES.
Mottura, G. and C. Marra. 2003. 'L'immigrazione albanese in Emilia-Romagna', in U. Melchionda (ed.), *Gli Albanesi in Italia: Inserimento Lavorativo e Sociale*. Milan: Franco Angeli, pp. 53–76.
Mottura, G. and P. Pinto. 2001. 'Aspetti salienti dell'immigrazione in Emilia Romagna', in F. Carchedi (ed.), *Progetti oltre Frontiera: L'Immigrazione Straniera nelle Regioni Adriatiche, vol. 2, La Ricerca*. Teramo: Inte.Mi.Gra, pp. 89–106.
Naficy, H. (ed.). 1999. *Home, Exile, Homeland*. New York and London: Routledge.
Nagi, D.L. 1988. *The Albanian-American Odyssey. A Pilot Study of the Albanian Community of Boston, Massachusetts*. New York: AMS Press.
Naldi, A. 2000. '"Clandestini" e "criminali"? La costruzione giornalistica dell'allarme sociale attorno alla figura dell'immigrato in Italia', in D. Scidà (ed.), *I Sociologi Italiani e le Dinamiche dei Processi Migratori*. Milan: Franco Angeli, pp. 143–152.
Nicholson, B. 2002. 'The wrong end of the telescope: economic migrants, immigration policy, and how it looks from Albania', *The Political Quarterly* 73(4): 436–444.
—. 2004a. 'Migrants as agents of development: Albanian return migrants and micro-enterprise', in D. Pop (ed.), *New Patterns of Labour Migration in Central and Eastern Europe*. Cluj Napoca: Public Policy Center, pp. 94–110.
—. 2004b. 'The tractor, the shop, and the filling-station: work migration and self-help development in Albania', *Europe-Asia Studies* 56(6): 877–890.
Nikas, C. and R. King. 2005. 'Economic growth through remittances: lessons from the Greek experience of the 1960s applied to the Albanian case', *Journal of Southern Europe and the Balkans* 7(2): 235–257.
Nyberg Sørensen, N., N. van Hear and P. Engberg-Pedersen. 2003. 'Migration, development and conflict: state-of-the-art overview', in N. van Hear and N. Nyberg Sørensen (eds), *The Migration–Development Nexus*. Geneva: United Nations and International Organization for Migration, pp. 5–50.
Olsen, N. 2000. *Albania*. Oxford: Oxfam Country Profile.

Orgocka, A. 2005. 'Albanian high-skilled migrant women in the US: the ignored experience', in R. King, N. Mai and S. Schwandner-Sievers (eds), *The New Albanian Migration*. Brighton: Sussex Academic Press, pp. 139–152.

—. 2006. *Children's Vulnerability to Trafficking Through Unaccompanied Migration – A Rapid Assessment in the North-East of Albania*. Tirana: CCF Albania.

Palomba, R. and A. Righi. 1992. *Quel giorno che gli Albanesi invasero l'Italia... Gli atteggiamenti dell'opinione pubblica e della stampa italiana sulla questione delle migrazioni dall'Albania*. Rome: Istituto di Ricerche sulla Popolazione, Working Paper 08/92.

Pandolfi, M. 1998. 'Two Italies: rhetorical figures of failed nationhood', in J. Schneider (ed.), *Italy's 'Southern Question': Orientalism in One Country*. Oxford: Berg, pp. 285–289.

Papailias, P. 2003. 'Money of *kurbet* is money of blood': the making of a "hero" of migration at the Greek–Albanian border', *Journal of Ethnic and Migration Studies* 29(6): 1059–1078.

Pastore, F. 1998. *Conflicts and Migrations: A Case Study on Albania*. Rome: Centro Studi Politica Internazionale, Occasional Paper.

Paterno, A. and M. Toigo. 2004. 'Le tre collettività a confronto', in O. Barsotti and E. Morretti (eds), *Rimesse e Cooperazione allo Sviluppo*. Milan: Franco Angeli, pp. 53–113.

Perlmutter, T. 1998. 'The politics of proximity: the Italian response to the Albanian crisis', *International Migration Review* 32(1): 203–222.

Però, D. 1999. 'Next to the dog pound: institutional discourses and practices about Rom refugees in left-wing Bologna', *Modern Italy* 4(2): 207–224.

—. 2001. 'Inclusionary rhetoric/exclusionary practice: an ethnographic critique of the Italian Left in the context of migration', in R. King (ed.), *The Mediterranean Passage: Migration and New Cultural Encounters in Southern Europe*. Liverpool: Liverpool University Press, pp. 162–185.

—. 2002. 'The Left and the political participation of immigrants in Italy: the case of the *Forum* of Bologna', in R. Grillo and J. Pratt (eds), *The Politics of Recognizing Difference: Multiculturalism Italian-Style*. Aldershot: Ashgate, pp. 95–113.

Perrone, L. 1996a. 'Migrazioni dall'Europa dell'Est', in K. Barjaba, G. Lapassade and L. Perrone (eds), *Naufragi Albanesi*. Rome: Sensibili alle Foglie, pp. 23–39.

—. 1996b. *Immigrati in Italia: il caso Salento*. Lecce: Argo.

—. 2001. 'La presenza immigrata nelle regioni adriatiche: il caso della Puglia', in F. Carchedi (ed.), *Progetti oltre Frontiera: L'Immigrazione Straniera nelle Regioni Adriatiche, vol. 2, La Ricerca*. Teramo: Inte.Mi.Gra, pp. 139–156.

—. 2003. 'La presenza immigrata nelle regioni adriatiche: il caso della Puglia', in U. Melchionda (ed.), *Gli Albanesi in Italia: Inserimento Lavorativo e Sociale*. Milan: Franco Angeli, pp. 122–157.

Pittau, F. and M. Reggio. 1992. 'Il caso Albania: emigrazione a due tempi', *Studi Emigrazione* 29(106): 227–239.

Portes, A. and M. Zhou. 1993. 'The new second generation: segmented assimilation and its variants among post-1965 immigrant youth', *Annals of the American Academy of Political and Social Sciences* 530: 74–96.

Pozzi, E. (ed.). 1997. *La Costruzione dello Straniero Interno. La Vicenda Albanese nella Stampa Italiana (Gennaio–Aprile 1997)*. Rome: Consiglio Regionale del Lazio and Università di Roma, Osservatorio sull'Identità degli Italiani.

Pratsinakis, E. 2005. 'Aspirations and strategies of Albanian immigrants in Thessaloniki', *Journal of Southern Europe and the Balkans* 7(2): 195–212.

Prifti, P. 1978. *Socialist Albania since 1944*. Cambridge, Mass: MIT Press.

Psimmenos, I. 2000. 'The making of periphractic spaces: the case of undocumented female migrants in the sex industry in Athens', in F. Anthias and G. Lazaridis (eds), *Gender and Migration in Southern Europe*. Oxford: Berg, pp. 81–101.

Psimmenos, I. and K. Kasimati. 2003. 'Immigration control pathways: organisational culture and work values of Greek welfare officers', *Journal of Ethnic and Migration Studies* 29(2): 337–371.

Pugliese, E. 1991. 'Le interpretazioni del razzismo nel dibattito italiano sulla immigrazione', *La Critica Sociologica* 99: 84–105.

Puri, S. and T. Ritzema. 1999. *Migrant Worker Remittances, Micro-Finance and the Informal Economy: Prospects and Issues*. Geneva: International Labour Office, Social Finance Unit, Working Paper 21.

Quassoli, F. 2004. 'Making the neighbourhood safer: social alarm, police practices and immigrant exclusion in Italy', *Journal of Ethnic and Migration Studies* 30(6): 1163–1181.

Ramamurthy, B. 2003. *International Labour Migrants: Unsung Heroes of Globalisation*. Stockholm: Swedish International Development Agency (SIDA Studies, 8).

Rapport, N. and A. Dawson (eds). 1998. *Migrants of Identity: Perceptions of Home in a World of Movement*. Oxford: Berg.

Regione Emilia-Romagna. 2002. *L'Immigrazione Straniera in Emilia-Romagna*. Milan: Franco Angeli.

Reilly, B., J. Litchfield and A. Castaldo. 2005. 'Who is most likely to emigrate from Albania? Evidence from the Albanian Living Standards Measurement Survey'. Brighton: University of Sussex, Development Research Centre on Migration, Globalisation and Poverty, Briefing no. 2.

Reyneri, E. 1998. 'The role of the underground economy in irregular migration to Italy: cause or effect?', *Journal of Ethnic and Migration Studies* 24(2): 313–331.

—. 2001. 'Il mercato di lavoro', in G. Zincone (ed.), *Secondo Rapporto sull'Integrazione degli Immigrati in Italia*. Bologna: Il Mulino, pp. 331–365.

—. 2004. 'Immigrants in a segmented and often undeclared labour market', *Journal of Modern Italian Studies* 9(1): 71–93.

Ribas Mateos, N. 2005. *The Mediterranean in the Age of Globalization: Migration, Welfare, and Borders*. New Brunswick NJ: Transaction Publishers.

Ricci, A. 2004. 'I flussi migratori: dall'Europa Centro Orientale e Orientale', in O.Forti, F. Pittau and A. Ricci (eds), *Europe: Allargamento a Est e Immigrazione*. Rome: Caritas Italiana, pp. 101–128.

Riccio, B. 1999. 'Senegalese street-sellers, racism and the discourse on "irregular trade" in Rimini', *Modern Italy* 4(2): 225–240.

—. 2001. 'Following the Senegalese migratory path through media representation', in R. King and N. Wood (eds), *Media and Migration: Constructions of Mobility and Difference*. London: Routledge, pp. 110–126.

Romania, V. 2004. *Fare Passari per Italiani. Strategie di Mimetismo Sociale*. Rome: Carocci.

Room, G. 1995. 'Poverty and social exclusion: the new European agenda for policy and research', in G. Room (ed.), *Beyond the Threshold: The Measurement and Analysis of Social Exclusion*. Bristol: Policy Press, pp. 1–9.

Salecl, R. 1993. 'National identity and socialist moral majority', in E. Carter, J. Donald and J. Squires (eds), *Space and Place: Theories of Identity and Location*. London: Lawrence and Wishart, pp. 101–109.

Saltmarshe, D. 2001. *Identity in a Post-Communist Balkan State: An Albanian Village Study*. Aldershot: Ashgate.

Samers, M. 1998. 'Immigration, "ethnic minorities" and "social exclusion" in the European Union: a critical perspective', *Geoforum* 29(2): 123–144.

Sampson, S. 1996. 'The social life of projects: importing civil society to Albania', in C. Haan and E. Dunn (eds), *Civil Society: Challenging Western Models*. London: Routledge, pp. 121–142.

Sampson, S. 1998. 'Exporting democracy, preventing Mafia: rebirth of Eastern Europe in the era of post-post-communism', in K. Karlsson, B. Petersson and B. Törnquist-Plewa (eds), *Collective Identities in an Era of Transformations: Analyzing Developments in East and Central Europe and the Former Soviet Union*. Lund: Lund University Press, pp. 151–186.

Sander, C. 2003. *Migrant Remittances to Developing Countries: A Scoping Study*. London: Bannock Consulting for the Department of International Development.

Sandström, P. and O. Sjöberg. 1991. 'Albanian economic performance: stagnation in the 1980s', *Soviet Studies* 43(5): 931–947.

Sauvy, A. 1980. 'La population d'Albanie', *Population* 35(2): 458–460.

Schmitter-Heisler, B. 2000. 'The sociology of immigration: from assimilation to segmented integration, from the American experience to the global arena', in C.B. Brettell and J.F. Hollifield (eds), *Migration Theory: Talking Across Disciplines*. New York: Routledge, pp. 77–96.

Schuster, L. 2005. 'The continuing mobility of migrants in Italy: shifting between places and statuses', *Journal of Ethnic and Migration Studies* 31(4): 757–774.

Schwandner-Sievers, S. 2001. 'The enactment of "tradition": Albanian constructions of identity, violence and power in times of crisis', in B.E. Schmidt and I.W. Schröder (eds), *Anthropology of Violence and Conflict*. London and New York: Routledge, pp. 97–120.

—. 2004. 'Albanians, Albanianism and the strategic subversion of stereotypes', in A. Hammond (ed.), *The Balkans and the West: Constructing the European Other, 1945–2003*. Aldershot: Ashgate, pp. 110–126.

Schwandner-Sievers, S. and B.J. Fischer (eds). 2002. *Albanian Identities: Myth and History*. London: Hurst.

Sciortino, G. 2003. 'Tra esclusione simbolica ed inclusione strutturale: gli albanesi in Friuli-Venezia Giulia', in U. Melchionda (ed.), *Gli Albanesi in Italia: Insediamento Lavorativo e Sociale*. Milan: Franco Angeli, pp. 148–172.

Shöpflin, G. 1997. 'The functions of myth and a taxonomy of myth', in G. Hosking and G. Shöpflin (eds), *Myth and Nationhood*. London: Hurst, pp. 19–35.

Silver, H. 1994. 'Social exclusion and social solidarity: three paradigms, *International Labour Review* 133(5–6): 531–578.

Silverstone, R. 1993. 'Time, information and communication technologies and the household', *Time and Society* 2(3): 283–311.

Sivignon, M. 1970. 'Quelques données démographiques sur la République Populaire d'Albanie', *Revue de Géographie de Lyon* 50(4): 332–343.

—. 1983. 'Evolution de la population d'Albanie', *Méditerranée* 50(4): 37–42.

—. 1995. 'La population d'Albanie: une ère nouvelle', *Méditerranée* 83(1–2): 47–52.

Sjöberg, O. 1989. 'A note about the regional dimensions of post-war demographic developments in Albania', *Nordic Journal of Soviet and East European Studies* 6(1): 91–121.
—. 1991. *Rural Change and Development in Albania*. Boulder: Westview Press.
—. 1992. 'Urbanisation and the zero urban growth hypothesis: diverted migration in Albania', *Geografiska Annaler* 74B(1): 3–19.
Sniderman, P., P. Peri, R.J.P. de Figueiredo and T. Piazza. 2000. *The Outsider: Prejudice and Politics in Italy*. Princeton: Princeton University Press.
Solomos, J. and L. Back. 1994. 'Conceptualising racisms: social theory, politics and research', *Sociology* 28(1): 143–161.
Solzhenitsyn, A. 1972. *One Word of Truth*. London: Bodley Head.
Stampini, M., B. Davis and G. Carletto. 2004. *Familiar Faces, Familiar Places: The Role of Family Networks and Previous Experience for Albanian Migrants*. Rome: FAO, ESA Working Paper.
Stark, D. 1992. 'Path dependence and privatisation strategies in East-Central Europe', *East European Politics and Societies* 6(1): 17–54.
Stella, G.A. 2002. *L'Orda. Quando gli Albanesi eravamo noi*. Milan: Rizzoli.
ter Wal, J. 1999. 'Attitudes towards Albanian refugees in political news discourse', in D. Melossi (ed.), *Migration, Interaction and Conflict in the Construction of a Democratic Europe*. Milan: Giuffré, pp. 719–750.
—. 2002a. 'Italy', in J. ter Wal (ed.), *Racism and Cultural Diversity in the Mass Media*. Vienna: European Monitoring Centre on Racism and Xenophobia, pp. 239–272.
—. 2002b. 'Conclusions', in J. ter Wal (ed.), *Racism and Cultural Diversity in the Mass Media*. Vienna: European Monitoring Centre on Racism and Xenophobia, pp. 31–73.
Thränhardt, D. and R. Miles. 1995. 'Introduction: European integration, migration and processes of inclusion and exclusion', in R. Miles and D. Thränhardt (eds), *Migration and European Integration: The Dynamics of Inclusion and Exclusion*. London: Pinter Publishers, pp. 1–12.
Tirta, M. 1999. *Migrime të Shqiptarëve*. Tirana: Shkeca (Ethnografia Shqiptare 18).
Todorova, M. 1997. *Imagining the Balkans*. New York: Oxford University Press.
Triandafyllidou, A. 2002. 'Greece', in J. ter Wal (ed.), *Racism and Cultural Diversity in the Mass Media*. Vienna: European Monitoring Centre on Racism and Xenophobia, pp. 149–171.
—. 2003. 'Immigration implementation policy in Italy: organisational culture, identity processes and labour market control', *Journal of Ethnic and Migration Studies* 29(2): 257–297.
Triandafyllidou, A. and M. Veikou. 2002. 'The hierarchy of Greekness: ethnic and national identity considerations in Greek immigration policy', *Ethnicities* 2(2): 189–208.
Trix, F. 2001. *The Albanians of Michigan*. East Lansing MI: Michigan State University Press.
UNDP. 1996. *Albanian Human Development Report 1996*. Tirana: UNDP.
—. 1998. *Albania Human Development Report*. Tirana: UNDP.
—. 2000a. *Human Development Report*. New York: Oxford University Press.
—. 2000b. *Albanian Human Development Report 2000*. Tirana: UNDP.
—. 2002. *Human Development Report: Albania 2002. Challenges of Local Governance and Regional Development*. Tirana: UNDP.

—. 2005. *National Human Development Report Albania 2005: Pro-Poor and Pro-Women Policies and Development in Albania*. Tirana: UNDP.
UNFPA. 1991. *Albania Report*. New York: UN Population Division.
UNICEF. 1998. *Children's and Women's Rights in Albania*. Tirana: UNICEF.
—. 2000. *Assessment of Social and Economic Conditions of Districts in Albania*. Tirana: UNICEF-Albania.
Uruçi, E. and I. Gedeshi. 2003. *Remittances Management in Albania*. Rome: CeSPI Working Paper 5/2003.
van Hear, N. 1998. *New Diasporas*. London: UCL Press.
van Hear, N. and N. Nyberg Sørensen (eds). 2003. *The Migration–Development Nexus*. Geneva: United Nations and International Organization for Migration.
Vasta, E. 1993. 'Rights and racism in a new country of immigration: the Italian case', in J. Solomos and J. Wrench (eds), *Racism and Migration in Western Europe*. Oxford: Berg, pp. 83–98.
Vaughan-Whitehead, D. 1999. *Albania in Crisis: The Predictable Fall of the Shining Star*. Cheltenham: Edward Elgar.
Vehbiu, A. and R. Devole. 1996. *La Scoperta dell'Albania. Gli Albanesi Secondo i Mass-Media*. Milan: Paoline.
Venturini, A. and C. Villosio. 2006. 'Labour market effects of immigration into Italy: an empirical analysis', *International Labour Review* 145(1–2): 91–118.
Verdicchio, P. 1997. 'The preclusion of postcolonial discourse in Southern Italy', in B. Allen and M. Russo (eds), *Revisioning Italy: National Identity and Global Culture*. Minneapolis: University of Minnesota Press, pp. 191–212.
Vermeulen, H. and R. Penninx (eds). 2000. *Immigrant Integration: The Dutch Case*. Amsterdam: Het Spinhuis.
Vickers, M. 1999. *The Albanians*. London: I.B. Tauris.
—. 2003. 'Albania's local elections: October 2003. A test of stability and democracy', *Besa* 7(2): 53–56.
Vickers, M. and J. Pettifer. 1997. *Albania: From Anarchy to a Balkan Identity*. London: Hurst.
Vullnetari, J. 2004. 'Like Stones in the Middle of the Road: the Impact of Migration on Older Persons in Rural SE Albania'. MSc dissertation in Migration Studies. Brighton: University of Sussex.
Waley, D. 1978. *The Italian City-Republics*. London: Longman.
Weiner, M. 1995. *The Global Migration Crisis*. New York: Harper Collins.
Whitaker, I. 1968. 'Tribal structure and national politics in Albania 1910–1950', in I. Lewis (ed.), *History and Social Anthropology*. London: Tavistock, pp. 253–293.
Wieviorka, M. 1994. 'Racism in Europe: unity and diversity', in A. Rattansi and S. Westwood (eds), *Racism, Modernity and Identity on the Western Front*. Cambridge: Cambridge University Press, pp. 173–188.
Winnifrith, T. 1992. 'Albania and the Ottoman Empire', in T. Winnifrith (ed.), *Perspectives on Albania*. Basingstoke: Macmillan, pp. 74–88.
World Bank. 1999. *Albania: Filling the Vulnerability Gap*. Tirana: The World Bank, Europe and Central Asia Region.
Yepez de Castillo, Y. 1994. 'A comparative approach to social exclusion: lessons from France and Belgium', *International Labour Review* 133(5–6): 613–633.
Zezza, A., G. Carletto and B. Davis. 2005. 'Moving away from poverty: a spatial analysis of poverty and migration in Albania', *Journal of Southern Europe and the Balkans* 7(2): 175–194.

Zincone, G. 2006. 'The making of policies: immigration and immigrants to Italy', *Journal of Ethnic and Migration Studies* 32(3): 347–375.

Zinn, D.L. 1994. 'The Senegalese immigrants in Bari: what happens when the Africans peer back', in R. Benmayor and A. Skotnes (eds), *Migration and Identity*. Oxford: Oxford University Press, pp. 53–68.

—. 1996. 'Adriatic brethren or black sheep? Migration in Italy and the Albanian crisis', *European Urban and Regional Studies* 3(3): 241–249.

—. 2005. 'The second generation of Albanians in Matera: the Italian experience and prospects for future ties to the homeland', *Journal of Southern Europe and the Balkans* 7(2): 259–277.

Zinn, D.L. and A. Rivera. 1995. 'Notes on a displaced womanhood: Albanian refugee women in Southern Italy', *Anthropology of East Europe Review* 13(1): 23–29.

Zolberg, A.R. 1989. 'The next waves: migration theory for a changing world', *International Migration Review* 23(3): 403–430.

INDEX

A
albanese, as derogatory term, 20, 114, 146, 188–91, 206
Albania
  agriculture, 39
  Albanian Party of Labour (APL), 44
  Census (2001), 65
  Chinese influence, 37, 39–40
  communist era, 32–40
  crime, 46, 246–47
  Democratic Party (DP), 44–45, 47, 249
  demography, 48–52, 77–82
  development assistance, 45
  'diaspora space', 207–8
  economic crisis (1991), 44–45
  economic impacts of migration, 223–34, 244, 246–47
  economic indicators, 27–28, 72
  economy under Hoxha, 39–40
  elderly people, 219–23
  elections, 47–48
  embassy occupation (1990), 43, 68, 85
  employment, 247
  and European Union, 243–44
  family relations, 220–22, 254n1
  fieldwork, 10–11, 216
  future of, 243–54
  gender and remittances, 231–34
  history, 28–48, 209–10
  homogeneous thought, 38–39
  household finances, 228–31, 244
  impacts of migration, 216–23, 240–41, 244–52
  industry, 39–40
  infrastructure problems, 239–40
  isolationism, 36–38
  Italian interests, 31–32, 113, 126n3
  lifestyles, 175–77
  migration from *see* migration from Albania
  myths of, 118–19, 209, 212–13n10
  National Strategy on Migration (2004) (NSM), 243, 245–47, 253, 255n8
  nationalism, 30, 209–10, 212–13n10
  politics, 248–49
  post-communist, 40–48, 243
  post-post-communism, 41, 59–61
  poverty as migration factor, 71–73, 82–84, 244
  pre-communist, 28–32
  prostitution, 219
  pyramid savings crisis, 46, 61, 69, 226–27
  regional divisions, 32–33, 62n6
  religion, 30, 35, 62n3, 118–19, 209–10, 212n10
  remittances, 47, 223–34, 244, 246, 255nn4-5
  return migration, 235–42, 247
  rural abandonment, 217–18, 240–41
  rural-urban migration, 36, 51–52, 250–51
  social polarisation, 249–52
  Socialist Party (SP), 45, 47, 249
  television, 10, 42, 53–61, 119, 207–8
  trafficking, 219, 246–47
  vulnerability caused by migration, 218–19
  women, 218–19
  young people, 42–43
Albanian associations in Italy
  and Albanian identity, 202–4
  development of, 194–97

help with finding work, 133
Italian views of, 199–202
and media representation, 204–5
political role, 197–99
Albanian Communist Party (ACP), 32–33
Albanian Living Standards Measurement Survey (LSMS), 70–71, 74, 98n4, 223
Albanian migrants
  access to public services, 182–87
  aggressive approach of, 185–87
  'boat-people' (1991), 1, 44, 68–69, 101, 105–10
  characteristics of, 74–76
  children in school, 89–90
  criminal stereotyping, 114–17, 126n4, 193–94, 206
  data sources, 84–85
  deportation, 151, 154
  documents, 138–39
  employment, 127–42, 157–58, 163–68
  evolution of (1990–2003), 85–88
  families, 88–89, 147–48, 160, 177–78, 180–81, 238–39
  gender divisions, 88–89, 128–29, 180–81, 223, 231–34
  grandparents, 223
  housing, 142–53, 160
  identity, 196, 202–11, 251–52
  illegal entry, 108–9, 126n1
  informal economy, 168–70
  intention to return, 236–37
  language of, 10, 104, 207
  lifestyles, 177–80
  media portrayal, 104–5, 112–17, 118–19, 193–94, 195, 204–5
  myth of, 117–19
  as 'other', 19, 103, 113, 122–23, 124–25
  prostitute stereotype, 147, 172n6
  qualifications, 130–32, 171n2
  racism towards, 186–94
  regional distribution, 90–95
  regularisation, 153–70
  relations with Italians, 179–82, 208–9, 211n1, 245
  religion, 209–10
  repatriation, 106–7, 235, 239
  return to Albania, 222–23, 235–42
  social and demographic characteristics, 88–90
  social inclusion and exclusion, 141–42, 205–11
  stereotyping, 114–17, 147, 172n6, 188–89, 193–94, 200–1
  stigmatisation, 104–5, 109–11, 114–17, 134, 179, 184, 187–94, 200
  students, 90, 109–10, 178–79, 192–93, 248
  visas, 154, 157, 159, 160–61
  wages, 135–38
  welcoming of, 107–8
  women, 88–89, 128–29, 181, 223
'Albanophobia', Italy, 21, 24, 114–17, 185, 204
Alia, Ramiz, 33, 40, 41–45
Alleanza Nazionale, 156, 172–73n9
Amato, Giuliano, 121
Anagrafe Informatizzata dei Lavoratori Extracomunitari (AILE), 163–65
Andall, Jacqueline, 112
Anderson, Benedict, 103
Apulia (Italy)
  field interviews, 6–7
  housing, 145–46
  as transit area, 148–49
Arbëresh, 29, 66–67, 252
Arrehag, L., 255n5
assimilation, 16

B

Bajram Curri (Albania), 251
Baldwin-Edwards, M., 95, 97
Balkanism, 124–25
Bari (Italy)
  Albanian 'boat people' (1991), 6, 69, 106–7
  housing, 145–46
Barjaba, Kosta, 68, 97, 236
Barroso, Jose Manuel, 243
Becker, J., 251, 252
Berghman, J., 12
Berisha, Sali, 40, 44, 45–46, 47
Berlusconi, Silvio, 63n14, 125, 156, 158, 172n9
besa (keeping one's word), 180, 211–12n2

Bilisht (Albania), 251
Bisceglie (Italy), 7, 133–34
Blumi, I., 23
Bonifazi, C., 87, 116
Borsellino, Paolo, 121
Bossi, Umberto, 172–73n9
Bota Shqiptare (The Albanian World), 195
brain drain, 248
Brindisi (Italy), Albanian 'boat people' (1991), 6, 69, 105
Buzan, B., 111, 112
Byrne, D., 14

C
Canada, Albanian migrants in, 98
Caracciolo, Lucio, 120
Caritas/Migrantes, migration figures, 70–71
Castles, S., 1, 13, 14, 19
Censis, 114
CGIL *see* Confederazione Generale Italiana del Lavoro
Chambers, Iain, 22
China, Albania's relations with, 37, 39–40
Cohen, Robin, 6
Cold War, end of, 2, 120
communism in Albania
  end of, 41–45
  Hoxha's regime, 33–40
  regionality, 32–33
comunitari, 13
Confederazione Generale Italiana del Lavoro (CGIL), 131, 145, 158, 169
Cotesta, V., 113
crime
  Albania, 46, 246–47
  Italy, 114–17
cultural integration, 17–18
cultural racism, 20–21

D
de Rapper, Gilles, 66
De Soto, H., 220
de Zwager, N., 228, 237, 255n4
Delle Donne, M., 112
demography
  Albania, 48–52

impact of migration, 77–82, 244
Derhemi, Eda, 67
development
  role of remittances, 223–26, 246
  role of return migrants, 247
Devole, R., 115, 117, 119
diaspora, Albanian, 252–54
differential exclusion, 14–15, 24–25
differential inclusion, 15, 16, 25
Drita Albanian association, Bologna, 195
Dukagjin, Lek, 29
Durrës (Albania)
  core-periphery polarisation, 250–51
  interviews in, 54–56, 176–77
  migration from, 44, 68, 81, 106, 222
  migration to, 82, 240
Dušan, Stefan, 28

E
Eastern Europe, shuttle migration, 2
Eco, Umberto, 125, 162
Edensor, T., 22–23
elderly people, Albania, 219–23
Emilia-Romagna (Italy)
  field sites, 7
  housing, 143–45
Engelberg, A., 251, 252
Eriksen, T.H., 23
Essed, P., 20
European Union (EU)
  and Albania, 243–44
  Albanian migrants, 97–98
  Italy's membership, 121
  social exclusion, 13–14
extracomunitari, 13–14, 19, 106

F
Falcone, Giovanni, 121
First World War, 30
Forza Italia, 156, 172–73n9
Fuga, Artan, 38

G
Gedeshi, I., 248
General Confederation of Italian Workers (CGIL) *see* Confederazione Generale Italiana del Lavoro

Ghegs, 62n6
Giorgio, A.G., 239
Gorbachev, Mikhail, 40
Greece
  Albanian migrants, 69, 76, 95–97, 172n4, 244–45
  census (2001), 96, 99n16
  as 'first destination' for migrants, 221
  regularisation (1998), 96
  remittances, 228
  return migration, 236–37
'guestworkers', 15, 157, 253

H
Hall, Derek, 33
Hall, Stuart, 21–22, 102
Hatziprokopiou, P., 97
Heckmann, F., 16, 18, 141, 175
homogeneous thought, 38–39
Hoxha, Enver, 33–40, 63n15

I
identificational integration, 17, 18
identity
  Albanian, 196, 202–11, 251–52
  concept of, 21–23
  Italian, 120–22, 124–25, 190–92
  media construction of, 102–3
Illyria Albanian association, Rome, 133, 197, 198–99
Illyrians, 28
integration, concept of, 15–18
interactive integration, 17, 18
International Organization for Migration (IOM), 163–64, 204
interviews in Albania, 10–11, 216
interviews in Italy, 8–10
Italian Confederation of Agriculture (CIA), 166
Italy
  agricultural sector, 166
  Albanian associations, 133, 194–205
  Albanian migrants *see* Albanian migrants
  Albanian television, 208
  'Albanophobia', 21, 24, 114–17, 185, 204
  Arbëresh immigrants, 29, 67, 252
  Bossi-Fini law (2002), 86, 153, 154–62
  census, 85, 87
  'contract to stay', 155, 157–58
  criminal stereotyping, 112–13, 114–17, 126n4, 193–94
  database of migrant workers, 163–65
  Dini Decree (1995), 86
  employment of immigrants, 127–42, 157–58, 163–68
  Erika and Omar case, 116–17, 193–94, 205
  field research sites, 6–8
  housing for immigrants, 142–53, 160
  identity formation, 102–3
  immigrants, nationality of, 86–87
  informal economy, 168–70
  interests in Albania, 113, 126n3
  legislation, immigration control, 153–57
  Martelli Law (1990), 85, 86, 106
  media representation of Albanian migrants, 104–5, 112–17, 118–19, 193–94, 195, 204–5
  municipal population registers, 84–85, 87
  national identity, 120–22, 124–25, 190–92
  North-South differences, 137–41, 152, 191–92
  'permits to stay', 84, 85, 99n10, 154–55, 157
  politics, 156, 158, 172–73n9
  Prodi decree, 151
  quotas for immigrants, 162–68
  racial stereotypes, 20, 26n6
  racism, 19–21, 186–94
  reception centres for migrants, 147, 172n5
  schools, Albanian pupils, 89–90
  seasonal migration, 96, 165–67, 236
  Second Republic, 120–22
  social exclusion, 13–14, 104, 141–42
  Southern identity, 122–23, 124
  television image of, 56–58, 103–4, 119, 207–8, 251–52
  Turko-Napolitano law (1998), 86, 153–54, 156, 159, 162
  universities, Albanian students, 90, 109–10, 192–93, 248

J
Jamieson, A., 115

K
Kadiu, Kledi, 204–5, 212n9
Kanun (customary law), 29, 211–12n2
Kastrioti dynasty, 29
Korçë (Albania), 81, 251, 255n5
Kosovan refugees, in Albania, 47, 69, 98n3, 126n3
Koumandraki, M., 19
kurbet, 66

L
Labrianidis, Lois, 244–45
language, of migrants, 10, 104, 207
Lazaridis, G., 19, 97
League of Nations, 30
Lecce (Italy)
  desire to move from, 140
  employment of Albanians, 128
  field interviews, 6–7, 8
  housing, 146, 149–50
  informal economy, 169–70
  Vëllazerimi Albanian association, 149, 195–96, 197–98
  wages, 137
Lega Nord, 156, 172–73n9
lifestyles
  Albania, 175–77
  Italy, 177–82
Lila, Elsa, 211
Limes, 200
Logoreci, A., 32
Lubonja, Fatos, 43, 209
Luisi, G., 239

M
Maastricht Treaty, 12, 121
Mac an Ghaill, M., 19
Marmullaku, R., 37
Maroukis, Thanos, 249
Maslo, Jerry, 19
Matteo, case of, 117
Mediterranean identity, 58, 251
Messia, Antonio, 134–35
methodology of research, 5–11
migrants *see* Albanian migrants

migration from Albania
  'boat-people' exodus (1991), 1, 44, 68–69, 101, 105–10
  brain drain, 248
  demographic and spatial impact, 77–82, 244
  district figures, 78–81
  during Hoxha regime, 36, 252
  impacts on Albania, 216–23, 240–41, 244–52
  internal, 78–82
  international outflows, 78–81
  motives and nature of, 71–76
  number of emigrants, 2–3
  and poverty, 71–73, 82–83, 244
  pre-communist period, 66–68
  pyramid savings crisis, 46, 61, 69
  as rite of passage, 66, 252
  seasonal, 96, 165–67, 236
  since 1990, 65, 68–71
  television's role, 57–58, 103–4, 207–8
  see also return migration
mikpritie (hospitality), 180, 211–12n2
Miles, R., 13
Miller, M.J., 1
Modena (Italy)
  employment of Albanians, 127–28
  field interviews, 7, 8
  housing, 143–45, 150–51
  wages, 137
Molfetta (Italy)
  desire to move from, 140–41, 161
  employment of Albanians, 128, 135
multiculturalism, 16
Mussolini, Benito, 31, 32
myths, Albanian, 117–19, 209, 212–13n10

N
Nano, Fatos, 40, 45, 47
Nicholson, Beryl, 247
Noli, Fan, 30–31
Nyberg Sørensen, N., 231

O
Operation Alba, 46, 62n8, 113
Operation Pelican, 45, 113
Ottoman Empire, 29–30, 67, 209–10

P

partial inclusion, 16
Pasha, Vaso, 212n10
Paterno, A., 236
Perrone, L., 236
Pivetti, Irene, 20
pluralism, 16
poverty, as migration factor, 71–73, 82–84, 244
Pozzi, Enrico, 115
prostitution, Albanian women, 147, 172n6, 219
pyramid savings crisis, 46, 61, 69, 226–27

Q

quotas for immigrants, Italy, 162–68

R

racial stereotypes, Italy, 20, 26n6
racism
 concept of, 18–19
 Italy, 19–21, 186–94
religion, Albania, 30, 35, 62n3, 118–19, 209–10, 212n10
remittances
 and Albanian economy, 47, 226–28, 244, 246
 development role, 223–26, 246
 gender divisions, 231–34
 government policy, 246
 and household survival, 228–31, 244, 255n5
 sending and receiving of, 231–34
return migration
 business attempts, 241–42
 development impacts, 247
 experiences of, 237–42
 types of, 235–37
Reyneri, Emilio, 167
Ribas Mateos, Natalia, 250–51
Roma, comparison with Albanians, 210–11
Romania, Vincenzo, 172n6
Rome
 Albanian community, 200
 employment of Albanians, 128
 field interviews, 7–8
 housing, 145, 151–52
 Illyria Albanian association, 133, 197, 198–99
 wages, 137–38
Room, G., 12
rural-urban migration, Albania, 36, 51–52, 250–51

S

Sabatino, D., 87, 116
Salecl, Renata, 122
Samers, Michael, 13, 14
Sampson, Steven, 41, 249
Sanremo song festival, on television, 55, 211
Sarandë (Albania), 79, 217, 251
Schengen Agreement, 121, 153
Second World War, 32
segmented assimilation, 16
segmented integration, 16
Shöpflin, George, 118
Sicily, Arbëresh immigrants, 29, 67, 252
Silj, A., 115
Sivignon, Michel, 48, 217
Sjöberg, Örjan, 48
Skanderbeg, 29, 62n2, 67, 212n10
social exclusion
 concept of, 12–15
 Italy, 13–14, 104, 141–42
Soviet Union, Albania's relations with, 36–37
spatial integration, 18
Stampini, M., 74, 96, 244
structural integration, 16–17

T

television
 Albanian in Italy, 208
 Italian in Albania, 10, 42, 53–61, 103–4, 207–8, 251–52
 as migration incentive, 57–58, 61, 207–8
 post-post-communism, 60–61
 unreality of image, 58–60, 119
ter Wal, Jessika, 112, 114
terrone (peasant), 191–92
Thränhardt, D., 13
Tirana
 core-periphery polarisation, 250–51
 desire to leave, 54–56

embassy occupation (1990), 43, 68
interviews in, 11, 54–60, 176–77, 216, 220
migration from, 74, 76, 81
migration to, 82, 83
population, 51
riots (1991), 44
Toigo, M., 236
Tosks, 33, 62n6
trafficking, Albania, 219, 246–47
Trix, Francis, 97

U
United Kingdom, Albanian migrants in, 97–98
United Nations Development Programme (UNDP), Human Development Report, 220, 250
United States
Albanian migrants, 67–68, 97, 100n19
Italian migrants, 200

V
van Hear, Nicholas, 215
Vehbiu, A., 117, 119
Vëllazerimi Albanian Association, Lecce, 149, 195–96, 197–98
Vickers, Miranda, 33, 37, 47
Vlorë (Albania), 81, 106, 109, 217, 230, 241
vu cumprà, 19, 26n5
Vullnetari, J., 220

W
Wieviorka, M., 19
women
in Albania, 218–19
Albanian migrants, 88–89, 128–29, 181, 223
World Bank, 27–28, 71, 219, 220, 224, 229

Y
Yugoslavia, Albania's relations with, 36, 243

Z
Zincone, Giovanna, 153
Zinn, Dorothy, 207
Zogu, Ahmed Bey (King Zog I), 30–31
Zolberg, Aristide, 1, 2

Printed in the United States
205499BV00002B/88-180/P